Survey of Economics

Select Chapters

9th Edition

Irvin B. Tucker

 CENGAGE
Learning·

Australia • Brazil • Japan • Korea • Mexico • Singapore • Spain • United Kingdom • United States

Survey of Economics: Select Chapters
9th Edition

Survey of Economics, Irvin B. Tucker
Irvin B. Tucker

© 2016, 2013 Cengage Learning. All rights reserved.

For product information and technology assistance, contact us at
Cengage Learning Customer & Sales Support, 1-800-354-9706

For permission to use material from this text or product,
submit all requests online at **cengage.com/permissions**
Further permissions questions can be emailed to
permissionrequest@cengage.com

This book contains select works from existing Cengage Learning resources and was produced by Cengage Learning Custom Solutions for collegiate use. As such, those adopting and/or contributing to this work are responsible for editorial content accuracy, continuity and completeness.

Compilation © 2015 Cengage Learning

ISBN: 978-1-305-75980-0

WCN: 01-100-101

Cengage Learning
20 Channel Center Street
Boston, MA 02210
USA

Cengage Learning is a leading provider of customized learning solutions with office locations around the globe, including Singapore, the United Kingdom, Australia, Mexico, Brazil, and Japan. Locate your local office at:
www.international.cengage.com/region.

Cengage Learning products are represented in Canada by Nelson Education, Ltd.

For your lifelong learning solutions, visit **www.cengage.com/custom.**

Visit our corporate website at **www.cengage.com.**

BRIEF CONTENTS

AVAILABLE VERSIONS

PREFACE

TEXT WITH A MISSION

The purpose of *Survey of Economics*, ninth edition, is to teach, in an engaging style, the basic operations of the U.S. economy to students who will take a one-term economics course. Rather than taking an encyclopedic approach to economic concepts, *Survey of Economics* focuses on the most important tool in economics—supply and demand analysis—and applies it to clearly explain real-world economic issues.

Every effort has been made to make *Survey of Economics* the most "student-friendly" text on the market. This text was written because so many others expose students to a confusing array of economic analyses that force students to simply memorize in order to pass the course. Instead, *Survey of Economics* presents a straightforward and unbiased approach that effectively teaches the application of basic economic principles. After reading this text, the student should be able to say "now that economics stuff in the news makes sense."

HOW IT FITS TOGETHER

This text presents the core principles of microeconomics, macroeconomics, and international economics. The first 10 chapters introduce the logic of economic analysis and develop the core of microeconomic analysis. Here students learn the role of demand and supply in determining prices in competitive versus monopolistic markets. This part of the book explores such issues as minimum wage laws, rent control, and pollution. The next 10 chapters develop the macroeconomics part of the text. Using the modern, yet simple, aggregate demand and aggregate supply model, the text explains measurement of and changes in the price level, national output, and employment in the economy. The study of macroeconomics also includes how the supply of and the demand for money influence the economy. Finally, this text concludes with three chapters devoted entirely to global issues. For example, students will learn how the supply of and demand for currencies determine exchange rates and what the complications of a strong or a weak dollar are.

TEXT FLEXIBILITY

Survey of Economics is easily adapted to an instructor's preference for the sequencing of microeconomics and macroeconomics topics. This text can be used in a macroeconomic–microeconomic sequence by teaching the first four chapters and then Parts 2, 3, and 4. Also, some instructors prefer to teach Chapter 22, Economies in Transition, after Chapter 1. Instructors should note the appendices on the self-correcting aggregate demand and supply model that follow Chapter 14, Aggregate Demand and Supply, and Chapter 20, Monetary Policy. This approach allows instructors to decide whether to cover this model. An alternative placement for Chapter 21, International Trade and Finance, is also possible. Some instructors say they prefer to emphasize international economics by placing it before the macroeconomic material in Parts 3 and 4. Other instructors believe that students should learn both the microeconomic and macroeconomic material before tackling Chapter 21. Also, a customized text might meet your needs. If so, contact your Cengage South-Western sales representative for information.

HOW NOT TO STUDY ECONOMICS

To some students, studying economics is a little frightening because many chapters are full of graphs. Students often make the mistake of preparing for tests by trying to memorize the lines of graphs. When their graded tests are returned, the students using this strategy will probably exclaim, "What happened?" The answer to this question is that the students should have learned the economic concepts *first*; then they would understand the graphs as *illustrations* of these underlying concepts. Stated simply, superficial cramming for economics quizzes does not work.

For students who are anxious about using graphs, the appendix to Chapter 1 provides a brief review of graphical analysis. In addition, the *Study Guide* contains step-by-step features on how to interpret graphs.

CHANGES TO THE NINTH EDITION

The basic layout of the ninth edition remains the same. The following are key changes.

- Chapter 1 Introducing the Economic Way of Thinking recognizes that students taking introductory college-level economics courses are considering their major. One reason to select economics is that the average starting salary for an undergraduate economics major is higher compared to many other majors. To aid their decision, current average starting salary figures for selected majors have been updated.

- Chapter 2 Production Possibilities, Opportunity Cost, and Economic Growth, has new questions added to the sample questions.

- Chapter 3 Market Demand and Supply ,has an updated global economics feature on organ shortages that includes the liver transplant experience of Apple CEO Steve Jobs. New questions have been added to the sample questions.

- Chapter 4 Markets in Action, has new questions added to the sample questions.

- Chapter 6 Production Costs, has new questions added to the sample questions.

- Chapter 8 Monopoly, has an example of the "sharing economy" added to the Economics in Practice on New York Taxicabs. This feature concludes with a discussion of the unregulated rideshares market with companies like Lyft sporting thick pink mustaches on the front grill.

- Chapter 10, Labor Markets and Income Distribution, has been updated with the latest figures on family income distribution and poverty rates. In addition, the feature article on fair pay for females has been updated. These are currently hot topics that generate great interest for students.

- Chapter 11 Gross Domestic Product, has a new heading on GDP alternatives to introduce and explain alternative measures for GDP.

- Chapter 12, Business Cycles and Unemployment, includes updated business cycle data. This chapter also includes updated unemployment rate data with a section on globalization. The graph showing the GDP gap has been updated and redrawn.

- Chapter 13, Inflation, updates data on inflation, including the Economics in Practice on "How Much More Does It Cost to Laugh?" In addition, here students enjoy learning how to convert Babe Ruth's 1932 salary into today's dollars.

- Chapter 16, The Public Sector, highlights the important current issue of the changing economic character of the United States with global comparisons to other countries. Here, for example, updated data traces the growth of U.S. government expenditures and taxes since the Great Depression. And global comparisons of spending and taxation exhibits have been revised. The chapter concludes with the latest tax rate data example for a single taxpayer. New questions have been added to the sample questions.

- Chapter 17, Federal Deficits, Surpluses, and the National Debt, focuses on the current "hot button" issues of federal deficits, the national debt, and the debt ceiling using updated data and exhibits. This chapter includes updated comparisons of the deficit and national debt as a percentage of GDP.

- Chapter 18, Money and the Federal Reserve System, has updated money supply figures and a updated Exhibit 18.4 listing the 10 top U.S. banks by asset size.

- Chapter 21 International Trade and Finance, updates and explains recent changes in the U.S. balance of trade. To simplify the U.S. balance of payments, the lines for Investment income (net) and Unilateral transfers (net) have been combined into a single line titled Income (net).

- Chapter 23 Growth and the Less-Developed Countries, presents updated data ranking countries by their GDP per capita. It also presents updated data comparing regions of the world by their average GDP per capita. Here updated data is used to explain to explain the link between economic freedom and quality-of-life indicators. New questions have been added to the sample questions.

ALTERNATE VERSIONS OF THE BOOK

For instructors who wish to spend various amounts of time for their courses and offer different topics of this text:

- *Economics for Today.* This complete version of the book contains all 30 chapters. It is designed for two-semester introductory courses that cover both microeconomics and macroeconomics.

- *Microeconomics for Today.* This version contains 17 chapters and is designed for one-semester courses in introductory microeconomics.

- *Macroeconomics for Today.* This version contains 20 chapters and is designed for one-semester courses in introductory macroeconomics.

- *Survey of Economics.* This version of the book contains 23 chapters. It is designed for one-semester courses that cover the basics of both microeconomics and macroeconomics.

- The accompanying table shows precisely which chapters are included in each book. Instructors who wish more information about these alternative versions should contact their local Cengage South-Western representative.

MOTIVATIONAL PEDAGOGICAL FEATURES

Survey of Economics strives to motivate and advance the boundaries of pedagogy with the following features.

PART OPENERS

Each part begins with a statement of the overall mission of the chapters in the part. In addition, there is a nutshell introduction of each chapter in relation to the part's learning objective.

CHAPTER PREVIEWS

Each chapter begins with a preview designed to pique the student's interest and reinforce how the chapter fits into the overall scheme of the book. Each preview appeals to the student's "Sherlock Holmes" impulses by posing several economics puzzles that can be solved by understanding the material presented in the chapter.

MARGIN DEFINITIONS AND FLASHCARDS

Key concepts introduced in the chapter are highlighted in bold type and then defined with the definitions again in the margins. This feature therefore serves as a quick reference. Key terms are also defined on the Tucker website with a Flashcard feature that is great for learning terms.

ECONOMICS IN PRACTICE

Each chapter includes boxed inserts that provide the acid test of "relevance to everyday life." This feature gives the student an opportunity to encounter timely, real-world extensions of economic theory. For example, students read about Fred Smith as he writes an economics term paper explaining his plan to create FedEx. To ensure that the student wastes no time figuring out which concepts apply to the article, applicable concepts are listed after each title. Many of these boxed features include quotes from newspaper articles over a period of years, demonstrating that economic concepts remain relevant over time.

CONCLUSION STATEMENTS

Throughout the chapters, highlighted conclusion statements of key concepts appear at the ends of sections and tie together the material just presented. Students will be able to see quickly if they have understood the main points of the section. A summary of these conclusion statements is provided at the end of each chapter.

GLOBAL ECONOMICS

GLOBAL ECONOMICS

Today's economic environment is global. *Survey of Economics* carefully integrates international topics throughout the text and presents the material using a highly readable and accessible approach designed for students with no training in international economics. All sections of the text that present global economics are identified by a special global icon in the text margin and in the Global Economics boxes. In addition, the final three chapters of the book are devoted entirely to international economics.

ANALYZE THE ISSUE

This feature follows each *Economics in Practice* and *Global Economics* feature and asks specific questions that require students to test their knowledge of how the material in the boxed insert is relevant to the applicable concept. So that these questions can be used in classroom discussions or homework assignments; answers are provided in the *Instructor's Manual* rather than in the text.

CHECKPOINT

Watch for these! Who said learning economics can't be fun? This feature is a unique approach to generating interest and critical thinking. These questions spark students to check their progress by asking challenging economics puzzles in game-like style. Students enjoy thinking through and answering the questions, and then checking the answers that can be found on the instructor's resource website. Students who answer correctly earn the satisfaction of knowing they have mastered the concepts.

ILLUSTRATIONS

Attractive large graphical presentations with grid lines and real-world numbers are essential for any successful economics textbook. Each exhibit has been carefully analyzed to ensure that the key concepts being represented stand out clearly. Brief descriptions are included with graphs to provide guidance for students as they study the graph. When actual data are used, the website reference is provided so that students can easily locate the data source.

KEY CONCEPTS

Key concepts introduced in the chapter are listed at the end of each chapter and are featured on the Tucker MindTap asset. As a study aid, you can use the key concepts as flashcards to test your knowledge. First state the definition and then click on the term to check for correctness.

VISUAL SUMMARIES

Each chapter ends with a brief point-by-point summary of the key concepts. Many of these summarized points include miniaturized versions of the important graphs and causation chains that illustrate many of the key concepts. These are intended to serve as visual reminders for students as they finish the chapters and are also useful in reviewing and studying for quizzes and exams.

STUDY QUESTIONS AND PROBLEMS

The end-of-chapter questions and problems offer a variety of levels ranging from straightforward recall to deeply thought-provoking applications. The answers to odd-numbered questions and problems are on the instructor's website and in the back of the book.

END-OF-CHAPTER SAMPLE QUIZZES

A great help before quizzes. Many instructors test students using multiple-choice questions. For this reason, the final section of each chapter provides the type of multiple-choice questions given in the instructor's Test Bank. The answers to all of these questions are given in the back of the book.

PART ROAD MAP

This feature concludes each part with review questions listed by chapter from the previous part. To reinforce the concepts, each set of questions relates to the interactive causation chain game. You can find the games on the MindTap asset for Tucker 9e. Answers to the questions are also on the instructor's website.

INTERACTIVE QUIZZES

In addition to the end-of-chapter sample quizzes, there are additional multiple-choice questions written by the author on the Tucker instructor's website. Each quiz contains multiple questions like those found in a typical exam. In addition, you may email yourself and/or your instructor the quiz results with a listing of correct and incorrect answers. Between this feature and the end-of-chapter practice quizzes, students are well prepared for tests.

ONLINE EXERCISES

These exercises for each chapter are designed to spark student's excitement about researching on the Internet by asking them to access online economic data and then answer questions related to the content of the chapter. All Internet exercises are on the Tucker instructor's website with direct links to the addresses so that students will not have the tedious and error-prone task of entering long website addresses.

A SUPPLEMENTS PACKAGE DESIGNED FOR SUCCESS

To access additional course material for *Survey of Economics*, visit www.cengagebrain.com. At the CengageBrain.com home page, search for the ISBN of your book using the search box at the top of the page. This will take you to the product page where these resources can be found. For additional information, contact your Cengage sales representative.

INSTRUCTOR RESOURCES

TUCKER WEBSITE

The Tucker website at www.cengagebrain.com provides open access to PowerPoint chapter review slides, study guide, Instructor's manual (prepared by Douglas Copeland of Johnson County Community College), direct links to the Internet activities mentioned in the text, updates to the text, Test Bank in PDF, and other downloadable teaching and learning resources.

COGNERO

Cengage Learning Testing Powered by Cognero is a flexible, online system that allows you to

- author, edit, and manage test bank content from multiple Cengage Learning solutions.
- create multiple test versions in an instant.
- deliver tests from your LMS, your classroom, or wherever you want.

Start right away!

Cengage Learning Testing Powered by Cognero works on any operating system or browser.

- No special installs or downloads needed
- Create tests from school, home, the coffee shop—anywhere with Internet access

What will you find?

- *Simplicity at every step*. A desktop-inspired interface features drop-down menus and familiar, intuitive tools that take you through content creation and management with ease.
- *Full-featured test generator*. Create ideal assessments with your choice of 15 question types (including true/false, multiple choice, opinion scale/likert, and essay). Multi-language support, an equation editor, and unlimited metadata help ensure your tests are complete and compliant.
- *Cross-compatible capability*. Import and export content into other systems.

STUDENT RESOURCES

MINDTAP FOR TUCKER

MindTap engages and empowers students to produce their best work consistently. By seamlessly integrating course material with videos, activities, apps, and much more, MindTap creates a unique learning path that fosters increased comprehension and efficiency.

- MindTap delivers real-world relevance with activities and assignments that help students build critical thinking and analytic skills that will transfer to other courses and their professional lives.

- MindTap helps students stay organized and efficient with a single destination that reflects what's important to the instructor, along with the tools students need to master the content.

- MindTap empowers and motivates students with information that shows where they stand at all times— both individually and compared to the highest performers in class.

- Relevant readings, multimedia, and activities are designed to take students up the levels of learning, from basic knowledge to analysis and application.

- Personalized teaching becomes yours through a Learning Path built with key student objectives and your syllabus in mind. Control what students see and when they see it.

- Analytics and reports provide a snapshot of class progress, time in course, engagement, and completion rates.

- Aplia generic homework and math and graphing tutorials.

- End of chapter homework, BBC videos with assessment, Concept Clips videos, Graphing-at-a-Glance Videos with assessment, Road Map Q&A, Checkpoint Q&A, and end of chapter questions and problems.

- Causation Chain Game: The highly successful causation chains are included under many graphs throughout the text. This pedagogical device helps students visualize complex economic relationships in terms of simple box diagrams that illustrate how one change causes another change. Each exhibit having a causation chain in the text is included in the Causation Chain Game within MindTap. This game makes it fun to learn.

APLIA

Created by Economist Paul Romer for his classroom, Aplia is the best-selling online economics product. In fact, Aplia is the most successful and widely used homework solution in the Economics marketing. Aplia provides automatically graded assignments that were written to make the most of the web medium and contain detailed immediate explanations of every question.

ACKNOWLEDGMENTS

A deep debt of gratitude is owed to the reviewers for their expert assistance. All comments and suggestions were carefully evaluated and served to improve the final product. To each of the reviewers of all five editions, I give my sincerest thanks.

SPECIAL THANKS

My appreciation goes to Michael Parthenakis and Steve Scoble, product managers for Cengage. My thanks also to Elizabeth Lowry, Content Developer; Joseph Malcolm, Project Manager; Mary Umbarger, Product Assistant; and Chris Walz, Marketing Coordinator, who put all the pieces of the puzzle together and brought their creative talent to this text. I am also grateful to John Carey for his skillful marketing. I especially wish to express my deepest appreciation to Douglas Copeland of Johnson County Community College for preparing the Instructor's Manual. Finally, I give my sincere thanks for a job well done to the entire team at Cengage.

ABOUT THE AUTHOR

IRVIN B. TUCKER

IRVIN B. TUCKER has over 30 years of experience teaching introductory economics at the University of North Carolina Charlotte. He earned his B.S. in Economics at NC State University and his M.A. and Ph.D. in Economics from the University of South Carolina. Dr. Tucker is former director of the Center for Economic Education at the University of North Carolina Charlotte and was a longtime member of the National Council on Economic Education. He is recognized for his ability to relate basic principles to economic issues and public policy. His work has received national recognition by being awarded the Meritorious Levy Award for Excellence in Private Enterprise Education, the Federation of Independent Business Award for Postsecondary Educator of the Year in Entrepreneurship and Economic Education, and the Freedom Foundation's George Washington Medal for Excellence in Economic Education. In addition, his research has been published in numerous professional journal articles on a wide range of topics including industrial organization, entrepreneurship, and economics of education. Dr. Tucker is also the author of the highly successful *Economics for Today*, Eight Edition, a text for the two-semester principles of economics courses, published by Cengage South-Western Publishing.

SURVEY *of* ECONOMICS

NINTH EDITION

PART 1

Introduction to Economics

The first two chapters introduce you to a foundation of economic knowledge vital to understanding the other chapters in the text. In these introductory chapters, you will begin to learn a valuable reasoning approach to solving economics puzzles that economists call "the economic way of thinking." Part 1 develops the cornerstone of this type of logical analysis by presenting basic economic models that explain such important topics as scarcity, opportunity cost, production possibilities, and economic growth.

Introducing the Economic Way of Thinking

In this chapter, you will learn to solve these economics puzzles:

- Can you prove there is no person worth a trillion dollars?
- Why would you purchase more Coca-Cola when the price increases?
- How can we explain the relationship between the Super Bowl winner and changes in the stock market?

CHAPTER PREVIEW

Welcome to an exciting and useful subject economists call "the economic way of thinking." As you learn this reasoning technique, it will become infectious. You will discover that the world is full of economics problems requiring more powerful tools than just common sense. As you master the methods explained in this book, you will appreciate economics as a valuable reasoning approach to solving economics puzzles. Stated differently, the economic way of thinking is important because it provides a logical framework for organizing your thoughts and understanding an economic issue or event. Just to give a sneak preview, in later chapters, you will study the perils of government price fixing for gasoline and health care. You will also find out why colleges and universities charge students different tuitions for the same education. You will investigate whether you should worry if the federal government fails to balance its budget. You will learn that the island of Yap uses large stones with holes in the center as money. In the final chapter, you will study why some countries grow rich while others remain poor and less developed. And the list of fascinating and relevant topics continues throughout each chapter.

As you read these pages, your efforts will be rewarded by an understanding of how economic theories and policies affect our daily lives—past, present, and future.

Chapter 1 acquaints you with the foundation of the economic way of thinking. The first building blocks joined are the concepts of scarcity and choice. The next building blocks are the steps in the model-building process that economists use to study the choices people make. Then we look at some pitfalls of economic reasoning and explain why economists might disagree with one another. The chapter concludes with a discussion of why you may want to be an economics major.

1-1 THE PROBLEM OF SCARCITY

Scarcity The condition in which human wants are forever greater than the available supply of time, goods, and resources.

Our world is a finite place where people, both individually and collectively, face the problem of scarcity. Scarcity is the condition in which human wants are forever greater than the available supply of time, goods, and resources. Because of scarcity, it is impossible to satisfy every desire. Pause for a moment to list some of your unsatisfied wants. Perhaps you would like a big home, gourmet meals, designer clothes, clean air, better health care, shelter for the homeless, and more leisure time. Unfortunately, nature does not offer the Garden of Eden, where every desire is fulfilled. Instead, there are always limits on the economy's ability to satisfy unlimited wants. Alas, scarcity is pervasive, so "you can't have it all."

You may think your scarcity problem would disappear if you were rich, but wealth does not solve the problem. No matter how affluent an individual is, the wish list continues to grow. We are familiar with the "rich and famous" who never seem to have enough. Although they live well, they still desire finer homes, faster planes, and larger yachts. In short, the condition of scarcity means all individuals, whether rich or poor, are dissatisfied with their material well-being and would like more. What is true for individuals also applies to society. Even Uncle Sam cannot escape the problem of scarcity. The federal government never has enough money to spend for the poor, education, highways, police, national defense, Social Security, and all the other programs it wishes to fund.

Scarcity is a fact of life throughout the world. In much of South America, Africa, and Asia, the problem of scarcity is often life threatening. On the other hand, North America, Western Europe, and some parts of Asia have achieved substantial economic growth and development. Although life is much less grueling in the more developed countries, the problem of scarcity still exists because individuals and countries never have as much of all the goods and services as they would like to have.

CONCLUSION The problem of scarcity and choice are basic economic problems faced by every society

1-2 SCARCE RESOURCES AND PRODUCTION

Resources The basic categories of inputs used to produce goods and services. Resources are also called *factors of production*. Economists divide resources into three categories: land, labor, and capital.

Because of the economic problem of scarcity, no society has enough resources to produce all the goods and services necessary to satisfy all human wants. Resources are the basic categories of inputs used to produce goods and services. Resources are also called *factors of production*. Economists divide resources into three categories: *land*, *labor*, and *capital* (see Exhibit 1-1).

1-2a Land

Land Any natural resource provided by nature used to produce goods and services.

Land is a shorthand expression for any natural resource provided by nature that is used to produce a good or service. Land includes those resources that are gifts of nature available for use in the production process. Farming, building factories, and constructing oil refineries would be impossible without land. Land includes

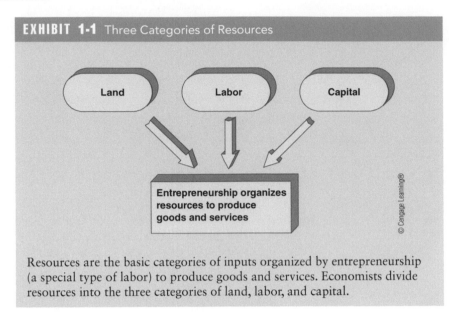

EXHIBIT 1-1 Three Categories of Resources

Land   Labor   Capital

Entrepreneurship organizes resources to produce goods and services

© Cengage Learning®

Resources are the basic categories of inputs organized by entrepreneurship (a special type of labor) to produce goods and services. Economists divide resources into the three categories of land, labor, and capital.

anything natural above or below the ground, such as forests, gold, diamonds, oil, coal, wind, and the sun. Two broad categories of natural resources are *renewable resources* and *nonrenewable resources*. Renewable resources are basic inputs that nature can automatically replace. Examples include lakes, crops, and clean air. Nonrenewable resources are basic inputs that nature cannot automatically replace. There is only so much coal, oil, and natural gas in the world. If these fossil fuels disappear, we must use substitutes.

1–2b Labor

Labor The mental and physical capacity of workers to produce goods and services.

Labor is the mental and physical capacity of workers to produce goods and services. The services of farmers, assembly-line workers, lawyers, professional football players, and economists are all *labor*. The labor resource is measured both by the number of people available for work and by the skills or quality of workers. One reason nations differ in their ability to produce is that human characteristics, such as the education, experience, health, and motivation of workers, differ among nations.

Entrepreneurship The creative ability of individuals to seek profits by taking risks and combining resources to produce innovative products.

Entrepreneurship is a special type of labor. Entrepreneurship is the creative ability of individuals to seek profits by taking risks and combining resources to produce innovative products. An *entrepreneur* is a motivated person who seeks profits by undertaking such risky activities as starting new businesses, creating new products, or inventing new ways of accomplishing tasks. Entrepreneurship is a scarce human resource because relatively few people are willing or able to innovate and make decisions involving greater-than-normal chances for failure. An important benefit of entrepreneurship is that it creates a growing economy.

Entrepreneurs are the agents of change who bring material progress to society. The birth of the Levi Strauss Company is a classic entrepreneurial success story. In 1853, at the age of 24, Levi Strauss sailed from New York to join the California Gold Rush. His intent was not to dig for gold but to sell cloth. By the time he arrived in San Francisco, he had sold most of his cloth to other people on the ship. The only cloth he had left was a roll of canvas for tents and covered wagons. On the dock, he met a miner who wanted sturdy pants that would last while digging for gold, so Levi made a pair from the canvas. Later, a customer gave Levi the idea of using little copper rivets to strengthen the seams. Presto! Strauss knew a good thing when he saw it, so he hired workers, built factories, and became one of the largest pants makers in the world. As a reward for taking business risks, organizing production, and introducing a product, the Levi Strauss Company earned profits, and Strauss became rich and famous.

1-2c Capital

Capital Human-made goods used to produce other goods and services.

Capital is a human-made good used to produce other goods and services. Capital includes the physical plants, machinery, and equipment used to produce other goods. Capital goods are human-made goods that do not directly satisfy human wants. Before the Industrial Revolution, *capital* meant a tool, such as a hoe, an axe, or a bow and arrow. In those days, these items served as capital to build a house or provide food for the dinner table. Today, capital also consists of factories, office buildings, warehouses, robots, trucks, roads, and distribution facilities. College buildings, the printing presses used to produce this textbook, and computers are also examples of capital.

The term *capital* as it is used in the study of economics can be confusing. Economists know that capital in everyday conversations means money or the money value of paper assets, such as stocks, bonds, or a deed to a house. This is actually *financial* capital. In the study of economics, capital does not refer to money assets. Capital in economics means a factor of production, such as a factory or machinery. Stated simply, you must pay special attention to this point: Money is not capital and is therefore not a resource. Instead, money is used to purchase land, labor, or capital.

CONCLUSION Money by itself does not produce goods and services; instead, it is only a paper means of buying capital.

1-3 ECONOMICS: THE STUDY OF SCARCITY AND CHOICE

Economics The study of how society chooses to allocate its scarce resources to the production of goods and services in order to satisfy unlimited wants.

The perpetual problem of scarcity forcing people to make choices is the basis for the definition of economics. Economics is the study of how society chooses to allocate its scarce resources to the production of goods and services to satisfy unlimited wants. You may be surprised by this definition. People often think economics means studying supply and demand, the stock market, money, and banking. In fact, there are many ways one could define *economics*, but economists accept the definition given here because it includes the link between *scarcity* and *choices*.

Society makes two kinds of choices: economywide, or macro, choices and individual, or micro, choices. The prefixes *macro* and *micro* come from the Greek words meaning "large" and "small," respectively. Reflecting the macro and micro perspectives, economics consists of two main branches: *macroeconomics* and *microeconomics*.

1-3a Macroeconomics

Macroeconomics The branch of economics that studies decision making for the economy as a whole.

The old saying "Looking at the forest rather than the trees" describes macroeconomics. Macroeconomics is the branch of economics that studies decision making for the economy as a whole. Macroeconomics applies an overview perspective to an economy by examining economywide variables, such as inflation, unemployment, growth of the economy, the money supply, and the national incomes of developing countries. Macroeconomic decision making considers such "big picture" policies as the effect that federal tax cuts will have on unemployment and the effect that changing the money supply will have on prices.

Microeconomics The branch of economics that studies decision making by a single individual, household, firm, industry, or level of government.

1-3b Microeconomics

Examining individual trees, leaves, and pieces of bark, rather than surveying the forest, illustrates **microeconomics**. Microeconomics is the branch of economics that studies decision making by a single individual, household, firm, industry, or level of government. Microeconomics applies a microscope to study specific parts of an economy, as one would examine cells in the body. The focus is on small economic units, such as economic decisions of particular groups of consumers and businesses. An example of microeconomic analysis would be to study economic units involved in the market for ostrich eggs. Will suppliers decide to supply more, less, or the same quantity of ostrich eggs to the market in response to price changes? Will individual consumers of these eggs decide to buy more, less, or the same quantity at a new price?

We have described macroeconomics and microeconomics as two separate branches, but they are related. Because the overall economy is the sum, or aggregation, of its parts, micro changes affect the macro economy, and macro changes produce micro changes.

1-4 THE METHODOLOGY OF ECONOMICS

As used by other disciplines, such as criminology, biology, chemistry, and physics, economists employ a step-by-step procedure for solving problems by identifying the problem, developing a model, gathering data, and testing whether the data are consistent with the model. Based on this analysis, economists formulate a conclusion. Exhibit 1-2 summarizes the model-building process.

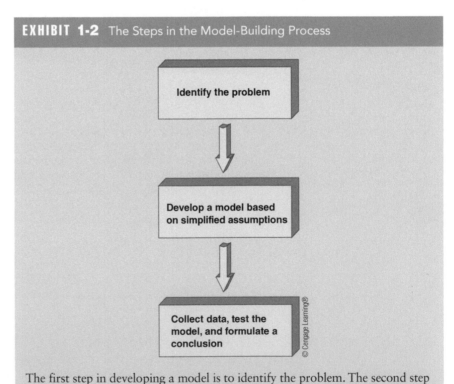

EXHIBIT 1-2   The Steps in the Model-Building Process

Identify the problem

Develop a model based on simplified assumptions

Collect data, test the model, and formulate a conclusion

© Cengage Learning®

The first step in developing a model is to identify the problem. The second step is to select the critical variables necessary to formulate a model that explains the problem under study. Eliminating other variables that complicate the analysis requires simplifying assumptions. In the third step, the researcher collects data and tests the model. If the evidence supports the model, the conclusion is to accept the model. If the evidence doesn't support, the model is rejected.

1–4a Problem Identification

The first step in applying the economic method is to define the issue. Suppose an economist wishes to investigate the microeconomic problem of why U.S. motorists cut back on gasoline consumption in a given year from, for example, 400 million gallons per day in May to 300 million gallons per day in December.

1–4b Model Development

Model A simplified description of reality used to understand and predict the relationship between variables.

The second step in our hypothetical example toward finding an explanation is for the economist to build a **model**. A model is a simplified description of reality used to understand and predict the relationship between variables. The terms *model* and *theory* are interchangeable. A model emphasizes only those variables that are most important to explaining an event. As Albert Einstein said, "Theories should be as simple as possible, but not more so." The purpose of a model is to construct an abstraction from real-world complexities and make events understandable. Consider a model airplane that is placed in a wind tunnel to test the aerodynamics of a new design. For this purpose, the model must represent only the shapes of the wings and fuselage, but it does not need to include tiny seats, electrical wiring, or other interior design details. A highway map is another example. To find the best route to drive between two distant cities, you do not want extraneous information on the location of all roads, streets, potholes, trees, stoplights, schools, hospitals, and firehouses. This would be too much detail, and the complexity would make it difficult to choose the best route.

A map is a model because it is an abstraction from reality.

©Marco Scisetti/Shutterstock.com

To be useful, a model requires simplified assumptions. Someone must decide, for example, whether a map will include only symbols for the major highways or the details of hiking trails through mountains. In our gasoline consumption example, several variables might be related to the quantity of gasoline consumed, including consumer incomes, the prices of substitutes for gasoline, the price of gasoline, the fuel economy of cars, and weather conditions. Because a theory focuses only on the main or critical variables, the economist must be a Sherlock Holmes and use a keen sense of observation to form a model. Using his or her expertise, the economist must select the relevant variables that are related to gasoline consumption and reject variables that have only slight or no relationship to gasoline consumption. In this simple case, the economist removes the cloud of complexity by formulating the theory that increases in the price of gasoline *cause* the quantity of gasoline consumed to decrease during the time period.

1–4c Testing a Theory

An economic model can be stated as a verbal argument, numerical table, graph, or mathematical equation. You will soon discover that a major part of this book is devoted to building and using economic models. The purpose of an economic model is to *forecast* or *predict* the results of various changes in variables. Note the appendix to this chapter provides a review of the graphical analysis. An economic theory can be expressed in the form "If *A*, then *B*, other things held constant." An economic model is useful only if it yields accurate predictions. When the evidence is consistent with the theory that *A* causes outcome *B*, there is confidence in the theory's validity. When the evidence is inconsistent with the theory that *A* causes outcome *B*, the researcher rejects this theory.

In the third step, the economist gathers data to test the theory that if the price of gasoline rises, then gasoline purchases fall—all other relevant factors held constant. Suppose the investigation reveals that the price of gasoline rose sharply between May and December of the given year. The data are therefore consistent with the theory that the quantity of gasoline consumed per month falls when its price rises, assuming no other relevant factors change. Thus, the conclusion is that the theory is valid if, for example, consumer incomes or population size does not change at the same time that gasoline prices rise.

CHECKPOINT

> **Can You Prove There Is No Trillion-Dollar Person?**
> Suppose a theory says that no U.S. citizen is worth $1 trillion. You decide to test this theory and send researchers to all corners of the nation to check financial records to see whether someone qualifies by owning assets valued at $1 trillion or more. After years of checking, the researchers return and report that not a single person is worth at least $1 trillion. Do you conclude that the evidence proves the theory? Explain.

1-5 HAZARDS OF THE ECONOMIC WAY OF THINKING

Models help us understand and predict the impact of changes in economic variables. A model is an important tool in the economist's toolkit, but it must be handled with care. The economic way of thinking seeks to avoid reasoning mistakes. Two of the most common pitfalls to clear thinking are (1) failing to understand the *ceteris paribus assumption* and (2) confusing *association* and *causation*.

1-5a The Ceteris Paribus Assumption

Ceteris paribus A Latin phrase that means while certain variables change, "all other things remain unchanged."

As you work through a model, try to think of a host of relevant variables assumed to be "standing still," or "held constant." **Ceteris paribus** is a Latin phrase that means while certain variables change, "all other things remain unchanged." In short, the ceteris paribus assumption allows us to isolate or focus attention on selected variables. In the gasoline example discussed earlier, a key simplifying assumption of the model is that changes in consumer incomes and certain other variables do not occur and complicate the analysis. The ceteris paribus assumption holds everything else constant and therefore allows us to concentrate on the relationship between two key variables: changes in the price of gasoline and the quantity of gasoline purchased per month.

Now suppose an economist examines a model explaining the relationship between the price and quantity purchased of Coca-Cola. The theory is "If the price increases, then the quantity of Coca-Cola purchased decreases, ceteris paribus." Now assume you observe that the price of Coca-Cola increased one summer and some people actually bought more, not less. Based on this real-world observation, you declare the theory is incorrect. Think again! The economist responds that this is a reasoning pitfall because the model is valid based on the assumption of ceteris paribus, and your observation gives us no reason to reject the model. The reason the model appeared flawed is because another factor, a sharp rise in the temperature, *caused* people to buy more Coca-Cola in spite of its higher price. If the temperature and all other factors are held constant as the price of Coca-Cola rises, then people will indeed buy less Coca-Cola, as the model predicts.

> **CONCLUSION** A theory cannot be tested legitimately unless its ceteris paribus assumption is satisfied.

1-5b Association versus Causation

Another common error in reasoning is confusing *association* (or correlation) and *causation* between variables. Stated differently, you err when you read more into a relationship between variables than is actually there. A model is valid only when a cause-and-effect relationship is stable or dependable over time, rather than being an association that occurs by chance and eventually disappears. Suppose a witch doctor performs a voodoo dance during three different months and stock market prices skyrocket during each of these months. The voodoo dance is *associated* with the increase in stock prices, but this does not mean the dance *caused* the event. Even though there is a statistical relationship between these two variables in a number of observations, eventually the voodoo dance will be performed, and stock prices will fall or remain unchanged. The reason is that there is no true systematic economic relationship between voodoo dances and stock prices.

Further investigation may reveal that stock prices actually responded to changes in interest rates during the months that the voodoo dances were performed. Changes in interest rates affect borrowing and, in turn, profits and stock prices. In contrast, there is no real economic relationship between voodoo dances and stock prices, and therefore, the voodoo model is not valid.

> **CONCLUSION** The fact that one event follows another does not necessarily mean that the first event caused the second event.

CHECKPOINT

Should Nebraska State Join a Big-Time Athletic Conference?
Nebraska State (a mythical university) stood by while Penn State, Florida State, the University of Miami, and the University of South Carolina joined big-time athletic conferences. Now Nebraska State officials are pondering whether to remain independent or to pursue membership in a conference noted for high-quality football and basketball programs. An editorial in the newspaper advocates joining and cites a study showing that universities belonging to major athletic conferences have higher graduation rates than nonmembers. Because educating its students is the number one goal of Nebraska State, will this evidence persuade Nebraska State officials to join a big-time conference? Why or why not?

Throughout this book, you will study economic models or theories that include variables linked by stable cause-and-effect relationships. For example, the theory that a change in the price of a good *causes* a change in the quantity purchased is a valid microeconomic model. The theory that a change in the money supply *causes* a change in interest rates is an example of a valid macroeconomic model. The following Economics in Practice gives some amusing examples of the "association means causation" reasoning pitfall.

1-6 WHY DO ECONOMISTS DISAGREE?

Why might one economist say a clean environment should be our most important priority and another economist say economic growth should be our most important goal? If economists share the economic way of thinking and carefully avoid reasoning pitfalls, then why do they disagree? Why are economists known for giving advice by saying, "On the one hand, if you do this, then *A* results, and on the other hand, doing this causes result *B*"? In fact, President Harry Truman once jokingly exclaimed, "Find me an economist with only one hand." George Bernard Shaw offered another famous line in the same vein: "If you took all the economists in the world and laid them end to end, they would never reach a conclusion." These famous quotes imply that economists should agree, but these quotes ignore the fact that physicists, doctors, business executives, lawyers, and all professionals often disagree.

Mops and Brooms, the Boston Snow Index, the Super Bowl, and Other Economic Indicators

Applicable concept: association versus causation

Although the Commerce Department, the Wharton School, the Federal Reserve Board, and other organizations publish economic forecasts and data on key economic indicators, they are not without armchair competition. For example, the chief executive of Standex International Corporation, Daniel E. Hogan, reported that his company can predict economic downturns and recoveries from sales reports of its National Metal Industries subsidiary in Springfield, Massachusetts. National makes metal parts for about 300 U.S. manufacturers of mops and brooms. A drop in National's sales always precedes a proportional fall in consumer spending. The company's sales always pick up slightly before consumer spending does.[1]

The Boston Snow Index (BSI) is the brainchild of a vice president of a New York securities firm. It predicts a rising economy for the next year if there is snow on the ground in Boston on Christmas Day. The BSI predicted correctly about 73 percent of the time over a 30-year period. However, its creator, David L. Upshaw, did not take it too seriously and views it as a spoof of other forecasters' methods.

Greeting card sales are another tried and true indicator, according to a vice president of American Greetings. Before a recession sets in, sales of higher-priced greeting cards rise. It seems that people substitute the cards for gifts, and since there is no gift, the card must be fancier.

A Super Bowl win by an NFC team predicts that in the following December the stock market will be higher than the year before. A win by an old AFL team predicts a dip in the stock market.

Several other indicators have also been proposed. For example, one economist suggested that the surliness of waiters is a countercyclical indicator. If they are nice, expect that bad times are coming, but if they are rude, expect an upturn. Waiters, on the other hand, counter that a fall in the average tip usually precedes a downturn in the economy.

Finally, Anthony Chan, chief economist for Bank One Investment Advisors, studied marriage trends over a 34-year period. He discovered that when the number of marriages increases, the economy rises significantly, and a slowdown in marriages is followed by a decline in the economy. Chan explains that there is usually about a one-year lag between a change in the marriage rate and the economy.[2]

ANALYZE the ISSUE Which of the above indicators are examples of causation? Explain.

[1] "Economic Indicators, Turtles, Butterflies, Monks, and Waiters," *The Wall Street Journal*, Aug. 27, 1979, pp. 1, 16.
[2] Sandra Block, "Worried? Look at Wedding Bell Indicator," *The Charlotte Observer*, Apr. 15, 1995, p. 8A.

Economists may appear to disagree more than other professionals partly because it is more interesting to report disagreements than agreements. Actually, economists agree on a wide range of issues. Many economists, for example, agree on free trade among nations, the elimination of farm subsidies and rent ceilings, government deficit spending to recover from a recession, and many other issues. When disagreements do exist, the reason can often be explained by the difference between *positive economics* and *normative economics*.

1-6a Positive Economics

Positive economics An analysis limited to statements that are verifiable.

Positive economics deals with facts and therefore addresses "what is" or "verifiable" questions. Positive economics is an analysis limited to statements that are verifiable. Positive statements can be proven either true or false. Often a positive statement is expressed: "If A, then B." For example, if the national unemployment rate rises to 9 percent, then teenage unemployment exceeds 80 percent. This is a positive "if-then" prediction, which may or may not be correct. Accuracy is not the criterion for a statement to be positive. The key consideration is whether the statement is *testable* and not whether it is true or false. Suppose the data show that when the nation's overall unemployment rate is close to 9 percent, the unemployment rate for teenagers never reaches 80 percent. For example, the overall unemployment rate was 9.3 percent in 2009, and the rate for teenagers was 24.3 percent—far short of 80 percent. Based on the facts, we would conclude that this positive statement is false.

Now we can explain one reason why economists' forecasts can diverge. The statement "If event *A* occurs, then event *B* follows" can be thought of as a *conditional* positive statement. For example, two economists may agree that if the federal government cuts spending by 10 percent this year, prices will fall about 2 percent next year. However, their predictions about the fall in prices may differ because one economist assumes Congress will not cut spending, while the other economist assumes Congress will cut spending by 10 percent.

> **CONCLUSION** Economists' forecasts can differ because, using the same methodology, economists can agree that event *A* causes event *B*, but disagree over the assumption that event *A* will occur.

1-6b Normative Economics

Normative economics An analysis based on value judgment.

Instead of using objective statements, an argument can be phrased subjectively. **Normative economics** attempts to determine "what should be." Normative economics is an analysis based on value judgments. Normative statements express an individual or collective opinion on a subject and cannot be proven by facts to be true or false. Certain words or phrases, such as *good*, *bad*, *need*, *should*, and *ought to*, tell us clearly that we have entered the realm of normative economics.

The point here is that people wearing different-colored glasses see the same facts differently. Each of us has individual subjective preferences that we apply to a particular subject. An animal rights activist says that no one *should* purchase a fur coat. Or one senator argues, "We *ought to* ensure that every teenager who wants a job has one." Another senator counters by saying, "Maintaining the purchasing power of the dollar is *more important* than teenage unemployment."

> **CONCLUSION** When opinions or points of view are not based on facts, they are scientifically untestable.

When considering a debate, make sure to separate the arguments into their positive and normative components. This distinction allows you to determine whether you are choosing a course of action based on factual evidence or on opinion. The material presented in this textbook, like most of economics, takes pains to stay within the boundaries of positive economic analysis. In our everyday lives, however, politicians, business executives, relatives, and friends use mostly normative statements to discuss economic issues. Economists also may associate themselves with a political position and use normative arguments for or against some economic policy. When using value judgments, an economist's arguments may have no greater validity than those of other people. Biases or preconceptions can cloud an economist's thinking about deficit spending or whether to increase taxes on gasoline. Like beginning economics students, economists are human.

1-7 CAREERS IN ECONOMICS

The author of this text entered college more years ago than I would like to admit. In those days, economics was not taught in high school, so I knew nothing of the subject. Like many students taking this course, I was uncertain about which major to pursue, but selected electrical engineering because I was an amateur radio operator and enjoyed building radio receivers and transmitters. My engineering curriculum required a course in economics. I signed up thinking that "econ is

Does the Minimum Wage Really Help the Working Poor?

Applicable concepts: positive and normative analyses

In 1938, Congress enacted the federal Fair Labor Standards Act, commonly known as the "minimum wage law." Today, a minimum-wage worker who works full time still earns a deplorably low annual income. One approach to help the working poor earn a living wage might be to raise the minimum wage.

The dilemma for Congress is that a higher minimum wage for the employed is enacted at the expense of jobs for unskilled workers. Opponents forecast that the increased labor cost from a large minimum wage hike would jeopardize hundreds of thousands of unskilled jobs. For example, employers may opt to purchase more capital and less expensive labor. Restaurants can use iPads instead of servers to take orders and install robotical burger flippers. The fear of such sizable job losses forces Congress to perform a difficult balancing act to ensure that a minimum-wage increase is large enough to help the working poor but not so large as to threaten their jobs.

Some politicians claim that raising the minimum wage is a way to help the working poor without cost to taxpayers. Others believe the cost is hidden in inflation and lost employment opportunities for marginal workers, such as teenagers, the elderly, and minorities. One study by economists, for example, examined 60 years of data and concluded that minimum wage increases resulted in reduced employment and hours of work for low-skilled workers.[1]

Another problem with raising the minimum wage to aid the working poor is that minimum wage is a blunt weapon for redistributing wealth. Studies show that only a small percentage of minimum-wage earners are full-time workers whose family income falls below the poverty line. This means that most increases in the minimum wage go to workers who are not poor. For example, many minimum wage workers are students living at home or workers whose spouse earns a much higher income. To help only the working poor, some economists argue that the government should target only those people who need assistance, rather than using the "shotgun" approach of raising the minimum wage.

Supporters of raising the minimum wage are not convinced by these arguments. They say it is outrageous that a worker can work full time and still live in poverty. Moreover, people on this side of the debate believe that opponents exaggerate the dangers to the economy from a higher minimum wage. For example, one could argue that a higher minimum wage will force employers to upgrade the skills and productivity of their workers. Increasing the minimum wage may therefore be a win-win proposition, rather than a win-lose proposition. Finally, across the United States in 2013 walkouts and protests by fast food workers demanded a higher minimum wage and collective bargaining rights.

ANALYZE the ISSUE

1. Identify two positive and two normative statements given above concerning raising the minimum wage. List other minimum-wage arguments not discussed in this Economics in Practice, and classify them as either positive or normative economics.

2. Give a positive and a normative argument why a business leader would oppose raising the minimum wage. Give a positive and a normative argument why a labor leader would favor raising the minimum wage.

3. Explain your position on this issue. Identify positive and normative reasons for your decision. Are there alternative ways to aid the working poor?

[1] David Newmark and William Wascher, *Minimum Wages*, Cambridge, MA. The MIT Press, 2008.

boring." Instead, it was an eye-opening experience that inspired me to change my major to economics and pursue an economics teaching career.

The study of economics has attracted a number of well-known people. For example, the Rolling Stones' Mick Jagger attended the London School of Economics, and other famous people who majored in economics include three former presidents—George H.W. Bush, Ronald Reagan, and Gerald Ford.

An economics major can choose many career paths. Most economics majors work for business firms. Because economists are trained in analyzing financial matters, they find good jobs in management, sales, or as a market analyst interpreting economic conditions relevant to a firm's markets. For those with an undergraduate degree, private sector job opportunities exist in banking, securities brokering, management consulting, computer and data processing firms, the power industry, market research, finance, health care, and many other industries. The remainder of economics majors work for government agencies or in colleges and universities.

EXHIBIT 1-3 Average Yearly Starting Salary for Selected Majors for 2013

Undergraduate Major	Salary ($)
Computer engineering	71,700
Computer science	64,800
Electrical engineering	63,400
Management information systems	63,100
Finance	57,400
Business administration	55,300
Economics	55,100
Accounting	53,300
Nursing	52,800
Marketing	51,000
Advertising	46,600
Special Education	46,100
International business	45,500
Communications	43,400
Journalism	40,400
Liberal arts	40,300
Political science	39,800
Criminal justice	35,200
Social work	35,100
Sociology	34,800
Conservation/renewable resources	30,900

Source: National Association of Colleges and Employers, *Salary Survey,* Spring 2013.

Government economists work for federal, state, and local governments. For example, a government economist might compile and report national statistics for economic growth or work on projects such as how to improve indexes to measure trends in consumer prices. Economists in academe not only enjoy the challenge of teaching economics but also have great freedom in selecting research projects.

Studying economics is also an essential preparation for other careers. Those preparing for law school, for example, find economics an excellent major because of its emphasis on a logical approach to problem solving. Economics is also great preparation for an MBA. In fact, students majoring in any field will benefit throughout their lives from learning how to apply the economic way of thinking to analyze real-world economic issues.

Finally, economics majors shine in salary offers upon graduation. Exhibit 1-3 shows average yearly starting salaries for bachelor's degree graduates for 2013.

Key Concepts

Scarcity	Entrepreneurship	Macroeconomics	Ceteris paribus
Resources	Capital	Microeconomics	Positive economics
Land	Economics	Model	Normative economics
Labor			

Summary

- **Scarcity** is the fundamental economic problem that human wants exceed the availability of time, goods, and resources. Individuals and society therefore can never have everything they desire.

- **Resources** are factors of production classified as land, labor, and capital. Entrepreneurship is a special type of labor. An entrepreneur seeks profits by taking risks and combining resources to produce innovative products.

- **Economics** is the study of how individuals and society choose to allocate scarce resources to satisfy unlimited wants. Faced with unlimited wants and scarce resources, we must make choices among alternatives.

- **Macroeconomics** applies an economywide perspective that focuses on such issues as inflation, unemployment, and the growth rate of the economy.

- **Microeconomics** examines individual decision-making units within an economy such as a consumer's response to changes in the price of coffee and the reasons for changes in the market price of personal computers.

- **Models** are simplified descriptions of reality used to understand and predict economic events. An economic model can be stated verbally or in a table, a graph, or an equation. If the evidence is not consistent with the model, the model is rejected.

- **Ceteris paribus** holds "all other factors unchanged" that might affect a particular relationship. If this assumption is violated, a model cannot be tested. Another reasoning pitfall is to think that *association* means *causation*.

- Use of positive versus normative economic analysis is a major reason for disagreements among economists. **Positive economics** uses testable statements. Often a positive argument is expressed as an *if-then* statement. **Normative economics** is based on value judgments or opinions and uses words such as *good*, *bad*, *ought to*, and *should*.

Study Questions and Problems

1. Explain why both nations with high living standards and nations with low living standards face the problem of scarcity. If you won $1 million in a lottery, would you escape the scarcity problem?
2. Why isn't money considered capital in economics?
3. Explain the difference between macroeconomics and microeconomics. Give examples of the areas of concern to each branch of economics.
4. Which of the following are microeconomic issues? Which are macroeconomic issues?
   a. How will an increase in the price of Coca-Cola affect the quantity of Pepsi-Cola sold?
   b. What will cause the nation's inflation rate to fall?
   c. How does a quota on textile imports affect the textile industry?
   d. Does a large federal budget deficit reduce the rate of unemployment in the economy?
5. Explain why it is important for an economic model to be an abstraction from the real world.
6. Explain the importance of the ceteris paribus assumption for an economic model.
7. Suppose Congress cuts spending for the military, and then unemployment rises in the U.S. defense industry. Is there causation in this situation, or are we observing an association between events?
8. Analyze the positive versus normative arguments in the following case. What statements of positive economics are used to support requiring air bags? What normative reasoning is used?

Should the Government Require Air Bags?

Technological advances continuously provide new high-tech options to save lives that add to the price of cars, such as cameras, radar, and airbags. Air bag advocates say air bags will save lives and the government should require them in all cars. Air bags add an estimated $600 to the cost of a car, compared to about $100 for a set of regular seat belts. Opponents argue that air bags are electronic devices that are subject to failure and have produced injuries and death. For example, air bags have killed both adults and children whose heads were within the inflation zone at the time of deployment. Opponents therefore believe the government should leave the decision of whether to spend an extra $600 or so for an air bag to the consumer. The role of the government should be limited to providing information on the risks of having versus not having air bags.

Sample Quiz

1. Which of the following illustrates the concept of scarcity?
   a. More clean air is wanted than is available in large polluted metropolitan areas such as Mexico City.
   b. There is usually more than one use of your "free" time in the evening.
   c. There are many competing uses for the annual budget of your city, county, or state.
   d. All of the answers are correct.

2. Which of the following are factors of production?
   a. The outputs generated by the production process transforming land, labor, and capital into goods and services.
   b. Restricted to the land resources such as natural resources that are unimproved by human economic activity.
   c. Land (natural resources), labor (human capital, entrepreneurship), and capital (constructed inputs such as factories).
   d. Just labor and capital in industrialized countries, where natural resources are no longer used to produce goods and services.

3. Which of the following is *not* an example of a capital input?
   a. A person's skills and abilities, which can be employed to produce valuable goods and services.
   b. Factories and offices where goods and services are produced.
   c. Tools and equipment.
   d. Computers used by a company to record inventory, sales, and payroll.

4. Which of the following is the *best* definition of economics?
   a. Economics is the study of how to manage corporations to generate the greatest return on shareholder investment.
   b. Economics is the study of how to manage city and county government to generate the greatest good to its citizens.
   c. Economics is the study of how society chooses to allocate its scarce resources.
   d. Economics is the study of how to track revenues and costs within a business.

5. Which of the following *best* illustrates the application of the model-building process to economics?
   a. Two economists with differing political agendas argue about the best way to solve the social security problem on a Sunday morning talk show.
   b. A labor economist notices that unemployment tends to be higher among teenagers than more experienced workers, develops a model, and gathers data to test the hypotheses in the model.
   c. A PhD student in economics develops a plausible mathematical model of an industry for his dissertation, but there is no data to test the model.
   d. Economists come to believe that some economic models are true simply because prominent leading economists say they are true.

6. Which of the following represents causality rather than association?
   a. In years that fashion dictates wider lapels on men's jackets, the stock market grows by at least 5 percent.
   b. Interest rates are higher in years ending with a 1 or a 6.
   c. Unemployment falls when the AFC champion wins the Super Bowl.
   d. Quantity demanded goes up when price falls because lower prices increase consumer purchasing power, and because some consumers of substitute goods switch.

7. Which of the following correctly describes the ceteris paribus assumption?
   a. If we increase the price of a good, reduce consumer incomes, and lower the price of substitutes, and if quantity demanded is observed to fall, we know that the price increase caused that decline in quantity demanded.
   b. If the federal government increases government spending, and the Federal Reserve Bank lowers interest rates, we know that the increase in government spending caused unemployment to fall.
   c. If a company reduces its labor costs, negotiates lower materials costs from its vendors, and advertises, we know that the reduced labor costs are why profits are higher.
   d. If we decrease the price of a good and observe that there is an increase in the quantity demanded, holding all other factors that influence this relationship constant.

8. The condition of scarcity
   a. cannot be eliminated.
   b. prevails in poor economies.
   c. prevails in rich economies.
   d. All of the answers above are correct.

9. Which of the following *best* describes an entrepreneur?
   a. A person who works as an office clerk at a major corporation.
   b. A person who combines the factors of production to produce innovative products.
   c. A special type of capital.
   d. Wealthy individuals who provide savings that stimulates the economy.

10. Which of the following is *true* about renewable natural resources?
    a. They are a type of land resource such as oil, coal, and natural gas that has a fixed stock.
    b. They are a type of capital resource such as irrigation networks and wastewater treatment plants that utilize water.
    c. They are a type of capital resource such as air filtration systems in buildings that renew and refresh polluted air from the outside.
    d. They are a type of land resource such as forests, range-lands, and marine fisheries that naturally regenerate and thus can tolerate a sustained harvest, but can be depleted from excessive harvest.

11. Because of scarcity,
    a. it is impossible to satisfy every desire and choices must be made.
    b. the available supply of time, good, and resources is greater than human wants.
    c. every desire is fulfilled.
    d. there are no limits on the economy's ability to satisfy unlimited wants.

12. Which of the following represents positive economics?
    a. Policy A is fair.
    b. Outcome B is the best objective to achieve.
    c. If policy A is followed, then outcome B results.
    d. All of these choices are positive economic analysis.

13. Which of the following is the last step in the model-building process?
    a. Collect data and test the model.
    b. Develop a model based on simplified assumptions.
    c. Identify the problem.
    d. Formulate an assumption.

14. Which of the following is *not* a type of economic analysis?
    a. Positive
    b. Resources
    c. Normative
    d. None of the above is a type of economic analysis.

15. Which word or phrase indicates that an economist is using positive economics?
    a. Good.
    b. Bad.
    c. If-then.
    d. Should.

16. Which of the following would eliminate scarcity as an economic problem?
    a. Moderation of people's competitive instincts.
    b. Discovery of sufficiently large new energy reserves.
    c. Resumption of the steady productivity growth.
    d. None of the answers above are correct.

17. Which resource is *not* an example of capital?
    a. Equipment.
    b. Machinery.
    c. Physical plants.
    d. Stocks or bonds.

18. Which of the following is the second step in the model-building process?
    a. Collect data and test the model.
    b. Develop a model based on simplified assumptions.
    c. Identify the problem.
    d. Include all possible variables that affect the model.

19. Which of the following is a type of economic analysis?
    a. Positive.
    b. Resources.
    c. Association.
    d. None of the above is a type of economic analysis.

20. Which of the following is a career that could result from majoring in economics?
    a. Management.
    b. Banking.
    c. Government.
    d. All of the answers above are correct.

APPENDIX 1

Applying Graphs to Economics

Economists are famous for their use of graphs. The reason is "a picture is worth a thousand words." Graphs are used throughout this text to present economics models. By drawing a line, you can use a two-dimensional illustration to analyze the effects of a change in one variable on another. You could describe the same information using other model forms, such as verbal statements, tables, or equations, but a graph is the simplest way to present and understand the relationship between economic variables.

Don't be worried that graphs will "throw you for a loop." Relax! This appendix explains all the basic graphical language you will need. The following illustrates the simplest use of graphs for economic analysis.

A1-1 A DIRECT RELATIONSHIP

Basic economic analysis typically concerns the relationship between two variables, both having positive values. Hence, we can confine our graphs to the upper-right (northeast) quadrant of the coordinate number system. In Exhibit 1A-1, notice that the scales on the horizontal axis (*x*-axis) and the vertical axis (*y*-axis) do not necessarily measure the same numerical values.

The horizontal axis in Exhibit 1A-1 measures annual income, and the vertical axis shows the amount spent per year for a personal computer (PC). In the absence of any established traditions, we could decide to measure income on the vertical axis and expenditure on the horizontal axis. The intersection of the horizontal and vertical axes is the *origin,* and the point at which both income and expenditure are zero. In Exhibit 1A-1, each point is a coordinate that matches the dollar value of income and the corresponding expenditure for a PC. For example, point *A* on the graph shows that people with an annual income of $10,000 spent $1,000 per year for a PC. Other incomes are associated with different expenditure levels. For example, at $30,000 per year (point *C*), $3,000 will be spent annually for a PC.

The straight line in Exhibit 1A-1 allows us to determine the direction of change in PC expenditure as annual income changes. This relationship is *positive* because PC expenditure, measured along the vertical axis, and annual income, measured along the horizontal axis, move in the same direction. PC expenditure increases as annual income increases. As income declines, so does the amount spent on a PC. Thus, the straight line representing the relationship between income and PC

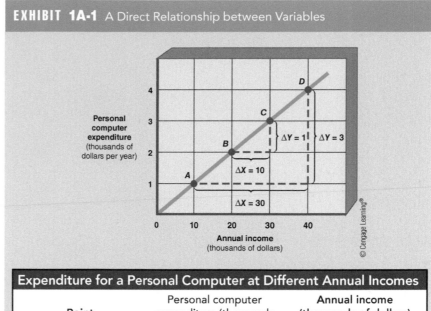

EXHIBIT 1A-1 A Direct Relationship between Variables

Expenditure for a Personal Computer at Different Annual Incomes		
Point	Personal computer expenditure (thousands of dollars per year)	Annual income (thousands of dollars)
A	$1	$10
B	2	20
C	3	30
D	4	40

The line with a positive slope shows that the expenditure per year for a personal computer has a direct relationship to annual income, ceteris paribus. As annual income increases along the horizontal axis, the amount spent on a PC also increases, as measured by the vertical axis. Along the line, each 10-unit increase in annual income results in a 1-unit increase in expenditure for a PC. Because the slope is constant along a straight line, we can measure the same slope between any two points. Between points B and C or between points A and D, the slope = $\Delta Y/\Delta X$ = +3/+30 = +1/+10 = 1/10.

Direct relationship A positive association between two variables. When one variable increases, the other variable increases, and when one variable decreases, the other variable decreases.

expenditure is a **direct relationship**. A direct relationship is a positive association between two variables. When one variable increases, the other variable increases, and when one variable decreases, the other variable decreases. In short, both variables change in the *same* direction.

Finally, this is an important point to remember: A two-variable graph, like any model, isolates the relationship between two variables and holds all other variables constant under the ceteris paribus assumption. In Exhibit 1A-1, for example, factors such as the prices of PCs and education are held constant by assumption. In Chapter 3, you will learn that allowing variables not shown in the graph to change can shift the position of the curve.

A1-2 AN INVERSE RELATIONSHIP

Now consider the relationship between the price of compact discs (CDs) and the quantity consumers will buy per year, shown in Exhibit 1A-2. These data indicate a *negative* relationship between the price and quantity variables. When the price is low, consumers purchase a greater quantity of CDs than when the price is high.

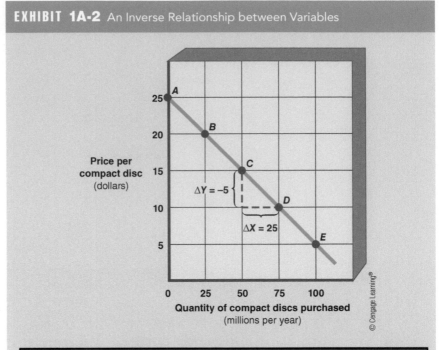

EXHIBIT 1A-2 An Inverse Relationship between Variables

The Quantity of Compact Discs Consumers Purchase at Different Prices

Point	Price per compact disc	Quantity of compact discs purchased (millions per year)
A	$25	0
B	20	25
C	15	50
D	10	75
E	5	100

The line with a negative slope shows an inverse relationship between the price per compact disc and the quantity of compact discs consumers purchase, ceteris paribus. As the price of a CD rises, the quantity of CDs purchased falls. A lower price for CDs is associated with more CDs purchased by consumers. Along the line, with each $5 decrease in the price of CDs, consumers increase the quantity purchased by 25 units. The slope = $\Delta Y/\Delta X = -5/+25 = -1/5$.

Inverse relationship A negative association between two variables. When one variable increases, the other variable decreases, and when one variable decreases, the other variable increases.

In Exhibit 1A-2, there is an **inverse relationship** between the price per CD and the quantity consumers buy. An inverse relationship is a negative association between two variables. When one variable increases, the other variable decreases, and when one variable decreases, the other variable increases. Stated simply, the variables move in *opposite* directions.

The line drawn in Exhibit 1A-2 is an inverse relationship. By long-established tradition, economists put price on the vertical axis and quantity on the horizontal axis. In Chapter 3, we will study in more detail the relationship between price and quantity called the *law of demand*.

In addition to observing the inverse relationship (slope), you must interpret the *intercept* at point *A* in the exhibit. The intercept in this case means that at a price of $25 no consumer is willing to buy a single CD.

A1–3 THE SLOPE OF A STRAIGHT LINE

Slope The ratio of the change in the variable on the vertical axis (the rise or fall) to the change in the variable on the horizontal axis (the run).

Plotting numbers gives a clear visual expression of the relationship between two variables, but it is also important to know how much one variable changes as another variable changes. To find out, we calculate the slope. The slope is the ratio of the change in the variable on the vertical axis (the rise or fall) to the change in the variable on the horizontal axis (the run). Algebraically, if Y is on the vertical axis and X is on the horizontal axis, the slope is expressed as follows (the delta symbol, Δ, means "change in"):

$$\text{Slope} = \frac{\text{rise}}{\text{run}} = \frac{\text{change in vertical axis}}{\text{change in horizontal axis}} = \frac{\Delta Y}{\Delta X}$$

Consider the slope between points B and C in Exhibit 1A-1. The change in expenditure for a PC, Y, is equal to +1 (from \$2,000 to \$3,000 per year), and the change in annual income, X, is equal to +10 (from \$20,000 to \$30,000 per year). The slope is therefore +1/+10. The sign is positive because computer expenditure is directly, or positively, related to annual income. The steeper the line, the greater the slope because the ratio of ΔY to ΔX rises. Conversely, the flatter the line, the smaller the slope. Exhibit 1A-1 also illustrates that the slope of a straight line is constant. That is, the slope between any two points along the line, such as between points A and D, is equal to +3/+30 = 1/10.

What does the slope of 1/10 mean? It tells you that a \$1,000 increase (decrease) in PC expenditure each year occurs for each \$10,000 increase (decrease) in annual income. The line plotted in Exhibit 1A-1 has a *positive slope*, and we describe the line as "upward sloping."

On the other hand, the line in Exhibit 1A-2 has a *negative slope*. The change in Y between points C and D is equal to −5 (from \$15 down to \$10), and the change in X is equal to +25 (from 50 million up to 75 million CDs purchased per year). The slope is therefore −5/+25 = −1/5, and this line is described as "downward sloping."

What does this slope of −1/5 mean? It means that raising (lowering) the price per CD by \$1 decreases (increases) the quantity of compact discs purchased by 5 million per year.

Suppose we calculate the slope between any two points on a flat line—for example, points B and C in Exhibit 1A-3. In this case, there is no change in Y (expenditure for toothpaste) as X (annual income) increases. Consumers spend \$20 per year on toothpaste regardless of annual income. It follows that $\Delta Y = 0$ for any ΔX, so the slope is equal to 0. The two variables along a flat line (horizontal or vertical) have an independent relationship. An independent relationship is a zero association between two variables. When one variable changes, the other variable remains unchanged.

Independent relationship A zero association between two variables. When one variable changes, the other variable remains unchanged.

A1–4 A THREE VARIABLE RELATIONSHIP IN ONE GRAPH

The two-variable relationships drawn so far conform to a two-dimensional flat piece of paper. For example, the vertical axis measures the price per CD variable, and the horizontal axis measures the quantity of CDs purchased variable. All other factors, such as consumer income, that may affect the relationship between the price and quantity variables are held constant by the ceteris paribus assumption. But reality is frequently not so accommodating. Often a model must take into account the impact of changes in a third variable (consumer income) drawn on a two-dimensional piece of graph paper.

Economists' favorite method of depicting a three-variable relationship is shown in Exhibit 1A-4. As explained earlier, the cause-and-effect relationship between price and quantity of CD purchases determines the downward-sloping

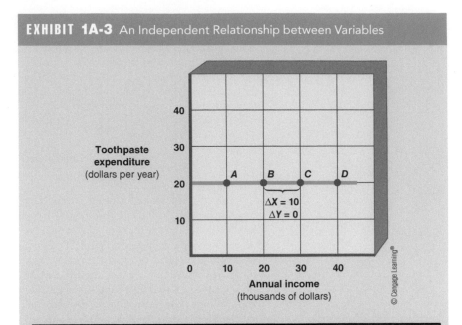

EXHIBIT 1A-3 An Independent Relationship between Variables

Expenditure for Toothpaste at Different Annual Incomes		
Point	Toothpaste expenditure (dollars per year)	Annual income (thousands of dollars)
A	$20	$10
B	20	20
C	20	30
D	20	40

The flat line with a zero slope shows that the expenditure per year for toothpaste is unrelated to annual income. As annual income increases along the horizontal axis, the amount spent each year for toothpaste remains unchanged at 20 units. If annual income increases 10 units, the corresponding change in expenditure is zero. The slope = $\Delta Y / \Delta X = 0/+10 = 0$.

curve. A change in the price per CD causes a movement downward along either of the two separate curves. As the price falls, consumers increase the quantity of CDs demanded. The location of each curve on the graph, however, depends on the annual income of consumers. As the annual income variable increases from $30,000 to $60,000 and consumers can afford to pay more, the price-quantity demanded curve shifts rightward. Conversely, as the annual income variable decreases and consumers have less to spend, the price-quantity demanded curve shifts leftward.

This is an extremely important concept that you must understand: Throughout this book, you must distinguish between *movements along* and *shifts in* a curve. Here's how to tell the difference. A change in one of the variables shown on either of the coordinate axes of the graph causes *movement along* a curve. On the other hand, a change in a variable not shown on one of the coordinate axes of the graph causes a *shift in* a curve's position on the graph.

CONCLUSION A shift in a curve occurs only when the ceteris paribus assumption is relaxed and a third variable not shown on either axis of the graph is allowed to change.

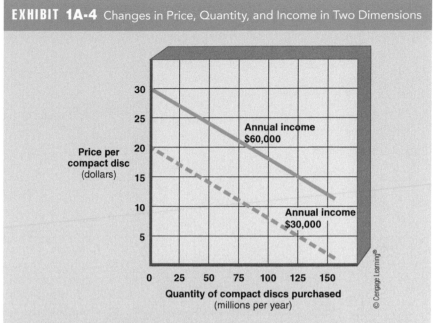

EXHIBIT 1A-4 Changes in Price, Quantity, and Income in Two Dimensions

Economists use a multicurve graph to represent a three-variable relationship in a two-dimensional graph. A decrease in the price per CD causes a movement downward along each curve. As the annual income of consumers rises, there is a shift rightward in the position of the demand curve.

A1-5 A HELPFUL STUDY HINT FOR USING GRAPHS

To some students, studying economics is a little frightening because many chapters are full of graphs. An often-repeated mistake is to prepare for tests by trying to memorize the lines of graphs. When their graded tests are returned, students using this strategy will probably exclaim, "What happened?" The answer is that if you learn the economic concepts first, then you will understand the graphs as illustrations of these underlying concepts. Stated simply, superficial cramming for economics quizzes does not work. For students who are anxious about using graphs, in addition to the brief review of graphical analysis in this appendix, the Graphing Workshop on the EconCentral Web site and the Study Guide contain step-by-step features on how to interpret graphs.

Key Concepts

Direct Relationship   Slope
Inverse Relationship   Independent Relationship

Summary

- **Graphs** provide a means to clearly show economic relationships in two-dimensional space. Economic analysis is often concerned with two variables confined to the upper-right (northeast) quadrant of the coordinate number system.

- A **direct relationship** occurs when two variables change in the *same* direction.

Direct Relationship

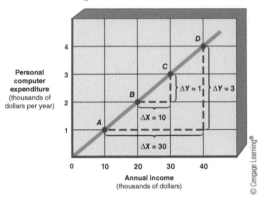

- An **inverse relationship** occurs when two variables change in *opposite* directions.

Inverse Relationship

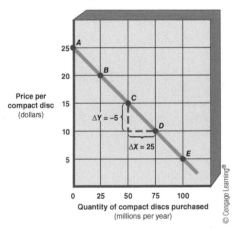

- An **independent relationship** occurs when two variables are unrelated. (Exhibit 1A-3)

Independent Relationship

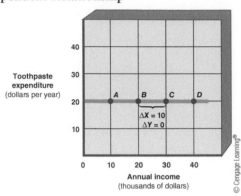

- **Slope** is the ratio of the vertical change (the rise or fall) to the horizontal change (the run). The slope of an *upward-sloping* line is *positive*, and the slope of a *downward-sloping* line is *negative*.

- A **three-variable relationship** is depicted by a graph showing a shift in a curve when the ceteris paribus assumption is relaxed and a third variable (such as annual income) not on either axis of the graph is allowed to change. (Exhibit 1A-4)

Three-Variable Relationship

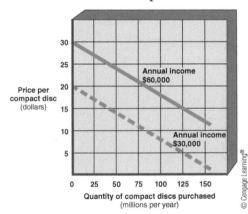

Study Questions and Problems

1. Draw a graph without specific data for the expected relationship between the following variables
   a. The probability of living and age
   b. Annual income and years of education
   c. Inches of snow and sales of bathing suits
   d. The number of football games won and the athletic budget
   In each case, state whether the expected relationship is *direct* or *inverse*. Explain an additional factor that would be included in the *ceteris paribus* assumption because it might change and influence your theory.

2. Assume a research firm collects survey sales data that reveal the relationship between the possible selling prices of hamburgers and the quantity of hamburgers consumers would purchase per year at alternative prices. The report states that if the price of a hamburger is $4, 20,000 hamburgers will be

bought. However, at a price of $3, 40,000 hamburgers will be bought. At $2, 60,000 hamburgers will be bought, and at $1, 80,000 hamburgers will be purchased.

Based on these data, describe the relevant relationship between the price of a hamburger and the quantity consumers are willing to purchase, using a verbal statement, a numerical table, and a graph. Which model do you prefer and why?

Sample Quiz

1. What is used to illustrate an independent relationship between two variables?
   a. An upward-sloping curve.
   b. A downward-sloping curve.
   c. A hill-shaped curve.
   d. A horizontal or vertical line.
2. Which of the following pairs is the *most* likely to exhibit an inverse relationship?
   a. The amount of time you study and your grade point average.
   b. People's annual income and their expenditure on personal computers.
   c. Baseball players' salaries and their batting averages.
   d. The price of a concert and the number of tickets people purchase.

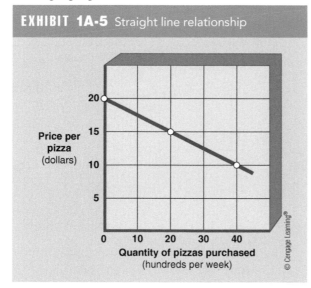

EXHIBIT 1A-5 Straight line relationship

Price per pizza (dollars)

Quantity of pizzas purchased (hundreds per week)

© Cengage Learning®

3. According to Exhibit 1A-5, the relationship between the price and quantity purchased of pizza is
   a. direct.
   b. inverse.
   c. complex.
   d. independent.

4. What is the slope of the line shown in Exhibit 1A-5?
   a. −1.
   b. −1/2.
   c. −1/4.
   d. 0.
5. Which of the following would cause a leftward shift in the relationship shown in Exhibit 1A-5?
   a. A fall in household incomes.
   b. A fall in the price of pizza.
   c. A fall in the quantity of pizza that people wish to purchase.
   d. All of the above would shift the line in the graph.
6. Suppose two variables are directly related. If one variable rises, then the other variable
   a. also rises.
   b. falls.
   c. remains unchanged.
   d. reacts unpredictably.
7. When an inverse relationship is graphed, the resulting line or curve is
   a. horizontal.
   b. vertical.
   c. upward-sloping.
   d. downward-sloping.

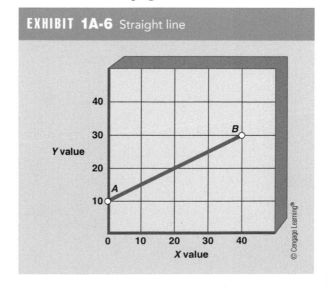

EXHIBIT 1A-6 Straight line

Y value

X value

© Cengage Learning®

8. Straight line AB in Exhibit 1A-6 shows that
   a. increasing values for *X* will decrease the values of *Y*.
   b. decreasing values for *X* will increase the values of *Y*.
   c. there is a direct relationship between *X* and *Y*.
   d. All of the answers above are correct.

9. In Exhibit 1A-6, the slope of straight line AB is
   a. positive.
   b. zero.
   c. negative.
   d. variable.

10. In Exhibit 1A-6, the slope of straight line AB is
    a. 1.
    b. 5.
    c. 1/2.
    d. −1.

11. As shown in Exhibit 1A-6, the slope of straight line AB
    a. decreases with increases in X.
    b. increases with increases in X.
    c. increases with decreases in X.
    d. remains constant with changes in X.

12. In Exhibit 1A-6, as *X* increases along the horizontal axis, the *Y* values increase. The relationship between the *X* and *Y* variables is
    a. direct.
    b. inverse.
    c. independent.
    d. variable.

EXHIBIT **1A-7** Straight line

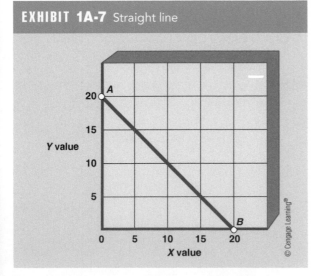

13. In Exhibit 1A-7, as *X* increases along the horizontal axis, the *Y* values decrease. The relationship between the *X* and *Y* variables is
    a. direct.
    b. inverse.
    c. independent.
    d. variable.

14. Straight line AB in Exhibit 1A-7 shows that
    a. increasing values for X reduces the value of Y.
    b. decreasing values for X increases the value of Y.
    c. there is an inverse relationship between X and Y.
    d. All of the answers above are correct.

15. As shown in Exhibit 1A-7, the slope of straight line AB
    a. decreases with increases in X.
    b. increases with increases in X.
    c. increases with decreases in X.
    d. remains constant with changes in X.

16. In Exhibit 1A-7, the slope for straight line AB is
    a. 3.
    b. 1.
    c. −1.
    d. −5.

17. In Exhibit 1A-7, the slope of straight line AB is
    a. positive.
    b. zero.
    c. negative.
    d. variable.

EXHIBIT **1A-8** Straight line

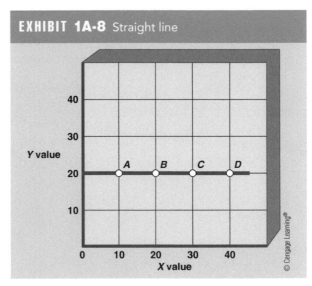

18. In Exhibit 1A-8, as X increases along the horizontal axis, corresponding to points A-D on the line, the Y values remain unchanged at 20 units. The relationship between the X and Y variables is
    a. direct.
    b. inverse.
    c. independent.
    d. undefined.

19. In Exhibit 1A-8, the slope of straight line A-D is
    a. greater than 1.
    b. equal to 1.
    c. less than 1.
    d. zero.

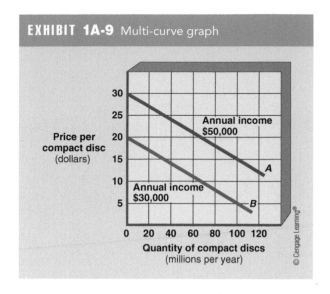

EXHIBIT 1A-9 Multi-curve graph

Price per compact disc (dollars)

Annual income $50,000

Annual income $30,000

A

B

Quantity of compact discs (millions per year)

© Cengage Learning®

20. Exhibit 1A-9 represents a three-variable relationship. As the annual income of consumers falls from $50,000 (line A) to $30,000 (line B), the result is a (an)
   a. upward movement along each curve.
   b. downward movement along each curve.
   c. leftward shift in curve A to curve B.
   d. rightward shift in curve A to curve B.

Production Possibilities, Opportunity Cost, and Economic Growth

In this chapter, you will learn to solve these economics puzzles:

- Why do so few rock stars and movie stars go to college?
- Why would you spend an extra hour reading this text rather than going to a movie or sleeping?
- Why are investment and economic growth so important?
- What does a war on terrorism really mean?

CHAPTER PREVIEW

This chapter continues building on the foundation laid in the preceding chapter. Having learned that *scarcity* forces *choices*, here you will study the choices people make in more detail. This chapter begins by examining the three basic choices: *What*, *How*, and *For Whom* to produce. The process of answering these basic questions introduces two other key building blocks in the economic way of thinking—*opportunity cost* and *marginal analysis*. Once you understand these important concepts stated in words, it will be easier to interpret our first formal economic model, the *production possibilities curve*. This model illustrates how economists use graphs as a powerful tool to supplement words and develop an understanding of basic economic principles. You will discover that the production possibilities model teaches many of the most important concepts in economics, including scarcity, the law of increasing opportunity costs, efficiency, investment, and economic growth. For example, the chapter concludes by using the production possibilities curve to explain why underdeveloped countries do not achieve economic growth and thereby improve their standard of living.

2-1 THREE FUNDAMENTAL ECONOMIC QUESTIONS

Because of the problem of scarcity, whether rich or poor, every nation must answer the same three fundamental economic questions: (1) *What* products will be produced? (2) *How* will they be produced? and (3) *For Whom* will they be produced? Later, the chapter on economies in transition introduces various types of economic systems and describes how each deals with these three economic choices.

2-1a What to Produce?

The *What* question requires an economy to decide the mix and quantity of goods and services it will produce. Should society devote its limited resources to producing more health care and fewer military goods? Should society produce more iPods and fewer Blu-rays? Should more capital goods be produced instead of consumer goods, or should small hybrid cars and fewer SUVs be produced? The problem of scarcity restricts our ability to produce everything we want during a given period, so the choice to produce "more" of one good requires producing "less" of another good. In the United States, consumer sovereignty answers the *What* question. In Cuba and North Korea, for example, the government, not the consumer, answers this question.

2-1b How to Produce?

After deciding which products to make, the second question for society to decide is *How* to mix technology and scarce resources in order to produce these goods. For instance, a towel can be sewn primarily by hand (labor), partially by hand and partially by machine (labor and capital), or primarily by machine (capital). In short, the *How* question asks whether a production technique will be more or less capital-intensive. The *How* question also concerns choices among resources for production. Should electricity be produced from oil, solar power, or nuclear power?

Education plays an important role in answering the *How* question. Education improves the ability of workers to perform their work. Variation in the quality and quantity of education among nations is one reason economies differ in their capacities to apply resources and technology to answer the *How* question. For example, the United States is striving to catch up with Japan in the use of robotics. Answering the question *How do we improve our robotics?* requires engineers and employees with the proper training in the installation and operation of robots.

2-1c For Whom to Produce?

Once the *What* and *How* questions are resolved, the third question is *For Whom*. Among all those desiring the produced goods, who actually receives them? This question concerns how the economic pie is divided. Who is fed well? Who drives a Mercedes? Who receives organ transplants? Should economics professors earn a salary of $1 million a year and others pay higher taxes to support economists? The *For Whom* question means that society must have a method to decide who will be "rich and famous" and who will be "poor and unknown." Chapter 10 returns to the *For Whom* question and discusses it in more detail.

2-2 OPPORTUNITY COST

Because of scarcity, the three basic questions cannot be answered without sacrifice or cost. But what does the term *cost* really mean? The common response would be to say that the purchase price is the cost. A movie ticket *costs* $8, or a shirt *costs* $50. Applying the economic way of thinking, however, *cost* is defined differently. A well-known phrase from Nobel Prize–winning economist Milton Friedman says, "There is no such thing as a free lunch." This expression captures the links among the concepts of scarcity, choice, and cost. Because of scarcity, people must make choices, and each choice incurs a cost (sacrifice). Once one option is chosen, another option is given up. The money you spend on a movie ticket cannot also buy a Blu-ray. A business may purchase a new textile machine to manufacture towels, but this same money cannot be used to buy a new recreation facility for employees.

Opportunity cost The best alternative sacrificed for a chosen alternative.

The Blu-ray and recreation facility examples illustrate that the true cost of these decisions is the **opportunity cost** of a choice, not the purchase price. Opportunity cost is the best alternative sacrificed for a chosen alternative. Stated differently, it is the cost of not choosing the next best alternative. This principle states that some highly valued opportunity must be forgone in all economic decisions. The actual good or use of time given up for the chosen good or use of time measures the opportunity cost. We may omit the word *opportunity* before the word *cost*, but the concept remains the same. Exhibit 2-1 illustrates the causation chain linking scarcity, choice, and opportunity cost.

Examples are endless, but let's consider a few. Suppose your economics professor decides to become a rock star in the Rolling in Dough band. Now all his or her working hours are devoted to creating hit music, and the opportunity cost is the educational services no longer provided. Now a personal example: The opportunity cost of dating a famous model or movie star (name your favorite) might be the loss of your current girlfriend or boyfriend. Opportunity cost also applies to national economic decisions. Suppose the federal government decides to spend tax revenues on a space station. The opportunity cost depends on the next best program *not* funded. Assume roads and bridges are the highest valued projects not built as a result of the decision to construct the space station. Then the opportunity cost of the decision to devote resources to the space station is the forgone roads and bridges and not the money actually spent to build the space station.

To personalize the relationship between time and opportunity cost, ask yourself what you would be doing if you were not reading this book. Your answer might be watching television or sleeping. If sleeping is your choice, the opportunity cost of studying this text is the sleep you sacrifice. Rock stars and movie stars, on the other hand, must forfeit a large amount of income to attend college. Now you know why you see so few of these stars in class.

Decisions often involve sacrifice of *both* goods and time. Suppose you decide to see a movie at a theater located 15 minutes from campus. If you had not spent the money at the movie theater, you could have purchased a Blu-ray and watched a movie at home. And the time spent traveling to and from the movie and sitting through it could have been devoted to studying for your economics exam. The opportunity cost of the movie consists of giving up (1) a Blu-ray and (2) study time needed to score higher on the economics exam.

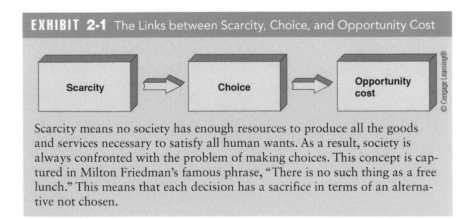

EXHIBIT 2-1 The Links between Scarcity, Choice, and Opportunity Cost

Scarcity means no society has enough resources to produce all the goods and services necessary to satisfy all human wants. As a result, society is always confronted with the problem of making choices. This concept is captured in Milton Friedman's famous phrase, "There is no such thing as a free lunch." This means that each decision has a sacrifice in terms of an alternative not chosen.

2-3 MARGINAL ANALYSIS

Marginal analysis An examination of the effects of additions to or subtractions from a current situation.

At the heart of many important decision-making techniques used throughout this text is **marginal analysis**. Marginal analysis examines the effects of additions to or subtractions from a current situation. This is a very valuable tool in the economic-way-of-thinking toolkit because it considers the "marginal" effects of change. The rational decision maker decides on an option only if the marginal benefit exceeds the marginal cost. For example, you must decide how to use your scarce time. Should you devote an extra hour to reading this book, going to a movie, watching television, texting, or sleeping? There are many ways to spend your time. Which option do you choose? The answer depends on marginal analysis. If you decide the benefit of a higher grade in economics exceeds the opportunity cost of, say, sleep, then you allocate the extra hour to studying economics. Excellent choice!

Businesses use marginal analysis. Hotels, for example, rent space to student groups for dances and other events. Assume you are the hotel manager and a student group offers to pay $400 to use the ballroom for a party. To decide whether to accept the offer requires marginal analysis. The marginal benefit of renting otherwise vacant space is $400, and the marginal cost is $300 for extra electricity and cleaning service. Since the marginal benefit exceeds the marginal cost, the manager sensibly accepts the offer.

Similarly, producers use marginal analysis. For example, a farmer must decide whether to add fertilizer when planting corn. Using marginal analysis, the farmer estimates that the corn revenue yield will be about $75 per acre without fertilizer and about $100 per acre using fertilizer. If the cost of fertilizer is $20 per acre, marginal analysis tells the farmer to fertilize. The addition of fertilizer will increase profit by $5 per acre because fertilizing adds $25 to the value of each acre at a cost of $20 per acre.

In Part 2, you will use marginal analysis to assess the microeconomic production choices that businesses make in order to maximize profits. Marginal analysis is an important concept when the government considers changes in various programs. For example, as demonstrated in the next section, it is useful to know that an increase in the production of military goods will result in an opportunity cost of fewer consumer goods produced.

2-4 THE PRODUCTION POSSIBILITIES CURVE

Production possibilities curve A curve that shows the maximum combinations of two outputs an economy can produce in a given period of time with its available resources and technology.

The economic problem of scarcity means that society's capacity to produce combinations of goods is constrained by its limited resources. This condition can be represented in a model called the **production possibilities curve**. The production possibilities curve shows the maximum combinations of two outputs that an economy can produce in a given period of time with its available resources and technology. Three basic assumptions underlie the production possibilities curve model:

1. **Fixed Resources.** The quantities and qualities of all resource inputs remain unchanged during the time period. But the "rules of the game" do allow an economy to shift any resource from the production of one output to the production of another output. For example, an economy might shift workers from producing consumer goods to producing capital goods. Although the number of workers remains unchanged, this transfer of labor will produce fewer consumer goods and more capital goods.

2. **Fully Employed Resources.** The economy operates with all its factors of production fully employed and producing the greatest output possible without waste or mismanagement.

Technology The body of knowledge applied to how goods are produced.

3. **Technology Unchanged.** Holding existing **technology** fixed creates limits, or constraints, on the amounts and types of goods any economy can produce. Technology is the body of knowledge applied to how goods are produced.

Exhibit 2-2 shows a hypothetical economy that has the capacity to manufacture any combination of military goods ("guns") and consumer goods ("butter") per year along its production possibilities curve (PPC), including points *A*, *B*, *C*, and *D*. For example, if this economy uses all its resources to make military goods, it can produce a *maximum* of 160 billion units of military goods and zero units of consumer goods (combination *A*). *Another* possibility is for the economy to use all its resources to produce a *maximum* of 100 billion units of consumer goods and

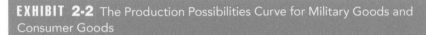

EXHIBIT 2-2 The Production Possibilities Curve for Military Goods and Consumer Goods

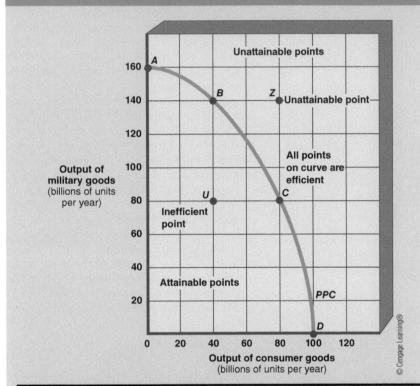

Production Possibilities Schedule for Military and Consumer Goods per Year				
	Production Possibilities			
Output (billions of units per year)	*A*	*B*	*C*	*D*
Military goods	160	140	80	0
Consumer goods	0	40	80	100

All points along the production possibilities curve (PPC) are maximum possible combinations of military goods and consumer goods. One possibility, point *A*, would be to produce 160 billion units of military goods and zero units of consumer goods each year. At the other extreme, point *D*, the economy uses all its resources to produce 100 billion units of consumer goods and zero units of military goods each year. Points *B* and *C* are obtained by using some resources to produce each of the two outputs. If the economy fails to utilize its resources fully, the result is the inefficient point *U*. Point *Z* lies beyond the economy's present production capabilities and is unattainable.

zero units of military goods (point *D*). Between the extremes of points *A* and *D* lie other production possibilities for combinations of military and consumer goods. If combination *B* is chosen, the economy will produce 140 billion units of military goods and 40 billion units of consumer goods. Another possibility (point *C*) is to produce 80 billion units of military goods and 80 billion units of consumer goods.

What happens if the economy does not use all its resources to their capacity? For example, some workers may not find work, or plants and equipment may be idle for any number of reasons. The result is that our hypothetical economy fails to reach any of the combinations along the PPC. In Exhibit 2-2, point *U* illustrates an *inefficient* output level for any economy operating without all its resources fully employed. At point *U*, our model economy is producing 80 billion units of military goods and 40 billion units of consumer goods per year. Such an economy is underproducing because it could satisfy more of society's wants if it were producing at some point along PPC.

Even if an economy fully employs all its resources, it is impossible to produce certain output quantities. Any point outside the production possibilities curve is *unattainable* because it is beyond the economy's present production capabilities. Point *Z*, for example, represents an unattainable output of 140 billion units of military goods and 80 billion units of consumer goods. Society would prefer this combination to any combination along, or inside, the PPC, but the economy cannot reach this point with its existing resources and technology.

> **CONCLUSION** Scarcity limits an economy to points on or below its production possibilities curve.

Because all the points along the curve are *maximum* output levels with the given resources and technology, they are all called *efficient* points. A movement between any two efficient points on the curve means that *more* of one product is produced only by producing *less* of the other product. In Exhibit 2-2, moving from point *A* to point *B* produces 40 billion additional units of consumer goods per year, but only at a cost of sacrificing 20 billion units of military goods. Thus, a movement between any two efficient points graphically illustrates "there is no such thing as a free lunch."

> **CONCLUSION** The production possibilities curve consists of all efficient output combinations at which an economy can produce more of one good only by producing less of the other good.

2-5 THE LAW OF INCREASING OPPORTUNITY COSTS

Why is the production possibilities curve shaped the way it is? Exhibit 2-3 will help us answer this question. It presents a production possibilities curve for a hypothetical economy that must choose between producing tanks and producing sailboats. Consider expanding the production of sailboats in 20,000-unit increments. Moving from point *A* to point *B*, the *opportunity cost* is 10,000 tanks; between point *B* and point *C*, the *opportunity cost* is 20,000 tanks; and the *opportunity cost* of producing at point *D*, rather than point *C*, is 50,000 tanks.

Law of increasing opportunity costs The principle that the opportunity cost increases as production of one output expands.

Exhibit 2-3 illustrates the law of increasing opportunity costs, which states that the opportunity cost increases as production of one output expands. Holding the stock of resources and technology constant (ceteris paribus), the law of increasing opportunity costs causes the production possibilities curve to display a *bowed-out* shape.

EXHIBIT 2-3 The Law of Increasing Opportunity Costs

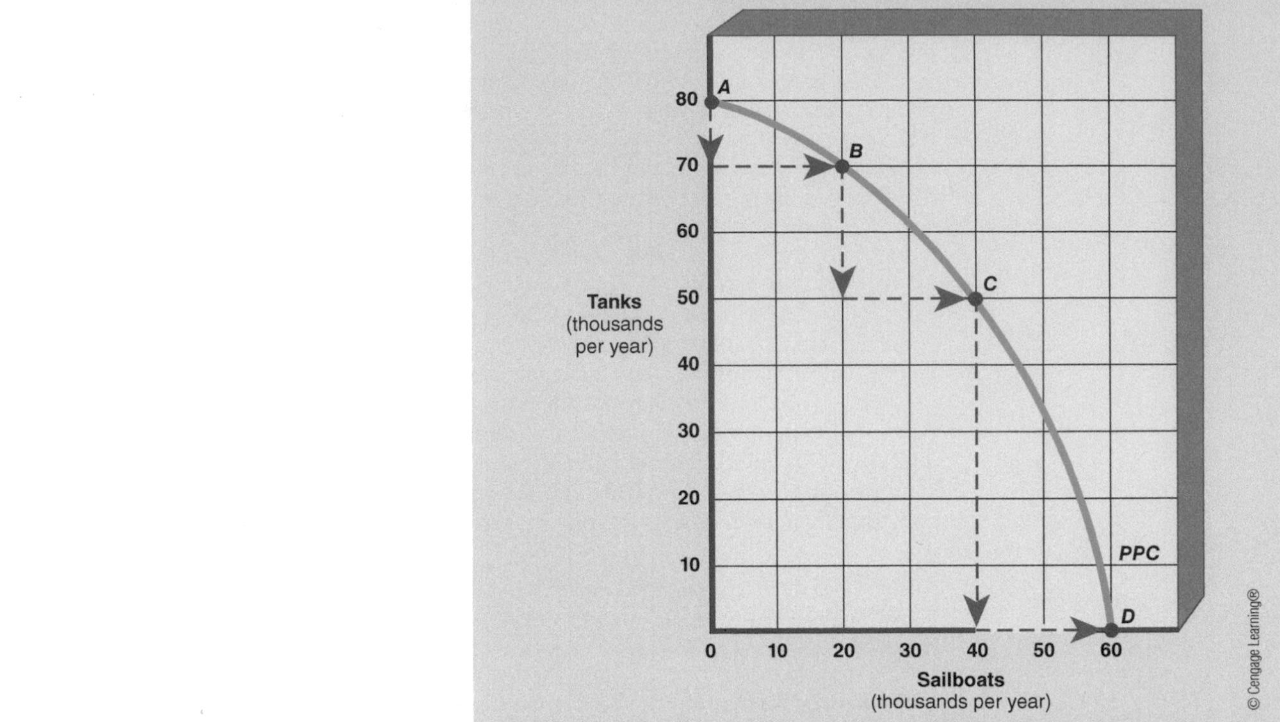

Production Possibilities Schedule for Tanks and Sailboats per Year				
	Production Possibilities			
Output (thousands per year)	A	B	C	D
Tanks	80	70	50	0
Sailboats	0	20	40	60

A hypothetical economy produces equal increments of 20,000 sailboats per year as we move from point *A* through point *D* on the production possibilities curve (PPC). If the economy moves from point *A* to point *B*, the opportunity cost of 20,000 sailboats is a reduction in tank output of 10,000 per year. This opportunity cost rises to 20,000 tanks if the economy moves from point *B* to point *C*. Finally, production at point *D*, rather than point *C*, results in an opportunity cost of 50,000 tanks per year. The opportunity cost rises because workers are not equally suited to making tanks and sailboats.

Why must our hypothetical economy sacrifice larger and larger amounts of tank output to produce each additional 20,000 sailboats? The reason is that all workers are not equally suited to producing one good, compared to another good. Expanding the output of sailboats requires the use of workers who are less suited to producing sailboats than producing tanks. Suppose our hypothetical economy produces no sailboats (point *A*) and then decides to start producing them. At first, the least-skilled tank workers are transferred to making sailboats, and 10,000 tanks are sacrificed at point *B*. As the economy moves from point *B* to point *C*, more highly skilled tank makers become sailboat makers, and the opportunity cost rises to 20,000 tanks. Finally, the economy can decide to move from point *C* to point *D*, and the opportunity cost increases even more to 50,000 tanks. Now the remaining tank workers, who are superb tank makers, but poor sailboat makers, must adapt to the techniques of sailboat production.

Finally, it should be noted that the production possibilities curve model could assume that resources can be substituted and the opportunity cost remains constant. In this case, the production possibilities curve would be a straight line, which is the model employed in Chapter 21 on international trade and finance.

> **CONCLUSION** The lack of perfect interchangeability between workers is the cause of increasing opportunity costs and the bowed-out shape of the production possibilities curve.

2-6 SOURCES OF ECONOMIC GROWTH

Economic growth The ability of an economy to produce greater levels of output, represented by an outward shift of its production possibilities curve.

The economy's production capacity is not permanently fixed. If either the resource base increases or technology advances, the economy experiences **economic growth**, and the production possibilities curve shifts outward. Economic growth is the ability of an economy to produce greater levels of output, represented by an outward shift of its production possibilities curve. Exhibit 2-4 illustrates the importance of an outward shift. (Note the causation chain, which is often used in this text to focus on a model's cause-and-effect relationship.) At point *A* on PPC_1, a hypothetical full-employment economy produces 40,000 computers and 200 million pizzas per year. If the curve shifts outward to the new curve PPC_2, the economy can expand its full-employment output options. One option is to produce at point *B* and increase computer output to 70,000 per year. Another possibility is to increase pizza output to 400 million per year. Yet another choice is to produce more of both at some point between points *B* and *C*.

2-6a Changes in Resources

One way to accelerate economic growth is to gain additional resources. Any increase in resources—for example, more natural resources, a baby boom, or more factories—will shift the production possibilities curve outward. In Exhibit 2-4, assume curve PPC_1 represents Japan's production possibilities for clothing and food in a given year. Suddenly, Japan discovers within its borders new sources of labor and other resources. As a result of the new resources, Japan will have an expanded capacity to produce any combination along an expanded curve, such as curve PPC_2.

Reductions in resources will cause the production possibilities curve to shift inward. Assume curve PPC_2 describes Japan's economy before World War II and the destruction of its factors of production in the war caused Japan's curve to shift leftward to curve PPC_1. Over the years, Japan trained its workforce, built new factories and equipment, and used new technology to shift its curve outward and surpass its original production capacity at curve PPC_2.

2-6b Technological Change

Another way to achieve economic growth is through research and development of new technologies. The knowledge of how to transform a stone into a wheel vastly improved the prehistoric standard of living. Technological change also makes it possible to shift the production possibilities curve outward by producing

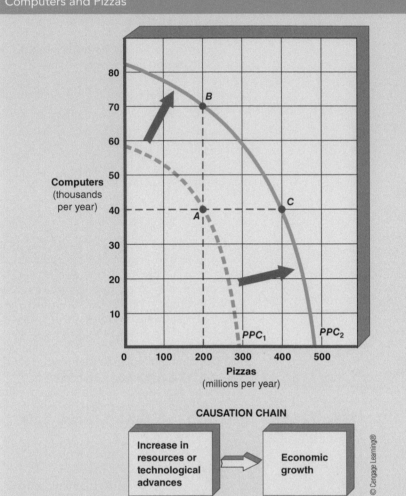

EXHIBIT 2-4 An Outward Shift of the Production Possibilities Curve for Computers and Pizzas

CAUSATION CHAIN

Increase in resources or technological advances ⟹ Economic growth

© Cengage Learning®

The economy begins with the capacity to produce combinations along the first production possibilities curve PPC₁. Growth in the resource base or technological advances can shift the production possibilities curve outward from PPC₁ to PPC₂. Points along PPC₂ represent new production possibilities that were previously impossible. This outward shift permits the economy to produce greater quantities of output. Instead of producing combination A, the economy can produce, for example, more computers at point B or more pizzas at point C. If the economy produces at a point between B and C, more of both pizzas and computers can be produced, compared to point A.

more from the same resources base. One source of technological change is *invention*. Computer chips, satellites, and the Internet are all examples of technological advances resulting from the use of science and engineering knowledge.

Technological change also results from the innovations of entrepreneurship, introduced in the previous chapter. Innovation involves creating and developing new products or productive processes. Seeking profits, entrepreneurs create new, better, or less expensive products. This requires organizing an improved mix of resources, which expands the production possibilities curve.

FedEx Wasn't an Overnight Success
Applicable concept: entrepreneurship

Frederick W. Smith is a classic entrepreneurial success story. Young Fred went to Yale University, had a good new idea, secured venture capital, worked like crazy, made a fortune, and the Smithsonian Institution rendered its ultimate accolade. It snapped up an early Federal Express jet for its collection, displaying it for a time in the Air and Space Museum in Washington, D.C., not far from the Wright brothers' first airplane.

Smith's saga began with a college economics term paper that spelled out a nationwide overnight parcel delivery system that would be guaranteed to "absolutely, positively" beat the U.S. Postal Service. People, he said, would pay much more if their packages would arrive at their destination the next morning. To accomplish his plan, planes would converge nightly on Memphis, Tennessee, carrying packages accepted at any location throughout the nation. Smith chose this city for its central U.S. location and because its airport has little bad weather to cause landing delays. In the morning hours, all items would be unloaded, sorted, and rerouted to other airports, where vans would

battle rush-hour traffic to make deliveries before the noon deadline.

Smith's college term paper only got a C grade. Perhaps the professor thought the idea was too risky, and lots of others certainly agreed. In 1969, after college and a tour as a Marine pilot in Vietnam, the 24-year-old Smith began pitching his parcel delivery plan to mostly skeptical financiers. Nevertheless, with $4 million of his family's money, he persuaded a few venture capitalists to put up $80 million. At this time, this was the largest venture capital package ever assembled. In 1973, delivery service began with 14 jets connecting 25 cities, but on the first night only 16 packages showed up.

It was years before Smith looked like a genius. The company posted a $27 million loss the first year, turned the corner in 1976, and then took off, helped by a 1981 decision to add letters to its basic package delivery service. Today, Smith's basic strategy hasn't changed, but the scale of the operation has exploded. FedEx is the world's largest express transportation company serving over 200 countries.

ANALYZE the ISSUE Draw a production possibilities curve for an economy producing only pizzas and computers. Explain how Fred Smith and other entrepreneurs affect the curve.

One entrepreneur, Henry Ford, changed auto industry technology by pioneering the use of the assembly line for making cars. Another entrepreneur, Chester Carlson, a law student, became so frustrated copying documents that he worked on his own to develop photocopying. After years of disappointment, a small firm named Xerox Corporation accepted Carlson's invention and transformed a good idea into a revolutionary product. These and a myriad of other business success stories illustrate that entrepreneurs are important because they transform their new ideas into production and practical use. Throughout history, technological advances have fostered economic growth by increasing our nation's productive power. Today, the Internet and computers are "new" technologies, but railroads, electricity, and automobiles, for example, were also "new" technologies in their time.

CHECKPOINT

What Does a War on Terrorism Really Mean?
With the disappearance of the former Soviet Union and the end of the Cold War, the United States became the world's only superpower and no longer engaged in an intense competition to build up its military. As a result, in the 1990s Congress and the White House had the opportunity to reduce the military's share of the budget and spend more funds for nondefense goods. This situation was referred to as the "peace dividend." Now consider that the need to combat terrorism diverts resources back to military and security output. Does a peace dividend or a reversal to more military spending represent a possible shift of the production possibilities curve or a movement along it?

2-7 PRESENT INVESTMENT AND THE FUTURE PRODUCTION POSSIBILITIES CURVE

GLOBAL ECONOMICS

When the decision for an economy involves choosing between capital goods and consumer goods, the output combination for the present period can determine future production capacity. Exhibit 2-5 compares two countries producing different combinations of capital and consumer goods. Part (a) shows the production possibilities curve for the low-investment economy of Alpha. This economy was producing combination A in 2000, which is an output of C_a of consumer goods and an output of K_a of capital goods per year. Let's assume K_a is just enough capital output to replace the capital being worn out each year (depreciation). As a result, Alpha fails to accumulate the net gain of factories and equipment required to expand its production possibilities curve outward in future years.[1] Why wouldn't Alpha simply move up along its production curve by shifting more resources to capital goods production? The problem is that sacrificing consumer goods for capital formation causes the standard of living to fall.

Comparing Alpha to Beta illustrates the importance of being able to do more than just replace worn-out capital. Beta operated in 2000 at point A in part (b), which is an output of C_b of consumer goods and K_b of capital goods. Assuming K_b is more than enough to replenish worn-out capital, Beta is a high-investment economy, adding to its capital stock and creating extra production capacity. This process of accumulating capital (*capital formation*) is **investment**. Investment is

Investment The accumulation of capital, such as factories, machines, and inventories, used to produce goods and services.

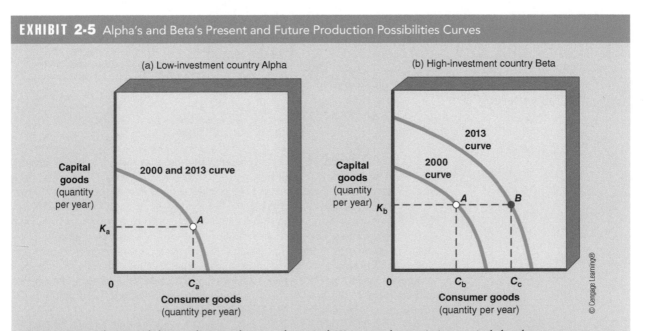

EXHIBIT 2-5 Alpha's and Beta's Present and Future Production Possibilities Curves

(a) Low-investment country Alpha

(b) High-investment country Beta

In part (a), each year Alpha produces only enough capital (K_a) to replace existing capital that has worn out. Without greater capital and assuming other resources remain fixed, Alpha is unable to shift its production possibilities curve outward. In part (b), each year Beta produces K_b capital, which is more than the amount required to replenish its depreciated capital. In 2013, this expanded capital provides Beta with the extra production capacity to shift its production possibilities curve to the right (outward). If Beta chooses point B on its curve, it has the production capacity to increase the amount of consumer goods from C_b to C_c without producing fewer capital goods.

---

[1] Recall from the Appendix to Chapter 1 that a third variable can affect the variables measured on the vertical and horizontal axes. In this case, the third variable is the quantity of capital worn out per year.

GLOBAL **ECONOMICS**

How Does Public Capital Affect a Nation's Curve?

Applicable concept: economic growth

©Zhangyang13576997233/Shutterstock.com

The discussion of low-investment country Alpha versus high-investment country Beta explained that sacrificing production of consumer goods for an increase in capital goods output can result in economic growth and a higher standard of living. Stated differently, there was a long-run benefit from the accumulation of capital that offset the short-run opportunity cost in terms of consumer goods. Here the analysis was in terms of investment in private capital such as factories, machines, and inventories. However, public or government capital can also influence the production of both capital goods and consumption goods. For example, the government provides infrastructure such as roads, schools, bridges, ports, dams, and sanitation that makes the accumulation process for private capital more efficient, and in turn, an economy grows at a greater rate.

Using data from 21 high-investment countries, a study by economists investigated how government investment policy affected the productivity of new private capital goods.[1] Countries included in the research were, for example, Canada, Japan, New Zealand, Spain, and the United States. A key finding was that a 1 percent increase in public investment increased the productivity of private investment by 27 percent. As a result, public capital caused the stock of private capital to rise more quickly over time.

Finally, economic growth and development is a major goal of countries throughout the world, and there are numerous factors that cause some countries to experience greater economic growth compared to other countries. Note that this topic is discussed in more depth in the last chapter of the text.

 Construct a production possibilities curve for a hypothetical country. Put public capital goods per year on the vertical axis and consumer goods per year on the horizontal axis. Not shown directly in your graph, assume that this country produces just enough private capital per year to replace its depreciated capital. Assume further that this country is without public capital and is operating at point *A* where consumer goods are at a maximum. Based on the above research and using a production possibilities curve show and explain what happens to this country's private capital, production possibilities curve, and standard of living if it increases its output of public capital.

[1] Stuart Fowler and Bichaka Fayissa, "Public Capital Spending Shocks and the Price of Investment: Evidence from a Panel of Countries," The 2007 Missouri Economics Conference.

the accumulation of capital, such as factories, machines, and inventories, used to produce goods and services. Newly built factories and machines in the present provide an economy with the capacity to expand its production options in the future. For example, the outward shift of its curve allows Beta to produce C_c consumer goods at point *B* in 2013. This means Beta will be able to improve its standard of living by producing $C_c - C_b$ extra consumer goods, while Alpha's standard of living remains unchanged because the production of consumer goods remains unchanged.

CONCLUSION A nation can accelerate its economic growth by increasing its production of capital goods in excess of the capital being worn out in the production process.

Key Concepts

What, How, and *For Whom*
    questions
Opportunity cost

Marginal analysis
Production possibilities curve
Technology

Law of increasing opportunity costs
Economic growth
Investment

Summary

- **Three fundamental economic questions** facing any economy are *What, How,* and *For Whom* to produce goods. The *What* question asks exactly which goods are to be produced and in what quantities. The *How* question requires society to decide the resource mix used to produce goods. The *For Whom* problem concerns the division of output among society's citizens.

- **Opportunity cost** is the best alternative forgone for a chosen option. This means no decision can be made without cost.

- **Marginal analysis** examines the impact of changes from a current situation and is a technique used extensively in economics. The basic approach is to compare the additional benefits of a change with the additional costs of the change.

- **A production possibilities curve** illustrates an economy's capacity to produce goods, subject to the constraint of scarcity. The production possibilities curve is a graph of the maximum possible combinations of two outputs that can be produced in a given period of time, subject to three conditions: (1) All resources are fully employed. (2) The resource base is not allowed to vary during the time period. (3) **Technology**, which is the body of knowledge applied to the production of goods, remains constant. **Inefficient** production occurs at any point inside the production possibilities curve. All points along the curve are **efficient** points because each point represents a maximum output possibility.

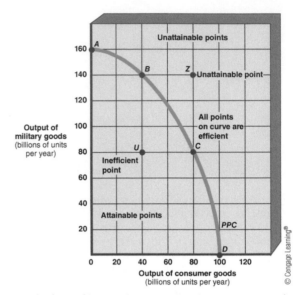

- The **law of increasing opportunity costs** states that the opportunity cost increases as the production of an output expands. The explanation for this law is that the suitability of resources declines sharply as greater amounts are transferred from producing one output to producing another output.

- **Economic growth** is represented by the production possibilities curve shifting outward as the result of an increase in resources or an advance in technology.

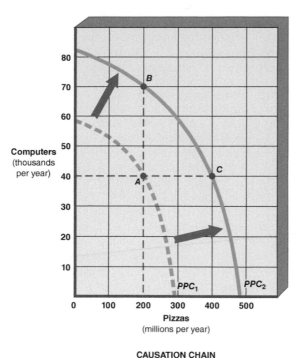

CAUSATION CHAIN

Increase in resources or technological advances → Economic growth

© Cengage Learning®

- **Investment** means that an economy is producing and accumulating capital. Investment consists of factories, machines, and inventories (capital) produced in the present that are used to shift the production possibilities curve outward in the future.

Study Questions and Problems

1. Explain why scarcity forces individuals and society to incur opportunity costs. Give specific examples.
2. Suppose a retailer promotes its store by advertising a drawing for a "free car." Is this car *free* because the winner pays *zero* for it?
3. Explain verbally the statement "There is no such thing as a free lunch" in relation to scarce resources.
4. Which of the following decisions has the greater opportunity cost? Why?
   a. A decision to use an undeveloped lot in Tokyo's financial district for an apartment building.
   b. A decision to use a square mile in the desert for a gas station.
5. Attending college is expensive, time consuming, and requires effort. So why do people decide to attend college?
6. The table below is a set of hypothetical production possibilities for a nation.

Combination	Automobiles (thousands)	Beef (thousands of tons)
A	0	10
B	2	9
C	4	7
D	6	4
E	8	0

a. Plot these production possibilities data. What is the opportunity cost of the first 2,000 automobiles produced? Between which points is the opportunity cost per thousand automobiles highest? Between which points is the opportunity cost per thousand tons of beef highest?
b. Label a point *F* inside the curve. Why is this an inefficient point? Label a point *G* outside the curve. Why is this point unattainable? Why are points *A* through *E* all efficient points?

c. Does this production possibilities curve reflect the law of increasing opportunity costs? Explain.

d. What assumptions could be changed to shift the production possibilities curve?

7. The following table shows the production possibilities for pies and flowerboxes. Fill in the opportunity cost (pies forgone) of producing the first through the fifth flowerbox.

Combination	Pies	Flowerboxes	Opportunity cost
A	30	0	_____
B	26	1	_____
C	21	2	_____
D	15	3	_____
E	8	4	_____
F	0	5	_____

8. Why does a production possibilities curve have a bowed-out shape?

9. Interpret the phrases "There is no such thing as a free lunch" and "A free lunch is possible" in terms of the production possibilities curve.

10. Suppose, unfortunately, your mathematics and economics professors have decided to give tests 2 days from now and you can spend only a total of 12 hours studying for both exams. After some thought, you conclude that dividing your study time equally between each subject will give you an expected grade of C in each course. For each additional 3 hours study time for one of the subjects, your grade will increase one letter for that subject, and your grade will fall one letter for the other subject.

a. Construct a table for the production possibilities and corresponding number of hours of study in this case.

b. Plot these production possibilities data in a graph.

c. Does this production possibilities curve reflect the law of increasing opportunity costs? Explain.

11. Draw a production possibilities curve for a hypothetical economy producing capital goods and consumer goods. Suppose a major technological breakthrough occurs in the capital goods industry and the new technology is widely adopted only in this industry. Draw the new production possibilities curve. Now assume that a technological advance occurs in consumer goods production, but not in capital goods production. Draw the new production possibilities curve.

12. The present choice between investing in capital goods and producing consumer goods now affects the ability of an economy to produce in the future. Explain.

Sample Quiz

1. Which of the following *best* describes the three fundamental economic questions?
   a. What to produce, when to produce, and where to produce.
   b. What time to produce, what place to produce, and how to produce.
   c. What to produce, when to produce, and for whom to produce.
   d. What to produce, how to produce, and for whom to produce.

2. Suppose that the alternative uses of an hour of your time in the evening, ranked from best to worst, are (1) study economics, (2) watch two half-hour TV sitcoms, (3) play pool, and (4) jog around town. You can only choose one activity. What is the opportunity cost of studying economics for one hour, given this information?
   a. Jogging around town.
   b. Watching two half-hour TV sitcoms.
   c. Playing pool.
   d. The sum of watching two half-hour TV sitcoms, playing pool, and jogging around town.

3. Which word or phrase *best* completes the following sentence? Marginal analysis means evaluating _____ changes from a current situation.
   a. positive or negative
   b. infinite
   c. no
   d. maximum

4. Which of the following is an example of an organization using marginal analysis?
   a. A hotel manager calculating the average cost per guest for the past year.
   b. A farmer hoping for rain.
   c. A government official considering about what effect an increase in military good production will have on the production of consumer goods.
   d. A businessperson calculating economic profits.

5. A production possibilities curve shows the various combinations of two outputs that
   a. Consumers would like to consume.
   b. Producers would like to produce.
   c. An economy can produce.
   d. An economy should produce.

6. A production possibilities curve is drawn based on which of the following assumptions?
   a. Resources are fixed and fully employed, and technology advances at the rate of growth of the economy overall.
   b. Resources such as nonrenewable resources will decline, but labor remains fully employed, and technology is unchanged.
   c. Resources can vary, most resources experience times of unemployment, and technology advances, particularly during wartime.
   d. Resources such as labor and capital will grow, are fully employed, and technology is unchanged.
   e. None of the answers above is correct.

7. If an economy can produce various combinations of food and shelter along a production possibilities curve (PPC), then if we increase the production of shelter along the PPC, which of the following is *true*?
   a. We also increase the production of food.
   b. We must decrease the production of food. This foregone food production represents the opportunity cost of the increase in shelter.
   c. We cannot change the production of food.
   d. The concept of opportunity cost does not apply along PPC.

8. An economy can produce various combinations of food and shelter along a production possibilities curve (PPC). We first increase the production of shelter along the PPC. If we then continue to shift more and more production to shelter, then which of the following will most likely happen to the opportunity cost of a unit of shelter?
   a. Opportunity cost will increase because as more and more shelter is produced, labor and capital that is highly productive at producing food is being shifted to shelter production, and so more and more food is being given up to produce a unit of shelter.
   b. Opportunity cost is the amount of labor (but not capital) that is used to produce the extra shelter.
   c. Opportunity cost must stay constant if we are to stay on the production possibilities curve.
   d. Opportunity cost includes all options given up to produce shelter.

9. An economy can produce various combinations of food and shelter along a production possibilities curve (PPC). Suppose a technological innovation resulted in a new, higher-yielding crop that generated more bushels of grain for a given set of land, labor, and capital resources. If this innovation did not affect the productivity of shelter production, then which of the following would be *true*?
   a. The production possibilities curve (PPC) will shift outward equally along both axes of the graph.
   b. The PPC will rotate inward along the food axis, but will not shift on the shelter axis.
   c. The PPC will rotate outward along the food axis, but will not shift on the shelter axis.
   d. The PPC will not change.

10. If a production possibilities curve (PPC) has capital on the vertical axis and consumer goods on the horizontal axis, which of the following is *true*?
   a. There is a tradeoff between emphasizing the production of capital today to benefit people today versus emphasizing the production of consumer goods today that will generate benefits in the future.
   b. Greater emphasis on the production of capital today leads to future inward shifts in the PPC, thus decreasing the wealth of people in the future.
   c. Greater emphasis on the production of consumer goods today leads to greater outward shifts in the PPC, thus increasing the wealth of people in the future.
   d. Greater emphasis on the production of capital today leads to greater outward shifts in the PPC, thus increasing the wealth of people in the future.

11. Which of the following reasons might explain why an economy would be operating inside its production possibilities curve (PPC)?
   a. Because shrinking population has reduced the number of productive workers in the economy.
   b. Because technological innovations have increased the productivity of labor and capital.
   c. Because damage to natural resources, such as might be caused by deforestation leading to erosion of topsoil, has shrunk the land resource.
   d. Because of unemployment or underemployment of labor, perhaps due to discrimination against employing workers of a certain race or gender.

12. Combinations of goods outside the production possibilities curve (PPC) have which of the following characteristics?
   a. They are only attainable today if we employ all unemployed or underemployed resources.
   b. They are not attainable given our existing stock of resources and technology.

   c. They imply that some resources, such as labor, are unemployed or underemployed.
   d. None of the answers above is correct.

13. Suppose that an economy can produce various combinations of fish and bread. If more people with strong fishing skills became employed in this economy, how would the production possibilities curve (PPC) change?
   a. The PPC would shift outward on the fish axis, but would not change on the bread axis.
   b. The PPC would shift outward equally along both the fish and the bread axes.
   c. The PPC would shift inward on the bread axis, but would not change on the fish axis.
   d. The PPC would shift inward equally along both the fish and the bread axes.

14. Three different economies have made choices about the production of capital goods. Which of the following is *most* likely to produce the greatest growth in the production possibilities curve (PPC)?
   a. Capital goods are produced at the exact rate needed to replace worn-out capital.
   b. Greater production of capital goods than what is needed to replace worn-out capital.
   c. Less production of capital goods than what is needed to replace worn-out capital.
   d. More production of consumption goods that replace worn-out capital.

15. In the study of economics, investment means
   a. the accumulation of capital that is used to produce goods and services.
   b. owning stocks and bonds.
   c. the principle that the opportunity cost increases as the production of one output expands.
   d. the effect of stock prices or the production possibilities curve.

16. Which of the following is *not* one of the three fundamental economic questions?
   a. What happens when you add to or subtract from a current situation?
   b. For whom to produce?
   c. How to produce?
   d. What to produce?

17. From the information in Exhibit 2-6, which of the following points are attainable with resources and technology currently available?
   a. A, B, C, E, U
   b. A, B, C, D, W
   c. E, U, W
   d. B, C, D, U
   e. A, B, C, E

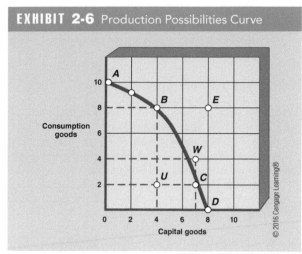

EXHIBIT 2-6 Production Possibilities Curve

© 2016 Cengage Learning®

18. In Exhibit 2-6, which of the following points on the production possibilities curve are efficient production points?
   a. A, B, C, U
   b. A, B, C, D, U
   c. E, U, W
   d. B, C, D, U
   e. A, B, C, D

19. In Exhibit 2-6, to move from U to B, the opportunity cost would be
   a. 4 units of consumption goods.
   b. 2 units of capital goods.
   c. zero.
   d. 5 units of capital goods.
   e. unable to be determined.

20. In Exhibit 2-6, which of the following points on the production possibilities are full-employment production points?
   a. A, B, C, D
   b. A, B, C, D, U
   c. E, U, W
   d. B, C, D, U
   e. A, B, C, U

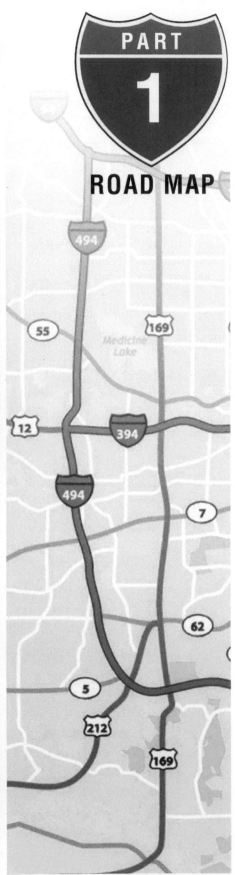

INTRODUCTION to Economics

This road map feature helps you tie together material in the part as you travel the Economic Way of Thinking Highway. The following are review questions listed by chapter from the previous part. The key concept in each question is given for emphasis, and each question or set of questions concludes with an interactive game to reinforce the concepts. Visit cengagebrain.com to purchase the MindTap product where you can select a chapter and play the visual causation chain game designed to make learning fun. The correct answers to the multiple choice questions are given in Appendix C on the instructor's resource site.

Chapter 1 Introducing the Economic Way of Thinking

1. Key Concept: Scarcity

Economists believe that scarcity forces everyone to

a. satisfy all their wants.
b. abandon consumer sovereignty.
c. lie about their wants.
d. create unlimited resources.
e. make choices.

2. Key Concept: Economics

The subject of economics is primarily the study of

a. the government decision-making process.
b. how to operate a business successfully.
c. decision making because of the problem of scarcity.
d. how to make money in the stock market.

CAUSATION CHAIN GAME:
The Relationship between Scarcity and Decision Making

3. Key Concept: Model

When building a model, an economist must

a. adjust for exceptional situations.
b. provide a complete description of reality
c. make simplifying assumptions.
d. develop a set of behavioral equations.

4. Key Concept: Ceteris paribus

If the price of a textbook rises and students purchase fewer textbooks, an economic model can show a cause-and-effect relationship only if which of the following conditions hold:

a. students' incomes fall.
b. tuition decreases.
c. the number of students increases.
d. everything else is constant.
e. the bookstore no longer accepts used book trade-ins.

5. Key Concept: Association vs. causation

Someone notices that sunspot activity is high just prior to recessions and concludes that sunspots cause recessions. This person has

a. confused association and causation.
b. misunderstood the ceteris paribus assumption.

c. used normative economics to answer a positive question.
d. built an untestable model.

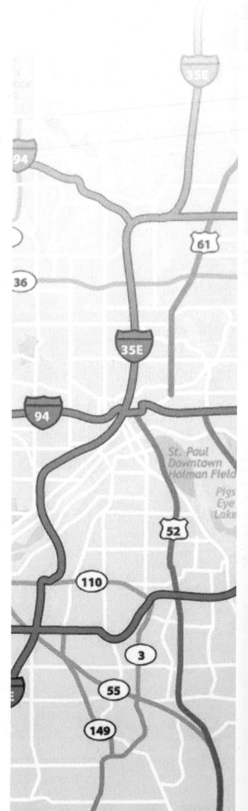

CAUSATION CHAIN GAME:
The Steps in the Model-Building Process—Exhibit 1.2

Chapter 2 Production Possibilities, Opportunity Cost, and Economic Growth

6. Key Concept: Production possibilities curve

Which of the following is *not true* about a production possibilities curve? The curve

a. indicates the combinations of goods and services that can be produced with a given technology.
b. indicates the efficient production points.
c. indicates the nonefficient production points.
d. indicates the feasible (attainable) and nonfeasible production points.
e. indicates which production point will be chosen.

7. Key Concept: Production possibilities curve

Which of the following is *true* about the production possibilities curve when a technological progress occurs?

a. Shifts inward to the left.
b. Becomes flatter at one end and steeper at the other end.
c. Becomes steeper.
d. Shifts outward to the right.
e. Does not change.

8. Key Concept: Shifting the production possibilities curve

An outward shift of an economy's production possibilities curve is caused by

a. entrepreneurship.
b. an increase in labor.
c. an advance in technology.
d. All of the above are correct.

9. Key Concept: Shifting the production possibilities curve

Which would be *least likely* to cause the production possibilities curve to shift to the right?

a. An increase in the labor force.
b. Improved methods of production.
c. An increase in the education and training of the labor force.
d. A decrease in unemployment.

10. Key Concept: Investment

A nation can accelerate its economic growth by

a. reducing the number of immigrants allowed into the country.
b. adding to its stock of capital.
c. printing more money.
d. imposing tariffs and quotas on imported goods.

CAUSATION CHAIN GAME:
Economic Growth and Technology—Exhibit 2.4

PART 2

The Microeconomy

In your study of the microeconomy, the chapters in Part 2 build on the basic concepts you learned in Part 1. Chapters 3 and 4 explain the market demand and supply model, which has a wide range of real-world applications. Chapter 5 takes a closer look at movements along the demand curve introduced in Chapter 3. Chapter 6 extends the concept of supply by developing a theory that explains how various costs of production change as output varies. Chapter 7 describes a highly competitive market consisting of an extremely large number of competing firms, and Chapter 8 explains the theory for a market with only a single seller. Between these extremes, Chapter 9 discusses two markets that have some characteristics of both competition and monopoly. Part 2 concludes by developing labor market theory and examining actual data on income and poverty in Chapter 10.

Market Demand and Supply

In this chapter, you will learn to solve these economics puzzles:

- What is the difference between a "change in quantity demanded" and a "change in demand"?
- Can Congress repeal the law of supply to control oil prices?
- Does the price system eliminate scarcity?

CHAPTER PREVIEW

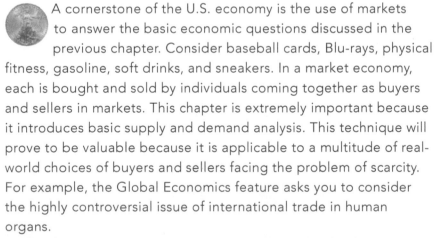

A cornerstone of the U.S. economy is the use of markets to answer the basic economic questions discussed in the previous chapter. Consider baseball cards, Blu-rays, physical fitness, gasoline, soft drinks, and sneakers. In a market economy, each is bought and sold by individuals coming together as buyers and sellers in markets. This chapter is extremely important because it introduces basic supply and demand analysis. This technique will prove to be valuable because it is applicable to a multitude of real-world choices of buyers and sellers facing the problem of scarcity. For example, the Global Economics feature asks you to consider the highly controversial issue of international trade in human organs.

Demand represents the choice-making behavior of consumers, while supply represents the choices of producers. The chapter begins by looking closely at demand and then supply. Finally, it combines these forces to see how prices and quantities are determined in the marketplace. Market demand and supply analysis is the basic tool of microeconomic analysis.

3-1 THE LAW OF DEMAND

Law of demand The principle that there is an inverse relationship between the price of a good and the quantity buyers are willing to purchase in a defined time period, ceteris paribus.

Economics might be referred to as "graphs and laughs" because economists are so fond of using graphs to illustrate demand, supply, and many other economic concepts. Unfortunately, some students taking economics courses say they miss the laughs.

Exhibit 3-1 reveals an important "law" in economics called the law of demand. The law of demand states there is an inverse relationship between the price of a good and the quantity buyers are willing to purchase in a defined time period, ceteris paribus. The law of demand makes good sense. At a "sale," consumers buy more when the price of merchandise is cut.

In Exhibit 3-1, the *demand curve* is formed by the line connecting the possible price and quantity purchased responses of an individual consumer. The demand curve therefore allows you to find the quantity demanded by a buyer at any possible selling price by moving along the curve. For example, Bob, a sophomore at Marketplace College, enjoys watching movies on Blu-rays. Bob's demand curve shows that at a price of $15 per Blu-ray, his quantity demanded is 6 Blu-rays purchased annually (point B). At the lower price of $10, Bob's quantity demanded increases to 10 Blu-rays per year (point C). Following this procedure, other price and quantity possibilities for Bob are read along the demand curve.

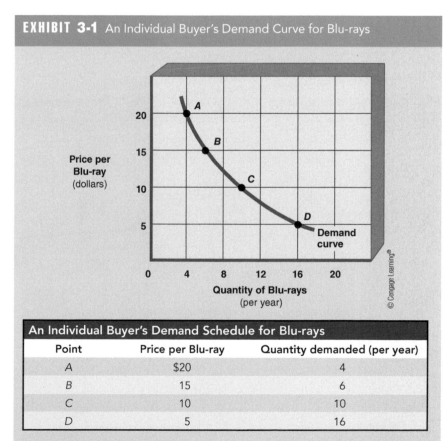

EXHIBIT 3-1 An Individual Buyer's Demand Curve for Blu-rays

An Individual Buyer's Demand Schedule for Blu-rays		
Point	Price per Blu-ray	Quantity demanded (per year)
A	$20	4
B	15	6
C	10	10
D	5	16

Bob's demand curve shows how many Blu-rays he is willing to purchase at different possible prices. As the price of Blu-rays declines, the quantity demanded increases, and Bob purchases more Blu-rays. The inverse relationship between price and quantity demanded conforms to the law of demand.

Note that until we know the actual price determined by both demand and supply, we do not know how many Blu-rays Bob will actually purchase annually. The demand curve is simply a summary of Bob's buying intentions. Once we know the market price, a quick look at the demand curve tells us how many Blu-rays Bob will buy.

Demand A curve or schedule showing the various quantities of product consumers are willing to purchase at possible prices during a specified period of time, ceteris paribus.

> **CONCLUSION** Demand is a curve or schedule showing the various quantities of a product consumers are willing to purchase at possible prices during a specified period of time, ceteris paribus.

3-1a Market Demand

To make the transition from an *individual* demand curve to a *market* demand curve, we total, or sum, the individual demand schedules. Suppose the owner of ZapMart, a small retail chain of stores serving a few states, tries to decide what to charge for Blu-rays and hires a consumer research firm. For simplicity, we assume Fred and Mary are the only two buyers in ZapMart's market, and they are sent a questionnaire that asks how many Blu-rays each would be willing to purchase at several possible prices. Exhibit 3-2 reports their price-quantity demanded responses in tabular and graphical form.

The market demand curve, D_{total}, in Exhibit 3-2 is derived by summing *horizontally* the two individual demand curves, D_1 and D_2, for each possible price. At a price of $20, for example, we sum Fred's 2 Blu-rays demanded per year and Mary's 1 Blu-ray demanded per year to find that the total quantity demanded at

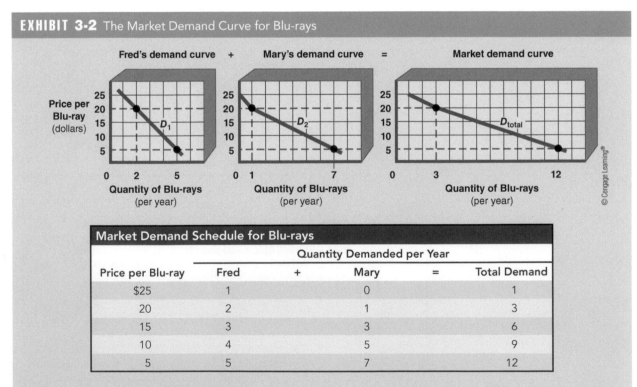

EXHIBIT 3-2 The Market Demand Curve for Blu-rays

Market Demand Schedule for Blu-rays					
	Quantity Demanded per Year				
Price per Blu-ray	Fred	+	Mary	=	Total Demand
$25	1		0		1
20	2		1		3
15	3		3		6
10	4		5		9
5	5		7		12

Individual demand curves differ for consumers Fred and Mary. Assuming they are the only buyers in the market, the market demand curve, D_{total}, is derived by summing horizontally the individual demand curves, D_1 and D_2.

$20 is 3 Blu-rays per year. Repeating the same process for other prices generates the market demand curve, D_{total}. For example, at a price of $5, the total quantity demanded is 12 Blu-rays.

3-2 THE DISTINCTION BETWEEN CHANGES IN QUANTITY DEMANDED AND CHANGES IN DEMAND

Change in quantity demanded A movement between points along a stationary demand curve, ceteris paribus.

Price is not the only variable that determines how much of a good or service consumers will buy. Recall from Exhibit 1A-4 of Appendix 1 that the price and quantity variables in our model are subject to the ceteris paribus assumption. If we relax this assumption and allow other variables held constant to change, a variety of factors can influence the position of the demand curve. Because these factors are not the price of the good itself, these variables are called *nonprice determinants*, or simply, *demand shifters*. The major nonprice determinants include (1) the number of buyers; (2) tastes and preferences; (3) income; (4) expectations of future changes in prices, income, and availability of goods; and (5) prices of related goods.

Before discussing these nonprice determinants of demand, we must pause to explain an important and possibly confusing distinction in terminology. We have been referring to a change in quantity demanded, which results solely from a change in the price. A change in quantity demanded is a movement between points along a stationary demand curve, ceteris paribus. In Exhibit 3-3(a), at the price of $15, the quantity demanded is 20 million Blu-rays per year. This is shown as point A on the demand curve, D. At a lower price of, say, $10, the quantity demanded increases to 30 million Blu-rays per year, shown as point B. Verbally, we describe the impact of the price decrease as an increase in the quantity demanded of 10 million Blu-rays per year. We show this relationship on the demand curve as a movement down along the curve from point A to point B.

> **CONCLUSION** Under the law of demand, any decrease in price along the vertical axis will cause an increase in quantity demanded, measured along the horizontal axis.

Change in demand An increase or a decrease in the quantity demanded at each possible price. An increase in demand is a rightward shift in the entire demand curve. A decrease in demand is a leftward shift in the entire demand curve.

A change in demand is an increase (rightward shift) or a decrease (leftward shift) in the quantity demanded at each possible price. If ceteris paribus no longer applies and if one of the five nonprice factors changes, the location of the demand curve shifts.

> **CONCLUSION** Changes in nonprice determinants can produce only a shift in the demand curve and not a movement along the demand curve, which is caused by a change in the price.

Comparing Parts (a) and (b) of Exhibit 3-3 is helpful in distinguishing between a change in quantity demanded and a change in demand. In Part (b), suppose the market demand curve for Blu-rays is initially at D_1 and there is a shift to the right (an increase in demand) from D_1 to D_2. This means that at *all* possible prices consumers wish to purchase a larger quantity than before the shift occurred. At $15 per Blu-ray, for example, 30 million Blu-rays (point B) will be purchased each year, rather than 20 million Blu-rays (point A).

Now suppose a change in some nonprice factor causes demand curve D_1 to shift leftward (a decrease in demand). The interpretation in this case is that at *all* possible prices consumers will buy a smaller quantity than before the shift occurred.

Exhibit 3-4 summarizes the terminology for the effects of changes in price and nonprice determinants on the demand curve.

EXHIBIT 3-3 Movement along a Demand Curve versus a Shift in Demand

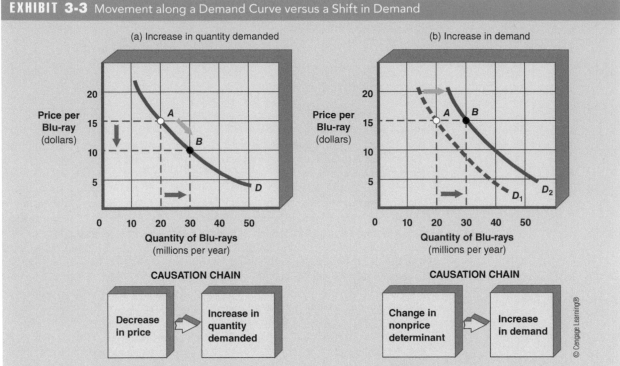

Part (a) shows the demand curve, *D*, for Blu-rays per year. If the price is $15 at point A, the quantity demanded by consumers is 20 million Blu-rays. If the price decreases to $10 at point B, the quantity demanded increases from 20 million to 30 million Blu-rays.

Part (b) illustrates an increase in demand. A change in some nonprice determinant can cause an increase in demand from D_1 to D_2. At a price of $15 on D_1 (point A), 20 million Blu-rays is the quantity demanded per year. At this price on D_2 (point B), the quantity demanded increases to 30 million.

3-3 NONPRICE DETERMINANTS OF DEMAND

Distinguishing between a change in quantity demanded and a change in demand requires some patience and practice. The following discussion of specific changes in nonprice factors or demand shifters will clarify how each nonprice variable affects demand.

3-3a Number of Buyers

Look back at Exhibit 3-2 and imagine the impact of adding more individual demand curves to the individual demand curves of Fred and Mary. At all possible prices, there is extra quantity demanded by the new customers, and the market demand curve for Blu-rays shifts rightward (an increase in demand). Population growth therefore tends to increase the number of buyers, which shifts the market demand curve for a good or service rightward. Conversely, a population decline shifts most market demand curves leftward (a decrease in demand).

The number of buyers can be specified to include both foreign and domestic buyers. Suppose the market demand curve D_1 in Exhibit 3-3(b) is for Blu-rays purchased in the United States by customers at home and abroad. Also assume Japan restricts the import of Blu-rays into Japan. What would be the effect of

EXHIBIT 3-4 Terminology for Changes in Price and Nonprice Determinants of Demand

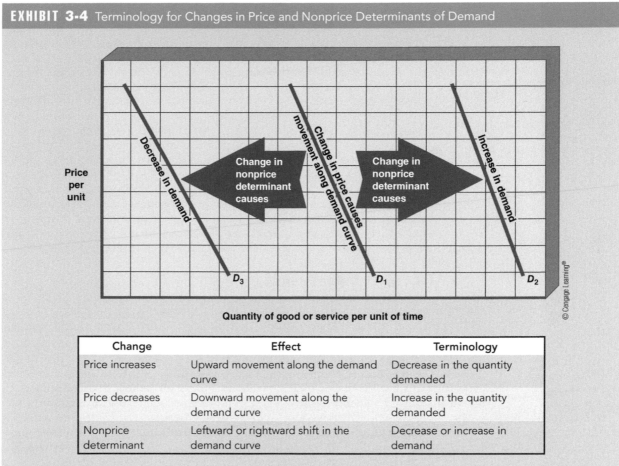

Change	Effect	Terminology
Price increases	Upward movement along the demand curve	Decrease in the quantity demanded
Price decreases	Downward movement along the demand curve	Increase in the quantity demanded
Nonprice determinant	Leftward or rightward shift in the demand curve	Decrease or increase in demand

Caution! It is important to distinguish between a change in quantity demanded, which is a movement along a demand curve (D_1) caused by a change in price, and a change in demand, which is a shift in the demand curve. An increase in demand (shift to D_2) or decrease in demand (shift to D_3) is not caused by a change in price. Instead, a shift is caused by a change in one of the nonprice determinants.

Japan removing this trade restriction? The answer is that the demand curve shifts rightward from D_1 to D_2 when Japanese consumers add their individual demand curves to the U.S. market demand for Blu-rays.

3–3b Tastes and Preferences

A favorable or unfavorable change in consumer tastes or preferences means more or less of a product is demanded at each possible price. Fads, fashions, advertising, and new products can influence consumer preferences to buy a particular good or service. Beanie Babies, for example, became the rage in the 1990s, and the demand curve for these products shifted to the right. When people tire of a product, the demand curve will shift leftward. The physical fitness trend has increased the demand for health clubs and exercise equipment. On the other hand, have you noticed many stores selling hula hoops? Advertising can also influence consumers' taste for a product. As a result, consumers are more likely to buy more at every price, and the demand curve for the product will shift to the right. Concern for global climate change has increased the demand for hybrid cars and recycling.

3-3c Income

Most students are all too familiar with how changes in income affect demand. There are two possible categories for the relationship between changes in income and changes in demand: (1) **normal goods** and (2) **inferior goods**.

A normal good is any good for which there is a direct relationship between changes in income and its demand curve. For many goods and services, an increase in income causes buyers to purchase more at any possible price. As buyers receive higher incomes, the demand curve shifts rightward for such *normal goods* as cars, steaks, vintage wine, cleaning services, and Blu-rays. A decline in income has the opposite effect, and the demand curve shifts leftward.

An inferior good is any good for which there is an inverse relationship between changes in income and its demand curve. A rise in income can result in reduced purchases of a good or service at any possible price. This might happen with such *inferior* goods as generic brands, Spam, discount clothes, and used cars. Instead of buying these inferior goods, higher incomes allow consumers to buy brand-name products, steaks, designer clothes, or new cars. Conversely, a fall in income causes the demand curve for inferior goods to shift rightward.

3-3d Expectations of Buyers

What is the effect on demand in the present when consumers anticipate future changes in prices, incomes, or availability? What happens when a war breaks out in the Middle East? Expectations that there will be a shortage of gasoline induce consumers to say "fill-er-up" at every opportunity, and demand increases. Suppose students learn that the prices of the textbooks for several courses they plan to take next semester will double soon. Their likely response is to buy now, which causes an increase in the demand curve for these textbooks. Another example is a change in the weather, which can indirectly cause expectations to shift demand for some products. Suppose severe weather destroys a substantial portion of the peach crop. Consumers reason that the reduction in available supply will soon drive up prices, and they dash to stock up before it is too late. This change in expectations causes the demand curve for peaches to increase. Prior to Hurricane Katrina hitting New Orleans, sales of batteries and flashlights soared.

3-3e Prices of Related Goods

Possibly the most confusing nonprice factor is the influence of other prices on the demand for a particular good or service. The term *nonprice* seems to forbid any shift in demand resulting from a change in the price of *any* product. This confusion exists when one fails to distinguish between changes in quantity demanded and changes in demand. Remember that ceteris paribus holds all prices of other goods constant. Therefore, movement along a demand curve occurs solely in response to changes in the price of a product, that is, its "own" price. When we draw the demand curve for Coca-Cola, for example, we assume the prices of Pepsi-Cola and other colas remain unchanged. What happens if we relax the ceteris paribus assumption and the price of Pepsi rises? Many Pepsi buyers switch to Coca-Cola, and the demand curve for Coca-Cola shifts rightward (an increase in demand). Coca-Cola and Pepsi-Cola are one type of related goods called **substitute goods**. A substitute good competes with another good for consumer purchases. As a result, there is a direct relationship between a price change for one good and the demand for its "competitor" good. Other examples of substitutes include margarine and butter, domestic cars and foreign cars, and Blu-rays and Internet movie downloads.

Blu-rays and Blu-ray players illustrate a second type of related goods called **complementary goods**. A complementary good is jointly consumed with another good. As a result, there is an inverse relationship between a price change for one good and the demand for its "go together" good. Although buying a Blu-ray

---

Normal goods Any good for which there is a direct relationship between changes in income and its demand curve.

Inferior goods Any good for which there is an inverse relationship between changes in income and its demand curve.

Substitute goods A good that competes with another good for consumer purchases. As a result, there is a direct relationship between a price change for one good and the demand for its "competitor" good.

Complementary goods A good that is jointly consumed with another good. As a result, there is an inverse relationship between a price change for one good and the demand for its "go together" good.

and buying a Blu-ray player can be separate decisions, these two purchases are related. The more Blu-ray players consumers buy, the greater the demand for Blu-rays. What happens when the price of Blu-ray players falls sharply? The market demand curve for Blu-rays shifts rightward (an increase in demand) because new owners of players add their individual demand curves to those of persons already owning players and buying Blu-rays. Conversely, a sharp rise in the price of deskjet printers would decrease the demand for ink cartridges.

Exhibit 3-5 summarizes the relationship between changes in the nonprice determinants of demand and the demand curve, accompanied by examples for each type of nonprice factor change.

EXHIBIT 3-5 Summary of the Impact of Changes in Nonprice Determinants of Demand on the Demand Curve

Nonprice Determinant of Demand	Relationship to Changes in Demand Curve	Shift in the Demand Curve	Examples
1. Number of buyers	Direct	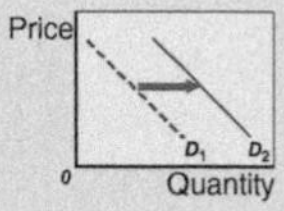	• Immigration from Mexico increases the demand for Mexican food products in grocery stores.
		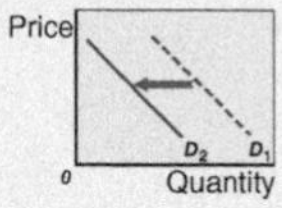	• A decline in the birthrate reduces the demand for baby clothes.
2. Tastes and preferences	Direct	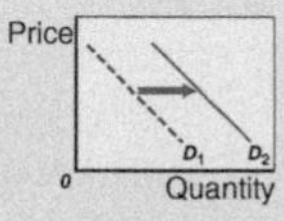	• For no apparent reason, consumers want Beanie Babies and demand increases.
		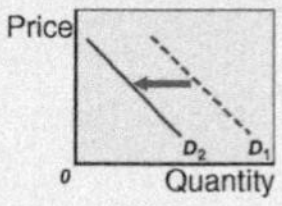	• After a while, the fad dies and demand declines.
3. Income a. Normal goods	Direct	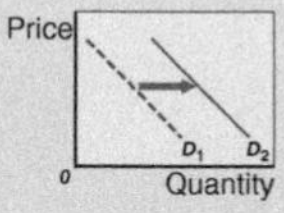	• Consumers' incomes increase, and the demand for steaks increases.
		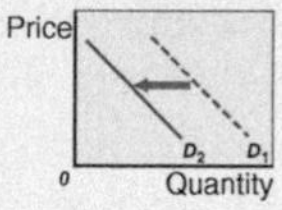	• A decline in income decreases the demand for air travel.
b. Inferior goods	Inverse	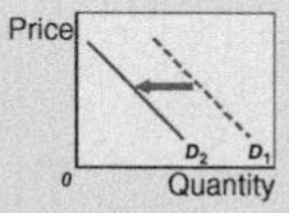	• Consumers' incomes increase, and the demand for hamburger decreases.
		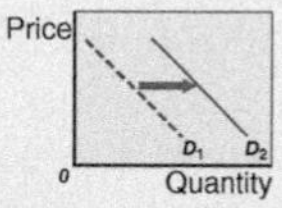	• A decline in income increases the demand for bus service.
4. Expectations of buyers	Direct	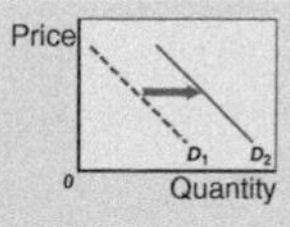	• Consumers expect that gasoline will be in short supply next month and that prices will rise sharply. Consequently, consumers fill the tanks in their cars this month, and there is an increase in demand for gasoline.

Continued

Continued from previous page

Nonprice Determinant of Demand	Relationship to Changes in Demand Curve	Shift in the Demand Curve	Examples
			• Months later consumers expect the price of gasoline to fall soon, and the demand for gasoline decreases.
5. Prices of related goods a. Substitute goods	Direct		• A reduction in the price of tea decreases the demand for coffee.
			• An increase in the price of airfares causes higher demand for bus transportation.
b. Complementary goods	Inverse		• A decline in the price of cellular service increases the demand for cell phones.
			• A higher price for peanut butter decreases the demand for jelly.

© Cengage Learning®

CHECKPOINT

Can Gasoline Become an Exception to the Law of Demand?
Suppose war in the Middle East threatened oil supplies and gasoline prices began rising. Consumers feared future oil shortages, and so they rushed to fill up their gas tanks. In this case, as the price of gas increased, consumers bought more, not less. Is this an exception to the law of demand?

3-4 THE LAW OF SUPPLY

Law of supply The principle that there is a direct relationship between the price of a good and the quantity sellers are willing to offer for sale in a defined time period, ceteris paribus.

In everyday conversations, the term *supply* refers to a specific quantity. A "limited supply" of golf clubs at a sporting goods store means there are only so many for sale and that's all. This interpretation of supply is *not* the economist's definition. To economists, supply is the relationship between ranges of possible prices and quantities supplied, which is stated as the **law of supply**. The law of supply states there is a direct relationship between the price of a good and the quantity sellers are willing to offer for sale in a defined time period, ceteris paribus. Interpreting the individual *supply curve* for ZapMart shown in Exhibit 3-6 is basically the same as interpreting Bob's demand curve shown in Exhibit 3-1. Each point on the curve represents a quantity supplied (measured along the horizontal axis) at a particular price (measured along the vertical axis). For example, at a price of $10 per Blu-ray (point C), the quantity supplied by the seller, ZapMart, is 35,000 Blu-rays per year. At the higher price of $15, the quantity supplied increases to 45,000 Blu-rays per year (point B).

Supply A curve or schedule showing the various quantities of a product sellers are willing to produce and offer for sale at possible prices during a specified period of time, ceteris paribus.

CONCLUSION Supply is a curve or schedule showing the various quantities of a product sellers are willing to produce and offer for sale at possible prices during a specified period of time, ceteris paribus.

EXHIBIT 3-6 An Individual Seller's Supply Curve for Blu-rays

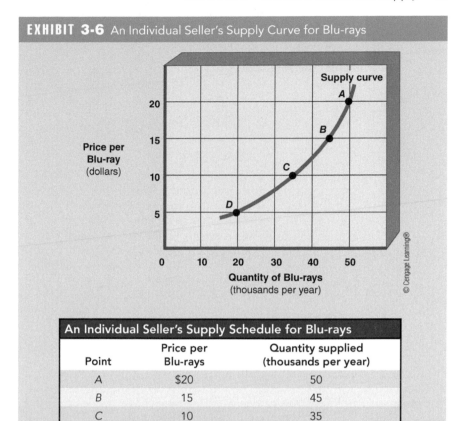

An Individual Seller's Supply Schedule for Blu-rays		
Point	Price per Blu-rays	Quantity supplied (thousands per year)
A	$20	50
B	15	45
C	10	35
D	5	20

The supply curve for an individual seller, such as ZapMart, shows the quantity of Blu-rays offered for sale at different possible prices. As the price of Blu-rays rises, a retail store has an incentive to increase the quantity of Blu-rays supplied per year. The direct relationship between price and quantity supplied conforms to the law of supply.

Why are sellers willing to sell more at a higher price? Suppose Farmer Brown is trying to decide whether to devote more of his land, labor, and barn space to the production of soybeans. Recall from Chapter 2 the production possibilities curve and the concept of increasing opportunity cost developed in Exhibit 2-3. If Farmer Brown devotes few of his resources to producing soybeans, the opportunity cost of, say, producing milk is small. But increasing soybean production means a higher opportunity cost, measured by the quantity of milk not produced. The logical question is: What would induce Farmer Brown to produce more soybeans for sale and overcome the higher opportunity cost of producing less milk? You guessed it! There must be the *incentive* of a higher price for soybeans.

CONCLUSION Only at a higher price will it be profitable for sellers to incur the higher opportunity cost associated with producing and supplying a larger quantity.

CHECKPOINT

Can the Law of Supply Be Repealed for the Oil Market?

The United States experienced two oil shocks during the 1970s in the aftermath of Middle East tensions. Congress said no to high oil prices by passing a law prohibiting prices above a legal limit. Supporters of such price controls said this was a way to ensure adequate supply without allowing oil producers to earn excess profits. Did price controls increase, decrease, or have no effect on U.S. oil production during the 1970s?

3–4a Market Supply

To construct a *market* supply curve, we follow the same procedure used to derive a market demand curve. That is, we *horizontally* sum all the quantities supplied at various prices that might prevail in the market.

Let's assume Entertain City and High Vibes are the only two firms selling Blu-rays in a given market. As you can see in Exhibit 3-7, the market supply curve, S_{total}, slopes upward to the right. At a price of $25, Entertain City will supply 25,000 Blu-rays per year, and High Vibes will supply 35,000 Blu-rays per year. Thus, summing the two individual supply curves, S_1 and S_2, *horizontally*, the total of 60,000 Blu-rays is plotted at this price on the market supply curve, S_{total}. Similar calculations at other prices along the price axis generate a market supply curve, telling us the total amount of Blu-rays these businesses offer for sale at different selling prices.

EXHIBIT 3-7 The Market Supply Curve for Blu-rays

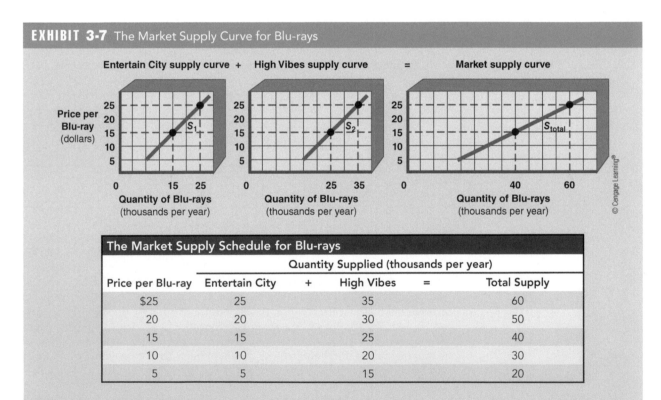

The Market Supply Schedule for Blu-rays

Price per Blu-ray	Entertain City	+	High Vibes	=	Total Supply
$25	25		35		60
20	20		30		50
15	15		25		40
10	10		20		30
5	5		15		20

Entertain City and High Vibes are two individual businesses selling Blu-rays. If these are the only two firms in the Blu-ray market, the market supply curve, S_{total}, can be derived by summing horizontally the individual supply curves, S_1 and S_2.

3-5 THE DISTINCTION BETWEEN CHANGES IN QUANTITY SUPPLIED AND CHANGES IN SUPPLY

Change in quantity supplied
A movement between points along a stationary supply curve, ceteris paribus.

Change in supply An increase or a decrease in the quantity supplied at each possible price. An increase in supply is a rightward shift in the entire supply curve. A decrease in supply is a leftward shift in the entire supply curve.

As in demand theory, the price of a product is not the only factor that influences how much sellers offer for sale. Once we relax the ceteris paribus assumption, there are six principal *nonprice determinants* (also called *supply shifters*) that can shift the supply curve's position: (1) the number of sellers, (2) technology, (3) resource prices, (4) taxes and subsidies, (5) expectations, and (6) prices of other goods. We will discuss these nonprice determinants in more detail momentarily, but first we must distinguish between a change in quantity supplied and a change in supply.

A change in quantity supplied is a movement between points along a stationary supply curve, ceteris paribus. In Exhibit 3-8(a), at the price of $10, the quantity supplied is 30 million Blu-rays per year (point A). At the higher price of $15, sellers offer a larger "quantity supplied" of 40 million Blu-rays per year (point B). Economists describe the effect of the rise in price as an increase in the quantity supplied of 10 million Blu-rays per year.

> **CONCLUSION** Under the law of supply, any increase in price along the vertical axis will cause an increase in the quantity supplied, measured along the horizontal axis.

EXHIBIT 3-8 Movement along a Supply Curve versus a Shift in Supply

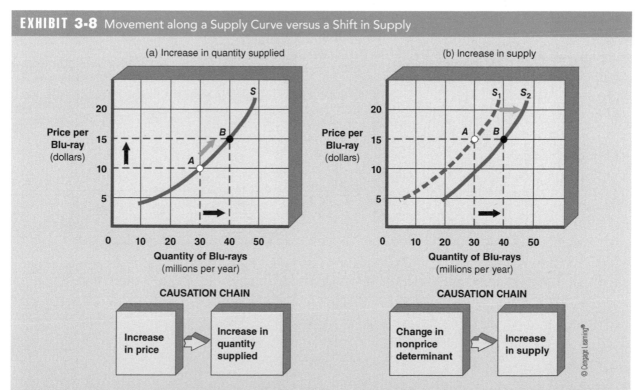

Part (a) presents the market supply curve, S, for Blu-rays per year. If the price is $10 at point A, the quantity supplied by firms will be 30 million Blu-rays. If the price increases to $15 at point B, the quantity supplied will increase from 30 million to 40 million Blu-rays.

Part (b) illustrates an increase in supply. A change in some nonprice determinant can cause an increase in supply from S_1 to S_2. At a price of $15 on S_1 (point A), the quantity supplied per year is 30 million Blu-rays. At this same price on S_2 (point B), the quantity supplied increases to 40 million.

A change in supply is an increase (rightward shift) or a decrease (leftward shift) in the quantity supplied at each possible price. If ceteris paribus no longer applies and if one of the six nonprice factors changes, the impact is to alter the supply curve's location.

> **CONCLUSION** Changes in nonprice determinants can produce only a shift in the supply curve and not in a movement along the supply curve.

In Exhibit 3-8(b), the rightward shift (an increase in supply) from S_1 to S_2 means that at all possible prices sellers offer a greater quantity for sale. At $15 per Blu-ray, for instance, sellers provide 40 million for sale annually (point B), rather than 30 million (point A).

Another case is that some nonprice factor changes and causes a leftward shift (a decrease in supply) from supply curve S_1. As a result, a smaller quantity will be offered for sale at any price.

Exhibit 3-9 summarizes the terminology for the effects of changes in price and nonprice determinants on the supply curve.

EXHIBIT 3-9 Terminology for Changes in Price and Nonprice Determinants of Supply

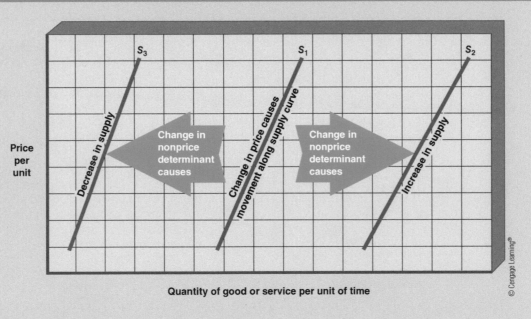

Change	Effect	Terminology
Price increases	Upward movement along the supply curve	Increase in the quantity supplied
Price decreases	Downward movement along the supply curve	Decrease in the quantity supplied
Nonprice determinant	Leftward or rightward shift in the supply curve	Decrease or increase in supply

Caution! As with demand curves, you must distinguish between a change in quantity supplied, which is a movement along a supply curve (S_1) in response to a change in price, and a shift in the supply curve. An increase in supply (shift to S_2) or decrease in supply occurs (shift to S_3) is caused by a change in some nonprice determinant and not by a change in the price.

3-6 NONPRICE DETERMINANTS OF SUPPLY

Now we turn to how each of the six basic nonprice factors affects supply.

3-6a Number of Sellers

What happens when a severe drought destroys wheat or a frost ruins the orange crop? The damaging effect of the weather may force orange growers out of business, and supply decreases. When the government eases restrictions on hunting alligators, the number of alligator hunters increases, and the supply curve for alligator meat and skins increases. Internationally, the United States may decide to lower trade barriers on textile imports, and this action increases supply by allowing new foreign firms to add their individual supply curves to the U.S. market supply curve for textiles. Conversely, higher U.S. trade barriers on textile imports shift the U.S. market supply curve for textiles leftward.

3-6b Technology

Never has society experienced such an explosion of new production techniques. Throughout the world, new and more efficient technology is making it possible to manufacture more products at any possible selling price. New, more powerful personal computers (PCs) reduce production costs and increase the supply of all sorts of goods and services. For example, computers are now milking cows. Computers admit the cows into the milking area and then activate lasers to guide milking cups into place. Dairy farmers no longer must wake up at 5:30 a.m., and cows get milked whenever they wish, day or night. As this technology spreads across the United States, it will be possible to offer more milk for sale at each possible price, and the entire supply curve for milk shifts to the right.

3-6c Resource Prices

Natural resources, labor, capital, and entrepreneurship are all required to produce products, and the prices of these resources affect supply. Suppose many firms are competing for computer programmers to design their software, and the salaries of these highly skilled workers increase. This increase in the price of labor adds to the cost of production. Along the original supply curve extra costs must be added to each possible price. As a result, the supply of computer software shifts leftward (decreases) because sellers must charge more than before for any quantity supplied. Any reduction in production cost caused by a decline in the price of resources will have an opposite effect on the supply curve and it shifts rightward (increases). Along the original supply curve cost declines so the price can be reduced at each possible price.

3-6d Taxes and Subsidies

Certain taxes, such as sales taxes, have the same effect on supply as an increase in the price of a resource. The impact of an increase in the sales tax is similar to a rise in the salaries of computer programmers. The higher sales tax imposes an additional production cost on, for example, Blu-rays, and the supply curve shifts leftward. Conversely, a payment from the government for each Blu-ray produced (an unlikely subsidy) would have the same effect as lower prices for resources or a technological advance. That is, the supply curve for Blu-rays shifts rightward.

3-6e Expectations of Producers

Expectations affect both current demand and current supply. Suppose a war in the Middle East causes oil producers to believe that oil prices will rise dramatically. Their initial response could be to hold back a portion of the oil in their storage tanks so they can sell more and make greater profits later when oil prices rise. One approach used by the major oil companies might be to limit the amount of gasoline delivered to independent distributors. This response by the oil industry shifts the current supply curve to the left. Now suppose farmers anticipate

PC Prices: How Low Can They Go?

Applicable concept: nonprice determinants of demand and supply

Radio was in existence for 38 years before 50 million people tuned in. Television took 13 years to reach that benchmark. Sixteen years after the first PC kit was introduced, 50 million people were using one. Once available to the public, the Internet crossed that line in four years.[1] Before 1999, there were no blogs, and now there are millions. Today, over 80 percent of U.S. households have a computer. Following are quotes from articles that illustrate changes in supply and demand for computers over time.

An Associated Press article reported in 1998:

Personal computers, which tumbled below the $1,000-price barrier just 18 months ago, now are breaking through the $400 price mark—putting them within reach of the average U.S. family. The plunge in PC prices reflects declining wholesale prices for computer parts, such as microprocessors, memory chips, and hard drives. "We've seen a massive transformation in the PC business," said Andrew Peck, an analyst with Cowen & Co., based in Boston.[2]

In 1999, an article in the *Wall Street Journal* reported that PC makers and distributors smashed their industry's time-honored sales channels. PC makers such as Hewlett-Packard Company began using the Internet to sell directly to consumers. In doing so, they are following the successful strategy of Dell, which for years bypassed storefront retailers and the PC distributors who traditionally keep them stocked, going instead straight to the consumer with catalogs, an 800 number, and Web sites.[3]

In 2001, an article in the *New York Times* described a computer price war:

We reached a situation where the market was saturated in 2000. People who needed computers had them. Vendors are living on sales of replacements, at least in the United States. But that doesn't give you the kind of growth these companies were used to. In the past, most price cuts came from falling prices for processors and other components. In addition, manufacturers have been narrowing profit margins for the last couple years. But when demand dried up last fall, the more aggressive manufacturers decided to try to gain market share by cutting prices to the bone. This is an all-out battle for market share.[4]

In 2012, an analyst in *USA Today* observed the following:

The TV market has been flat for the past two years, while PC sales—despite the enthusiasm for next generation products such as tablets and smartphones—are growing.

The way consumers are actually using PCs "is expanding, not contracting," says Matt McRae, Vizio's chief technology officer. "They come home and use their PC for e-mail, but they're also using it for entertainments experiences."[5]

Finally, Wikipedia reports that over time changes in supply and demand have continued to reduce PC prices. In 1982, for example, Dell offered a $3,000 PC. By 1998, the average selling price was below $1,000. Today, computers selling for less than $300 outperform computers from only a few years previously.

ANALYZE the ISSUE Identify changes in quantity demanded, changes in demand, changes in quantity supplied, and changes in supply described in the article. For any change in demand or supply, also identify the nonprice determinant causing the change.

[1] The Emerging Digital Economy (U.S. Department of Commerce, 1998), Chap. 1, p. 1.
[2] David E. Kalish, "PC Prices Fall below $400, Luring Bargain-Hunters," Associated Press/*Charlotte Observer*, Aug. 25, 1998, p. 3D.
[3] George Anders, "Online Web Seller Asks: How Low Can PC Prices Go?" *The Wall Street Journal*, Jan. 19, 1999, p. B1.
[4] Barnaby J. Feder, "Five Questions for Martin Reynolds: A Computer Price War Leaves Buyers Smiling," *The New York Times*, May 13, 2001.
[5] Jefferson Graham, "Plans to Sell Budget, High-Performance PCs," *USA Today*, Jan. 9, 2012, p. 1B.

that the price of wheat will soon fall sharply. The reaction is to sell their inventories stored in silos today before the price declines tomorrow. Such a response shifts the supply curve for wheat to the right.

3–6f Prices of Other Goods the Firm Could Produce

Businesses are always considering shifting resources from producing one good to producing another good. A rise in the price of one product relative to the prices of other products signals to suppliers that switching production to the product with the higher relative price yields higher profit. Suppose the price of corn rises because of government incentives to grow corn for ethanol while the price of wheat remains the same, then many farmers will divert more of their land to corn and less to wheat. The result is an increase in the supply of corn and a decrease in the supply of wheat. This happens because the opportunity cost of growing wheat, measured in forgone corn profits, increases.

Exhibit 3-10 summarizes the relationship between changes in the nonprice determinants of supply and the supply curve, accompanied by examples for each type of nonprice factor change.

EXHIBIT 3-10 Summary of the Impact of Changes in Nonprice Determinants of Supply on the Supply Curve

Nonprice Determinant of Supply	Relationship to Changes in Supply Curve	Shift in the Supply Curve	Examples
1. Number of sellers	Direct		• The United States lowers trade restrictions on foreign textiles, and the supply of textiles in the United States increases.
			• A severe drought destroys the orange crop, and the supply of oranges decreases.
2. Technology	Direct		• New methods of producing automobiles reduce production costs, and the supply of automobiles increases.
			• Technology is destroyed in war, and production costs increase; the result is a decrease in the supply of good X.
3. Resource prices	Inverse		• A decline in the price of computer chips increases the supply of computers.
			• An increase in the cost of farm equipment decreases the supply of soybeans.
4. Taxes and subsidies	Inverse		• An increase in the per-pack tax on cigarettes reduces the supply of cigarettes.
	Direct		• A government payment to dairy farmers based on the number of gallons produced increases the supply of milk.
5. Expectations	Inverse		• Oil companies anticipate a substantial rise in future oil prices, and this expectation causes these companies to decrease their current supply of oil.
			• Farmers expect the future price of wheat to decline, so they increase the present supply of wheat.

Continued

Continued from previous page

Nonprice Determinant of Supply	Relationship to Changes in Supply Curve	Shift in the Supply Curve	Examples
6. Prices of other goods and services	Inverse	Price s_2 s_1 0 Quantity	• A rise in the price of brand-name drugs causes drug companies to decrease the supply of generic drugs.
		Price s_1 s_2 0 Quantity	• A decline in the price of tomatoes causes farmers to increase the supply of cucumbers.

© Cengage Learning®

3-7 A MARKET SUPPLY AND DEMAND ANALYSIS

Market Any arrangement in which buyers and sellers interact to determine the price and quantity of goods and services exchanged.

Surplus A market condition existing at any price where the quantity supplied is greater than the quantity demanded.

"Teach a parrot to say 'supply and demand' and you've got an economist." A drumroll please! Buyer and seller actors are on center stage to perform a balancing act in a **market**. A market is any arrangement in which buyers and sellers interact to determine the price and quantity of goods and services exchanged. Let's consider the retail market for sneakers. Exhibit 3-11 displays hypothetical market demand and supply data for this product. Notice in column 1 of the exhibit that price serves as a common variable for both supply and demand relationships. Columns 2 and 3 list the quantity demanded and the quantity supplied for pairs of sneakers per year.

The important question for market supply and demand analysis is: Which selling price and quantity will prevail in the market? Let's start by asking what will happen if retail stores supply 75,000 pairs of sneakers and charge $105 a pair. At this relatively high price for sneakers, consumers are willing and able to purchase only 25,000 pairs. As a result, 50,000 pairs of sneakers remain as unsold inventory on the shelves of sellers (column 4), and the market condition is a **surplus** (column 5). A surplus is a market condition existing at any price where the quantity supplied is greater than the quantity demanded.

How will retailers react to a surplus? Competition forces sellers to bid down their selling price to attract more sales (column 6). If they cut the selling price to $90, there will still be a surplus of 40,000 pairs of sneakers, and pressure on sellers to cut their selling price will continue. If the price falls to $75, there will still

EXHIBIT 3-11 Demand, Supply, and Equilibrium for Sneakers (pairs per year)

(1) Price per Pair	(2) Quantity Demanded	(3) Quantity Supplied	(4) Difference (3) − (2)	(5) Market Condition	(6) Pressure on Price
$105	25,000	75,000	+50,000	Surplus	Downward
90	30,000	70,000	+40,000	Surplus	Downward
75	40,000	60,000	+20,000	Surplus	Downward
60	50,000	50,000	0	Equilibrium	Stationary
45	60,000	35,000	−25,000	Shortage	Upward
30	80,000	20,000	−60,000	Shortage	Upward
15	100,000	5,000	−95,000	Shortage	Upward

© Cengage Learning®

be an unwanted surplus of 20,000 pairs of sneakers remaining as inventory, and pressure to charge a lower price will persist.

Now let's assume sellers slash the price of sneakers to $15 per pair. This price is very attractive to consumers, and the quantity demanded is 100,000 pairs of sneakers each year. However, sellers are willing and able to provide only 5,000 pairs at this price. The good news is that some consumers buy these 5,000 pairs of sneakers at $15. The bad news is that potential buyers are willing to purchase 95,000 more pairs at that price but cannot because the shoes are not on the shelves for sale. This out-of-stock condition signals the existence of a **shortage**. A shortage is a market condition existing at any price where the quantity supplied is less than the quantity demanded.

In the case of a shortage, unsatisfied consumers compete to obtain the product by bidding to pay a higher price. Because sellers are seeking the higher profits that higher prices make possible, they gladly respond by setting a higher price of, say, $30 and increasing the quantity supplied to 20,000 pairs annually. At the price of $30, the shortage persists because the quantity demanded still exceeds the quantity supplied. Thus, a price of $30 will also be temporary because the unfulfilled quantity demanded provides an incentive for sellers to raise their selling price further and offer more sneakers for sale. Suppose the price of sneakers rises to $45 a pair. At this price, the shortage falls to 25,000 pairs, and the market still gives sellers the message to move upward along their market supply curve and sell for a higher price.

3-7a Equilibrium Price and Quantity

Assuming sellers are free to sell their products at any price, trial and error will make all possible price-quantity combinations unstable except at **equilibrium**. Equilibrium occurs at any price and quantity where the quantity demanded and the quantity supplied are equal. Economists also refer to *equilibrium* as *market clearing*.

In Exhibit 3-11, $60 is the *equilibrium* price, and 50,000 pairs of sneakers is the *equilibrium* quantity per year. Equilibrium means that the forces of supply and demand are "in balance" or "at rest" and there is no reason for price or quantity to change, ceteris paribus. In short, all prices and quantities except a unique equilibrium price and quantity are temporary. Once the price of sneakers is $60, this price will not change unless a nonprice factor changes demand or supply.

English economist Alfred Marshall (1842–1924) compared supply and demand to a pair of scissor blades. He wrote, "We might as reasonably dispute whether it is the upper or the under blade of a pair of scissors that cuts a piece of paper, as whether value is governed by utility [demand] or cost of production [supply]."[1] Joining market supply and market demand in Exhibit 3-12 allows us to clearly see the "two blades," that is, the demand curve, *D*, and the supply curve, *S*. We can measure the amount of any surplus or shortage by the horizontal distance between the demand and supply curves. At any price *above* equilibrium—say, $90—there is an *excess quantity supplied* (surplus) of 40,000 pairs of sneakers. For any price *below* equilibrium—$30, for example—the horizontal distance between the curves tells us there is an *excess quantity demanded* (shortage) of 60,000 pairs. When the price per pair is $60, the market supply curve and the market demand curve intersect at point *E*, and the quantity demanded equals the quantity supplied at 50,000 pairs per year.

CONCLUSION Graphically, the intersection of the supply curve and the demand curve is the market equilibrium price-quantity point. When all other nonprice factors are held constant, this is the only stable coordinate on the graph.

Shortage A market condition existing at any price at where the quantity supplied is less than the quantity demanded.

Equilibrium A market condition that occurs at any price and quantity at which the quantity demanded and the quantity supplied are equal.

[1] Alfred Marshall, *Principles of Economics*, 8th ed. (New York: Macmillan, 1982), p. 348.

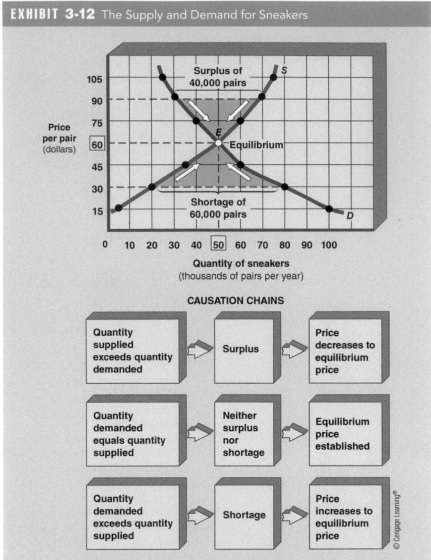

EXHIBIT 3-12 The Supply and Demand for Sneakers

CAUSATION CHAINS

| Quantity supplied exceeds quantity demanded | → | Surplus | → | Price decreases to equilibrium price |

| Quantity demanded equals quantity supplied | → | Neither surplus nor shortage | → | Equilibrium price established |

| Quantity demanded exceeds quantity supplied | → | Shortage | → | Price increases to equilibrium price |

© Cengage Learning®

The supply and demand curves represent a market for sneakers. The intersection of the demand curve, *D*, and the supply curve, *S*, at point E indicates the equilibrium price of $60 and the equilibrium quantity of 50,000 pairs bought and sold per year. At any price above $60, a surplus prevails and pressure exists to push the price downward. At $90, for example, the excess quantity supplied of 40,000 pairs remains unsold. At any price below $60, a shortage provides pressure to push the price upward. At $30, for example, the excess quantity demanded of 60,000 pairs encourages consumers to bid up the price.

3–7b Rationing Function of the Price System

Our analysis leads to an important conclusion. The predictable or stable outcome in the sneakers example is that the price will eventually come to rest at $60 per pair. All other factors held constant, the price may be above or below $60, but the forces of surplus or shortage guarantee that any price other than the equilibrium price is temporary. This is the theory of how the price system operates, and

Price system A mechanism that uses the forces of supply and demand to create an equilibrium through rising and falling prices.

GLOBAL ECONOMICS

The Market Approach to Organ Shortages

Applicable concept: price system

There is a global market in human organs in spite of attempts to prevent these transactions. For example, China banned organ sales in 2006, and India did the same in 1994. The National Transplant Organ Act of 1984 made sale of organs illegal in the United States. Economist James R. Rinehart wrote the following on this subject:

If you were in charge of a kidney transplant program with more potential recipients than donors, how would you allocate the organs under your control? Life and death decisions cannot be avoided. Some individuals are not going to get kidneys regardless of how the organs are distributed because there simply are not enough to go around. Persons who run such programs are influenced in a variety of ways. It would be difficult not to favor friends, relatives, influential people, and those who are championed by the press. Dr. John la Puma, at the Center for Clinical Medical Ethics, University of Chicago, suggested that we use a lottery system for selecting transplant patients. He feels that the present rationing system is unfair.

The selection process frequently takes the form of having the patient wait at home until a suitable donor is found. What this means is that, at any given point in time, many potential recipients are just waiting for an organ to be made available. In essence, the organs are rationed to those who are able to survive the wait. In many situations, patients are simply screened out because they are not considered to be suitable candidates for a transplant. For instance, patients with heart disease and overt psychosis often are excluded. Others with end-stage liver disorders are denied new organs on the grounds that the habits that produced the disease may remain to jeopardize recovery....

Under the present arrangements, owners receive no monetary compensation; therefore, suppliers are willing to supply fewer organs than potential recipients want. Compensating a supplier monetarily would encourage more people to offer their organs for sale. It also would be an excellent incentive for us to take better care of our organs. After all, who would want an enlarged liver or a weak heart...?[1]

The following illustrates the controversy: Apple CEO Steve Jobs had a temporary deliverance from death thanks to a liver transplant. This illustrates how the organ-donations system can be heavily weighted against poor potential recipients. Affluent patients like Steve Jobs can win the "transplant lottery" by listing simultaneously in different regions to increase their odds of finding a donor. In this case, a Palo Alto, Californian found his organ donor in Tennessee. The rules require that a prospective patient must be able to get to a center within seven or eight hours when an organ becomes available. This means a patient must be able to afford a private jet on standby and rent a place nearby the hospital. Such a system can be considered highly unfair. It should be noted that it is not known if Jobs was on more than one list, but this was allowed under the rules.

Based on altruism, the organ donor distribution system continues to result in shortages. In 2014, there were over 134,000 patients waiting on the list for organs. To address the shortage of organ donation, some European countries such as Spain, Belgium, and Austria have implemented an "opt-out" organ donation system. In the "opt-out" system, people are automatically considered to be organ donors unless they officially declare that they do not wish to be donors. Also, Facebook encourages everyone on Facebook to advertise their donor status on their pages.

 ANALYZE the ISSUE

1. Draw supply and demand curves for the U.S. organ market and compare the U.S. market to the market in a country where selling organs is legal.
2. What are some arguments against using the price system to allocate organs?
3. Should foreigners have the right to buy U.S. organs and U.S. citizens have the right to buy foreign organs?

[1] James R. Rinehart, "The Market Approach to Organ Shortages," *Journal of Health Care Marketing* 8, no. 1, March 1988, pp. 72–75.

it is the cornerstone of microeconomic analysis. The price system is a mechanism that uses the forces of supply and demand to create an equilibrium through rising and falling prices. Stated simply, price plays a *rationing* role. The price system is important because it is a mechanism for distributing scarce goods and services. At the equilibrium price of $60, only those consumers willing to pay $60 per pair get sneakers, and there are no shoes for buyers unwilling to pay that price.

Why would you prefer a world with all markets in equilibrium? If all markets are in equilibrium, there would be no shortages or surpluses for any good or service. In this world, consumers are not frustrated because they want to buy something and it is not on the shelf. Sellers are not upset because unsold merchandise is piling up unsold in their storerooms. Everyone is happy!

CHECKPOINT

Can the Price System Eliminate Scarcity?
You visit Cuba and observe that at "official" prices there is a constant shortage of consumer goods in government stores. People explain that in Cuba scarcity is caused by low prices combined with low production quotas set by the government. Many Cuban citizens say that the condition of scarcity would be eliminated if the government would allow markets to respond to supply and demand. Can the price system eliminate scarcity?

Key Concepts

Law of demand	Substitute good	Market
Demand	Complementary good	Surplus
Change in quantity demanded	Law of supply	Shortage
Change in demand	Supply	Equilibrium
Normal good	Change in quantity supplied	Price system
Inferior good	Change in supply	

Summary

- The **law of demand** states there is an inverse relationship between the price and the quantity demanded, ceteris paribus. A market demand curve is the horizontal summation of individual demand curves.

- A **change in quantity demanded** is a movement along a stationary demand curve caused by a change in price. When any of the nonprice determinants of demand changes, the demand curve responds by shifting. An *increase in demand* (rightward shift) or a *decrease in demand* (leftward shift) is caused by a change in one of the nonprice determinants.

Change in Quantity Demanded

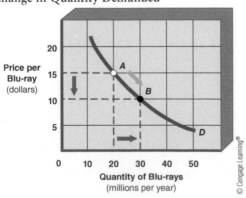

Change in Demand

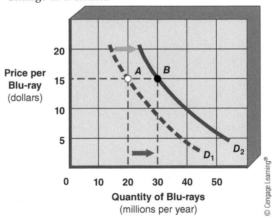

- Nonprice determinants of demand are as follows:
  a. Number of buyers
  b. Tastes and preferences
  c. Income (normal and inferior goods)
  d. Expectations of future price and income changes
  e. Prices of related goods (substitutes and complements)

- The **law of supply** states there is a direct relationship between the price and the quantity supplied, ceteris paribus. The market supply curve is the horizontal summation of individual supply curves.

- A **change in quantity supplied** is a movement along a stationary supply curve caused by a change in price. When any of the nonprice determinants of supply changes, the supply curve responds by shifting. An *increase in supply* (rightward shift) or a *decrease in supply* (leftward shift) is caused by a change in one of the nonprice determinants.

Change in Quantity Supplied

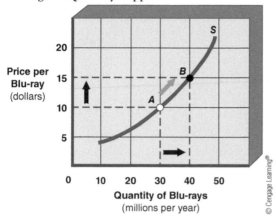

Change in Supply

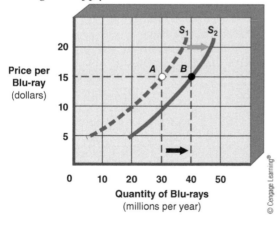

- Nonprice determinants of supply are as follows:
  a. Number of sellers
  b. Technology
  c. Resource prices
  d. Taxes and subsidies
  e. Expectations of future price changes
  f. Prices of other goods and services

- A **surplus** or **shortage** exists at any price where the quantity demanded and the quantity supplied are not equal. When the price of a good is higher than the equilibrium price, there is an excess quantity supplied, or *surplus*. When the price is less than the equilibrium price, there is an excess quantity demanded, or *shortage*.

- **Equilibrium** is the unique price and quantity established at the intersection of the supply and demand curves. Only at equilibrium does quantity demanded equal quantity supplied.

Equilibrium

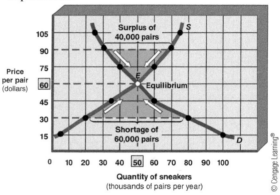

- The **price system** is the supply and demand mechanism that establishes equilibrium through the ability of prices to rise and fall.

Study Questions and Problems

1. Some people will pay a higher price for brand-name goods. For example, some people buy Rolls Royces and Rolex watches to impress others. Does knowingly paying higher prices for certain items just to be a "snob" violate the law of demand?
2. Draw graphs to illustrate the difference between a decrease in the quantity demanded and a decrease in demand for Mickey Mantle baseball cards. Give a possible reason for change in each graph.
3. Suppose oil prices rise sharply for years as a result of a war in the Persian Gulf region. What happens and why to the demand for each of the following?

   a. cars
   b. home insulation
   c. coal
   d. tires
4. Draw graphs to illustrate the difference between a decrease in quantity supplied and a decrease in supply for condominiums. Give a possible reason for change in each graph.
5. Use supply and demand analysis to explain why the quantity of word processing software exchanged increases from one year to the next.

6. Predict the direction of change for either supply or demand in the following situations:
   a. Several new companies enter the cell phone industry.
   b. Consumers suddenly decide SUVs are unfashionable.
   c. The U.S. Surgeon General issues a report stating that tomatoes prevent colds.
   d. Frost threatens to damage the coffee crop, and consumers expect the price to rise sharply in the future.
   e. The price of tea falls. What is the effect on the coffee market?
   f. The price of sugar rises. What is the effect on the coffee market?
   g. Tobacco lobbyists convince Congress to remove the tax paid by sellers on each carton of cigarettes sold.
   h. A new type of robot is invented that will pick peaches.
   i. Nintendo anticipates that the future price of its games will fall much lower than the current price.

7. Explain the effect of the following situations:
   a. Population growth surges rapidly.
   b. The prices of resources used in the production of good X increase.
   c. The government is paying a $1-per-unit subsidy for each unit of a good produced.
   d. The incomes of consumers of normal good X increase.
   e. The incomes of consumers of inferior good Y decrease.
   f. Farmers are deciding what crop to plant and learn that the price of corn has fallen relative to the price of cotton.

8. Explain why the market price may not be the same as the equilibrium price.

9. If a new breakthrough in manufacturing technology reduces the cost of producing Blu-ray players by half, what will happen to each of the following?
   a. supply of Blu-ray players
   b. demand for Blu-ray players
   c. equilibrium price and quantity of Blu-ray player
   d. demand for Blu-rays

10. The U.S. Postal Service is facing increased competition from firms providing overnight delivery of packages and letters. Additional competition has emerged because communications can be sent by emails, fax machines, and text messaging. What will be the effect of this competition on the market demand for mail delivered by the post office?

11. There is a shortage of college basketball and football tickets for some games, and a surplus occurs for other games. Why do shortages and surpluses exist for different games?

12. Explain the statement "People respond to incentives and disincentives" in relation to the demand curve and supply curve for good X.

Sample Quiz

1. Which of the following causes the demand for veggie-burgers to increase?
   a. A decline in the price of veggie-burgers.
   b. An increase in the price of tofu-burgers, perceived as a substitute by veggie-burger consumers.
   c. An increase in the price of burger buns.
   d. A technological innovation that lowers the cost of producing veggie-burgers.

2. Which of the following would *not* cause market demand for a normal good to decline?
   a. An increase in the price of a substitute.
   b. An increase in the price of a complement.
   c. A decline in consumer income.
   d. Consumer expectations that the good will go on sale in the near future.
   e. An announcement by the Surgeon General that the product contributes to premature death.

3. Low-income families consume proportionately more of which of the following kinds of goods?
   a. Luxury goods.
   b. Substitute goods.
   c. Normal goods.
   d. Inferior goods.

4. Suppose that each of the seven dwarfs buys 4 mugs of ginger ale per week from Snow White's cafe, when the price per mug is $2. If the seven dwarfs are the entire market demand for Snow White's ginger ale, then which of the following is the correct value for market quantity demanded of ginger ale at a price of $2?
   a. 4.
   b. 8.
   c. 28.
   d. 7.

5. Which of the following increases the supply of corn?
   a. The farm worker's union successfully negotiates a pay increase for corn harvest workers.
   b. The Surgeon General announces that eating corn bread contributes to baldness in men.
   c. Congress and the President eliminate subsidies formerly paid to corn farmers.
   d. Farmers that grow soybeans can also grow corn, and the price of soybeans drops by 75 percent.
6. With an upward-sloping supply curve, which of the following is *true*?
   a. An increase in price results in a decrease in quantity supplied.
   b. An increase in price results in an increase in supply.
   c. A decrease in price results in a decrease in quantity supplied.
   d. A decrease in price results in an increase in supply.
7. A rightward shift in the demand curve is called
   a. A decrease in output.
   b. A decrease in demand.
   c. An increase in demand.
   d. An increase in income.
8. A surplus occurs when
   a. The quantity demanded exceeds the quantity supplied.
   b. Price is below the equilibrium price.
   c. Price is at the equilibrium.
   d. Price is above the equilibrium.
9. A shortage occurs when
   a. The quantity supplied exceeds the quantity demanded.
   b. Price is below the equilibrium price.
   c. Price is at the equilibrium.
   d. Price is above the equilibrium.
10. Which of the following decreases supply in the market for pizza?
   a. Pizza shop employees successfully organize a union and negotiate a pay increase.
   b. The Surgeon General announces that eating pizza reduces the incidence of stomach cancer.
   c. Cheese prices drop because price supports for dairy farmers are removed.
   d. Suppose that some hot sandwich shops can also produce pizzas, and consumer demand for hot sandwiches declines sharply, reducing the profitability of producing hot sandwiches.

11. Which of the following results from an increase in the price of a one-week vacation at beach resorts on the coast of Mexico?
   a. An increase in the supply of bicycle tires in Toledo, Ohio.
   b. An increase in the demand for vacations at resorts on Caribbean islands.
   c. An increase in the supply of vacation opportunities at resorts on the coast of Mexico.
   d. A decrease in the demand for vacations at resorts on Caribbean islands.
12. There is news that the price of Tucker's Root Beer will increase significantly next week. If the demand for Tucker's Root Beer reacts *only* to this factor and shifts to the right, the position of this demand curve has reacted to a change in
   a. tastes.
   b. income levels.
   c. the prices of related goods.
   d. the number of buyers.
   e. expectations.
13. Which of the following causes a shortage to become larger?
   a. An increase in market price.
   b. An increase in supply.
   c. A decrease in demand.
   d. A decrease in price.
14. Which of the following is *true* in ski-towns such as Crested Butte, Colorado, and Whistler, British Columbia during the peak winter ski season as compared to the months of May and June?
   a. Demand for motel rooms is higher.
   b. Demand for motel rooms is lower.
   c. There is a surplus of motel rooms.
   d. The price of motel rooms will be lower.
15. In moving from a shortage toward the market equilibrium, which of the following is *true*?
   a. Price falls.
   b. Price rises.
   c. Quantity demanded increases.
   d. Quantity supplied decreases.
16. The law of demand is the principle that there is _____ relationship between the price of a good and the quantity buyers are willing to purchase in a defined time period, ceteris paribus.
   a. a direct
   b. no
   c. an inverse
   d. independent

17. A curve that is derived by summing horizontally individual demand curves is called
    a. aggregate supply.
    b. market supply.
    c. aggregate demand.
    d. market demand.

18. A leftward shift in the demand curve is called
    a. a decrease in demand.
    b. a decrease in output.
    c. an increase in demand.
    d. an increase in income.

19. Under the law of demand, any increase in price will cause _____ in quantity demanded.
    a. a decrease
    b. an increase
    c. no change
    d. constant change

20. The law of supply is the principle that there is _____ relationship between the price of a good and the quantity sellers are willing to offer for sale in a defined time period, ceteris paribus.
    a. an inverse
    b. a direct
    c. no
    d. an independent

EXHIBIT 3-13 Demand and Supply Data for Video Games

Price ($)	Quantity Demanded of Video Games	Quantity Supplied of Video Games
75	400	900
70	450	850
65	500	800
60	550	750
55	600	700
50	650	650
45	700	600
40	750	550

© Cengage Learning®

21. Exhibit 3-13 presents supply and demand data for the video game market. If the price of video games was currently $70, there would be an _____ of _____ video games in this market.
    a. excess demand; 450
    b. excess demand; 500
    c. excess supply; 400
    d. excess supply; 850
    e. excess demand; 400

22. In Exhibit 3-13, if the price of video games was currently $45, there would be an _____ of _____ video games in this market.
    a. excess demand; 700
    b. excess demand; 500
    c. excess supply; 100
    d. excess supply; 600
    e. excess demand; 100

23. In Exhibit 3-13, at any market price of video games above $50, a(an) _____ would result, causing price to _____.
    a. excess demand; rise
    b. excess supply; rise
    c. excess demand; fall
    d. excess supply; fall
    e. shortage; rise

24. In Exhibit 3-13, at any market price of video games below $50, a (an) _____ would result, causing price to _____.
    a. excess demand; rise
    b. excess supply; rise
    c. excess demand; fall
    d. excess supply; fall
    e. surplus; rise

25. In Exhibit 3-13, if there is a shortage of video games of 200 units, the current price of video games must be
    a. $60.
    b. $55.
    c. $50.
    d. $45.
    e. $40.Exhibit 3-13

CHAPTER

4

Markets in Action

In this chapter, you will learn to solve these economics puzzles:

- How can a spotted owl affect the price of homes?
- How do demand and supply affect the price of ethanol fuel?
- Why might government warehouses overflow with cheese and milk?
- What do ticket scalping and rent controls have in common?
- Can vouchers fix our schools?

CHAPTER PREVIEW

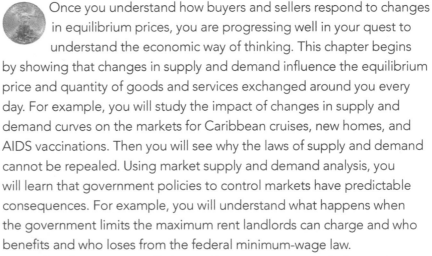

Once you understand how buyers and sellers respond to changes in equilibrium prices, you are progressing well in your quest to understand the economic way of thinking. This chapter begins by showing that changes in supply and demand influence the equilibrium price and quantity of goods and services exchanged around you every day. For example, you will study the impact of changes in supply and demand curves on the markets for Caribbean cruises, new homes, and AIDS vaccinations. Then you will see why the laws of supply and demand cannot be repealed. Using market supply and demand analysis, you will learn that government policies to control markets have predictable consequences. For example, you will understand what happens when the government limits the maximum rent landlords can charge and who benefits and who loses from the federal minimum-wage law.

In this chapter, you will also study situations in which the market mechanism fails. Have you visited a city and lamented the smog that blankets the beautiful surroundings? Or have you ever wanted to swim or fish in a stream, but could not because of industrial waste? These are obvious cases in which market-system magic failed and the government must consider cures to reach socially desirable results.

4-1 CHANGES IN MARKET EQUILIBRIUM

Using market supply and demand analysis is like putting on glasses if you are nearsighted. Suddenly, the fuzzy world around you comes into clear focus. Many people believe that prices are set by sellers adding a certain percentage to their costs. If sellers, costs rise, they simply raise their prices by that percentage. In free markets, there is more to the story. In the following examples, you will open your eyes and see that economic theory has something important to say about so many things in the real world.

4-1a Changes in Demand

The Caribbean cruise market shown in Exhibit 4-1(a) assumes market supply, S, is constant and market demand increases from D_1 to D_2. Why has the demand curve shifted rightward in the figure? We will assume the popularity of cruises to these vacation islands has suddenly risen sharply due to extensive advertising that influenced tastes and preferences. Given supply curve S and demand curve D_1, the initial equilibrium price is $600 per cruise, and the initial equilibrium quantity is 8,000 cruises per year, shown as point E_1. After the impact of advertising, the new equilibrium point, E_2, becomes 12,000 cruises per year at a price of $900 each. Thus, the increase in demand causes both the equilibrium price and the equilibrium quantity to increase.

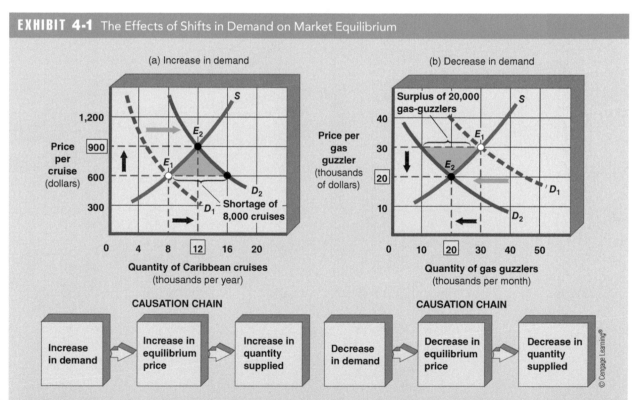

EXHIBIT 4-1 The Effects of Shifts in Demand on Market Equilibrium

In part (a), demand for Caribbean cruises increases because of extensive advertising and the demand curve shifts rightward from D_1 to D_2. This shift in demand causes a temporary shortage of 8,000 cruises per year at the initial equilibrium of E_1. This disequilibrium condition encourages firms in the cruise business to move upward along the supply curve to a new equilibrium at E_2.

Part (b) illustrates a decrease in the demand for gas-guzzling automobiles (SUVs) caused by a sharp rise in the price of gasoline (a complement). This leftward shift in demand from D_1 to D_2 results in a temporary surplus of 20,000 gas guzzlers per month at the initial equilibrium of E_1. This disequilibrium condition forces sellers of these autos to move downward along the supply curve to a new equilibrium at E_2.

It is important to understand the force that caused the equilibrium to shift from E_1 to E_2. When demand initially increased from D_1 to D_2, there was a temporary shortage of 8,000 cruises at $600 per cruise. Firms in the cruise business responded to the excess demand by hiring more workers, offering more cruises to the Caribbean, and raising the price. The cruise lines therefore move upward along the supply curve (increasing quantity supplied, but *not* changing supply). During some period of trial and error, Caribbean cruise sellers increase their price and quantity supplied until a shortage no longer exists at point E_2. Therefore, the increase in demand causes both the equilibrium price and the equilibrium quantity to increase.

What will happen to the demand for gas-guzzling automobiles (e.g., SUVs) if the price of gasoline triples? Because gasoline and automobiles are complements, a rise in the price of gasoline decreases the demand for such automobiles from D_1 to D_2 in Exhibit 4-1(b). At the initial equilibrium price of $30,000 per gas guzzler ($E_1$), the quantity supplied now exceeds the quantity demanded by 20,000 automobiles per month. This unwanted inventory forces automakers to reduce the price and quantity supplied. As a result of this movement downward on the supply curve, market equilibrium changes from E_1 to E_2. The equilibrium price falls from $30,000 to $20,000, and the equilibrium quantity falls from 30,000 to 20,000 gas guzzlers per month.

EXHIBIT 4-2 The Effects of Shifts in Supply on Market Equilibrium

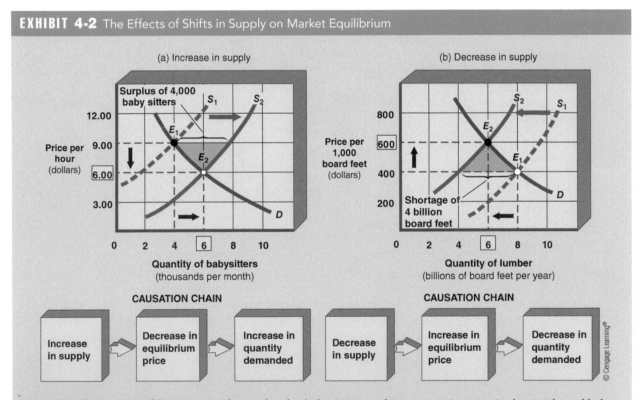

In part (a), begin at equilibrium E_1 in the market for babysitters, and assume an increase in the number of babysitters shifts the supply curve rightward from S_1 to S_2. This shift in supply causes a temporary surplus of 4,000 unemployed babysitters per month. This disequilibrium condition causes a movement downward along the demand curve to a new equilibrium at E_2. At E_2, the equilibrium price declines and the equilibrium quantity rises.

In part (b), steps to protect the environment cause the supply curve for lumber to shift leftward from S_1 to S_2. This shift in supply results in a temporary shortage of 4 billion board feet per year. Customer bidding for the available lumber raises the price. As a result, the market moves upward along the demand curve to a new equilibrium at E_2, and the quantity demanded falls.

4-1b Changes in Supply

Now reverse the analysis by assuming demand remains constant and allow some nonprice determinant to shift the supply curve. In Exhibit 4-2(a), begin at point E_1 in a market for babysitting services at an equilibrium price of $9 per hour and 4,000 babysitters hired per month. Then assume there is a population shift and the number of people available to babysit rises. This increase in the number of sellers shifts the market supply curve rightward from S_1 to S_2 and creates a temporary surplus of 4,000 babysitters at point E_1 who offer their services but are not hired. The unemployed babysitters respond by reducing the price and the number of babysitters available for hire, which is a movement downward along S_2. As the price falls, buyers move down along their demand curve and hire more babysitters per month. When the price falls to $6 per hour, the market is in equilibrium again at point E_2, instead of E_1, and consumers hire 6,000 babysitters per month.

Exhibit 4-2(b) illustrates the market for lumber. Suppose this market is at equilibrium at point E_1, where the going price is $400 per thousand board feet, and 8 billion board feet are bought and sold per year. Now consider the impact of the Endangered Species Act, and the federal government setting aside huge forest resources to protect the spotted owl and other wildlife. This means the market supply curve shifts leftward from S_1 to S_2, and a temporary shortage of 4 billion board feet of lumber exists at point E_1. Suppliers respond by hiking their price from $400 to $600 per thousand board feet, and a new equilibrium is established at E_2, where the quantity is 6 billion board feet per year. This higher cost of lumber, in turn, raises the price of a new home.

Exhibit 4-3 gives a concise summary of the impact of changes in demand or supply on market equilibrium.

CHECKPOINT

Why the Higher Price for Ethanol Fuel?

Suppose more consumers purchased ethanol fuel for their cars, and at the same time, producers switched to ethanol fuel production. Within a year period, the price of ethanol fuel shot up $2 per gallon. During this period, which increased more—demand, supply, or neither?

4-1c Trend of Prices over Time

Basic demand and supply analysis allows us to explain a trend in prices over a number of years. Exhibit 4-4 shows the effect of changes in nonprice determinants that increase both the demand and supply curves for good X between 2005, 2010, and 2015. A line connects the equilibrium prices for each year in order to summarize the trend of equilibrium price changes over this time period. In this case, the observed prices trace an upward-sloping trend line.

EXHIBIT 4-3   Effect of Shifts in Demand or Supply on Market Equilibrium

Change	Effect on Equilibrium Price	Effect on Equilibrium Quantity
Demand increases	Increases	Increases
Demand decreases	Decreases	Decreases
Supply increases	Decreases	Increases
Supply decreases	Increases	Decreases

© Cengage Learning®

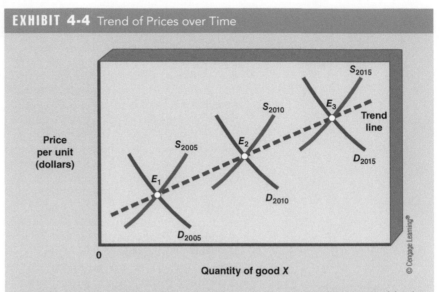

EXHIBIT 4-4 Trend of Prices over Time

Nonprice determinants of demand and supply for good X have caused both the demand and supply curves to shift rightward between 2005 and 2015. As a result, the equilibrium price in this example rises along the upward-sloping trend line connecting each observed equilibrium price.

4-2 CAN THE LAWS OF SUPPLY AND DEMAND BE REPEALED?

The government intervenes in some markets with the objective of preventing prices from rising to the equilibrium price. In other markets, the government's goal is to intervene and maintain a price higher than the equilibrium price. Market supply and demand analysis is a valuable tool for understanding what happens when the government fixes prices. There are two types of price controls: *price ceilings* and *price floors*.

4-2a Price Ceilings
Case 1: Rent Control

What happens if the government prevents the price system from setting a market price "too high" by mandating a **price ceiling**? A price ceiling is a legally established maximum price a seller can charge. Rent controls are an example of the imposition of a price ceiling in the market for rental units. New York City, Washington, D.C., Los Angeles, San Francisco, and other communities in the United States have some form of rent control. Since World War I, rent controls have been widely used in Europe. The rationale for rent controls is to provide an "essential service" that would otherwise be unaffordable by many people at the equilibrium rental price. Let's see why most economists believe that rent controls are counterproductive.

Exhibit 4-5 is a supply and demand diagram for the quantity of rental units demanded and supplied per month in a hypothetical city. We begin the analysis by assuming no rent controls exist and equilibrium is at point *E*, with a monthly rent of $1,200 per month and 6 million units occupied. Next, assume the city council imposes a rent control (ceiling price) that by law forbids any landlord from renting a unit for more than $800 per month. What does market supply and demand theory predict will happen? At the low rent ceiling of $800, the quantity demanded of rental units will be 8 million, but the quantity supplied

Price ceiling A legally established maximum price a seller can charge.

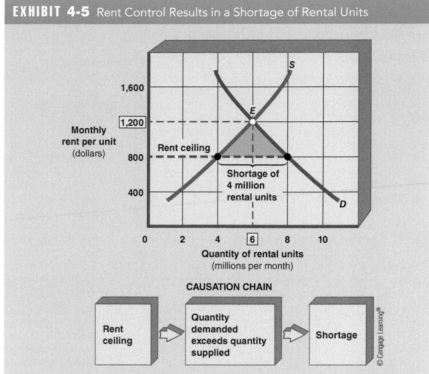

EXHIBIT 4-5 Rent Control Results in a Shortage of Rental Units

If no rent controls exist, the equilibrium rent for a hypothetical apartment is $1,200 per month at point *E*. However, if the government imposes a rent ceiling of $800 per month, a shortage of 4 million rental units occurs. Because rent cannot rise by law, one outcome is that consumers must search for available units instead of paying a higher rent. Other outcomes include a black market, bribes, discrimination, and other illegal methods of dealing with a shortage of 4 million rental units per month.

will be only 4 million. Consequently, the price ceiling creates a persistent market shortage of 4 million rental units because suppliers cannot raise the rental price without being subjected to legal penalties.

Note that a rent ceiling at or above $1,200 per month would have no effect. If the ceiling is set at the equilibrium rent of $1,200, the quantity of rental units demanded and the quantity of rental units supplied are equal regardless of the rent control. If the rent ceiling is set above the equilibrium rent, the quantity of rental units supplied exceeds the quantity of rental units demanded, and this surplus will cause the market to adjust to the equilibrium rent of $1,200.

What is the impact of rent controls on consumers? First, as a substitute for paying higher prices, consumers must spend more time on waiting lists and searching for housing. This means consumers incur an *opportunity cost* added to the $800 rent set by the government. Second, an illegal market, or *black market*, can arise because of the excess quantity demanded. Because the price of rental units is artificially low, the profit motive encourages tenants to risk breaking the law by subletting their unit to the highest bidder over $800 per month.

From the seller's perspective, rent control encourages two undesirable effects. First, faced with a mandated low rent, landlords may cut maintenance expenses, and housing deterioration will reduce the stock of rental units in the long run. Second, landlords may use discriminatory practices to replace the price system. Once owners realize there is an excess quantity demanded for rentals at the

Who Turned Out the Lights in California?
Applicable concept: price ceiling

In order to keep electricity cheap for its state, the California legislature in 1996 set a retail ceiling price of 10 cents per kilowatt-hour. Moreover, no new plants or hydroelectric plants were built during the 1990s. Also, the plan was to require utilities to sell their power plants and import electricity as needed from the "spot market" through high-speed transmission lines from other states. In the deregulated wholesalers electricity market, a spot market is one in which the price of electricity is determined by supply and demand conditions each hour.

The stage was set for the forces of supply and demand to "turn out the lights." First, demand soared during a heat wave in the summer of 2000 as consumers turned on their air conditioners. Second, there was a leftward shift in supply. High natural gas prices increased the cost of producing electricity in all states. Also, low snowpacks and a drought in the Northwest reduced the capacity of hydroelectric dams in this region.

Facing shortages from both increased demand and decreased supply, California utilities had no choice but to buy electricity on the spot market as prices soared tenfold over their normal levels. Because customer rates were capped, the price paid by consumers did not cover what the utilities were paying for electricity. The utilities quickly found themselves facing bankruptcy, and this threat caused

additional spot rate increases. Duke Power Company of North Carolina, for example, has stated that 8 percent of its spot price was a premium to cover the risk of selling to California utilities that might not repay. Also, a subsequent investigation by the Federal Energy Regulatory Commission (FERC) reported evidence that power companies such as Enron developed strategies to drive up prices.

Faced with this crisis, former governor Gray Davis of California called for more price caps. He convinced the FERC to cap wholesale prices in the west during hours of highest demand, combined with a daily regime of rolling blackouts and calls for conservation. In April 2001, Governor Davis abandoned the 1996 price ceiling, thus sharply increasing the retail electric price.

 **ANALYZE the ISSUE** Put price of electricity (cents per kilowatt-hour) on the vertical axis and quantity of electricity (megawatts per hour) on the horizontal axis of a graph. Draw the changes in demand and supply for electricity in California described above. [Hint: Begin the graph in equilibrium below the price ceiling.]

controlled price, they may resort to preferences based on pet ownership, or family size to allocate scarce rental space.

Case 2: Gasoline Price Ceiling

The government placed ceilings on most nonfarm prices during World War II and, to a lesser extent, during the Korean War. In 1971, President Nixon "froze" virtually all wages, prices, and rents until 1973 in an attempt to control inflation. As a result of an oil embargo in late 1973, the government imposed a price ceiling of 55 cents per gallon of gasoline. To deal with the shortage, nonprice rationing schemes were introduced in 1974. Some states used a first-come, first-served system, while other states allowed consumers with even-numbered license plates to buy gas on even-numbered days and those with odd-numbered license plates to buy on odd-numbered days. Gas stations were required to close on Friday night and not open until Monday morning. Regardless of the scheme, long waiting lines for gasoline formed, just as the supply and demand model predicts. Finally, in the past, legally imposed price ceilings have been placed on such items as natural gas shipped in interstate commerce and on interest rates for loans. Maximum interest rate laws are called *usury laws*, and state governments have adopted these ceilings in the past to regulate home mortgages and other types of loans. Internationally, as discussed later in Chapter 22 on economies in transition, price ceilings on food and rent were common in the former Soviet Union. Soviet sociologists estimated that members of a typical urban household spent a combined total of 40 hours per week standing in lines to obtain various goods and services.

4-2b Price Floors

Price floor A legally established minimum price a seller can be paid.

The other side of the price-control coin is a **price floor** set by government because it fears that the price system might establish a price viewed as "too low."

A price floor is a legally established minimum price a seller can be paid. We now turn to two examples of price floors. The first is the minimum wage, and the second is agricultural price supports.

Case 1: The Minimum-Wage Law

In the first chapter, the second Economics in Practice applied *normative* and *positive* reasoning to the issue of the minimum wage. Now you are prepared to apply market supply and demand analysis (positive reasoning) to this debate. Begin by noting that the demand for unskilled labor is the downward-sloping curve shown in Exhibit 4-6. The wage rate on the vertical axis is the price of unskilled labor, and the amount of unskilled labor employers are willing to hire varies inversely with the wage rate. At a higher wage rate, businesses will hire fewer workers. At a lower wage rate, they will employ a larger quantity of workers.

On the supply side, the wage rate determines the number of unskilled workers willing and able to work per year. At higher wages, workers will give up leisure or schooling to work, and at lower wages, fewer workers will be available for hire. The upward-sloping curve in Exhibit 4-6 is the supply of labor.

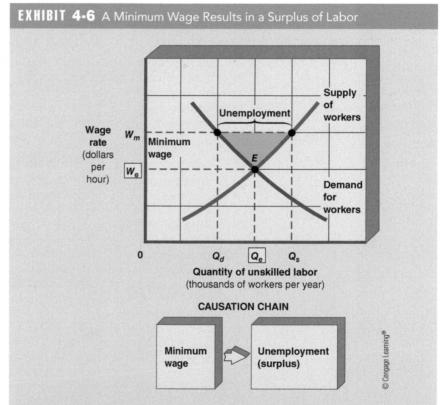

EXHIBIT 4-6 A Minimum Wage Results in a Surplus of Labor

When the federal or state government sets a wage-rate floor above the equilibrium wage, a surplus of unskilled labor develops. The supply curve is the number of workers offering their labor services per year at possible wage rates. The demand curve is the number of workers employers are willing and able to hire at various wage rates. Equilibrium wage, W_e, will result if the price system is allowed to operate without government interference. At the minimum wage of W_m, there is a surplus of unemployed workers, $Q_s - Q_d$.

Assuming the freedom to bargain, the price system will establish an equilibrium wage rate of W_e and an equilibrium quantity of labor employed of Q_e. But suppose the government enacts a minimum wage, W_m, which is a price floor above the equilibrium wage, W_e. The intent of the legislation is to "wave a carrot" in front of people who will not work at W_e and to make lower-paid workers better off with a higher wage rate. But consider the undesirable consequences. One result of an artificially high minimum wage is that the number of workers willing to offer their labor increases upward along the supply curve to Q_s, but there are fewer jobs because the number of workers firms are willing to hire decreases to Q_d on the demand curve. The predicted outcome is a labor surplus of unskilled workers, $Q_s - Q_d$, who are unemployed. Moreover, employers are encouraged to substitute machines and skilled labor for the unskilled labor previously employed at equilibrium wage W_e. The minimum wage is therefore considered counterproductive because employers lay off the lowest-skilled workers, who ironically are the type of workers minimum-wage legislation intends to help. Also, loss of minimum-wage jobs represents a loss of entry-level jobs to those who seek to enter the workforce.

Supporters of the minimum wage are quick to point out that those employed (Q_d) are better off. Even though the minimum wage causes a reduction in employment, some economists argue that a more equal or fairer income distribution is worth the loss of some jobs. Moreover, the shape of the labor demand curve may be much more vertical than shown in Exhibit 4-6. If this is the case, the unemployment effect of a rise in the minimum wage would be small. In addition, they claim opponents ignore the possibility that unskilled workers lack bargaining power versus employers.

Finally, a minimum wage set at or below the equilibrium wage rate is ineffective. If the minimum wage is set at the equilibrium wage rate of W_e, the quantity of labor demanded and the quantity of labor supplied are equal regardless of the minimum wage. If the minimum wage is set below the equilibrium wage, the forces of supply of and demand for labor establish the equilibrium wage regardless of the minimum wage rate.

Case 2: Agricultural Price Supports

A farm price support is a well-known example of a price floor, which results in government purchases of surplus food and in higher food prices. Agricultural price support programs began in the 1930s as a means of raising the income of farmers, who were suffering from low market prices during the Great Depression. Under these programs, the government guarantees a minimum price above the equilibrium price and agrees to purchase any quantity the farmer is unable to sell at the legal price.

A few of the crops that have received price supports are corn, peanuts, soybeans, wheat, cotton, rice, tobacco, and dairy products. As predicted by market supply and demand analysis, a price support above the equilibrium price causes surpluses. Government warehouses therefore often overflow with such perishable products as butter, cheese, and dry milk purchased with taxpayers' money. The Economics in Practice on the dairy industry examines one of the best-known examples of U.S. government interference with agricultural market prices.

CONCLUSION A price ceiling or price floor prevents market adjustment in which competition among buyers and sellers bids the price upward or downward to the equilibrium price.

CHECKPOINT

Is There Price Fixing at the Ticket Window?

At sold-out concerts, sports contests, and other events, some ticket holders try to resell their tickets for more than they paid—a practice known as scalping. For scalping to occur, must the original ticket price be legally set by a price floor, at the equilibrium price, or by a price ceiling?

Rigging the Market for Milk
Applicable concept: price supports

"I always wondered how the government set milk prices."

Each year the milk industry faces an important question. What does the federal government plan to do about its dairy price support program, which has helped boost farmers' income since 1949? Under the price support program, the federal government agrees to buy storable milk products, such as cheese, butter, and dry milk. If the farmers cannot sell all their products to consumers at a price exceeding the price support level, the federal government will purchase any unsold grade A milk production. Although state-run dairy commissions set their own minimum prices for milk, state price supports closely follow federal levels and are kept within 3 percent of levels in bordering states to reduce interstate milk price competition.

Members of Congress who advocate changes in the price support programs worry that milk surpluses are costing taxpayers too much. Each year the federal government pays billions of dollars to dairy farmers for milk products held in storage at a huge cost. Moreover, the problem is getting worse because the federal government encourages dairy farmers to use ultramodern farming techniques to increase the production per cow. Another concern is the biggest government support checks go to the largest farmers, while the number of dairy farmers continues to decline.

Congress is constantly seeking a solution to the milk price support problem. The following are some of the ideas that have been considered:

- Freeze the current price support level. This prospect dismays farmers, who are subject to increasing expenses for feed, electricity, and other resources.
- Eliminate the price supports gradually in yearly increments over the next five years. This would subject the milk market to the price fluctuations of the free market, and farmers would suffer some bad years from low milk prices.
- Have the Department of Agriculture charge dairy farmers a tax of 50 cents for every 100 pounds of milk they produce. The farmers oppose this approach because it would discourage production and run small farmers out of business.
- Have the federal government implement a "whole herd buyout" program. The problem is that using taxpayers' money to get farmers out of the dairy business pushes up milk product prices and rewards dairy farmers who own a lot of cows. Besides, what does the government do with the cows after it purchases them?

Finally, opponents of the dairy price support program argue that the market for milk is inherently a competitive industry and that consumers and taxpayers would be better served without government price supports for milk.

ANALYZE the ISSUE

1. Draw a supply and demand graph to illustrate the problem described in the case study, and prescribe your own solution.
2. Which proposal do you think best serves the interests of the small dairy farmers? Why?
3. Which proposal do you think best serves the interests of the consumers? Why?
4. Which proposal do you think best serves the interests of members of Congress? Why?

4-3 MARKET FAILURE

Market failure A situation in which market equilibrium results in too few or too many resources being used in the production of a good or service. This inefficiency may justify government intervention.

In this chapter and the previous chapter, you have gained an understanding of how markets operate. Through the price system, society coordinates economic activity, but markets are not always "Prince Charmings" that achieve *market efficiency* without a misallocation of resources. It is now time to step back with a critical eye and consider markets that become "ugly frogs" by allocating resources inefficiently. Market failure occurs when market equilibrium results in too few or too many resources being used in the production of a good or service. In this section, you will study four important cases of market failure: lack of competition, externalities, public goods, and income inequality. A word of caution: Do not assume that government intervention always corrects an alleged market failure. The topic of government failure is discussed in Chapter 16.

Adam Smith (1723–1790) The father of modern economics who wrote *The Wealth of Nations*, published in 1776.

4–3a Lack of Competition

There must be competition among both producers and consumers for markets to function properly. But what happens if the producers fail to compete? In *The Wealth of Nations*, Adam Smith states, "People of the same trade seldom meet together, even for merriment and diversion, but the conversation ends in a conspiracy against the public, or in some diversion to raise prices."[1] This famous quotation clearly underscores the fact that in the real world businesses seek ways to replace consumer sovereignty with "big business sovereignty." What happens when a few firms rig the market and they become the market's boss? By restricting supply through artificial limits on the output of a good, firms can enjoy higher prices and profits. As a result, firms may waste resources and retard technology and innovation.

Exhibit 4-7 illustrates how IBM, Apple, Dell, and other suppliers of personal computers (PCs) could benefit from rigging the market. Without collusive action, the competitive price for PCs is $1,500, the quantity of 200,000 per month is sold, and efficient equilibrium prevails at point E_1. It is in the best interest of sellers, however, to take steps that would make PCs artificially scarce and raise the price. Graphically, the sellers wish to shift the competitive supply curve, S_1, leftward to the restricted supply curve, S_2. This could happen for a number of reasons, including an agreement among sellers to restrict supply (collusion) and government action. For example, the sellers could lobby the government to pass a law allowing an association of PC suppliers to set production quotas. The proponents

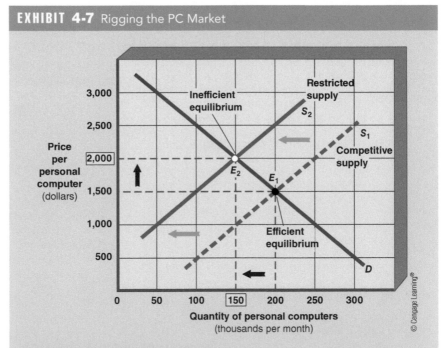

EXHIBIT 4-7 Rigging the PC Market

At efficient equilibrium point E_1, sellers compete. As a result, the price charged per PC is $1,500, and the quantity of PCs exchanged is 200,000. Suppose suppliers use collusion, government intervention, or other means to restrict the supply of this product. The decrease in supply from S_1 to S_2 establishes inefficient market equilibrium E_2. At E_2, firms charge the higher price of $2,000, and the equilibrium quantity of PCs falls to 150,000. Thus, the outcome of restricted supply is that the market fails because firms use too few resources to produce PCs at an artificially higher price.

---

[1] Adam Smith, *An Inquiry into the Nature and Causes of the Wealth of Nations* (1776; reprint, New York: Random House, The Modern Library, 1937), p. 128.

might argue this action raises prices and, in turn, profits. Higher profits enable the industry to invest in new capital and become more competitive in world markets.

Opponents of artificially restricted supply argue that, although the producers benefit, the lack of competition means the economy loses. The result of restricting supply is that the efficient equilibrium point, E_1, changes to the inefficient equilibrium point, E_2. At point E_2, the higher price of $2,000 is charged, and the lower equilibrium quantity means that firms devote too few resources to producing PCs and charge an artificially high price. Note that under U.S. antitrust laws, the Justice Department is responsible for prosecuting firms that collude to restrict supply to force higher prices.

4–3b Externalities

Externalities A cost or benefit imposed on people other than the consumers and producers of a good or service.

Even when markets are competitive, some markets may still fail because they suffer from the presence of side effects economists call **externalities**. An externality is a cost or benefit imposed on people other than the consumers and producers of a good or service. Externalities are also called *spillover effects* or *neighborhood effects*. People other than consumers and producers who are affected by these side effects of market exchanges are called *third parties*. Externalities may be either negative or positive; that is, they may be detrimental or beneficial. Suppose you are trying to study and your roommate is listening to Steel Porcupines at full blast. The action of your roommate is imposing an unwanted *external cost* or *negative externality* on you and other third parties who are trying to study or sleep. Externalities can also result in an *external benefit* or *positive externality* to nonparticipating parties. When a community proudly displays its neat lawns, gorgeous flowers, and freshly painted homes, visitors are third parties who did none of the work but enjoy the benefit of the pleasant scenery.

A Graphical Analysis of Pollution

Exhibit 4-8 provides a graphical analysis of two markets that fail to include externalities in their market prices unless the government takes corrective action. Exhibit 4-8(a) shows a market for steel in which steel firms burn high-sulfur coal and pollute the environment. Demand curve D and supply curve S_1 establish the inefficient equilibrium, E_1, in the steel market. Not included in S_1 are the *external costs* to the public because the steel firms are not paying for the damage from smoke emissions. If steel firms discharge smoke and ash into the atmosphere, foul air reduces property values, raises health care costs, and generally erodes the quality of life. Because supply curve S_1 does not include these external costs, they are also not included in the price of steel, P_1. In short, the absence of the cost of pollution in the price of steel means the firms produce more steel and pollution than is socially desirable.

S_2 is the supply curve that would exist if the external costs of respiratory illnesses, dirty homes, and other undesirable side effects were included. Once S_2 includes the charges for environmental damage, the equilibrium price rises to P_2, and the equilibrium quantity becomes Q_2.

At the efficient equilibrium point, E_2, the steel market achieves allocative efficiency. At E_2, steel firms are paying the full cost and using fewer resources to produce the lower quantity of steel at Q_2.

> **CONCLUSION** When the supply curve fails to include external costs, the equilibrium price is artificially low and the equilibrium quantity is artificially high.

Regulation and pollution taxes are two ways society can correct the market failure of pollution:

1. **Regulation.** Legislation can set standards that force firms to clean up their emissions as a condition of remaining in business. This means firms must buy, install, and maintain pollution control equipment. When the extra cost

EXHIBIT 4-8 Externalities in the Steel and AIDS Vaccination Markets

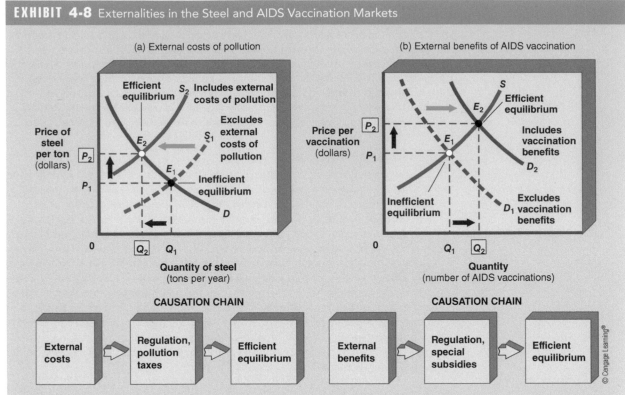

In Part (a), resources are overallocated at inefficient market equilibrium E_1 because steel firms do not include the cost per ton of pollution in the cost per ton of steel. Supply curve S_2 includes the external costs of pollution. If firms are required to purchase equipment to remove the pollution or to pay a tax on pollution, the economy achieves the efficient equilibrium of E_2.

Part (b) demonstrates that external benefits cause an underallocation of resources. The efficient output at equilibrium point E_2 is obtained if people are required to purchase AIDS shots or if the government pays a subsidy equal to the external benefit per shot.

of the pollution equipment is added to the production cost per ton of steel, the initial supply curve, S_1, shifts leftward to supply curve S_2. This means regulation has forced the market equilibrium to change from E_1 to E_2. At point E_2, the firms use fewer resources to produce Q_2 compared to Q_1 output of steel per year, and, therefore, the firms operate efficiently.

2. **Pollution Taxes.** Another approach would be for the government to levy a tax per ton of steel equal to the external cost imposed on society when the firm emits pollution into the air. This action inhibits production by imposing an additional production cost per ton of steel from the pollution taxes and shifts the supply curve leftward from S_1 to S_2. Again, the objective is to change the equilibrium from E_1 to E_2 and eliminate the overuse of resources devoted to steel production and its pollution. The tax revenue could be used to compensate those damaged by the pollution.

A Graphical Analysis of AIDS Vaccinations

As explained above, the supply curve can understate the *external costs* of a product. Now you will see that the demand curve can understate the *external benefits* of a product. Suppose a vaccination is discovered that prevents AIDS. Exhibit 4-8(b) illustrates the market for immunization against AIDS. Demand curve D_1 reflects the price consumers would pay for shots to receive the benefit of a reduced probability of infection by AIDS. Supply curve S shows the quantities of shots suppliers offer for sale at different prices. At equilibrium point E_1, the market fails to achieve an efficient allocation of resources. The reason is that when buyers are vaccinated, other people who do not purchase AIDS shots (called *free riders*) also benefit because this disease is less likely to spread. Once demand curve D_2 includes external benefits to nonconsumers of AIDS vaccinations (increase in the number of buyers), the efficient equilibrium of E_2 is established. At Q_2, sellers devote greater resources to AIDS vaccinations, and the underallocation of resources is eliminated.

How can society prevent the market failure of AIDS vaccinations? Two approaches follow:

1. **Regulation.** The government can boost consumption and shift the demand curve rightward by requiring all citizens to purchase AIDS shots each year. This approach to capturing external benefits in market demand explains why all school-age children must have polio and other shots before entering school.
2. **Special Subsidies.** Another possible solution would be for the government to increase consumer income by paying consumers for each AIDS vaccination. This would mean the government pays each citizen a dollar payment equal to the amount of external benefits per shot purchased. Because the subsidy amount is payable at any price along the demand curve, the demand curve shifts rightward until the efficient equilibrium price and quantity are reached.

> **CONCLUSION** When externalities are present, market failure gives incorrect price and quantity signals, and as a result, resources are misallocated. External costs cause the market to overallocate resources, and external benefits cause the market to underallocate resources.

4-3c Public Goods

Public good A good or service with two properties: (1) users collectively consume benefits, and (2) there is no way to bar people who do not pay (free riders) from consuming the good or service.

Private goods are produced through the price systems. In contrast, national defense is an example of a public good provided by the government because of its special characteristics. A public good is a good or service that, once produced, has two properties: (1) users collectively consume benefits and (2) there is no way to bar people who do not pay (free riders) from consuming the good or service.

To see why the marketplace fails, imagine that Patriot Missiles Inc. offers to sell missile defense systems to people who want private protection against attacks from incoming missiles. First, once the system is operational, everyone in the defense area benefits from increased safety. Second, the *nonexclusive* nature of a public good means it is impossible or very costly for any owner of a Patriot missile defense system to prevent nonowners, the free riders, from reaping the benefits of its protection.

Given the two properties of a public good, why would any private individual purchase a Patriot missile defense system? Why not take a free ride and wait until someone else buys a missile system? Thus, each person wants a Patriot system but does not want to bear the cost of the system when everyone shares in the benefits. As a result, the market fails to provide Patriot missile defense systems, and everyone hopes no missile attacks occur before someone finally decides to purchase one. Government can solve this public goods problem by producing Patriot missiles and taxing the public to pay. Unlike a private citizen, the government can use force to collect payments and prevent the free rider problem. Other examples of public goods include global agreements to reduce emissions, the judicial system, the national emergency warning system, air traffic control, prisons, and traffic lights.

> **CONCLUSION** If public goods are available only in the marketplace, people wait for someone else to pay, and the result is an underproduction or zero production of public goods.

ECONOMICS IN PRACTICE

Can Vouchers Fix Our Schools?

Applicable concept: public goods versus private goods

© AWAVA,2010/Shutterstock.com

In their book *Free to Choose*, published in 1980, economists Milton Friedman and his wife Rose Friedman proposed a voucher plan for schools.[1] The objective of their proposal was to retain government financing, but give parents greater freedom to choose the schools their children attend. The Friedmans pointed out that under the current system parents face a strong incentive not to remove their children from the public schools. The reason is because, if parents decide to withdraw their children from a public school and send them to a private school, they must pay private tuition in addition to the taxes that finance children enrolled in the public schools.

To remove the financial penalty that limits the freedom of parents to choose schools, the government could give parents a voucher, which is a piece of paper redeemable for a sum of money payable to any approved school. For example, if the government spends $6,000 per year to educate a student, then the voucher could be for this amount. The voucher plan embodies the same principle as the GI Bill that provides educational benefits to military veterans. The veteran receives a voucher good only for educational expenses and is free to choose the school where it is used, provided the school satisfies certain standards.

The Friedmans argue that parents could, and should, be permitted to use the vouchers not only at private schools but also at other public schools—and not only at schools in their own district, city, or state but at any school that is willing to accept their child. That option would give every parent a greater opportunity to choose and at the same time would require public schools to charge tuition. The tuition would be competitive because public schools must compete for students both with one another and with private schools. It is important to note that this plan relieves no one of the burden of taxation to pay for schooling. It simply gives parents a wider choice as to which competing schools their children attend, given the amount of funding per student that the community has obligated itself to provide. The plan also does not affect the present standards imposed on

private schools to ensure that students attending them satisfy the compulsory attendance laws.

In 1990, Milwaukee began an experiment with school vouchers. The program gave selected children from low-income families taxpayer-funded vouchers to allow them to attend private schools. There has been a continuing heated debate among parents, politicians, and educators over the results. In 1998, Wisconsin's highest court ruled in a 4–2 decision that Milwaukee could use public money for vouchers for students who attend religious schools without violating the constitutional separation of church and state.

A 2002 article in *USA Today* reported:

> Opponents of vouchers have repeatedly argued that they would damage the public schools, draining them of resources and better students. A recent study of the Milwaukee voucher program by Caroline Hoxby, a Harvard economist, suggests just the opposite. She wrote that "schools that faced the most potential competition from vouchers had the best productivity response." No doubt, the nation's experience with vouchers is limited, yet the evidence cited in a recent Brookings Institution report shows that they do seem to benefit African-American youngsters.[2]

The controversy continues: For example, in a landmark 2002 case, the U.S. Supreme Court ruled that government vouchers for private or parochial schools are constitutional. In 2003, however, a Denver judge struck down Colorado's new school voucher law, ruling that it violated the state's constitution by stripping local school boards of their control over education. In 2006, the Florida Supreme Court ruled that Florida's voucher program for students in the lowest rated public schools was unconstitutional. Then in 2010, Florida legislated a tax-credit voucher plan for low-income students. And in 2013, the Indiana Supreme Court upheld the state's voucher program, which is the nation's broadest school voucher program.

ANALYZE *the* ISSUE

1. In recent years, school choice has been a hotly debated issue. Explain whether education is a public good. If education is not a public good, why should the government provide it?
2. The Freidmans present a one-sided view of the benefits of a voucher system. Other economists disagree about the potential effectiveness of vouchers. Do you support a voucher system for education? Explain your reasoning.

[1] Milton Friedman and Rose Friedman, *Free to Choose: A Personal Statement* (New York: Harcourt Brace Jovanovich, 1980), pp. 160–161.
[2] Robert J. Bresler, "Vouchers and the Constitution," *USA Today*, May 2002, p. 15.

4-3d Income Inequality

In the cases of insufficient competition, externalities, and public goods, the marketplace allocates too few or too many resources to producing output. The market may also result in a very unequal distribution of income, thereby raising a very controversial issue. Under the impersonal price system, movie stars earn huge incomes for acting in movies, while homeless people roam the streets penniless. The controversy is therefore over how equal the distribution of income should be and how much government intervention is required to achieve this goal. Some people wish to remove most inequality of income. Others argue for the government to provide a "safety net" minimum income level for all citizens. Still others see high income as an incentive and a "fair" reward for productive resources.

To create a more equal distribution of income, the government uses various programs to transfer money from people with high incomes to those with low incomes. Unemployment compensation and food stamps are examples of such programs. The federal minimum wage is another example of a government attempt to raise the earnings of low-income workers.

CHECKPOINT

Should There Be a War on Drugs?
The U.S. government fights the use of drugs, such as marijuana and cocaine, in a variety of ways, including spraying crops with poisonous chemicals; imposing jail sentences for dealers and users; and confiscating drug-transporting cars, boats, and planes. Which market failure motivates the government to interfere with the market for drugs: lack of competition, externalities, public goods, or income inequality?

Key Concepts

Price ceiling
Price floor

Market failure
Externality

Public good

Summary

- **Price ceilings** and **price floors** are maximum and minimum prices enacted by law, rather than allowing the forces of supply and demand to determine prices. A *price ceiling* is a maximum price mandated by government, and a *price floor*, or *support price* for agricultural products, is a minimum legal price. If a price ceiling is set below the equilibrium price, a shortage will persist. If a price floor is set above the equilibrium price, a surplus will persist.

Price Ceiling

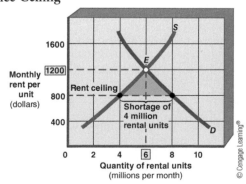

Price Floor

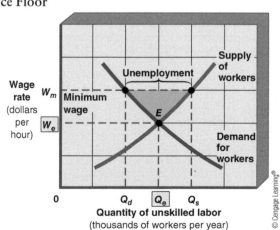

- **Market failure** occurs when the market mechanism does not achieve an efficient allocation of resources. Sources of market failure include lack of competition, externalities, public goods, and income inequality. Although controversial, government intervention is a possible way to correct market failure.

• An **externality** is a cost or benefit of a good imposed on people who are not buyers or sellers of that good. Pollution is an example of an *external cost*, which means too many resources are used to produce the product responsible for the pollution. Two basic approaches to solve this market failure are regulation and pollution taxes. Vaccinations provide *external benefits*, which mean sellers devote too few resources to produce this product. Two basic solutions to this type of market failure are laws to require consumption of shots and special subsidies.

Externalities

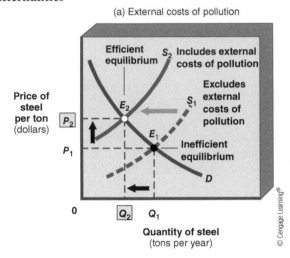

(a) External costs of pollution

(b) External benefits of AIDS vaccination

• **Public goods** are goods that are consumed by all people in a society regardless of whether they pay or not. National defense, air traffic control, and other public goods can benefit many individuals simultaneously and are provided by the government.

Study Questions and Problems

1. Market researchers have studied the market for milk, and their estimates for the supply of and the demand for milk per month are as follows:

Price per Gallon	Quantity Demanded (millions of gallons)	Quantity Supplied (millions of gallons)
$10.00	100	500
8.00	200	400
6.00	300	300
4.00	400	200
2.00	500	100

a. Using the above data, graph the demand for and the supply of milk. Identify the equilibrium point as *E*, and use dotted lines to connect *E* to the equilibrium price on the price axis and the equilibrium quantity on the quantity axis.

b. Suppose the government enacts a milk price support of $8 per gallon. Indicate this action on your graph, and explain the effect on the milk market. Why would the government establish such a price support?

c. Now assume the government decides to set a price ceiling of $4 per gallon. Show and explain how this legal price affects your graph of the milk market. What objective could the government be trying to achieve by establishing such a price ceiling?

2. Use a graph to show the impact on the price of Japanese cars sold in the United States if the United States imposes import quotas on Japanese cars. Now draw another graph to show how the change in the price of Japanese cars affects the price of American-made cars in the United States. Explain the market outcome in each graph and the link between the two graphs.

3. Using market supply and demand analysis, explain why labor union leaders are strong advocates of raising the minimum wage above the equilibrium wage.

4. What are the advantages and disadvantages of the price system?

5. Suppose a market is in equilibrium and both the demand and the supply curves increase. What happens to the equilibrium price if demand increases more than supply?

6. Consider this statement: "Government involvement in markets is inherently inefficient." Do you agree or disagree? Explain.
7. Suppose coal-burning firms are emitting excessive pollution into the air. Suggest two ways the government can deal with this market failure.
8. Explain the impact of external costs and external benefits on resource allocation.

9. Why are public goods not produced in sufficient quantities by private markets?
10. Which of the following are public goods?
   a. Air bags.
   b. Pencils.
   c. Cycle helmets.
   d. City streetlights.
   e. Contact lenses.

Sample Quiz

1. Suppose that X and Y are substitutes. If the price of Y increases, how will this change the market equilibrium for X?
   a. Equilibrium price and quantity both decline.
   b. Equilibrium price and quantity both rise.
   c. Equilibrium price declines, and equilibrium quantity rises.
   d. Equilibrium price rises, and equilibrium quantity falls.
2. If the cost of producing a good rises for sellers, then how will this affect the market equilibrium for that good?
   a. Price will rise and quantity will fall.
   b. Price will fall and quantity will rise.
   c. Price and quantity will both rise.
   d. Price and quantity will both fall.
3. If goods A and B are complements, and if the price of good B rises, how will this affect the market equilibrium for good A?
   a. Price will rise and quantity will fall.
   b. Price will fall and quantity will rise.
   c. Price and quantity will both rise.
   d. Price and quantity will both fall.
4. Suppose that Big-Cat and Fat-Cat are rival cat food brands, and the price of Fat-Cat is reduced. Following this price drop, is there a shortage or a surplus of Big-Cat at the old price of Big-Cat?
   a. Shortage.
   b. Surplus.
   c. Neither, equilibrium exists.
   d. Neither, a price drop cannot cause a shortage or surplus.
5. Suppose that the average equilibrium monthly rental price of apartments and rooms in a college town had been steady at $600, but then the college expanded enrollment from 10,000 to 12,000, and suddenly there was a shortage of rental housing at the prevailing price of $600. Which of the following is most likely to be *true*?
   a. The shortage occurred because demand increased, and a new market equilibrium will feature higher rental prices and more rental units available on the market.

   b. The shortage occurred because supply increased, and a new market equilibrium will feature lower rental prices and fewer rental units available on the market.
   c. The shortage occurred because demand decreased, and a new market equilibrium will feature lower rental prices and fewer rental units available on the market.
   d. The shortage occurred because demand increased, and a new market equilibrium will feature higher rental prices and fewer rental units available on the market.
6. If a price ceiling is set at $10, and the equilibrium market price is $8, then which of these is the price that consumers actually pay?
   a. $10.
   b. $8.
   c. $18.
   d. $2.
7. Suppose that the State of California imposes a minimum wage of $15 per hour. In the entry-level labor market in California fast-food restaurants, the quantity of labor demanded at $15 per hour is 800 thousand, and the quantity of labor supplied is 1.2 million. Which of the following is *true*?
   a. There is a shortage of 800 thousand workers in the labor market.
   b. There is a surplus of 400 thousand workers in the labor market.
   c. There is a shortage of 400 thousand workers in the labor market.
   d. There is a surplus of 1.2 million workers in the labor market.
8. Suppose that the federal government imposes a price floor (support price) in the milk market at a price of $3 per gallon. If market quantity demanded at $3 is 1 billion gallons, and if market quantity supplied is 1.5 billion gallons, then which of the following is *true*?
   a. There is a shortage of 500 million gallons of milk, and the federal government will buy 1 billion gallons to maintain the $3 price.
   b. There is a surplus of 500 million gallons of milk, and the federal government will buy this 500 million gallons to maintain the $3 price.

c. There is a shortage of 500 million gallons of milk, and the federal government will buy an additional 500 million gallons to maintain the $3 price.

d. There is a surplus of 1 billion gallons of milk, and the federal government will buy 1.5 billion gallons to maintain the $3 price.

9. Suppose that the City of Arcata, California, imposes rent control so that rents cannot exceed $500 per month on one-bedroom rental units. Suppose that $500 had also been the equilibrium rental price in Arcata before a huge new apartment complex was built in the nearby town of McKinleyville, where rents are $400 per month. Which of the following is most likely to be *true*?

a. There will be a shortage of rental housing in Arcata at the rent-control price of $500.

b. There will be a lasting surplus of rental housing in Arcata after the new apartment complex is built in McKinleyville.

c. The equilibrium rental price in Arcata will fall below $500, and thus rent control will not affect the rental market in Arcata.

d. The equilibrium price of $500 per month in Arcata will not change.

10. Suppose that the federal government provides wheat farmers with a price floor above the market equilibrium price of wheat, creating a surplus. Which of the following causes a reduction in the surplus of wheat?

a. Elimination of the price floor.

b. An increase in the price of wheat.

c. A decrease in the demand for wheat.

d. An increase in the supply of wheat.

11. If society allows firms to freely pollute the environment, then which of the following is *true*?

a. Market equilibrium output will be too high relative to the efficient output level.

b. Market equilibrium output will be too low relative to the efficient output level.

c. Market equilibrium output will be equivalent to the efficient output level.

d. The efficient output level can be achieved by giving firms a subsidy for the pollution they generate.

12. If there are external benefits for good X, then which of the following would be *true*?

a. The socially efficient amount of good X can be achieved if society taxes consumers of good X.

b. The socially efficient amount of good X can be achieved if society subsidizes consumers of good X.

c. The socially efficient amount of good X will be equivalent to the free market equilibrium quantity.

d. The socially efficient amount of good X does not exist.

13. Suppose a new pollution tax of $0.01 per kilowatt-hour of electricity is imposed on coal-fired power producers by the federal government. Which of the following correctly describes how this tax will affect the market for electricity served by these power plants?

a. Demand for electricity will decrease.

b. Demand for electricity will increase.

c. The supply of electricity will decrease.

d. The supply of electricity will increase.

14. Why don't competitive markets do a good job providing public goods?

a. Because people do not receive benefits from public goods.

b. Because firms cannot produce enough to satisfy market demand.

c. Because public goods generate negative externalities, and pollution taxes reduce the incentive for firms to supply public goods.

d. Because it is difficult to exclude people from gaining benefits from public goods without paying for them, and so market demand does not reflect the benefits to society from the public good.

15. Which of the following is *not* an example of market failure?

a. Lack of competition.

b. Externalities.

c. Efficient equilibrium.

d. Extreme income inequality.

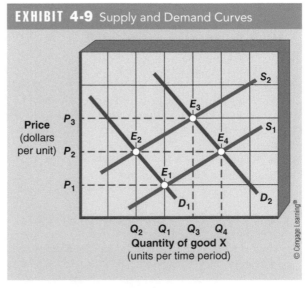

EXHIBIT 4-9 Supply and Demand Curves

© Cengage Learning®

16. In Exhibit 4-9, which of the following might cause a shift from S_1 to S_2?

a. A decrease in input prices.

b. An improvement in technology.

c. An increase in input prices.

d. An increase in consumer income.

17. The market shown in Exhibit 4-9 is initially in equilibrium at point E_1. Union negotiations for workers producing good X result in a wage increase. Other things being equal, which of the following is the new equilibrium after this wage increase is in effect?
    a. E_1.
    b. E_2.
    c. E_3.
    d. E_4.

18. The market shown in Exhibit 4-9 is initially in equilibrium at E_1. Changes in market conditions result in a new equilibrium at E_2. This change is stated as a(an)
    a. increase in supply and an increase in quantity demanded.
    b. increase in supply and a decrease in demand.
    c. decrease in supply and a decrease in quantity demanded.
    d. increase in demand and an increase in supply.

19. The market shown in Exhibit 4-9 is initially in equilibrium at E_3. Changes in market conditions result in a new equilibrium at E_4. This change is stated as a(an)
    a. increase in demand and an increase in supply.
    b. decrease in demand and a decrease in quantity supplied.
    c. increase in quantity demanded and an increase in quantity supplied.
    d. decrease in supply and a decrease in quantity demanded.
    e. increase in supply and an increase in quantity demanded.

20. In Exhibit 4-9, a decrease in quantity demanded would cause a movement from which equilibrium point to another, other things being equal?
    a. E_1 to E_2.
    b. E_1 to E_3.
    c. E_4 to E_1.
    d. E_3 to E_4.

Applying Supply and Demand Analysis to Health Care

One out of every six dollars spent in the United States is spent for health care services. This is a greater percentage than in any other industrialized country.[1] And in 2010, a historic health care legislation (the Affordable Care Act, commonly called Obamacare) was enacted to dramatically reform the U.S. system. The topic of health care arouses deep emotions and generates intense media coverage. How can we understand many of the important health care issues? One approach is to listen to the normative statements made by politicians and other concerned citizens. Another approach is to use supply and demand theory to analyze the issue. Here again the objective is to bring textbook theory to life and use it to provide you with a deeper understanding of third-party health service markets.

A4-1 THE IMPACT OF HEALTH INSURANCE

There is a downward-sloping demand curve for health care services just as there is for other goods and services. Following the same law of demand that applies to cars, clothing, entertainment, and other goods and services, movements along the demand curve for health care occur because consumers respond to changes in the price of health care. As shown in Exhibit 4A-1, we assume that health care, including doctor visits, medicine, hospital bills, and other medical services, can be measured in units of health care. Without health insurance, consumers buy Q_1 units of health care services per year at a price of P_1 per unit. Assuming supply curve S represents the quantity supplied, the market is in equilibrium at point A. At this point, the total cost of health care can be computed by the price of health care (P_1) times the quantity demanded (Q_1) or represented geometrically by the rectangle $0P_1AQ_1$.

Analysis of the demand curve for health care is complicated by the way health care is financed. About 80 percent of all health care is paid for by *third parties*, including private insurance companies and government programs, such as Medicare and Medicaid. The price of health care services therefore depends on the *copayment rate*, which is the percentage of the cost of services consumers pay out of pocket. To understand the impact, it is more realistic to assume consumers are insured and extend the analysis represented in Exhibit 4A-1. Because patients pay only 20 percent of the bill, the quantity of health care demanded in the figure increases to

---

[1] U.S. Census Bureau, *Statistical Abstract of the United States*, 2013, http://www.census.gov/compendia/statab/, Table 1345.

Q_2 at a lower price of P_2. At point B on the demand curve, insured consumers pay an amount equal to rectangle $0P_2BQ_2$, and insurers pay an amount represented by rectangle P_2P_3CB. Health care providers respond by increasing the quantity supplied from point A to point C on the supply curve S, where the quantity supplied equals the quantity demanded of Q_2. The reason that there is no shortage in the health care market is that the combined payments from the insured consumers and insurers equal the total payment required for the movement upward along the supply curve. Stated in terms of rectangles, the total health care payment of $0P_3CQ_2$ equals $0P_2BQ_2$ paid by consumers plus P_2P_3CB paid by insurers.

> **CONCLUSION** Compared to a health care market without insurance, the quantity demanded, the quantity supplied, and the total cost of health care are increased by copayment health care insurance.

Finally, note that Exhibit 4A-1 represents an overall or general model of the health care market. Individual health care markets are subjected to *market failure*. For example, there would be a lack of competition if hospitals, doctors, or drug companies conspired to fix prices. Externalities provide another source of market failure, as illustrated previously for vaccinations in Exhibit 4-8(b). We are also concerned that health care be distributed in a fair way. This concern explains why the government Medicare and Medicaid programs help the elderly and poor afford health care.

EXHIBIT 4A-1 The Impact of Insurance on the Health Care Market

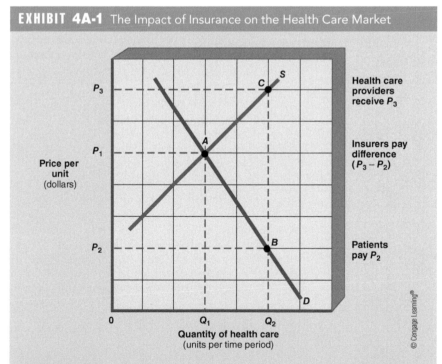

Without health insurance, the market is in equilibrium at point A, with a price of P_1 and a quantity demanded of Q_1. Total spending is $0P_1AQ_1$. With copayment health insurance, consumers pay the lower price of P_2, and the quantity demanded increases to Q_2. Total health care costs rise to $0P_3CQ_2$, with $0P_2BQ_2$ paid by consumers and P_2P_3CB paid by insurers. As a result, the quantity supplied increases from point A to point C, where it equals the quantity demanded of Q_2.

A4–2 SHIFTS IN THE DEMAND FOR HEALTH CARE

While changes in the price of health care cause movements along the demand curve, other factors can cause the demand curve to shift. The following are some of the nonprice determinants that can change the demand for health care.

A4–2a Number of Buyers

As the population increases, the demand for health care increases. In addition to the total number of people, the distribution of older people in the population is important. As more people move into the 65-and-older age group, the demand for health care services becomes greater because older people have more frequent and prolonged spells of illness. An increase in substance abuse involving alcohol, tobacco, or drugs also increases the demand for health care. For example, if the percentage of babies born into drug-prone families increases, the demand for health care will shift rightward.

A4–2b Tastes and Preferences

Changes in consumer attitudes toward health care can also change demand. For example, television, movies, magazines, and advertising may be responsible for changes in people's preferences for cosmetic surgery. Moreover, medical science has improved so much that we believe there must be a cure for most ailments. As a result, consumers are willing to buy larger quantities of medical services at each possible price.

Doctors also influence consumer preferences by prescribing treatment. It is often argued that some doctors guard against malpractice suits or boost their incomes by ordering more tests or office visits than are really needed. Some estimates suggest that fraud and abuse account for about 10 percent of total health care spending. These studies reveal that as many as one-third of some procedures are inappropriate.

A4–2c Income

Health care is a normal good. Rising inflation-adjusted incomes of consumers in the United States cause the demand curve for health care services to shift to the right. On the other hand, if real median family income remains unchanged, there is no influence on the demand curve.

A4–2d Prices of Substitutes

The prices of medical goods and services that are substitutes can change and, in turn, influence the demand for other medical services. For example, treatment of a back problem by a chiropractor is an alternative for many of the treatments provided by orthopedic doctors. If the price of orthopedic therapy rises, then some people will switch to treatment by a chiropractor. As a result, the demand curve for chiropractic therapy shifts rightward.

A4–3 SHIFTS IN THE SUPPLY OF HEALTH CARE

Changes in the following nonprice factors change the supply of health care.

A4–3a Number of Sellers

Sellers of health care include hospitals, nursing homes, physicians in private practice, drug companies, chiropractors, psychologists, and a host of other suppliers. To ensure the quality and safety of health care, virtually every facet of the industry is regulated and licensed by the government or controlled by the American Medical Association (AMA).

Primarily through medical school accreditation and licensing requirements, the AMA limits the number of persons practicing medicine. The federal Food and Drug Administration (FDA) requires testing that delays the introduction of new drugs. Tighter restrictions on the number of sellers shift the health care supply curve leftward and reduced restrictions shift the supply curve rightward.

A4–3b Resource Prices

An increase in the costs of resources underlying the supply of health care shifts the supply curve leftward. By far the single most important factor behind increasing health care spending has been technological change. New diagnostic, surgical, and therapeutic equipment is used extensively in the health care industry, and the result is higher costs. Wages, salaries, and other costs, such as the costs of malpractice suits, also influence the supply curve. If hospitals, for example, are paying higher prices for inputs used to produce health care, the supply curve shifts to the left because the same quantities may be supplied only at higher prices.

CHAPTER 5

Price Elasticity of Demand

In this chapter, you will learn to solve these economics puzzles:

- Can total revenue from a Steel Porcupines concert remain unchanged regardless of changes in the ticket price?
- How sensitive is the quantity of cigarettes demanded to changes in the price of cigarettes?
- What would happen to the sales of Mercedes, BMWs, and Jaguars in the United States if Congress prohibited sales of Japanese luxury cars in this country?

CHAPTER PREVIEW

Elasticity concerns how *sensitive* changes in quantity are to changes in price. Suppose you are the manager of the Steel Porcupines rock group. You are considering raising your ticket price, and you wonder how the fans will react. You have studied economics and know the law of demand. When the price of a ticket rises, the quantity demanded goes down, ceteris paribus. So you really need to know how many tickets fans will purchase if the band boosts the ticket price. If the lawn seating ticket price for a Steel Porcupines concert is $25, you will sell 20,000 tickets. At $30 per ticket, only 10,000 tickets will be sold. Thus, a $5 increase per ticket cuts the number of tickets sold in half.

Which ticket price should you choose? Is it better to charge a higher ticket price and sell fewer tickets or to charge a lower ticket price and sell more tickets? The answer depends on changes in *total revenue*, or sales, as we move upward along points on Steel Porcupines' demand curve. At $30 per ticket, sales will be $300,000. If you charge $25, the group will take in $500,000 for a concert. Okay, you say, what happens at $20 per ticket?

This chapter teaches you to calculate the percentage change in the quantity demanded when the price changes by a given percentage. Then you will see how this relates to total revenue. This knowledge of the sensitivity of demand is vital for pricing and targeting markets for goods and services. The chapter concludes by relating the concept of price elasticity determinants such as availability of substitutes and share of one's budget spent on the product.

5-1 PRICE ELASTICITY OF DEMAND

In Chapter 3, when you studied the demand curve, the focus was on the law of demand. This law states there is an inverse relationship between the price and the quantity demanded of a good or service. In this chapter, the emphasis is on measuring the *relative size* of changes in the price and the quantity demanded. Now we ask: By *what percentage* does the quantity demanded rise when the price falls by, say, 10 percent?

5-1a The Price Elasticity of Demand Midpoints Formula

Price elasticity of demand The ratio of the percentage change in the quantity demanded of a product to a percentage change in its price.

Economists use a **price elasticity of demand** formula to measure the degree of consumer responsiveness, or sensitivity, to a change in price. Price elasticity of demand is the ratio of the percentage change in the quantity demanded of a product to a percentage change in its price. Elasticity of demand explains how strongly consumers react to a change in price. Think of quantity demanded as a rubber band. Price elasticity of demand measures how "stretchy" the rubber band is when the price changes. Suppose a university's enrollment drops by 20 percent because tuition rises by 10 percent. Therefore, the price elasticity of demand is 2 (-20 percent/$+10$ percent). The number 2 means that the quantity demanded (enrollment) changes 2 percent for each 1 percent change in price (tuition). Note there should be a minus sign in front of the 2 because, under the law of demand, price and quantity move in *opposite* directions. However, economists drop the minus sign because we know from the law of demand that quantity demanded and price are inversely related.

The number 2 is an *elasticity coefficient*, which economists use to measure the degree of elasticity. The elasticity formula is

$$E_d = \frac{\text{percentage change in quantity demanded}}{\text{percentage change in price}}$$

where E_d is the elasticity of demand coefficient. Here you must take care. *There is a problem using this formula.* Let's return to the rock group example from the Chapter Preview. Suppose Steel Porcupines raises its ticket price from $25 to $30 and the number of seats sold falls from 20,000 to 10,000. We can compute the elasticity coefficient as

$$E_d = \frac{\%\Delta Q}{\%\Delta P} = \frac{\dfrac{10{,}000 - 20{,}000}{20{,}000}}{\dfrac{30 - 25}{25}} = \frac{50\%}{20\%} = 2.5$$

Now consider the elasticity coefficient computed between these same points on Steel Porcupines' demand curve when the price is lowered. Starting at $30 per ticket and lowering the ticket price to $25 causes the number of seats sold to rise from 10,000 to 20,000. In this case, the rock group computes a much different elasticity coefficient, as

$$E_d = \frac{\%\Delta Q}{\%\Delta P} = \frac{\dfrac{20{,}000 - 10{,}000}{10{,}000}}{\dfrac{25 - 30}{30}} = \frac{100\%}{17\%} = 5.9$$

There is a reason for the different elasticity coefficients between the same two points on a demand curve (2.5 if price is raised, 5.9 if price is cut). The natural approach is to select the initial point as the base and then compute a percentage change. But price elasticity of demand involves changes between two possible initial base points (P_1, Q_1 or P_2, Q_2). Economists solve this problem of different base points by using the *midpoints* as the base points of changes in prices and quantities demanded. The *midpoints formula* for price elasticity of demand is

$$E_d = \frac{\text{change in quantity}}{\text{sum of quantities}/2} \div \frac{\text{change in price}}{\text{sum of prices}/2}$$

which can be expressed as

$$E_d = \frac{\%\Delta Q}{\%\Delta P} = \frac{\dfrac{Q_2 - Q_1}{Q_1 + Q_2}}{\dfrac{P_2 - P_1}{P_1 + P_2}}$$

where Q_1 represents the first quantity demanded, Q_2 represents the second quantity demanded, and P_1 and P_2 are the first and second prices. Expressed this way, we divide the change in quantity demanded by the *average* quantity demanded. Then this value is divided by the change in the price divided by the *average* price.[1]

It does not matter if Q_1 or P_1 is the first or second number in each term because we are finding averages. Also note that you can drop the 2 as a divisor of both the $(Q_1 + Q_2)$ and $(P_1 + P_2)$ terms because the 2s in the numerator and the denominator cancel out. Now we can use the midpoints formula to calculate the price elasticity of demand of 3.7 regardless of whether Steel Porcupines raises the ticket price from $25 to $30 or lowers it from $30 to $25.

$$E_d = \frac{\dfrac{Q_2 - Q_1}{Q_1 + Q_2}}{\dfrac{P_2 - P_1}{P_1 + P_2}} = \frac{\dfrac{10,000 - 20,000}{20,000 + 10,000}}{\dfrac{30 - 25}{25 + 30}} = \frac{33\%}{9\%} = 3.7$$

and

$$E_d = \frac{\dfrac{Q_2 - Q_1}{Q_1 + Q_2}}{\dfrac{P_2 - P_1}{P_1 + P_2}} = \frac{\dfrac{20,000 - 10,000}{10,000 + 20,000}}{\dfrac{25 - 30}{30 + 25}} = \frac{33\%}{9\%} = 3.7$$

5-1b The Total Revenue Test of Price Elasticity of Demand

As reflected in the midpoints formula, the *responsiveness* of the quantity demanded to a change in price determines the value of the elasticity coefficient. There are three possibilities: (1) the numerator is greater than the denominator, (2) the numerator is less than the denominator, and (3) the numerator equals the denominator. Exhibit 5-1 presents three cases that the Steel Porcupines rock band may confront.

5-1c Elastic Demand ($E_d > 1$)

Suppose the Steel Porcupines' demand curve is as depicted in Exhibit 5-1(a). Using the above midpoints formula, which drops the 2 as a divisor, if the group lowers its ticket price from $30 to $20, the quantity demanded increases from

---

[1]The midpoints formula is also commonly called the *arc elasticity formula*.

EXHIBIT 5-1 The Impact of a Decrease in Price on Total Revenue

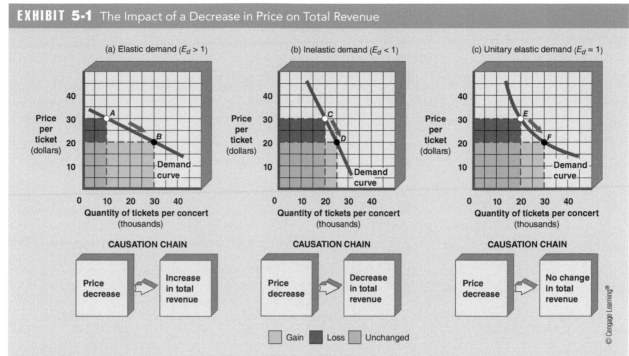

These three different demand curve graphs show the relationship between a decrease in concert ticket price and a change in total revenue.

In part (a), the demand curve is elastic between points A and B. The percentage change in quantity demanded is greater than the revenue percentage change in price, $E_d > 1$. As the ticket price falls from $30 to $20, total revenue increases from $300,000 to $600,000.

Part (b) shows a case in which the demand curve is inelastic between points C and D. The percentage change in quantity demanded is less than the percentage change in price, $E_d < 1$. As the ticket price decreases over the same range, total revenue falls from $600,000 to $500,000.

Part (c) shows a unitary elastic demand curve. The percentage change in quantity demanded equals the percentage change in price between points E and F, $E_d = 1$. As the concert ticket price decreases, total revenue remains unchanged at $600,000.

Elastic A condition in which the percentage change in quantity demanded is greater than the percentage change in price.

Total revenue (TR) The total number of dollars a firm earns from the sale of a good or service, which is equal to its price multiplied by the quantity demanded.

10,000 to 30,000. Using the midpoints formula, this means that a 20 percent reduction in ticket price brings a 50 percent increase in quantity demanded. Thus, $E_d = 2.5$, and demand is **elastic**. Elastic demand is a condition in which the percentage change in quantity demanded is greater than the percentage change in price. Demand is elastic when the elasticity coefficient is greater than 1. Because the percentage change in quantity demanded is greater than the percentage change in price, the drop in price causes **total revenue (TR)** to rise. Total revenue is the total number of dollars a firm earns from the sale of a good or service, which is equal to the price multiplied by the quantity demanded. Perhaps the simplest way to tell whether demand is elastic, unitary elastic, or inelastic is to observe the response of total revenue as the price of a product changes. For example, in Exhibit 5-1(a), the total revenue at $30 is $300,000. The total revenue at $20 is $600,000. Compare the shaded rectangles under the demand curve, representing total revenue at each price. The blue area is an amount of total revenue unaffected by the price change. Note that the green shaded area gained at $20 per ticket ($400,000) is greater than the red area lost at $30 per ticket ($100,000). This net gain of $300,000 causes the total revenue to increase by this amount when Steel Porcupines lowers the ticket price from $30 to $20.

5-1d Inelastic Demand ($E_d < 1$)

The demand curve in Exhibit 5-1(b) is inelastic. The quantity demanded is less responsive to a change in price. Here a fall in Steel Porcupines ticket price from $30 to $20 causes the quantity demanded to increase by just 5,000 tickets (20,000 to 25,000 tickets). Using the midpoints formula, a 20 percent fall in the ticket price causes an 11 percent rise in the quantity demanded. This means $E_d = 0.55$ and demand is inelastic. Inelastic demand is a condition in which the percentage change in quantity demanded is less than the percentage change in price. Demand is inelastic when the elasticity coefficient is less than 1. When demand is inelastic, the drop in price causes total revenue to fall from $600,000 to $500,000. Note the net change in the shaded rectangles.

Inelastic A condition in which the percentage change in quantity demanded is less than the percentage change in price.

5-1e Unitary Elastic Demand ($E_d = 1$)

An interesting case exists when a demand curve is neither elastic nor inelastic. Exhibit 5-1(c) shows a demand curve for which any percentage change in price along the curve causes an exact proportional change in quantity demanded. When this situation occurs, the total amount of money spent on a good or service does not vary with changes in price. If Steel Porcupines drops the ticket price from $30 to $20, the quantity demanded rises from 20,000 to 30,000. Therefore, using the midpoints formula, a 20 percent decrease in price brings about a 20 percent increase in quantity demanded. If this is the case, demand is unitary elastic ($E_d = 1$), and the total revenue remains unchanged at $600,000. Unitary elastic demand is defined as a condition in which the percentage change in quantity demanded is equal to the percentage change in price. Because the percentage change in price equals the percentage change in quantity, total revenue does not change regardless of changes in price.

Unitary elastic A condition in which the percentage change in quantity demanded is equal to the percentage change in price.

5-1f Perfectly Elastic Demand ($E_d = \infty$)

Two extreme cases are shown in Exhibit 5-2. These represent the limits between which the three demand curves explained above fall. Suppose for the sake of argument that a demand curve is perfectly horizontal, as shown in Exhibit 5-2(a). At a price of $20, buyers are willing to buy as many tickets as the Steel Porcupines band is willing to offer for sale. At higher prices, buyers buy nothing. For example, at $20.01 per ticket or higher buyers will buy zero tickets. If so, ($E_d = \infty$), and demand is perfectly elastic. Perfectly elastic demand is a condition in which a small percentage change in price brings about an infinite percentage change in quantity demanded.

Perfectly elastic A condition in which a small percentage change in price brings about an infinite percentage change in quantity demanded.

5-1g Perfectly Inelastic Demand ($E_d = 0$)

Exhibit 5-2(b) shows the other extreme case, which is a perfectly vertical demand curve. No matter how high or low the Steel Porcupines' ticket price is, the quantity demanded is 20,000 tickets. Such a demand curve is perfectly inelastic, and $E_d = 0$. Perfectly inelastic demand is a condition in which the quantity demanded does not change as the price changes.

Exhibit 5-3 summarizes the ranges for price elasticity of demand.

Perfectly inelastic A condition in which the quantity demanded does not change as the price changes.

5-2 PRICE ELASTICITY OF DEMAND VARIATIONS ALONG A DEMAND CURVE

The price elasticity of demand for a downward-sloping straight-line demand curve varies as we move along the curve. Look at Exhibit 5-4, which shows a linear demand curve in part (a) and the corresponding total revenue curve in part (b). Begin at $40 on the demand curve and move down to $35, to $30, to $25, and so on. The table in Exhibit 5-4 lists variations in the total revenue

EXHIBIT 5-2 Perfectly Elastic and Perfectly Inelastic Demand

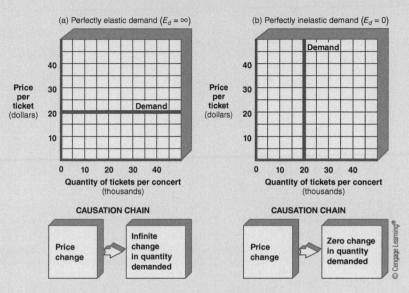

Here two extreme demand curves for Steel Porcupines concert tickets are presented.

Part (a) shows a demand curve that is a horizontal line. Such a demand curve is perfectly elastic. At $20 per ticket, the Steel Porcupines can sell as many concert tickets as it wishes. At any price above $20, the quantity demanded falls from an infinite number to zero.

Part (b) shows a demand curve that is a vertical line. This demand curve is perfectly inelastic. No matter what the ticket price, the quantity demanded remains unchanged at 20,000 tickets.

EXHIBIT 5-3 Price Elasticity of Demand Terminology

Elasticity coefficient	Definition	Demand	Graph
$E_d > 1$	Percentage change in quantity demanded is greater than the percentage change in price	Elastic	
$E_d < 1$	Percentage change in quantity demanded is less than the percentage change in price	Inelastic	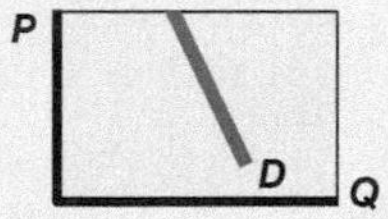
$E_d = 1$	Percentage change in quantity demanded is equal to the percentage change in price	Unitary elastic	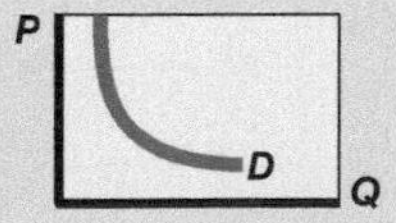
$E_d = \infty$	Percentage change in quantity demanded is infinite in relation to the percentage change in price	Perfectly elastic	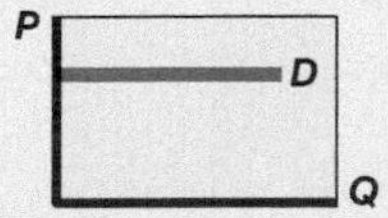
$E_d = 0$	Quantity demanded does not change as the price changes	Perfectly inelastic	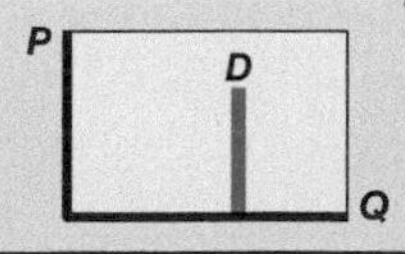

© Cengage Learning®

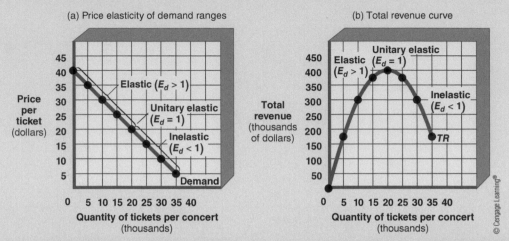

EXHIBIT 5-4 The Variation in Elasticity and Total Revenue along a Hypothetical Demand Curve

Calculation of Total Revenue and Elasticity along a Hypothetical Demand Curve

Price	Quantity (thousands of tickets)	Total Revenue (thousands of dollars)	Elasticity Coefficient (E_d)	Price Elasticity of Demand
$40	0	$0		
			15.00	Elastic
35	5	175		
			4.33	Elastic
30	10	300		
			2.20	Elastic
25	15	375		
			1.29	Elastic
20	20	400		
			1.00	Unitary elastic
15	25	375		
			0.78	Inelastic
10	30	300		
			0.45	Inelastic
5	35	175		
			0.23	Inelastic

Part (a) shows a straight-line demand curve and its three elasticity ranges. In the $40–$20 price range, demand is elastic. As price decreases in this range, total revenue increases. At $20, demand is unitary elastic, and total revenue is at its maximum. In the $20–$5 price range, demand is inelastic. As price decreases in this range, total revenue decreases. The total revenue curve (TR) is plotted in part (b) to trace its relationship to price elasticity.

and the elasticity coefficient (E_d) at different ticket prices. As we move down the upper segment of the demand curve, price elasticity of demand falls, and total revenue rises. For example, measured over the price range of $35 to $30, the price elasticity of demand is 4.33, so this segment of demand is elastic ($E_d > 1$). Between these two prices, total revenue increases from $175,000 to $300,000. At $20, price elasticity is unitary elastic ($E_d = 1$), and total revenue is maximized at $400,000. As we move down the lower segment of the demand curve, price elasticity of demand falls below a value of 1.0, and total revenue falls. Over the price range of $15 to $10, for example, the price elasticity of demand is 0.45, and, therefore, this segment of demand is inelastic ($E_d < 1$). Between these two prices, total revenue decreases from $375,000 to $300,000.

CONCLUSION The price elasticity coefficient of demand applies only to a specific range of prices.

It is no coincidence that the demand curve in Exhibit 5-4(a) has elastic, unitary elastic, and inelastic segments. In fact, *any downward-sloping straight-line demand curve has ranges of all three of these types of price elasticity of demand.* As we move downward, first, there is an elastic range; next, a unitary elastic range; and finally, an inelastic range. Why? Recall that price elasticity of demand is a ratio of percentage changes. At the upper end of the demand curve, quantities demanded are lower, and prices are higher. A change of 1 unit in quantity demanded is a large percentage change. On the other hand, a $1 price change is a relatively small percentage change. At the lower end of the curve, the situation reverses. A 1-unit change in quantity demanded is a small percentage change. A $1 price change is a relatively larger percentage change. Now pause and refer back to parts (a) and (b) of Exhibit 5-1. If we examine changes in price along the entire length of these demand curves, we will find elastic, unitary elastic, and inelastic segments.

Exhibit 5-5 summarizes the relationships between elasticity, price change, and total revenue.

EXHIBIT 5-5 Relationships between Elasticity, Price Change, and Total Revenue

Price elasticity of demand	Elasticity coefficient	Price	Total revenue
Elastic	$E_d > 1$	↑	↓
Elastic	$E_d > 1$	↓	↑
Unitary elastic	$E_d = 1$	↑↓	No change
Inelastic	$E_d < 1$	↑	↑
Inelastic	$E_d < 1$	↓	↓

© Cengage Learning®

CHECKPOINT

Will Fliers Flock to Low Summer Fares?
American Airlines is concerned over low sales and announces special cuts in its fares this summer. The New York to Los Angeles fare, for example, is reduced from $500 to $420. Does American Airlines think demand is elastic, unitary elastic, or inelastic?

5-3 DETERMINANTS OF PRICE ELASTICITY OF DEMAND

Economists have estimated price elasticity of demand for various goods and services. Exhibit 5-6 presents some of these estimates, and as you can see, the elasticity coefficients vary a great deal. For example, the demand for automobiles and for chinaware is elastic. On the other hand, the demand for jewelry and watches and for theater and opera tickets is inelastic. The demand for tires is approximately unitary elastic. Why do the price elasticities of demand for these products vary so much? The following factors cause these differences.

5-3a Availability of Substitutes
By far the most important influence on price elasticity of demand is the availability of substitutes. Demand is more elastic for a good or service with close

EXHIBIT 5-6 Estimated Price Elasticities of Demand

| | Elasticity Coefficient | |
Item	Short Run	Long Run
Automobiles	1.87	2.24
Chinaware	1.54	2.55
Movies	0.87	3.67
Tires	0.86	1.19
Commuter rail fares	0.62	1.59
Jewelry and watches	0.41	0.67
Medical care	0.31	0.92
Housing	0.30	1.88
Gasoline	0.20	0.70
Theater and opera tickets	0.18	0.31
Foreign travel	0.14	1.77
Air travel	0.10	2.40

Sources: Robert Archibald and Robert Gillingham, "An Analysis of the Short-Run Consumer Demand for Gasoline Using Household Survey Data," *Review of Economics and Statistics* 62 (November 1980): 622–628; Hendrik S. Houthakker and Lester D. Taylor, *Consumer Demand in the United States: Analyses and Projections* (Cambridge, MA: Harvard University Press, 1970, pp. 56–149; Richard Voith, "The Long-Run Elasticity of Demand for Commuter Rail Transportation," *Journal of Urban Economics* 30 (November 1991): 360–372.

substitutes. If the price of cars rises, consumers can switch to buses, trains, bicycles, and walking. The more public transportation is available, the more responsive quantity demanded is to a change in the price of cars. When consumers have limited alternatives, the demand for a good or service is more price inelastic. If the price of tobacco rises, people addicted to it have few substitutes because not smoking is unappealing to most users.

CONCLUSION The price elasticity coefficient of demand is directly related to the availability of good substitutes for a product.

Price elasticity also depends on the market used to measure demand. For example, studies show the price elasticity of Chevrolets is greater than that of automobiles in general. Chevrolets compete with other cars sold by GM, Ford, Chrysler, Toyota, and other automakers and with buses and trains—all of which are substitutes for Chevrolets. But using the broad class of cars eliminates these specific types of cars as competitors. Instead, substitutes for automobiles include buses and trains, which are also substitutes for Chevrolets. In short, there are more close substitutes for Chevrolets than there are for all cars.

CHECKPOINT

Can Trade Sanctions Affect Elasticity of Demand for Cars?
Assume Congress prohibits the sale of Japanese luxury cars, such as Lexus, Acura, and Infiniti, in the United States. How would this affect the price elasticity of demand for Mercedes, BMWs, and Jaguars in the United States?

Cigarette Smoking Price Elasticity of Demand
Applicable concept: price elasticity of demand

Tobacco use is one of the chief preventable causes of death in the world. Since 1964, health warnings have been mandated in the United States on tobacco advertising, including billboards and printed advertising. In 1971, television advertising was prohibited. Most states have banned smoking in state buildings, and the federal government has restricted smoking in federal offices and military facilities. In 1998, the Senate engaged in heated debate over proposed legislation to curb smoking by teenagers. This bill would have raised the price of cigarettes by $1.10 a pack over five years, and the tobacco industry would have paid $369 billion over the next 25 years. Opponents argued that this price increase would be a massive tax on low-income Americans that would generate huge revenues to finance additional government programs and spending. Proponents countered that the bill was not about taxes. Instead, the bill was an attack on the death march of Americans who die early from tobacco-related diseases. Ultimately, the Senate was so divided on the issue that it was impossible, at least for that year, to pass a tobacco bill.

Estimates of the price elasticity of demand for cigarettes in the United States and other high-income countries fall in the inelastic range of 0.62. This means that if prices rise by 10 percent, cigarette consumption will fall by about 6 percent.[1] Moreover, estimates of the price

elasticity of demand range significantly across states from 2.00 (Kentucky) to 0.09 (Mississippi).[2] The price elasticity of demand for cigarettes also appears to vary by education. Less-educated adults are more responsive to price changes than better educated adults. This finding supports the theory that less-educated people are more present-oriented, or "myopic," than people with more education. Thus, less-educated individuals tend to be more influenced by current changes in the price of a pack of cigarettes.[3] Another study in 2000 confirmed that education has strong negative effects on the quantity of cigarettes smoked, especially for high-income individuals. The presence of young children reduces smoking, with the effect most pronounced for women.[4]

A study published in *Health Economics* estimated the relationship between cigarette smoking and price for 34,145 respondents, aged 15–29 years. The price elasticity of smoking was inelastic and varied inversely with age: 0.83 for ages 15–17, 0.52 for ages 18–20, 0.37 for ages 21–23, 0.20 for ages 24–26, and 0.09 for ages 27–29. Thus, younger people were more likely to reduce the number of cigarettes smoked in response to increased prices.[5]

ANALYZE the ISSUE According to the above discussion, what factors influence the price elasticity of demand for cigarettes? What other factors not mentioned in the article might also influence the price elasticity of demand for cigarettes?

[1] Jon P. Nelson, "Cigarette Demand, Structural Change, and Advertising Bans: International Evidence, 1970–1995," *Contribution to Economic Analysis and Policy* 2, no. 1 (2003): article 10.
[2] Craig A. Gallet, "Health Information and Cigarette Consumption: Supply and Spatial Considerations," *Empirica* 33, no. 1 (March 2006): 35–47.
[3] Frank Chaloupka, et al., "Tax, Price and Cigarette Smoking," *Tobacco Control* 11, no. 1 (March 2002): 62–73.
[4] Joni Hersch, "Gender, Income Levels, and the Demand for Cigarettes," *Journal of Risk and Uncertainty* 21, no. 2–3 (November 2000): 263–282.
[5] Jeffrey E. Harris and Sandra W. Chan, "The Continuum of Addiction: Cigarette Smoking in Relation to Price among Americans Aged 15–29," *Health Economics* 8, no. 1 (February 1999): 81–86.

5-3b Share of Budget Spent on the Product

When the price of salt changes, consumers pay little attention. Why should they notice? The price of salt or matches can double, and this purchase will remain a small percentage of one's budget. If, however, college tuition, the price of dinners at restaurants, or housing prices double, people will look for alternatives. These goods and services account for a large part of people's budgets.

CONCLUSION The price elasticity coefficient of demand is directly related to the percentage of one's budget spent for a good or service.

5-3c Adjustment to a Price Change over Time

Exhibit 5-6 separates the elasticity coefficients into short-run and long-run categories. As time passes, buyers can respond fully to a change in the price of a product by finding more substitutes. Consider the demand for gasoline. In the short run, people find it hard to cut back the amount they buy when the price rises sharply. They are accustomed to driving back and forth to work alone in their cars. The typical short-run response is to cut luxury travel and reduce speed on trips. If high prices persist over time, car buyers will find ways to cut back. They can buy cars with better fuel economy (more miles per gallon), form car pools, and ride buses or commuter trains. This explains why the short-run elasticity coefficient of gasoline in the exhibit is more inelastic at 0.2 than the long-run elasticity coefficient of 0.7.

CONCLUSION In general, the price elasticity coefficient of demand is higher the longer a price change persists.

Key Concepts

Price elasticity of demand

Elastic demand

Total revenue

Inelastic demand

Unitary elastic demand

Perfectly elastic demand

Perfectly inelastic demand

Summary

- **Price elasticity of demand** is a measure of the responsiveness of the quantity demanded to a change in price. Specifically, price elasticity of demand is the ratio of the percentage change in quantity demanded to the percentage change in price.

$$E_d = \frac{\%\Delta Q}{\%\Delta P} = \frac{\dfrac{Q_2 - Q_1}{Q_1 + Q_2}}{\dfrac{P_2 - P_1}{P_1 + P_2}}$$

- **Elastic demand** occurs when there is a change of more than 1 percent in quantity demanded in response to a 1 percent change in price. Demand is elastic when the elasticity coefficient is greater than 1, and *total revenue* (price times quantity) varies inversely with the direction of the price change.

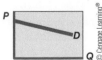

- **Inelastic demand** occurs when there is a change of less than 1 percent in quantity demanded in response to a 1 percent change in price. Demand is inelastic when the elasticity coefficient is less

than 1 and total revenue varies directly with the direction of the price change.

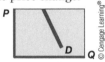

- **Unitary elastic demand** occurs when there is a 1 percent change in quantity demanded in response to a 1 percent change in price. Demand is unitary elastic when the elasticity coefficient equals 1 and total revenue remains constant as the price changes.

- **Perfectly elastic demand** occurs when the quantity demanded declines to zero for even the slightest rise or fall in price. This is an extreme case in which the demand curve is horizontal and the elasticity coefficient equals infinity.

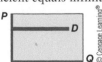

- **Perfectly inelastic demand** occurs when the quantity demanded does not change in response to price changes. This is an extreme case in which the demand curve is vertical and the elasticity coefficient equals zero.

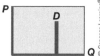

- **Determinants of price elasticity of demand** include (a) the availability of substitutes, (b) the percentage of one's budget spent on the product, and (c) the length of time allowed for adjustment. Each of these factors is directly related to the elasticity coefficient.

Study Questions and Problems

1. If the price of a good or service increases and the total revenue received by the seller declines, is the demand for this good over this segment of the demand curve elastic or inelastic? Explain.
2. Suppose the price elasticity of demand for farm products is inelastic. If the federal government wants to follow a policy of increasing income for farmers, what type of programs will the government enact?
3. Suppose the price elasticity of demand for used cars is estimated to be 3. What does this mean? What will be the effect on the quantity demanded for used cars if the price rises by 10 percent?
4. Consider the following demand schedule:

Price	Quantity Demanded	Elasticity Coefficient
$25	20	
20	40	_____
15	60	_____
10	80	_____
5	100	_____

What is the price elasticity of demand between
a. P = $25 and P = $20?
b. P = $20 and P = $15?
c. P = $15 and P = $10?
d. P = $10 and P = $5?
5. Suppose a university raises its tuition from $3,000 to $3,500. As a result, student enrollment falls from 5,000 to 4,500. Calculate the price elasticity

of demand. Is demand elastic, unitary elastic, or inelastic?
6. Will each of the following changes in price cause total revenue to increase, decrease, or remain unchanged?
a. Price falls, and demand is elastic.
b. Price rises, and demand is elastic.
c. Price falls, and demand is unitary elastic.
d. Price rises, and demand is unitary elastic.
e. Price falls, and demand is inelastic.
f. Price rises, and demand is inelastic.
7. Suppose a movie theater raises the price of popcorn 10 percent, but customers do not buy any less popcorn. What does this tell you about the price elasticity of demand? What will happen to total revenue as a result of the price increase?
8. Charles loves Mello Yello and will spend $10 per week on the product no matter what the price. What is his price elasticity of demand for Mello Yello?
9. Which of the following pairs of goods has the higher price elasticity of demand?
a. Oranges or Sunkist oranges.
b. Cars or salt.
c. Foreign travel in the short run or foreign travel in the long run.
10. The Energizer Bunny that "keeps on going and going" has been a very successful ad campaign for batteries. Explain the relationship between this slogan and the firm's price elasticity of demand and total revenue.

Sample Quiz

1. A perfectly elastic demand curve has an elasticity coefficient of
   a. 0.
   b. 1.
   c. less than 1.
   d. infinity.
2. If the percentage change in the quantity demanded of a good is less than the percentage change in price, price elasticity of demand is
   a. elastic.
   b. inelastic.
   c. perfectly inelastic.
   d. unitary elastic.

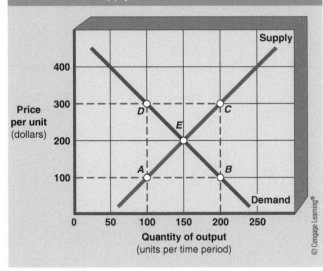

EXHIBIT 5-7 Supply and Demand Curves for Good X

© Cengage Learning®

3. As shown in Exhibit 5-7, the price elasticity of demand for good X between points E and B is
   a. 3/7 = 0.43.
   b. 7/3 = 2.33.
   c. 1/2 = 0.50.
   d. 1.
4. Which of the following is *true* about the price elasticity of demand on the top part of a linear demand curve?
   a. Demand is inelastic.
   b. Demand is unitary elastic.
   c. Demand is elastic.
   d. It is impossible to tell.

5. Price elasticity of demand tends to be larger in the long run than in the short run. Which of the following is consistent with the reason why?
   a. Because over time people's incomes rise.
   b. Because if price rises, over time producers will be able to offer more substitutes.
   c. Because over time the good will become a smaller and smaller share of peoples' budget.
   d. Because people see fewer and fewer substitutes for the good in the long run.
6. If a decrease in the price of movie tickets increases the total revenue of movie theaters, this is evidence that demand is
   a. price elastic.
   b. price inelastic.
   c. unit elastic with respect to price.
   d. perfectly inelastic.
7. Suppose the president of a college argues that a 25 percent tuition increase will raise revenues for the college. It can be concluded that the president thinks that demand to attend this college is
   a. elastic.
   b. inelastic, but not perfectly inelastic.
   c. unitary elastic.
   d. perfectly elastic.
8. The president of Tucker Motors says, "Lowering the price won't sell a single additional Tucker car." The president believes that the price elasticity of demand is
   a. perfectly elastic.
   b. perfectly inelastic.
   c. unitary elastic.
   d. elastic.
9. If a straight-line demand curve slopes down, price elasticity will
   a. remain the same at all points on the demand curve.
   b. change between points along the demand curve.
   c. always be greater than one.
   d. always equal one.
10. On a part of the demand curve where the price elasticity of demand is less than 1, a decrease in price
    a. is impossible.
    b. will increase total revenue.
    c. will decrease total revenue.
    d. decreases quantity demanded.

11. If Stimpson University increases tuition in order to increase its revenue, it will
    a. not be successful if the demand curve slopes downward.
    b. be successful if demand is elastic.
    c. be successful if demand is inelastic.
    d. be successful if supply is elastic.
12. A demand curve that has constant price elasticity of demand coefficient equals to one at *all* points is a (an)
    a. rectangular hyperbola.
    b. downward-sloping straight line.
    c. upward-sloping straight line.
    d. None of the answers above are correct.

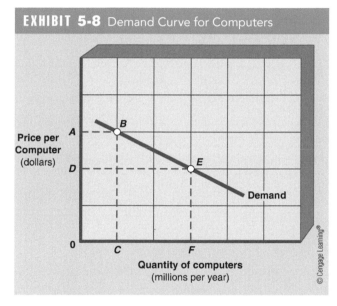

EXHIBIT 5-8 Demand Curve for Computers

Price per Computer (dollars)

Quantity of computers (millions per year)

© Cengage Learning®

13. In Exhibit 5-8, if the area OABC equals the area ODEF, the demand curve is
    a. elastic.
    b. inelastic.
    c. unitary elastic.
    d. nonelastic.
14. In Exhibit 5-8, the change in total revenue resulting from a change in price from A to D indicates that the demand curve is
    a. elastic.
    b. inelastic.
    c. unitary elastic.
    d. quasielastic.

15. If the price elasticity of demand is elastic, then
    a. $E_d < 1$.
    b. consumers are relatively not very responsive to a price increase.
    c. an increase in the price will increase total revenue.
    d. there are likely a large number of substitute products available.
16. If the quantity of bread demanded rises 2 percent when the price of bread declines 10 percent, then the price elasticity of demand is
    a. 0.2.
    b. 1.
    c. 2.
    d. 10.
    e. Cannot be determined.
17. Suppose that Sally always buys exactly 5 bars of English toffee each week, regardless of whether the toffee bars are regularly priced at $1 or on sale for $0.50. Based on this information, what is Sally's price elasticity of demand for English toffee in this price range?
    a. 0.
    b. 1.
    c. Infinity.
    d. Cannot be determined.
18. Suppose that Bill budgets exactly $50 each month for fresh shrimp, regardless of whether shrimp is priced at $10 per pound, or is on sale for $4 per pound. Based on this information, Bill's price elasticity of demand is
    a. 0.
    b. 1.
    c. Infinite.
    d. Cannot be determined.
19. What is the price elasticity of demand for a vertical demand curve?
    a. Perfectly inelastic.
    b. Inelastic, but not perfectly inelastic.
    c. Unitary elastic.
    d. Elastic, but not perfectly elastic.
    e. Perfectly elastic.
20. A perfectly price-elastic demand is consistent with which of the following?
    a. A horizontal demand curve.
    b. Few close substitutes.
    c. Inferior goods.
    d. A low cross-price elasticity of demand.

Production Costs

In this chapter, you will learn to solve these economics puzzles:

- Why would an accountant say a firm is making a profit and an economist say it is losing money?

- What is the difference between the short run and the long run?

- How can a company make a profit with a free Web site?

CHAPTER PREVIEW

Suppose you dream of owning your own company. That's right! You want to be an entrepreneur. You crave the excitement of starting your own firm and making it successful. Instead of working for someone else, you want to be your own boss. You are under no illusions; it is going to take hard work and sacrifice.

You are an electrical engineer who is an expert at designing electronic components for cell phones and similar applications. So you quit your job and invest your nest egg in starting Computech (a mythical company). You lease factory space, hire employees, and purchase raw materials, and soon your company's products begin rolling off the assembly line. And then you find that production cost considerations influence each decision you make in this new business venture.

The purpose of this chapter is to study production and its relationship to various types of costs. Whether your company is new and small or an international giant, understanding costs is essential for success. In this chapter and the next two chapters, you will follow Computech and learn the basic principles of production and the way various types of costs vary with output.

6-1 COSTS AND PROFIT

A basic assumption in economics is that the motivation for business decisions is profit maximization. Economists realize that managers of firms sometimes pursue other goals, such as contributing to the United Way or building an empire for the purpose of ego satisfaction. Nevertheless, the profit maximization goal has proved to be the best theory to explain why managers of firms choose a particular level of output or price. To understand profit as a driving force for business firms, we must distinguish between the way economists measure costs and the way accountants measure costs.

6-1a Explicit and Implicit Costs

Explicit costs Payments to nonowners of a firm for their resources.

Economists define the total opportunity cost of a business as the sum of *explicit costs* and *implicit costs*. Explicit costs are payments to nonowners of a firm for their resources. In our Computech example, explicit costs include the wages paid to labor, the rental charges for a plant, the cost of electricity, the cost of materials, and the cost of medical insurance. These resources are owned outside the firm and must be purchased with actual payments to these "outsiders."

Implicit costs The opportunity costs of using resources owned by a firm.

Implicit costs are the opportunity costs of using resources owned by a firm. These are opportunity costs of resources because the firm makes no actual payment to outsiders. When you started Computech, you gave up the opportunity to earn a salary as an electrical engineer for someone else's firm. When you invested your nest egg in your own enterprise, you gave up the opportunity to earn interest. You also used a building you own to warehouse Computech products. Although you made no payment to anyone, you gave up the opportunity to earn rental payments.

6-1b Economic and Accounting Profit

In everyday use, the word *profit* is defined as follows:

$$\text{Profit} = \text{total revenue} - \text{total cost}$$

Economists call this concept *accounting profit*. This popular formula is expressed in economics as

$$\text{Accounting profit} = \text{total revenue} - \text{total explicit cost}$$

Economic profit Total revenue minus explicit and implicit costs.

Because economic decisions include implicit as well as explicit costs, economists use the concept of economic profit instead of accounting profit. Economic profit is total revenue minus explicit and implicit costs. Economic profit can be positive, zero, or negative (an economic loss). Expressed as an equation:

$$\text{Economic profit} = \text{total revenue} - \text{total opportunity costs}$$

or

$$\text{Economic profit} = \text{total revenue} - (\text{explicit costs} + \text{implicit costs})$$

Exhibit 6-1 illustrates the importance of the difference between accounting profit and economic profit. Computech must know how well it is doing, so you hire an accounting firm to prepare a financial report. The exhibit shows that Computech earned total revenue of $500,000 in its first year of operation. Explicit costs for wages, materials, interest, and other payments totaled $470,000. Based on standard accounting procedures, this left an accounting profit of $30,000.

If the analysis ends with accounting profit, Computech is profitable. But accounting practice overstates profit. Because implicit costs are subjective and therefore difficult to measure, accounting profit ignores implicit costs. A few examples will illustrate the importance of implicit costs. Your $50,000-a-year

EXHIBIT 6-1 Computech's Accounting Profit versus Economic Profit

Item	Accounting Profit	Economic Profit
Total revenue	$500,000	$500,000
Less explicit costs:		
Wages and salaries	400,000	400,000
Materials	50,000	50,000
Interest paid	10,000	10,000
Other payments	10,000	10,000
Less implicit costs:		
Forgone salary	0	50,000
Forgone rent	0	10,000
Forgone interest	0	5,000
Equals profit	$ 30,000	−$ 35,000

© Cengage Learning®

salary as an electrical engineer was forgone in order to spend all your time as owner of Computech. Also forgone were $10,000 in rental income and $5,000 in interest that you would have earned during the year by renting your building and putting your savings in the bank. Subtracting both explicit and implicit costs from total revenue, Computech had an economic loss of $35,000. The firm is failing to cover the opportunity costs of using its resources in the electronics industry. Thus, the firm's resources would earn a higher return if used for other alternatives.

How would you interpret a zero economic profit? It's not as bad as it sounds. Economists call this condition **normal profit**. Normal profit is the minimum profit necessary to keep a firm in operation. Zero economic profit signifies there is just enough total revenue to pay the owners for all explicit and implicit costs. Stated differently, there is no benefit from reallocating resources to another use. For example, assume an owner earns zero economic profit, including an implicit (forfeited) cost of $50,000 per year that could have been earned working for someone else. This means the owner earned as much as would have been earned in the next best employment opportunity.

Normal profit The minimum profit necessary to keep a firm in operation. A firm that earns normal profits earns total revenue equal to its total opportunity cost.

CONCLUSION Since business decision making is based on economic profit, rather than accounting profit, the word *profit* in this text always means economic profit.

CHECKPOINT

Should the Professor Go or Stay?

Professor Martin is considering leaving the university and opening a consulting business. For her services as a consultant, she would be paid $75,000 a year. To open this business, Professor Martin must convert a house from which she collects rent of $20,000 per year into an office and hire a part-time secretary at a salary of $15,000 per year. The university pays Professor Martin $50,000 a year. Based only on economic decision making, do you predict the professor will leave the university to start a new business?

6-2 SHORT-RUN PRODUCTION COSTS

Having presented the basic definitions of total cost, the next step is to study cost theory. In this section, we explore the relationship between output and cost in the short run. In the next section, the time horizon shifts to the long run.

6-2a Short Run versus Long Run

Fixed input Any resource for which the quantity cannot change during the period of time under consideration.

Suppose I asked you, "What is the difference between the short run and the long run?" Your answer might be that the short run is less than a year and the long run is over a year. Good guess, but wrong! Economists do not partition production decisions based on any specific number of days, months, or years. Instead, the distinction depends on the ability to vary the quantity of inputs or resources used in production. There are two types of inputs—*fixed inputs* and *variable inputs*. A fixed input is any resource for which the quantity cannot change during the period of time under consideration. For example, the physical size of a firm's plant and the production capacity of heavy machines cannot easily change within a short period of time. They must remain as fixed amounts while managers decide to vary output. In addition to fixed inputs, the firm uses variable inputs in the production process. A variable input is any resource for which the quantity can change during the period of time under consideration. For example, managers can hire fewer or more workers during a given year. They can also change the amount of materials and electricity used in production.

Variable input Any resource for which the quantity can change during the period of time under consideration.

Short run A period of time so short that there is at least one fixed input.

Long run A period of time so long that all inputs are variable.

Now we can link the concepts of fixed and variable inputs to the *short run* and the *long run*. The short run is a period of time so short that there is at least one fixed input. For example, the short run is a period of time during which a firm can increase output by hiring more workers (variable input), while the size of the firm's plant (fixed input) remains unchanged. The firm's plant is the most difficult input to change quickly. The long run is a period of time so long that all inputs are variable. In the long run, the firm can build new factories or purchase new machinery. New firms can enter the industry, and existing firms may leave the industry.

6-2b The Production Function

Production function The relationship between the maximum amounts of output that a firm can produce and various quantities of inputs.

Having defined inputs, we can now describe how these inputs are transformed into outputs using a concept called a production function. A production function is the relationship between the maximum amounts of output a firm can produce and various quantities of inputs. An assumption of the production function model we are about to develop is that the level of technology is fixed. Technological advances would mean more output is possible from a given quantity of inputs.

Exhibit 6-2(a) presents a short-run production function for Eaglecrest Vineyard. The variable input is the number of workers employed per day, and each worker is presumed to have equal job skills. The acreage, amount of fertilizer, and all other inputs are assumed to be fixed; therefore, our production model is operating in the short run. Employing zero workers produces no bushels of grapes. A single worker can produce 10 bushels per day, but a lot of time is wasted when one worker picks, loads containers, and transports the grapes to the winery. Adding a second worker raises output to 22 bushels per day because the workers divide the tasks and specialize. Adding four more workers raises total product to 50 bushels per day.

6-2c Marginal Product

Marginal product The change in total output produced by adding one unit of a variable input, with all other inputs used being held constant.

The relationship between changes in total output and changes in labor is called the marginal product of labor. Marginal product is the change in total output produced by adding one unit of a variable input, with all other inputs used being

EXHIBIT 6-2 A Production Function and the Law of Diminishing Returns

Short-Run Production Function of Eaglecrest Vineyard

(1) Labor Input (number of workers per day)	(2) Total Output (bushels of grapes per day)	(3) Marginal Product (bushels of grapes per day) [Δ(2)/Δ(1)]
0	0	
		10
1	10	
		12
2	22	
		11
3	33	
		9
4	42	
		6
5	48	
		2
6	50	

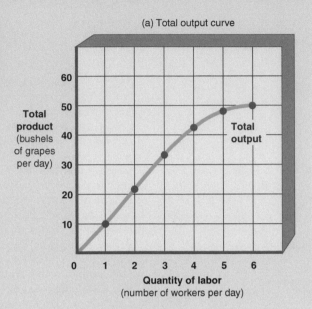

(a) Total output curve

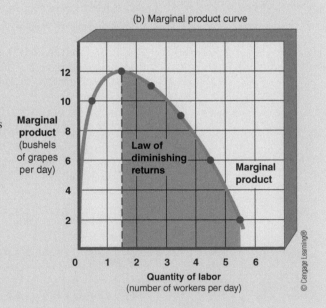

(b) Marginal product curve

Part (a) shows how the total output of bushels of grapes per day increases and the number of workers increases while all other inputs remain constant. This figure is a short-run production function, which relates outputs to a one-variable input while all other inputs are fixed.

Part (b) illustrates the law of diminishing returns. The first worker adds 10 bushels of grapes per day, and marginal product is 10 bushels per day. Adding a second worker adds another 12 bushels of grapes per day to total output. This is the range of increasing marginal returns. After two workers, diminishing marginal returns set in, and marginal product declines continuously.

held constant. When Eaglecrest increases labor from zero to one worker, output rises from 0 to 10 bushels produced per day. This increase is the result of the addition of one more worker. Therefore, the marginal product so far is 10 bushels per worker. Similar marginal product calculations generate the marginal product curve shown in Exhibit 6-2(b). Note that marginal product is plotted at the midpoints shown in the table because the change in total output occurs between each additional unit of labor used.

6-2d The Law of Diminishing Returns

Law of diminishing returns The principle that beyond some point the marginal product decreases as additional units of a variable factor are added to a fixed factor.

A long-established economic law called the **law of diminishing returns** determines the shape of the marginal product curve. The law of diminishing returns states that beyond some point the marginal product decreases as additional units of a variable factor are added to a fixed factor. Because the law of diminishing returns assumes fixed inputs, this principle is a short-run, rather than a long-run, concept.

This law applies to production of both agricultural and nonagricultural products. Returning to Exhibit 6-2, we can identify and explain the law of diminishing returns in our Eaglecrest example. Initially, the total output curve rises quite rapidly as this firm hires the first two workers. The marginal product curve reflects the change in the total output curve because marginal product is the slope of the total output curve. As shown in Exhibit 6-2(b), the range from zero to two workers hired is called *increasing marginal returns*. In this range of output, the last worker hired adds more to total output than the previous worker.

Diminishing returns begin after the second worker is hired and the marginal product reaches its peak. Beyond two workers, diminishing returns occur, and the marginal product declines. The short-run assumption guarantees this condition. Eventually, marginal product falls because the amount of land per worker falls as more workers are added to fixed quantities of land and other inputs used to produce wine. Similar reasoning applies to the Computech example introduced in the chapter preview. Assume Computech operates with a fixed plant size and a fixed number of machines and all other inputs except the number of workers are fixed. Those in the first group of workers hired divide the most important tasks among themselves, specialize, and achieve increasing returns. Then diminishing returns begin and continue as Computech employs each additional worker. The reason is that as more workers are added, they must share fixed inputs, such as machinery. Some workers are underemployed because they are standing around waiting for a machine to become available. Also, as more workers are hired, there are fewer important tasks to perform. As a result, marginal product declines. In the extreme case, marginal product would be negative. At some number of workers, they must work with such limited floor space, machines, and other fixed inputs that they start stepping on each other's toes. No profit-seeking firm would ever hire workers with zero or negative marginal product. Chapter 10 explains the labor market in more detail and shows how Computech decides exactly how many workers to hire.

6-3 SHORT-RUN COST FORMULAS

To make production decisions in either the short run or the long run, a business must determine the costs associated with producing various levels of output. Using Computech, you will study the relationship between two "families" of short-run costs and output: first, the total cost curves, and next, the average cost curves.

6-3a Total Cost Curves
Total Fixed Cost

Total fixed cost (TFC) Costs that do not vary as output varies and that must be paid even if output is zero. These are payments that the firm must make in the short run, regardless of the level of output.

As production expands in the short run, costs are divided into two basic categories—*total fixed cost* and *total variable cost*. **Total fixed cost (TFC)** consists of costs that do not vary as output varies and that must be paid even if output is zero. These are payments that the firm must make in the short run regardless of the level of output. Even if a firm, such as Computech, produces nothing, it must still pay rent, interest on loans, property taxes, and fire insurance. Fixed costs are therefore beyond management's control in the short run. The total fixed cost for Computech is $100, as shown in column 2 of Exhibit 6-3.

EXHIBIT 6-3 Short-Run Cost Schedule for Computech

(1) Total Product (Q)	(2) Total Fixed Cost (TFC)	(3) Total Variable Cost (TVC)	(4) Total Cost (TC)	(5) Marginal Cost (MC)	(6) Average Fixed Cost (AFC)	(7) Average Variable Cost (AVC)	(8) Average Total Cost (ATC)
0	$100	$ 0	$100		—	—	—
				$50			
1	100	50	150		$ 100	$ 50	$ 150
				34			
2	100	84	184		50	42	92
				24			
3	100	108	208		33	36	69
				19			
4	100	127	227		25	32	57
				23			
5	100	150	250		20	30	50
				30			
6	100	180	280		17	30	47
				38			
7	100	218	318		14	31	45
				48			
8	100	266	366		13	33	46
				59			
9	100	325	425		11	36	47
				75			
10	100	400	500		10	40	50
				95			
11	100	495	595		9	45	54
				117			
12	100	612	712		8	51	59

© Cengage Learning®

Total Variable Cost

Total variable cost (TVC) Costs that are zero when output is zero and vary as output varies.

As the firm expands from zero output, total variable cost is added to total fixed cost. **Total variable cost (TVC)** consists of costs that are zero when output is zero and vary as output varies. These costs relate to the costs of variable inputs. Examples include wages for hourly workers, electricity, fuel, and raw materials. As a firm uses more input to produce output, its variable costs will increase. Management can control variable costs in the short run by changing the level of output. Exhibit 6-3 lists the total variable cost for Computech in column 3.

Total Cost

Total cost (TC) The sum of total fixed cost and total variable cost at each level of output.

Given total fixed cost and total variable cost, the firm can calculate **total cost (TC)**. Total cost is the sum of total fixed cost and total variable cost at each level of output. As a formula:

$$TC = TFC + TVC$$

Total cost for Computech is shown in column 4 of Exhibit 6-3. Exhibit 6-4(a) uses the data in Exhibit 6-3 to construct graphically the relationships between total cost, total fixed cost, and total variable cost. Note that the *TVC* curve varies with the level of output and the *TFC* curve does not. The *TC* curve is simply the *TVC* curve plus the vertical distance between the *TC* and *TVC* curves, which represents *TFC*.

6-3b Average Cost Curves

In addition to total cost, firms are interested in the *per-unit cost* or *average cost*. Average cost, like product price, is stated on a per-unit basis. The last three columns in Exhibit 6-3 are *average fixed cost* (AFC), *average variable cost* (AVC), and *average total cost* (ATC). These average, or per-unit, curves are also shown in Exhibit 6-4(b). These three concepts are defined as follows:

Average Fixed Cost

Average fixed cost (AFC) Total fixed cost divided by the quantity of output produced.

As output increases, average fixed cost (AFC) falls continuously. Average fixed cost is total fixed cost divided by the quantity of output produced. Written as a formula:

$$AFC = \frac{TFC}{Q}$$

As shown in Exhibit 6-4(b), the *AFC* curve approaches the horizontal axis as output expands. This is because larger output numbers divide into *TFC* and cause *AFC* to become smaller and smaller.

Average Variable Cost

Average variable cost (AVC) Total variable cost divided by the quantity of output produced.

The average variable cost (AVC) in our example forms a U-shaped curve. Average variable cost is total variable cost divided by the quantity of output produced. Written as a formula:

$$AVC = \frac{TVC}{Q}$$

The *AVC* curve is also drawn in Exhibit 6-4(b). At first, the *AVC* curve falls, and then after an output of 6 units per hour, the *AVC* curve rises. Thus, the *AVC* curve is U-shaped.

Average Total Cost

Average total cost (ATC) Total cost divided by the quantity of output produced.

Average total cost (ATC) is sometimes referred to as *per-unit cost*. The average total cost is total cost divided by the quantity of output produced. Written as a formula:

$$ATC = \frac{TC}{Q}$$

or

$$ATC = AFC + AVC$$

Like the *AVC* curve, the *ATC* curve is U-shaped, as shown in Exhibit 6-4(b). At first, the *ATC* curve falls because its component parts—*AVC* and *AFC*—are falling. As output continues to rise, the *AVC* curve begins to rise, while the *AFC* curve falls continuously. Beyond the output of 7 units per hour, the rise in the *AVC* curve is greater than the fall in the *AFC* curve, which causes the *ATC* curve to rise in a U-shaped pattern.

Marginal Cost

Marginal cost (MC) The change in total cost when one additional unit of output is produced.

Marginal analysis asks how much it costs to produce an *additional* unit of output. Column 5 in Exhibit 6-3 is marginal cost (MC). Marginal cost is the change

EXHIBIT 6-4 Short-Run Cost Curves

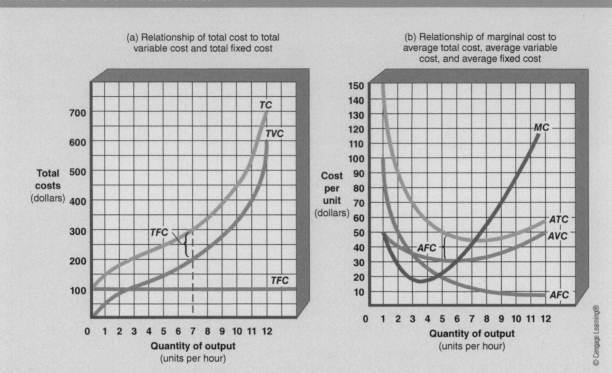

The curves in this exhibit are derived by plotting data from Exhibit 6-3. Part (a) shows that the total cost (*TC*) at each level of output is the sum of total variable cost (*TVC*) and total fixed cost (*TFC*). Because the *TFC* curve does not vary with output, the shape of the *TC* curve is determined by the shape of the *TVC* curve. The vertical distance between the *TC* and the *TVC* curves is *TFC*.

In part (b), the marginal cost (*MC*) curve decreases at first, reaches a minimum, and then increases as output increases. The *MC* curve intersects both the average variable cost (*AVC*) curve and the average total cost (*ATC*) curve at the minimum point on each of these cost curves. The average fixed cost (*AFC*) curve declines continuously as output expands. *AFC* is also the difference between the *ATC* and the *AVC* curves at any quantity of output.

in total cost when one additional unit of output is produced. Stated differently, marginal cost is the ratio of the change in total cost to a one-unit change in output. Written as a formula:

$$MC = \frac{\text{change in } TC}{\text{change in } Q}$$

Changing output by one unit at a time simplifies the marginal cost calculations in our Computech example. The marginal cost data are listed between output levels to show that marginal cost is the change in total cost as the output level changes. Exhibit 6-4(b) shows this marginal cost schedule graphically. In the short run, a firm's marginal cost initially falls as output expands, eventually reaches a minimum, and then rises, forming a J-shaped curve. Note that marginal cost is plotted at the midpoints because the change in cost actually occurs between each additional unit of output.

Exhibit 6-5 summarizes a firm's short-run cost relationships.

EXHIBIT 6-5 Short-Run Cost Formulas

Cost Concept	Formula	Graph
Total cost (TC)	$TC = TFC + TVC$	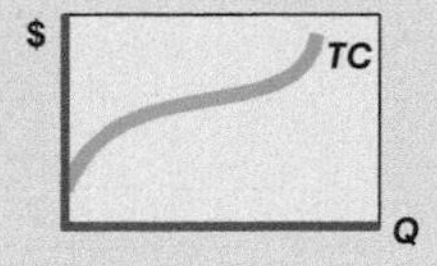
Marginal cost (MC)	$\dfrac{\text{change in } TC}{\text{change in } Q}$	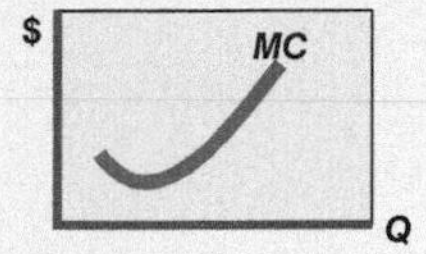
Average fixed cost (AFC)	$AFC = \dfrac{TFC}{Q}$	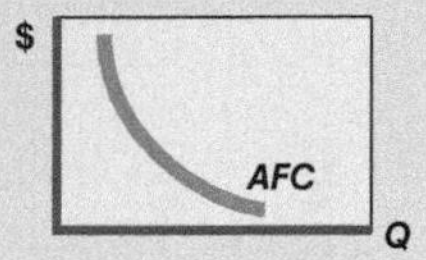
Average variable cost (AVC)	$AVC = \dfrac{TVC}{Q}$	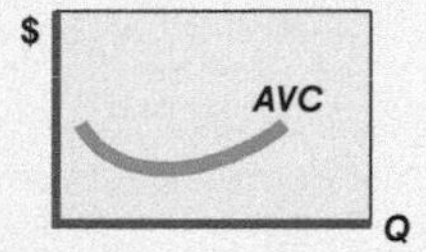
Average total cost (ATC)	$ATC = \dfrac{TC}{Q}$	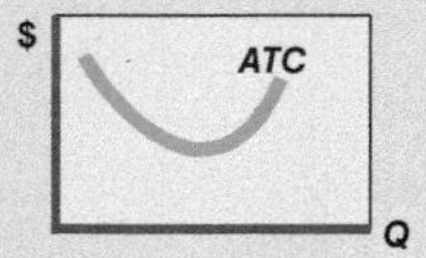

© Cengage Learning®

6-4 LONG-RUN PRODUCTION COSTS

As explained earlier in this chapter, the long run is a time period long enough to change the quantity of all fixed inputs. A firm can, for example, build a larger or smaller factory or vary the capacity of its machinery. In this section, we will discuss how varying factory size and *all* other inputs in the long run affects the relationship between production and costs.

6-4a Long-Run Average Cost Curves

Suppose Computech is making its production plans for the future. Taking a long-run view of production means the firm is not locked into a small, medium-sized, or large factory. However, once a factory of any particular size is built, the firm operates in the short run because the plant becomes a fixed input.

CONCLUSION A firm operates in the short run when there is insufficient time to alter some fixed input. The firm plans in the long run when all inputs are variable.

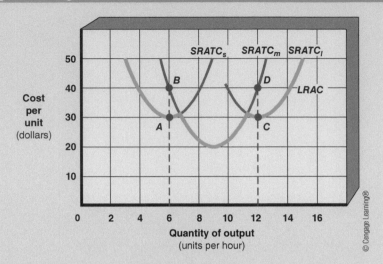

EXHIBIT 6-6 The Relationship between Three Factory Sizes and the Long-Run Average Cost Curve

Each of the three short-run *ATC* curves in the exhibit corresponds to a different plant size. Assuming these are the only three plant-size choices, a firm can choose any one of these plant sizes in the long run. For example, a young firm may operate a small plant represented by the U-shaped short-run average total cost curve $SRATC_s$. As a firm matures and demand for its product expands, it can decide to build a larger factory, corresponding to either $SRATC_m$ or $SRATC_l$. The long-run average cost curve (*LRAC*) is the green scalloped curve joining the short-run curves below their intersections.

Exhibit 6-6 illustrates a situation in which there are only three possible factory sizes Computech might select. Short-run cost curves representing these three possible plant sizes are labeled $SRATC_s$, $SRATC_m$, and $SRATC_l$. *SR* is the abbreviation for short run, and *ATC* stands for average total cost. The subscripts s, m, and l represent small, medium, and large plant size, respectively. In the previous sections, there was no need to use *SR* for short run because we were discussing only short-run cost curves and not long-run cost curves.

Suppose Computech estimates that it will be producing an output level of 6 units per hour for the foreseeable future. Which plant size should the company choose? It will build the plant size represented by $SRATC_s$ because this affords a lower cost of $30 per unit (point A) than the factory size represented by $SRATC_m$, which is $40 per unit (point B).

What if production is expected to be 12 units per hour? In this case, the firm will choose the plant size represented by $SRATC_l$. At this plant size, the cost is $30 per unit (point C), which is lower than $40 per unit (point D).

CONCLUSION The plant size selected by a firm in the long run depends on the expected level of production.

Using the three short-run average cost curves shown in Exhibit 6-6, we can construct the firm's **long-run average cost curve (LRAC)**. The long-run average cost curve traces the lowest cost per unit at which a firm can produce any level of output after the firm can build any desired plant size. The *LRAC* curve is often called the firm's planning curve. In Exhibit 6-6, the green curve represents the *LRAC* curve.

Long-run average cost curve (LRAC) The curve that traces the lowest cost per unit at which a firm can produce any level of output when the firm can build any desired plant size.

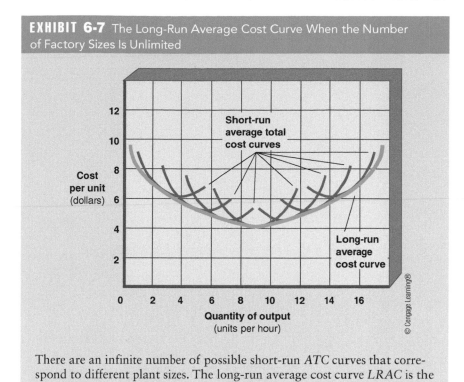

EXHIBIT 6-7 The Long-Run Average Cost Curve When the Number of Factory Sizes Is Unlimited

There are an infinite number of possible short-run *ATC* curves that correspond to different plant sizes. The long-run average cost curve *LRAC* is the green curve tangent to each of the possible red short-run *ATC* curves.

Exhibit 6-7 shows there are actually an infinite number of possible plant sizes from which managers can choose in the long run. As the intersection points of the short-run *ATC* curves move closer and closer together, the lumps in the *LRAC* curve in Exhibit 6-7 disappear. With a great variety of plant sizes, the corresponding short-run *ATC* curves trace a smooth *LRAC* curve in Exhibit 6-8. When the *LRAC* curve falls, the tangency points are to the left of the minimum points on the short-run *ATC* curves. As the *LRAC* curve rises, the tangency points are to the right of the minimum points on the short-run *ATC* curves.

6-5 DIFFERENT SCALES OF PRODUCTION

Exhibit 6-7 depicts long-run average cost as a U-shaped curve. In this section, we will discuss the reasons why the *LRAC* curve first falls and then rises when output expands in the long run. In addition, we will learn that the *LRAC* curve can have a variety of shapes. Note that the law of diminishing returns is not an explanation here because in the long run there are no fixed inputs.

For simplicity, Exhibit 6-8 excludes possible short-run *ATC* curves that touch points along the *LRAC* curve. Typically, a young firm starts small and builds larger plants as it matures. As the scale of operation expands, the *LRAC* curve can follow three different patterns. Over the lowest range of output from zero to Q_1, the firm experiences **economies of scale**. Economies of scale exist when the long-run average cost curve declines as the firm increases output.

There are several reasons for economies of scale. First, a larger firm can increase its *division of labor* and *use of specialization*. Adam Smith noted in *The Wealth of Nations*, published in 1776, that the output of a pin factory is greater when one worker draws the wire, a second straightens it, a third cuts it, a fourth grinds the point, and a fifth makes the head of the pin. As a firm initially

Economies of scale A situation in which the long-run average cost curve declines as the firm increases output.

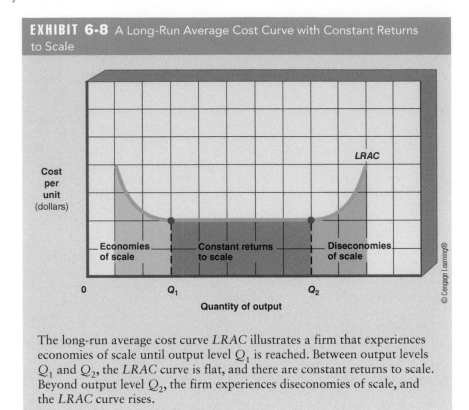

EXHIBIT 6-8 A Long-Run Average Cost Curve with Constant Returns to Scale

The long-run average cost curve *LRAC* illustrates a firm that experiences economies of scale until output level Q_1 is reached. Between output levels Q_1 and Q_2, the *LRAC* curve is flat, and there are constant returns to scale. Beyond output level Q_2, the firm experiences diseconomies of scale, and the *LRAC* curve rises.

expands, having more workers allows managers to break a job into small tasks. Then each worker—including managers—can specialize by mastering narrowly defined tasks rather than trying to be a jack-of-all-trades.[1] The classic example is Henry Ford's assembly line, which greatly reduced the cost of producing automobiles. Today, McDonald's trains its workers at "Hamburger University"; then some workers prepare food, some specialize in taking orders, and a few workers specialize in the drive-through window operation.

Second, economies of scale results from greater *efficiency of capital*. Suppose machine A costs $1,000 and produces 1,000 units per day. Machine B costs $4,000, but it is technologically more efficient and has a capacity of 8,000 units per day. The low-output firm will find it too costly to purchase machine B, so it uses machine A, and its average cost is $1. The large-scale firm can afford to purchase machine B and produce more efficiently at a per-unit cost of only $0.50.

The *LRAC* curve may not turn upward and form the U-shaped cost curve in Exhibit 6-7. Between some levels of output, such as Q_1 and Q_2 in Exhibit 6-8, the *LRAC* curve no longer declines. In this range of output, the firm increases its plant size, but the *LRAC* curve remains flat. Economists call this situation **Constant returns to scale**. Constant returns to scale exist when the long-run average cost curve does not change as the firm increases output. Economists believe this is the shape of the *LRAC* curve in many real-world industries. The scale of operation is important for competitive reasons. Consider a young firm producing less than output Q_1 and competing against a more established firm producing in

Constant returns to scale A situation in which the long-run average cost curve does not change as the firm increases output.

---

[1] Adam Smith, *An Inquiry into the Nature and Causes of the Wealth of Nations* (1776; reprint, New York: Random House, 1937), pp. 4–6.

ECONOMICS IN PRACTICE

Why Is That Web Site You're Using Free?
Applicable concepts: economies and diseconomies of scale

Pick the best price that you wish to pay for a product. Is zero reserved only for those who believe in Santa Claus? Recall the famous saying by economist Milton Friedman that "there's no such thing as a free lunch." Well, today more and more Web companies are using digital technology and the principles of *freeconomics* to make profits by giving something away free of charge. And the key to understanding this radical business model is the concept of economies of scale.

How is it possible for companies to cover their production costs with a price of zero? Don't Web businesses have huge fixed costs to buy computer servers and design Web pages? This is true, but once the servers are powered up and the sites are online, the cost of logging in each additional customer is very small. Then as the companies' scale expands over time, the cost of servers, bandwidth, and software is spread out over millions of users, and the long-run cost curve declines to almost zero, which is economies of scale.[1]

In the Web land of free payments called *freemiums*, the basic idea is to shift from the view of a market price matching buyers and sellers of a product to a free system with many participants and only a few who exchange cash. After customers get used to the free services, the companies hope that people will pay for more advanced services. Examples of freemiums are Adobe Reader, search engines, blogging platforms, and Skype-to-Skype phone calls. The revenue from the premiums for more powerful services covers the cost of both the premium and free activities. This is

the cross-subsidy approach. A legendary example of this marketing strategy is King Gillette who in the early 1900s was having no success selling men on the idea of shaving with disposable thin blades rather than with a straight razor. The solution was to bundle free razors with gum, coffee, marshmallows, and even new bank deposits with the slogan "Shave and Save" attached. The freebie razor without blades was useless so customers bought the blades and the rest of this success story is history.

Another approach is to use free services to deliver advertising, just like traditional broadcast TV or radio. One company that has very successfully applied the advertising approach to freemiums is Google. There is no cost to use its search engine, but the results pages feature "Sponsored Links," which are advertisements paid for by Web sites related to your search terms. Google used this model to achieve impressive financial results.

ANALYZE the ISSUE Suppose a hugely successful Web company has used freeconomics, expanded its scale of operations, and spread its long-run costs over larger and larger audiences. After years of profits, the company's profits fell continuously. Using production costs theory, explain why this situation might be occurring.

[1] Chris Anderson, "Why $0.00 Is the Future of Business," March 2008, http://www.wired.com/images/press/pdf/free.pdf.

---

the constant-returns-to-scale range of output. The *LRAC* curve shows that the older firm has an average cost advantage.

As a firm becomes large and expands output beyond some level, such as Q_2 in Exhibit 6-8, it encounters diseconomies of scale. Diseconomies of scale exists when the long-run average cost curve rises as the firm increases output. A very large-scale firm becomes harder to manage. As the firm grows, the chain of command lengthens, and communication becomes more complex. People communicate through forms instead of direct conversation. The firm becomes too bureaucratic, and operations bog down in red tape. Layer upon layer of managers are paid big salaries to shuffle papers that have little or nothing to do with beating the competition by producing output at a lower price. Consequently, it is no surprise that a firm can become too big, and these management problems can cause the average cost of production to rise.

Steven Jobs, founder of Apple Computer Company, stated:

> *When you are growing [too big], you start adding middle management like crazy. ... People in the middle have no understanding of the business, and because of that, they screw up communications. To them, it's just a job. The corporation ends up with mediocre people that form a layer of concrete.*[2]

Diseconomies of scale A situation in which the long-run average cost curve rises as the firm increases output.

[2] Deborah Wise and Catherine Harris, "Apple's New Crusade," *Business Week*, Nov. 26, 1984, p. 156.

Key Concepts

Explicit costs	Production function	Average total cost (ATC)
Implicit costs	Marginal product	Marginal cost (MC)
Economic profit	Law of diminishing returns	Long-run average cost curve (LRAC)
Normal profit	Total fixed cost (TFC)	Economies of scale
Fixed input	Total variable cost (TVC)	Constant returns to scale
Variable input	Total cost (TC)	Diseconomies of scale
Short run	Average fixed cost (AFC)	
Long run	Average variable cost (AVC)	

Summary

- **Economic profit** is equal to total revenue minus both *explicit* and *implicit* costs. **Implicit costs** are the opportunity costs of forgone returns to resources owned by a firm. Economic profit is important for decision-making purposes because it includes implicit costs and accounting profit does not. Accounting profit equals total revenue minus explicit costs.

- The **short run** is a time period during which a firm has at least one fixed input, such as its factory size. The **long run** for a firm is defined as a period during which all inputs are variable.

- A **production function** is the relationship between output and inputs. Holding all other factors of production constant, the production function shows the total output as the amount of one input, such as labor, varies.

- **Marginal product** is the change in total output caused by a one-unit change in a variable input, such as the number of workers hired. **The law of diminishing returns** states that after some level of output in the short run, each additional unit of the variable input yields less and less marginal product. This range of declining marginal product is the region of diminishing returns.

- **Total fixed cost (TFC)** consists of costs that cannot vary with the level of output, such as rent for office space. Total fixed cost is the cost of inputs that do not change as the firm changes output in the short run. **Total variable cost (TVC)** consists of costs that vary with the level of output, such as wages. Total variable cost is the cost of variable inputs used in production. **Total cost (TC)** is the sum of total fixed cost (TFC) and total variable cost (TVC).

Total Cost Curves

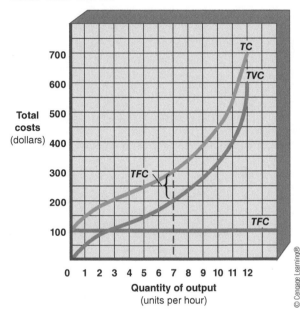

- **Marginal cost (MC)** is the change in total cost associated with one additional unit of output. **Average fixed cost (AFC)** is the total fixed cost divided by total output. **Average variable cost (AVC)** is the total variable cost (TVC) divided by total output. **Average total cost (ATC)** is the total cost, or the sum of average fixed cost and average variable cost, divided by output.

Average and Marginal Cost Curves

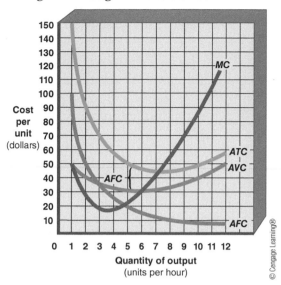

Quantity of output
(units per hour)

© Cengage Learning®

- The **long-run average cost curve (LRAC)** is a curve drawn tangent to all possible short-run

average total cost curves. When the long-run average cost curve decreases as output increases, the firm experiences **economies of scale.** If the long-run average cost curve remains unchanged as output increases, a firm experiences **constant returns to scale.** If the long-run average cost curve increases as output increases, a firm experiences **diseconomies of scale.**

Long-Run Average Cost Curve

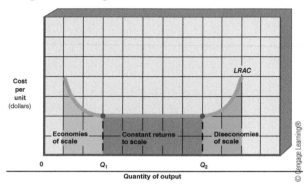

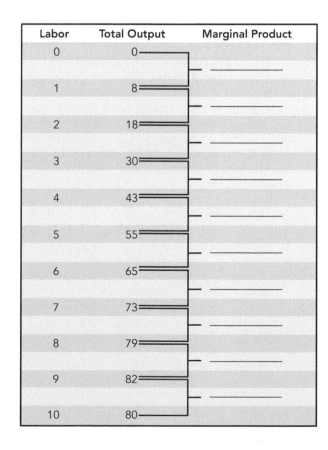

Quantity of output

© Cengage Learning®

Study Questions and Problems

1. Indicate whether each of the following is an explicit cost or an implicit cost.
   a. A manager's salary.
   b. Payments to Dell for computers.
   c. A salary forgone by the owner of a firm by operating his or her own company.
   d. Interest forgone on a loan an owner makes to his or her own company.
   e. Medical insurance payments a company makes for its employees.
   f. Income forgone while going to college.
2. Suppose you own a video game store. List some of the fixed inputs and variable inputs you would use in operating the store.
3. a. Construct the marginal product schedule for the production data in the following table.
   b. Graph the total output and marginal product curves, and identify increasing and diminishing marginal returns.
4. Consider this statement: "Total output starts falling when diminishing returns occur." Do you agree or disagree? Explain.
5. What effect might a decrease in the demand for high definition television have on the short-run average total cost curve for this product?
6. a. Construct the cost schedule using the data below for a firm operating in the short run.
   b. Graph the average variable cost, average total cost, and marginal cost curves.

Labor	Total Output	Marginal Product
0	0	
1	8	
2	18	
3	30	
4	43	
5	55	
6	65	
7	73	
8	79	
9	82	
10	80	

Total Output (Q)	Total Fixed Cost (TFC)	Total Variable Cost (TVC)	Total Cost (TC)	Marginal Cost (MC)	Average Fixed Cost (AFC)	Average Variable Cost (AVC)	Average Total Cost (ATC)
0	$ 50	$ _____	$ 50		$ _____	$ _____	$ _____
				$ _____			
1	_____	_____	$ 70		_____	_____	_____
				_____			
2	_____	_____	$ 85		_____	_____	_____
				_____			
3	_____	_____	$ 95		_____	_____	_____
				_____			
4	_____	_____	$ 100		_____	_____	_____
				_____			
5	_____	_____	$110		_____	_____	_____
				_____			
6	_____	_____	$130		_____	_____	_____
				_____			
7	_____	_____	$165		_____	_____	_____
				_____			
8	_____	_____	$ 215		_____	_____	_____
				_____			
9	_____	_____	$ 275		_____	_____	_____

7. Explain why the average total cost curve and the average variable cost curve move closer together as output expands.
8. Ace Manufacturing produces 1,000 hammers per day. The total fixed cost for the plant is $5,000 per day, and the total variable cost is $15,000 per day. Calculate the average fixed cost, average variable cost, average total cost, and total cost at the current output level.
9. An owner of a firm estimates that the average total cost is $6.71 and the marginal cost is $6.71 at the current level of output. Explain the relationship between these marginal cost and average total cost figures.
10. What short-run effect might a decline in the demand for electronic components for automated teller machines have on Computech's average total cost curve?
11. For mathematically minded students, what is the algebraic relationship between the equation for output and the equation for marginal product in Exhibit 6-2?

Sample Quiz

1. A firm has $200 million in total revenue and explicit costs of $190 million. Suppose its owners have invested $100 million in the company at an opportunity cost of 10 percent interest rate per year. The firm's economic profit is
   a. $400 million.
   b. $100 million.
   c. $80 million.
   d. zero.

2. If the units of variable input in a production process are 1, 2, 3, 4, and 5, and the corresponding total outputs are 30, 34, 37, 39, and 40, respectively. The marginal product of the fourth unit is
   a. 2.
   b. 1.
   c. 37.
   d. 39.

3. The situation in which the marginal product of labor is greater than zero and declining as more labor is hired is called the law of
   a. negative response.
   b. inverse return to labor.
   c. diminishing returns.
   d. demand.

4. Which of the following is *true* if the total variable cost curve is rising?
   a. Average fixed cost is increasing.
   b. Marginal cost is decreasing.
   c. Marginal cost is increasing.
   d. Average fixed cost is constant.

5. If the minimum points of all the possible short-run average total cost curves become successively lower as quantity of output increases, then
   a. the firm should try to produce less output.
   b. total fixed costs are constant along the LRAC curve.
   c. there are economies of scale.
   d. the firm is probably having significant management problems.

6. A young chef is considering opening his own sushi bar. To do so, he would have to quit his current job, which pays $20,000 a year, and take over a store building that he owns and currently rents to his brother for $6,000 a year. His expenses at the sushi bar would be $50,000 for food and $2,000 for gas and electricity. What are his explicit costs?
   a. $26,000.
   b. $66,000.
   c. $78,000.
   d. $52,000.

7. An economist left his $100,000-a-year teaching position to work full-time in his own consulting business. In the first year, he had total revenue of $200,000 and business expenses of $150,000. He made a (an)
   a. implicit profit.
   b. economic loss.
   c. economic profit.
   d. accounting loss but not an economic loss.

8. Which of the following *best* describes total fixed cost?
   a. The change in total cost when one additional unit of output is produced.
   b. Total cost divided by the quantity of output produced.
   c. Total variable cost divided by the quantity of output produced.
   d. Total fixed cost divided by the quantity of output produced.
   e. Costs that do not vary as output varies.

9. A farm can produce 10,000 bushels of wheat per year with 5 workers and 13,000 bushels with 6 workers. The marginal product of the sixth worker for this farm is
   a. 10,000 bushels.
   b. 3,000 bushels.
   c. 500 bushels.
   d. 23,000 bushels.

10. The law of diminishing returns applies to which of the following segments of the marginal product of labor curve?
    a. The entire curve.
    b. The downward-sloping segment only.
    c. The upward-sloping segment only.
    d. The point where labor input is zero.

11. Which of the following is *true* at the point where diminishing returns set in?
    a. Both marginal product and marginal cost are at a maximum.
    b. Both marginal product and marginal cost are at a minimum.
    c. Marginal product is at a maximum and marginal cost at a minimum.
    d. Marginal product is at a minimum and marginal cost at a maximum.

12. In the long run, total fixed cost
    a. falls.
    b. rises.
    c. is constant.
    d. does not exist.

13. Which of the following is considered to be a fixed cost of operating an automobile?
    a. Gasoline.
    b. Tires.
    c. Oil change.
    d. Maintenance.
    e. Registration fees.
14. Which of the following is an example of a fixed cost for a fishing company?
    a. The cost of hiring a fishing crew.
    b. The fuel costs of running the boat.
    c. The monthly loan payment on the boat.
    d. The supply of nets, hooks, and fishing lines.
15. The decreasing portion of a firm's long-run average cost curve is attributable to
    a. increasing marginal cost.
    b. economies of scale.
    c. diseconomies of scale.
    d. constant returns to scale.
16. Diseconomies of scale exists over the range of output for which the long-run average cost curve is
    a. constant.
    b. falling.
    c. rising.
    d. None of the answers above are correct.
17. Assume both the marginal cost and the average variable cost curves are U-shaped. At the minimum point on the *AVC* curve, marginal cost must be
    a. greater than the average variable cost.
    b. less than the average variable cost.
    c. equal to the average variable cost.
    d. at its minimum.

EXHIBIT 6-9 Costs Schedules for Producing Pizza

Pizzas	Fixed cost	Variable cost	Total cost	Marginal cost
0	$	$	$	$
1		5		
2		13		
3				10
4	100		140	
5				20
6		85		
7			215	

© Cengage Learning®

18. By filling in the blanks in Exhibit 6-9, the total cost of producing zero pizzas is shown to be equal to
    a. zero.
    b. $100.
    c. $5.
    d. $105.
    e. $95.
19. By filling in the blanks in Exhibit 6-9, the fixed cost of producing 6 pizzas is shown to be equal to
    a. $100.
    b. $150.
    c. $200.
    d. $185.
    e. $85.
20. By filling in the blanks in Exhibit 6-9, the average variable cost of producing 4 pizzas is shown to be equal to
    a. $10.
    b. $15.
    c. $20.
    d. $40.
    e. $85.
21. By filling in the blanks in Exhibit 6-9, the average total cost of producing 5 pizzas is shown to be equal to
    a. $12.
    b. $15.
    c. $32.
    d. $85.
    e. $160.
22. By filling in the blanks in Exhibit 6-9, the marginal cost of the fourth pizza is shown to be equal to
    a. $10.
    b. $15.
    c. $17.
    d. $23.
    e. $40.
23. In Exhibit 6-10, which firm's long-run average cost curve experiences constant returns to scale?
    a. Firm A.
    b. Firm B.
    c. Firm C.
    d. Firms A and C.
24. Which firm in Exhibit 6-10 displays a long-run average cost curve with diseconomies of scale beginning at 2,000 units of output per week?
    a. Firm A.
    b. Firm B.
    c. Firm C.
    d. Firms A and C.

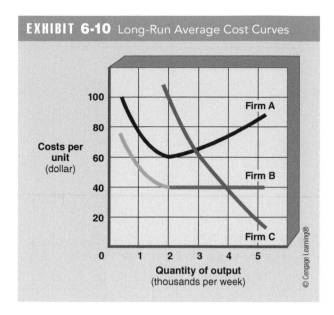

EXHIBIT 6-10 Long-Run Average Cost Curves

Costs per unit (dollar)

Firm A

Firm B

Firm C

Quantity of output (thousands per week)

© Cengage Learning®

25. Which firm in Exhibit 6-10 displays a long-run average cost curve with economies of scale throughout the range of output shown?
   a. Firm A.
   b. Firm B.
   c. Firm C.
   d. Firms A and B.

Perfect Competition

© Florinikus/Shutterstock.com

In this chapter, you will learn to solve these economics puzzles:

* Why is the demand curve horizontal for a firm in a perfectly competitive market?

* Why would a firm stay in business while losing money?

* In the long run, can alligator farms earn an economic profit?

CHAPTER PREVIEW

Ostrich farmers in Iowa, Texas, Oklahoma, and other states in the Midwest "stuck their necks out." Many invested millions of dollars converting a portion of their farms into breeding grounds for ostriches. The reason was that mating pairs of ostriches were selling for $75,000 during the early 1990s. Ostrich breeders claimed that ostrich meat would become the low-cholesterol, low-fat health treat, and ostrich prices rose. The higher prices fueled profit expectations, and many cattle ranchers deserted their cattle and went into the ostrich business.

Adam Smith concluded that competitive forces are like an "invisible hand" that leads people who simply pursue their own interests and, in the process, serve the interests of society. In a competitive market, when the profit potential in the ostrich business looked good, firms entered this market and started raising ostriches. Over time, more and more ostrich farmers flocked to this market, and the population of these flightless birds exploded. As a result, the price of a breeding pair plummeted to only a few thousand dollars, profits tumbled, and the number of ostrich farms declined. A decade later demand increased unexpectedly because mad cow disease plagued Europe, and people

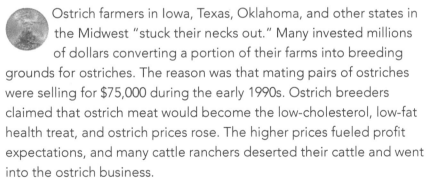

bought alternatives to beef. Suppliers could not meet the demand for ostrich burgers and profits rose again, causing farmers to increase supply by investing in more ostriches.

This chapter combines the demand, cost of production, and marginal analysis concepts from previous chapters to explain how competitive markets determine prices, output, and profits. Here firms are small, like an ostrich ranch or an alligator farm, rather than huge, like Wal-Mart, Exxon, Mobil, or Microsoft. Other types of markets in which large and powerful firms operate are discussed in the next two chapters.

7-1 PERFECT COMPETITION

Market structure A classification system for the key traits of a market, including the number of firms, the similarity of the products they sell, and the ease of entry into and exit from the market.

Perfect competition A market structure characterized by (1) a large number of small firms, (2) a homogeneous product, and (3) very easy entry into or exit from the market. Perfect competition is also referred to as *pure competition*.

Firms sell goods and services under different market conditions, which economists call market structures. A market structure describes the key traits of a market, including the number of firms, the similarity of the products they sell, and the ease of entry into and exit from the market. Examination of the business sector of our economy reveals firms operating in different market structures. In this chapter and the two chapters that follow, we will study four market structures. The first is perfect competition, to which this entire chapter is devoted. Perfect, or pure, competition is a market structure characterized by (1) a large number of small firms, (2) a homogeneous product, and (3) very easy entry into or exit from the market. Let's discuss each of these characteristics.

7-1a Characteristics of Perfect Competition

Large Number of Small Firms

How many sellers is a large number? And how small is a small firm? Certainly, one, two, or three firms in a market would not be a large number. In fact, the exact number cannot be stated. This condition is fulfilled when each firm in a market has no significant share of total output and, therefore, no ability to affect the product's price. Each firm acts independently, rather than coordinating decisions collectively. For example, there are thousands of independent egg farmers in the United States. If any single egg farmer raises the price, the going market price for eggs is unaffected.

> **CONCLUSION** The large-number-of-sellers condition is met when each firm is so small relative to the total market that no single firm can influence the market price.

Homogeneous Product

In a perfectly competitive market, all firms produce a standardized or homogeneous product. This means the good or service of each firm is identical. Farmer Brown's wheat is identical to Farmer Jones's wheat. Buyers may believe the transportation services of one independent trucker are about the same as another's services. This assumption rules out rivalry among firms in advertising and quality differences.

> **CONCLUSION** If a product is homogeneous, buyers are indifferent as to which seller's product they buy.

Very Easy Entry and Exit

Barrier to entry Any obstacle that makes it difficult for a new firm to enter a market.

Very easy entry into a market means that a new firm faces no barrier to entry. A barrier to entry is any obstacle that makes it difficult for a new firm to enter a market. Barriers can be financial, technical, or government-imposed barriers, such as licenses, permits, and patents. Such barriers do not exist for ostrich farming. Anyone who wants to try his or her hand at raising ostriches needs only a plot of land and feed.

CONCLUSION Perfect competition requires that resources be completely mobile to freely enter or exit a market.

No real-world market exactly fits the three assumptions of perfect competition. The perfectly competitive market structure is a theoretical or ideal model, but some actual markets do approximate the model fairly closely. Examples include farm products markets, the stock market, and the foreign exchange market.

7-1b The Perfectly Competitive Firm as a Price Taker

Price taker A seller that has no control over the price of the product it sells.

For model-building purposes, suppose a firm operates in a market that conforms to all three of the requirements for perfect competition. This means that the perfectly competitive firm is a **price taker**. A price taker is a seller that has no control over the price of the product it sells. From the individual firm's perspective, the price of its products is determined by market supply and demand conditions over which the firm has no influence. Look again at the characteristics of a perfectly competitive firm: A small firm that is one among many firms, sells a homogeneous product, and is exposed to competition from new firms entering the market. These conditions make it impossible for the perfectly competitive firm to have the market power to affect the market price. Instead, the firm must adjust to, or "take," the market price.

Exhibit 7-1 is a graphical presentation of the relationship between the market supply and demand for electronic components and the demand curve facing a firm in a perfectly competitive market. Here we will assume that the electronic components industry is perfectly competitive, keeping in mind that the real-world market does not exactly fit the model. Exhibit 7-1(a) shows market supply and

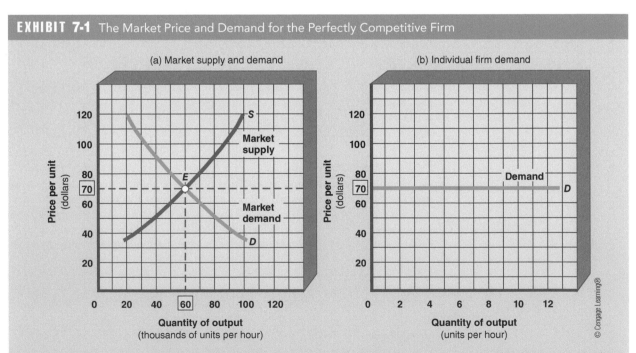

EXHIBIT 7-1 The Market Price and Demand for the Perfectly Competitive Firm

In part (a), the market equilibrium price is $70 per unit. The perfectly competitive firm in part (b) is a price taker because it is so small relative to the market. At $70, the individual firm faces a horizontal demand curve, *D*. This means that the firm's demand curve is perfectly elastic. If the firm raises its price even one penny, it will sell zero output.

demand curves for the quantity of output per hour. The theoretical framework for this model was explained in Chapter 4. The equilibrium price is $70 per unit, and the equilibrium quantity is 60,000 units per hour.

Because the perfectly competitive firm "takes" the equilibrium price, the individual firm's demand curve in Exhibit 7-1(b) is *perfectly elastic* (horizontal) at the $70 market equilibrium price. (Note the difference between the firm's units per hour and the industry's thousands of units per hour.) Recall from Chapter 5 that when a firm facing a perfectly elastic demand curve tries to raise its price one penny higher than $70, no buyer will purchase its product [Exhibit 5-2(a) in Chapter 5]. The reason is that many other firms are selling the same product at $70 per unit. Hence, the perfectly competitive firm will not set the price above the prevailing market price and risk selling zero output. Nor will the firm set the price below the market price because a lower price would reduce the firm's revenue and the firm can sell all it wants to at the going price.

7-2 SHORT-RUN PROFIT MAXIMIZATION FOR A PERFECTLY COMPETITIVE FIRM

Since the perfectly competitive firm has no control over price, what does the firm control? The firm makes only one decision—what quantity of output to produce that maximizes profit. This section develops two profit-maximization methods that determine the output level for a competitive firm. We begin by examining the total revenue–total cost approach for finding the profit-maximizing level of output. Next, marginal analysis is used to show another method for determining the profit-maximizing level of output. The framework for the analysis is the short run with some fixed input, such as factory size.

7-2a The Total Revenue–Total Cost Method

Exhibit 7-2 provides hypothetical data on output, total revenue, total cost, and profit for our typical electronic components producer—Computech. Using Computech as our example allows us to extend the data and analysis presented in previous chapters. The cost figures are taken from Exhibit 6-3 in Chapter 6. Total fixed cost at zero output is $100. Total revenue is reported in column 3 of Exhibit 7-2 and is computed as the product price times the quantity. In this case, we assume the market equilibrium price is $70 per unit, as determined in Exhibit 7-1. Because Computech is a price taker, the total revenue from selling 1 unit is $70, from selling 2 units is $140, and so on. Subtracting total cost in column 6 from total revenue in column 3 gives the total profit or loss (column 9) that the firm earns at each level of output. From zero to 2 units, the firm incurs losses, and then a *break-even point* (zero economic profit) occurs at about 3 units per hour. If the firm produces 9 units per hour, it earns the maximum profit of $205 per hour. Recall from the previous chapter that at zero economic profit the firm earns only a normal profit, which is the minimum profit necessary to keep a firm in operation. As output expands between 9 and 12 units of output, the firm's profit diminishes. Exhibit 7-3 illustrates graphically that the maximum profit occurs where the vertical distance between the total revenue and the total cost curves is at a maximum.

7-2b The Marginal Revenue Equals Marginal Cost Method

A second approach uses *marginal analysis* to determine the profit-maximizing level of output by comparing marginal revenue (marginal benefit) and marginal cost. Recall from the previous chapter that marginal cost is the change in total cost as the output level changes one unit. Also, recall that these marginal cost data are listed between the quantity of output line entries because the change in

EXHIBIT 7-2 Short-Run Profit-Maximization Schedule for Computech as a Perfectly Competitive Firm

(1) Output (units per hour) (Q)	(2) Price per Unit (P)	(3) Total Revenue (TR)	(4) Marginal Revenue (MR)	(5) Marginal Cost (MC)	(6) Total Cost (TC)	(7) Average Variable Cost (AVC)	(8) Average Total Cost (ATC)	(9) Profit (+) or Loss (−) [(3) − (6)]
0	$70	$0			$100	—	—	− $100
			$70	$50				
1	70	70			150	$50	$150	−80
			70	34				
2	70	140			184	42	92	−44
			70	24				
3	70	210			208	36	69	2
			70	19				
4	70	280			227	32	57	53
			70	23				
5	70	350			250	30	50	100
			70	30				
6	70	420			280	30	47	140
			70	38				
7	70	490			318	31	45	172
			70	48				
8	70	560			366	33	46	194
			70	59				
9	70	630	70	70	425	36	47	205
			70	75				
10	70	700			500	40	50	200
			70	95				
11	70	770			595	45	54	175
			70	117				
12	70	840			712	51	59	128

© Cengage Learning®

total cost occurs between each additional whole unit of output rather than exactly at each listed output level.

Now we introduce **marginal revenue (MR)**, a concept similar to marginal cost. Marginal revenue is the change in total revenue from the sale of one additional unit of output. Stated another way, marginal revenue is the ratio of the change in total revenue to a change in output.

Mathematically,

$$\text{MR} = \frac{\text{change in total revenue}}{\text{change in output}}$$

As shown in Exhibit 7-1(b), the perfectly competitive firm faces a perfectly elastic demand curve. Because the competitive firm is a price taker, the sale of

Marginal revenue (MR) The change in total revenue from the sale of one additional unit of output.

EXHIBIT 7-3 Short-Run Profit Maximization Using the Total Revenue–Total Cost Method for a Perfectly Competitive Firm

This exhibit shows the profit-maximizing level of output chosen by a perfectly competitive firm, Computech. Part (a) shows the relationships between total revenue, total cost, and output, given a market price of $70 per unit. The maximum short-run profit is earned by producing 9 units per hour. At this level of output, the vertical distance between the total revenue and the total cost curves is the greatest. At an output level below 3 units per hour, the firm incurs losses.

Profit maximization is also shown in part (b). The maximum profit of $205 per hour corresponds to the profit-maximizing output of 9 units per hour, represented in part (a).

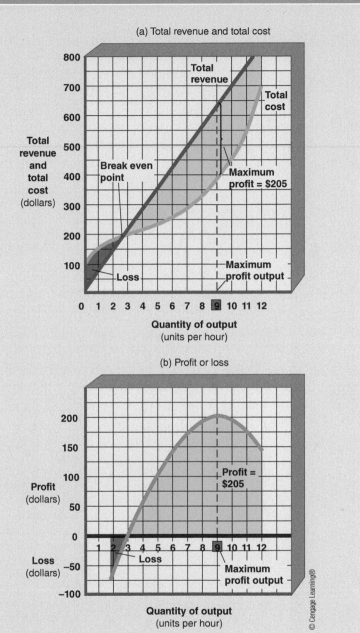

each additional unit adds to total revenue an amount equal to the price (average revenue, TR/Q). In our example, Computech adds $70 to its total revenue each time it sells one unit. Therefore, $70 is the marginal revenue for each additional unit of output in column 4 of Exhibit 7-2. As with MC, MR is also listed between the quantity of output line entries because the change in total revenue occurs between each additional unit of output.

> **CONCLUSION** In perfect competition, the firm's marginal revenue equals the price that the firm views as a horizontal demand curve.

Columns 3 and 6 in Exhibit 7-2 show that both total revenue and total cost rise as the level of output increases. Now compare marginal revenue and marginal cost in columns 4 and 5. As explained, marginal revenue remains equal to the price, but marginal cost follows the J-shaped pattern introduced in Exhibit 6-4 of Chapter 6. At first, marginal cost is below marginal revenue, and this means that producing each additional unit adds less to total cost than to total revenue. Economic profit therefore increases as output expands from zero until the output level reaches 9 units per hour. Over this output range, Computech moves from a $100 loss to a $205 profit per hour. Beyond an output level of 9 units per hour, marginal cost exceeds marginal revenue, and profit falls. This is because each additional unit of output raises total cost by more than it raises total revenue. In this case, profit falls from $205 to only $128 per hour as output increases from 9 to 12 units per hour.

Our example leads to this question: How does the firm use its marginal revenue and marginal cost curves to determine the profit-maximizing level of output? The answer is that the firm follows a guideline called the *MR = MC rule: The firm maximizes profit by producing the output where marginal revenue equals marginal cost.* Exhibit 7-4 relates the marginal revenue curve equals marginal cost curve condition to profit maximization. In Exhibit 7-4(a), the perfectly elastic demand is drawn at the industry-determined price of $70. The average total cost (*ATC*) and average variable cost (*AVC*) curves are traced from Exhibit 6-2. Using marginal analysis, we can relate the *MR = MC* rule to the same profit data given in Exhibit 7-2. Between 8 and 9 units of output, the *MC* curve is below the *MR* curve ($59 < $70), and the profit curve rises to its peak at $205. Beyond 9 units of output, the *MC* curve is above the *MR* curve, and the profit curve falls. For example, between 9 and 10 units of output, marginal cost is $75 and marginal revenue is $70. Therefore, if the firm produces at 9 units of output rather than, say, 8 or 10 units of output, the *MR* curve equals the *MC* curve, and the profit is maximized.

You can also calculate profit directly from Exhibit 7-4(a). At the profit-maximizing level of output of 9 units, the vertical distance between the demand curve and the *ATC* curve is the *average profit per unit.* Multiplying the average profit per unit times the quantity of output gives the profit [($70 − $47.22) × 9 = $205.02].[1] The shaded rectangle also represents the maximum profit of $205 per hour. Note that we have arrived at the same profit-maximization amount ($205) derived by comparing the total revenue and the total cost curves.

7-3 SHORT-RUN LOSS MINIMIZATION FOR A PERFECTLY COMPETITIVE FIRM

Because the perfectly competitive firm must take the price determined by market supply and demand forces, market conditions can change the prevailing price. When the market price drops, the firm can do nothing but adjust its output to make the best of the situation. Here only the marginal approach is used to predict output decisions of firms. Our model therefore assumes that business managers

---

[1] In Exhibit 6-3 in Chapter 6, the average total cost figure at 9 units of output was rounded to $47. It also should be noted that there is often no level of output for which marginal revenue exactly equals marginal cost when dealing with whole units of output.

EXHIBIT 7-4 Short-Run Profit Maximization Using the Marginal Revenue Equals Marginal Cost Method for a Perfectly Competitive Firm

In addition to comparing total revenue and total cost, a firm can find the profit-maximizing level of output by comparing marginal revenue (MR) and marginal cost (MC). As shown in part (a), profit is at a maximum where marginal revenue equals marginal cost at $70 per unit. The intersection of the marginal revenue and the marginal cost curves establishes the profit-maximizing output at 9 units per hour and short-run profit is $205 per hour.

A profit curve is depicted separately in part (b) to show that the maximum profit occurs when the firm produces at the level of output corresponding to the marginal revenue equals marginal cost point. Below 9 units per hour output, the firm incurs losses.

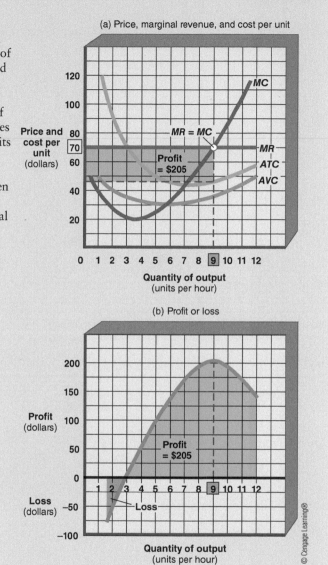

(a) Price, marginal revenue, and cost per unit

(b) Profit or loss

CAUSATION CHAIN

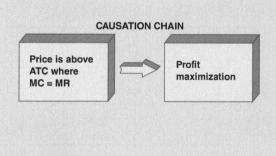

Price is above ATC where MC = MR ⟹ Profit maximization

make their output decisions by comparing the *marginal* effect on profit of a *marginal* change in output.

7-3a A Perfectly Competitive Firm Facing a Short-Run Loss

Suppose a decrease in the market demand for electronic components causes the market price to fall to $35. As a result, the firm's horizontal demand curve shifts downward to the new position shown in Exhibit 7-5(a). In this case, there is no level of output at which the firm earns a profit because any price along the demand curve is below the *ATC* curve.

EXHIBIT 7-5 Short-Run Loss Minimization Using the Marginal Revenue Equals Marginal Cost Method for a Perfectly Competitive Firm

If the market price is less than the average total cost, the firm will produce a level of output that keeps its loss to a minimum. In part (a), the given price is $35 per unit, and marginal revenue (MR) equals marginal cost (MC) at an output of 6 units per hour and the short-run loss is $70 per hour.

Part (b) shows that the firm's loss will be greater at any output other than where the marginal revenue and the marginal cost curves intersect. Because the price is above the average variable cost, each unit of output sold pays for the average variable cost and a portion of the average fixed cost.

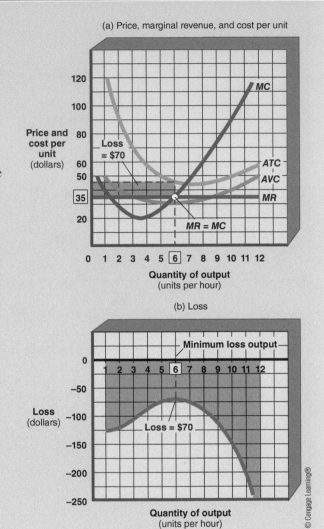

(a) Price, marginal revenue, and cost per unit

(b) Loss

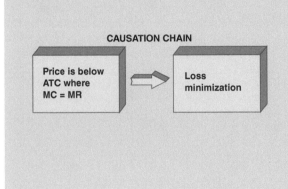

CAUSATION CHAIN

| Price is below ATC where MC = MR | ⟹ | Loss minimization |

Since Computech cannot make a profit, what output level should it choose? The logic of the $MR = MC$ rule given in the profit-maximization case applies here as well. At a price of $35, $MR = MC$ at 6 units per hour. Comparing parts (a) and (b) of Exhibit 7-5 shows that the firm's loss will be minimized at this level of output. The minimum loss of $70 per hour is equal to the shaded area, which is the *average loss per unit* times the quantity of output [($35 − $46.66) × 6 = −$70].

Note that although the price is not high enough to pay the average total cost, the price is high enough to pay the average variable cost. Each unit sold also contributes to paying a portion of the average fixed cost, which is the vertical distance between the *ATC* and the *AVC* curves. This analysis leads us to extend the $MR = MC$ rule: *The firm maximizes profit or minimizes loss by producing the output where marginal revenue equals marginal cost.*

7-3b A Perfectly Competitive Firm Shutting Down

What happens if the market price drops below the *AVC* curve, as shown in Exhibit 7-6? For example, if the price is $25 per unit, should Computech produce some level of output? The answer is no. The best course of action is for the firm to shut down following this rule: *If the price is below the minimum point on the AVC curve, each unit produced would not cover the variable cost per unit; therefore, operating would increase losses.* The firm is better off shutting down and producing zero output. While shut down, the firm might keep its factory, pay fixed costs, and hope for higher prices soon. If the firm does not believe market conditions will improve, it will avoid fixed costs by going out of business.

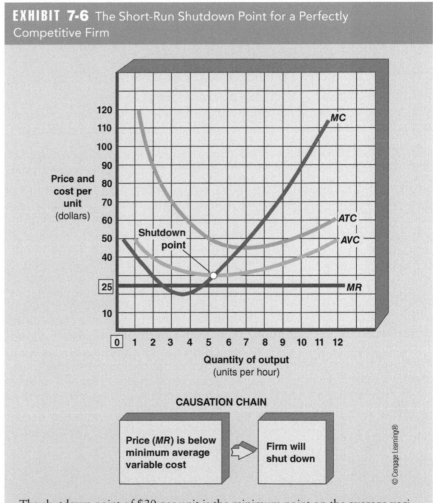

EXHIBIT 7-6 The Short-Run Shutdown Point for a Perfectly Competitive Firm

CAUSATION CHAIN

Price (*MR*) is below minimum average variable cost ⟹ Firm will shut down

The shutdown point of $30 per unit is the minimum point on the average variable cost curve (AVC). If the price falls below this price, the firm shuts down. The reason is that operating losses are now greater than the total fixed cost. In this exhibit, the price of $25 per unit (MR) is below the average variable cost curve at any level of output, and the firm would shut down at this price.

Should Motels Offer Rooms at the Beach for Only $50 a Night?
Myrtle Beach, South Carolina, with its famous Grand Strand and seafood, is lined with virtually identical motels. Summertime rates run about $200 a night. During the winter, one can find rooms for as little as $50 a night. Assume the average fixed cost of a room per night, including insurance, taxes, and depreciation, is $50. The average guest-related cost for a room each night, including cleaning service and linens, is $45. Would these motels be better off renting rooms for $50 in the offseason or shutting down until summer?

7-4 SHORT-RUN SUPPLY CURVES UNDER PERFECT COMPETITION

The preceding examples provide a framework for a more complete explanation of the supply curve than was given earlier in Chapter 3. We now develop the short-run supply curve for an individual firm and then derive it for an industry.

7-4a The Perfectly Competitive Firm's Short-Run Supply Curve

Exhibit 7-7 reproduces the cost curves from our Computech example. Also represented in the exhibit are three possible demand curves the firm might face—MR_1, MR_2, and MR_3. As the marginal revenue curve moves upward along the marginal cost curve, the $MR = MC$ point changes.

Suppose demand for electronic components begins at a market price close to $30. Point A therefore corresponds to a price equal to MR_1, which equals MC at the lowest point on the AVC curve. At any lower price, the firm cuts its loss by shutting down. At a price of about $30, however, the firm produces 5.5 units per hour. Point A is therefore the lowest point on the individual firm's short-run supply curve.

If the price rises to $45, represented in the exhibit by MR_2, the firm breaks even and earns a normal profit at point *B* with an output of 7 units per hour. As the marginal revenue curve rises, the firm's supply curve is traced by moving upward along its MC curve. At a price of $90, point *C* is reached. Now MR_3 intersects the MC curve at an output of 10 units per hour, and the firm earns an economic profit. If the price rises higher than $90, the firm will continue to increase the quantity supplied and increase its maximum profit.

We can now define a **perfectly competitive firm's short-run supply curve**. The perfectly competitive firm's short-run supply curve is its marginal cost curve above the minimum point on its average variable cost curve.

Perfectly competitive firm's short-run supply curve The firm's marginal cost curve above the minimum point on its average variable cost curve.

7-4b The Perfectly Competitive Industry's Short-Run Supply Curve

Understanding that the firm's short-run supply curve is the segment of its MC curve above its AVC curve sets the stage for derivation of the **perfectly competitive industry's short-run supply curve**. The perfectly competitive industry's short-run supply curve is the horizontal summation of the marginal cost curves of all firms in the industry above the minimum point of each firm's average variable cost curve.

In Exhibit 3-7 in Chapter 3, we drew a market supply curve. Now we will reconstruct this market, or industry, supply curve using more precision. Although in perfect competition there are many firms, we suppose for simplicity that the industry has only two firms, Computech and Western Computer Co. Exhibit 7-8

Perfectly competitive industry's short-run supply curve The supply curve derived from horizontal summation of the marginal cost curves of all firms in the industry above the minimum point of each firm's average variable cost curve.

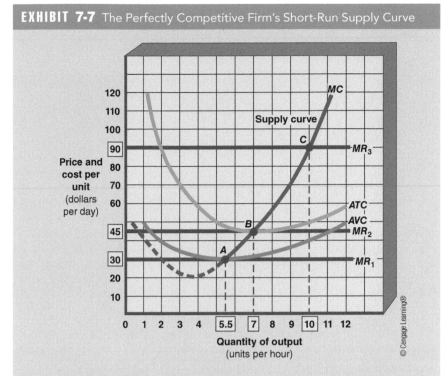

EXHIBIT 7-7 The Perfectly Competitive Firm's Short-Run Supply Curve

This exhibit shows how the short-run supply curve for Computech is derived. When the price is $30, the firm will produce 5.5 units per hour at point *A*. If the price rises to $45, the firm will move upward along its marginal cost (*MC*) curve to point *B* and produce 7 units per hour. At $90, the firm continues to set price equal to marginal cost, and it produces 10 units per hour. Thus, the firm's short-run supply curve is the *MC* curve above its *AVC* curve.

illustrates the *MC* curves for these two firms. Each firm's *MC* curve is drawn for prices above the minimum point on the *AVC* curve. At a price of $40, the quantity supplied by Computech is 7 units, and the quantity supplied by Western Computer Co. is 11 units. Now horizontally add these two quantities and obtain one point on the industry supply curve corresponding to a price of $40 and 18 units. Following this procedure for all prices, we generate the short-run industry supply curve.

Note that the industry supply curve derived above is based on the assumption that input prices remain unchanged as output expands. In the next section, we will learn how changes in input prices affect derivation of the supply curve.

7-4c Short-Run Equilibrium for a Perfectly Competitive Firm

Exhibit 7-9 illustrates a condition of short-run equilibrium under perfect competition. Exhibit 7-9(a) represents the equilibrium price and cost situation for one of the many firms in an industry. As shown in the exhibit, the firm earns an economic profit in the short run by producing 9 units. Exhibit 7-9(b) depicts short-run equilibrium for the industry. As explained earlier, the industry supply curve is the aggregate of each firm's *MC* curve above the minimum point on the *AVC* curve. Including industry demand establishes the equilibrium

EXHIBIT 7-8 Deriving the Industry Short-Run Supply Curve

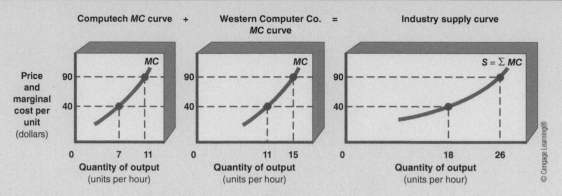

Assuming input prices remain constant as output expands, the short-run supply curve for an industry is derived by horizontally summing the quantities supplied at each price by all firms in the industry. In this exhibit, we assume there are only two firms in an industry. At $40, Computech supplies 7 units of output, and Western Computer Co. supplies 11 units. The quantity supplied by the industry is therefore 18 units. Other points forming the industry short-run supply curve are obtained similarly.

EXHIBIT 7-9 Short-Run Perfectly Competitive Equilibrium

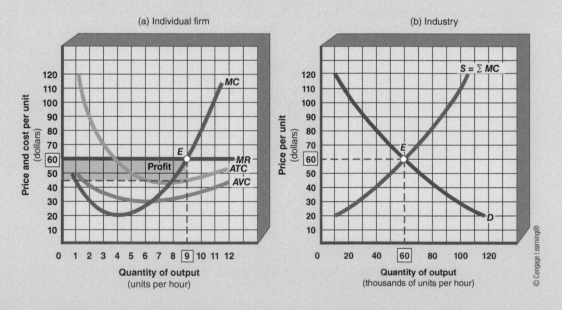

Short-run equilibrium occurs at point *E*. The intersection of the industry supply and demand curves shown in part (b) determines the price of $60 facing the firm shown in part (a). Given this equilibrium price, the firm represented in part (a) establishes its profit-maximizing output at 9 units per hour and earns an economic profit shown by the shaded area. Note in part (b) that the short-run industry supply curve is the horizontal summation of the marginal cost curves (MC) of all individual firms above their minimum average variable cost points.

price of $60 that all firms in the industry must take. The industry's equilibrium quantity supplied is 60,000 units. This state of short-run equilibrium will remain until some factor changes and causes a new equilibrium condition in the industry.

7-5 LONG-RUN SUPPLY CURVES UNDER PERFECT COMPETITION

Recall from Chapter 6 that *all* inputs are variable in the long run. Existing firms in an industry can react to profit opportunities by building larger or smaller plants, buying or selling land and equipment, or varying other inputs that are fixed in the short run. Profits also attract new firms to an industry, while losses cause some existing firms to leave the industry. As you will now see, the free entry and exit characteristic of perfect competition is a crucial determinant of the shape of the long-run supply curve.

7-5a Long-Run Equilibrium for a Perfectly Competitive Firm

As discussed in Chapter 6, in the long run a firm can change its plant size or any input used to produce a product. This means that an established firm can decide to *leave* an industry if it earns below normal profits (negative economic profits) and that new firms may enter an industry in which earnings of established firms exceed normal profits (positive economic profits). This process of entry and exit of firms is the key to long-run equilibrium. If there are economic profits, new firms enter the industry and shift the short-run industry supply curve to the right. This increase in short-run supply causes the price to fall until economic profits reach zero in the long run. On the other hand, if there are economic losses in an industry, existing firms leave, causing the short-run supply curve to shift to the left, and the price rises. This adjustment continues until economic losses are eliminated and economic profits equal zero in the long run.

Exhibit 7-10 shows a typical firm in long-run equilibrium. Supply and demand for the market as a whole set the equilibrium price. Thus, in the long run, the firm faces an equilibrium price of $60. Following the $MR = MC$ rule, the firm produces an equilibrium output of 6 units per hour. At this output level, the firm earns a normal profit (zero economic profit) because marginal revenue (price) equals the minimum point on both the short-run average total cost curve and the long-run average cost curve (LRAC). Given the U-shaped $LRAC$ curve, the firm is producing with the optimal factory size.

These conditions for long-run perfectly competitive equilibrium can also be expressed as an equality:

$$P = MR = SRMC = SRATC = LRAC$$

As long as none of the variables in the above formula changes, there is no reason for a perfectly competitive firm to change its output level, factory size, or any aspect of its operation. Everything is just right! Because the typical firm is in a state of equilibrium, the industry is also at rest. Under long-run equilibrium conditions, there are neither positive economic profits to attract new firms to enter the industry nor negative economic profits to force existing firms to leave. In long-run equilibrium, maximum efficiency is achieved. The adjustment process of firms moving into or out of the industry is complete, and the firms charge the lowest possible price to consumers.

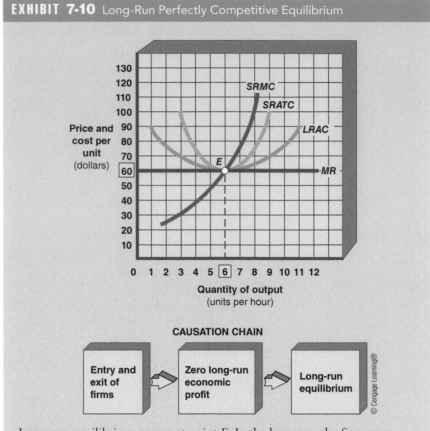

EXHIBIT 7-10 Long-Run Perfectly Competitive Equilibrium

CAUSATION CHAIN

Entry and exit of firms ⇒ Zero long-run economic profit ⇒ Long-run equilibrium

© Cengage Learning®

Long-run equilibrium occurs at point *E*. In the long run, the firm earns a normal profit. The firm operates where the price equals the minimum point on its long-run average cost (LRAC) curve (LRAC). At this point, the short-run marginal cost curve (SRMC) intersects both the short-run average total cost curve (SRATC) and the long-run average cost curve (LRAC) at their minimum points.

CHECKPOINT

Are You in Business for the Long Run?

You are considering building a Rent Your Own Storage Center. You are trying to decide whether to build 50 storage units at a total economic cost of $200,000, 100 storage units at a total economic cost of $300,000, or 200 storage units at a total economic cost of $700,000. If you wish to survive in the long run, which size will you choose?

ECONOMICS IN PRACTICE

Recession Takes a Bite Out of Gator Profits

Applicable concepts: short-run and long-run competitive equilibrium

In the late 1980s, many farmers who were tired of milking cows, roping steers, and slopping hogs decided to try their hands at a new animal. Anyone feeding this animal, however, could require a gun for protection.

Prior to the late 1970s, alligators were on the endangered species list. Under this protection, their numbers grew so large that wandering alligators became pests in Florida neighborhoods and police were exhausted from chasing them around. Consequently, the ban on hunting was removed, and shrewd entrepreneurs began seeking big profits by turning gators into farm animals. In fact, gator farming became one of Florida's fastest-growing businesses.

The gators spawned several hot industries. The lizard "look" came back into vogue, and the fashionable sported gator-skin purses, shoes, and belts. Chic didn't come cheap. In New York, gator cowboy boots sold for $1,800, and attaché cases retailed for $4,000. And you could order gator meat at trendy restaurants all along the East Coast. "Why not gator?" asked Red Lobster spokesman Dick Monroe. "Today's two-income households are looking for more variety. And they think it's neat to eat an animal that can eat them."

To meet the demand, Florida doubled the number of its licensed alligator farms compared to the previous four years when they functioned almost entirely as tourist attractions. In 1985, Florida farmers raised 37,000 gators; in 1986, that figure increased by 50 percent. Revenues soared as well. Frank Godwin, owner of Gatorland in Orlando, netted an estimated $270,000 from the 1,000 animals he harvested annually. Improved technology was applied to gator farming in order to boost profits even higher. Lawler Wells, for example, owner of Hilltop Farms in Avon Park, raised 7,000 gators in darkened hothouses that accelerated their growth.[1]

Seven years later, a 1993 article in the Washington Post continued the gator tale: "During the late 1980s, gator ranching was booming, and the industry was being compared to a living gold mine. People rushed into the industry. Some farmers became temporarily rich."[2]

In 1995, a USA Today interview with a gator hunter provided evidence of long-run equilibrium: "Armed with a pistol barrel attached to the end of an 8-foot wooden pole, alligator hunter Bill Chaplin fires his 'bankstick' and dispatches a six-footer with a single round of .44 magnum ammunition. What's in it for him? Financially, very little. At $3.50 a pound for the meat and $45 a foot for the hide, an alligator is worth perhaps $100 a foot. After paying for skinning and processing, neither hunter nor landowner gets rich."[3]

A 2000 article in The Dallas Morning News provided further evidence: Mark Glass, who began raising gators in 1995 south of Atlanta, stated, "I can honestly say I haven't made any money yet, but I hope that's about to change."[4] And a 2003 article from Knight Ridder/Tribune Business News gave a pessimistic report for Florida: "Revenue from alligator harvesting has flattened in recent years, despite Florida's efforts to promote the alligator as part of a viable 'aquaculture' industry. It's a tough business."[5] And beginning in 2009, alligator skin bags, belts, shoes, watch straps, and purses were victims of the recession. As a result, many alligator farms were overrun with an unprecedented surplus of unsold alligators and falling prices. Wayne Sagrera, co-owner of Vermilion Gator Farm near Lafayette, Louisiana, stated, "We can't invest in eggs if the demand is not there. They're just not selling."[6]

ANALYZE the ISSUE

1. Draw short-run firm and industry competitive equilibriums for a perfectly competitive gator-farming industry before the number of alligator farms in Florida doubled. For simplicity, assume the gator farm is earning zero economic profit. Now show the short-run effect of an increase in demand for alligators.

2. Assuming gator farming is perfectly competitive, explain the long-run competitive equilibrium condition for the typical gator farmer and the industry as a whole.

[1] Ron Moreau and Penelope Wang, "Gators: Snapping Up Profits," Newsweek, Dec. 8, 1986, p. 68.
[2] William Booth, "Bag a Gator and Save the Species," The Washington Post, Aug. 25, 1993, p. A1.
[3] J. Taylor Buckley, "S. Carolina Lets Hunters Go for Gators Again," USA Today, Sept. 21, 1995, News Section, p. A1.
[4] "More Bite for the Buck," Dallas Morning News, Dec. 6, 2000, p. 2A.
[5] Jerry W. Jackson, "Alligators are Growing Part of Florida's Agricultural Landscape," Knight Ridder/Tribune Business News, Jan. 26, 2003.
[6] Rick Jervis, "Recession Eats into Gator Market," USA Today, Oct. 22, 2009, News Section, p. 2A.

Key Concepts

Market structure

Perfect competition

Barrier to entry

Price taker

Marginal revenue (MR)

Perfectly competitive firm's short-run supply curve

Perfectly competitive industry's short-run supply curve

Summary

- **Market structure** consists of three market characteristics: (1) the number of sellers, (2) the nature of the product, and (3) the ease of entry into or exit from the market.

- **Perfect competition** is a market structure in which an individual firm cannot affect the price of the product it produces. Each firm in the industry is very small relative to the market as a whole, all the firms sell a homogeneous product, and firms are free to enter and exit the industry.

- A **price-taker firm** in perfect competition faces a perfectly elastic demand curve. It can sell all it wishes at the market-determined price, but it will sell nothing above the given market price. This is because so many competitive firms are willing to sell the same product at the going market price.

- The **total revenue–total cost method** is one way a firm determines the level of output that maximizes profit. Profit reaches a maximum when the vertical difference between the total revenue and the total cost curves is at a maximum.

Total Revenue–Total Cost Method

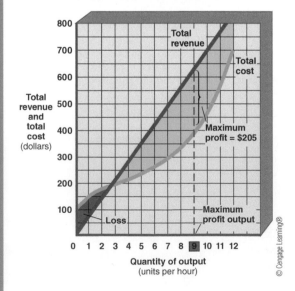

- The **marginal revenue equals marginal cost method** is a second approach to finding where a firm maximizes profits. **Marginal revenue (MR)** is the change in total revenue from a one-unit change in output. Marginal revenue for a perfectly competitive firm equals the market price. The $MR = MC$ rule states that the firm maximizes profit or minimizes loss by producing the output where marginal revenue equals marginal cost. If the price (average revenue) is below the minimum point on the average variable cost curve, the $MR = MC$ rule does not apply, and the firm shuts down to minimize its losses.

Marginal Revenue Equals Marginal Cost Method

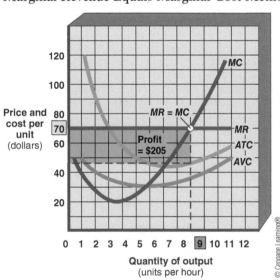

- The **perfectly competitive firm's short-run supply curve** shows the relationship between the price of a product and the quantity supplied in the short run. The individual firm always produces along its marginal cost curve above its intersection with the average variable cost curve. The **perfectly competitive industry's short-run supply** curve is the horizontal summation of the short-run supply curves of all firms in the industry.

Firm's Short-Run Supply Curve

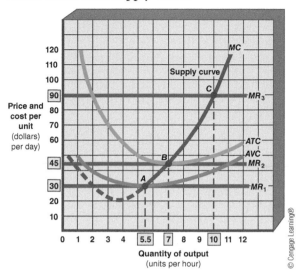

Long-Run Perfectly Competitive Equilibrium

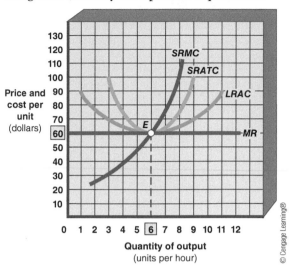

- **Long-run perfectly competitive equilibrium** occurs when a firm earns a normal profit by producing where price equals minimum long-run average cost equals minimum short-run average total cost equals short-run marginal cost.

Study Questions and Problems

1. Explain why a perfectly competitive firm would or would not advertise.
2. Does a Kansas wheat farmer fit the perfectly competitive market structure? Explain.
3. Suppose the market equilibrium price of wheat is $2 per bushel in a perfectly competitive industry. Draw the industry supply and demand curves and the demand curve for a single wheat farmer. Explain why the wheat farmer is a price taker.
4. Assuming the market equilibrium price for wheat is $5 per bushel, draw the total revenue and the marginal revenue curves for the typical wheat farmer in the same graph. Explain how marginal revenue and price are related to the total revenue curve.
5. Consider the cost data below for a perfectly competitive firm in the short run: If the market price is $150, how many units of output will the firm produce in order to maximize profit in the short run? Specify the amount of economic profit or loss. At what level of output does the firm break even?
6. Consider this statement: "A firm should increase output when it makes a profit." Do you agree or disagree? Explain.
7. Consider this statement: "When marginal revenue equals marginal cost, total cost equals total revenue, and the firm makes zero profit." Do you agree or disagree? Explain.

Output (Q)	Total Fixed Cost (TFC)	Total Variable Cost (TVC)	Total Cost (TC)	Total Revenue (TR)	Profit
1	$100	$120	$_____	$_____	$_____
2	100	200	_____	_____	_____
3	100	290	_____	_____	_____
4	100	430	_____	_____	_____
5	100	590	_____	_____	_____

8. Consider Exhibit 7-11, which shows the graph of a perfectly competitive firm in the short run.
   a. If the firm's demand curve is MR_3, does the firm earn an economic profit or loss?
   b. Which demand curve(s) indicate(s) the firm incurs a loss?
   c. Which demand curve(s) indicate(s) the firm would shut down?
   d. Identify the firm's short-run supply curve.

9. Consider this statement: "The perfectly competitive firm will sell all the quantity of output consumers will buy at the prevailing market price." Do you agree or disagree? Explain your answer.
10. Suppose a perfectly competitive firm's demand curve is below its average total cost curve. Explain the conditions under which a firm continues to produce in the short run.
11. Suppose the industry equilibrium price of residential housing construction is $100 per square foot and the minimum average variable cost for a residential construction contractor is $110 per square foot. What would you advise the owner of this firm to do? Explain.
12. Suppose independent truckers operate in a perfectly competitive industry. If these firms are earning positive economic profits, what happens in the long run to the following: the price of trucking services, the industry quantity of output, and the profits of trucking firms?

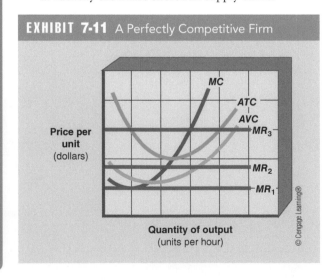

EXHIBIT 7-11 A Perfectly Competitive Firm

Sample Quiz

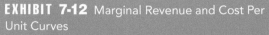

EXHIBIT 7-12 Marginal Revenue and Cost Per Unit Curves

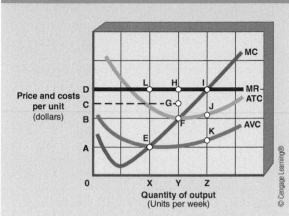

© Cengage Learning®

1. As shown in Exhibit 7-12, suppose the firm's price is OB. The firm's total economic profit at this price is equal to the area of
   a. CJID.
   b. BFHD.
   c. AEXD.
   d. CGHD.
   e. zero.
2. The firm shown in Exhibit 7-12 will
   a. produce where marginal cost equals marginal revenue.
   b. be a price taker.
   c. not produce below a price of OA.
   d. All the answers above are correct.
3. As shown in Exhibit 7-12, if the price is OD, a perfectly competitive firm maximizes profit at which point on its marginal cost curve?
   a. E.
   b. F.
   c. I.
   d. Between E and I.
4. As shown in Exhibit 7-12, if the price is OD, the firm's total cost of producing at its *most* profitable level of output is
   a. YF.
   b. XL.
   c. OYHD.
   d. OXEA.
5. As shown in Exhibit 7-12, if the price is OD, the firm's total revenue at its *most* profitable level of output is
   a. OZID.
   b. OYHD.
   c. OXLD.
   d. OYFB.

6. As shown in Exhibit 7-12, suppose the firm's price is OD. The firm's total economic profit at this price is equal to the area of
   a. CJID.
   b. BFHD.
   c. AEXD.
   d. CGHD.
   e. BJID
7. As shown in Exhibit 7-12, if the price is OB, the firm's total cost of producing at its *most* profitable level of output is
   a. YF.
   b. XL.
   c. OYFB.
   d. OXEA.
8. As shown in Exhibit 7-12, the firm will *not* produce in the short-run if the price is below
   a. OD.
   b. OB.
   c. OC.
   d. OA.
9. Perfect competition is defined as market structure in which
   a. there are many small sellers.
   b. the product is homogeneous.
   c. it is very easy for firms to enter or exit the market.
   d. All of the answers above are correct.
10. Under perfect competition, which of the following are the same (equal) at *all* levels of output?
    a. Price and marginal cost.
    b. Price and marginal revenue.
    c. Marginal cost and marginal revenue.
    d. All of the answers above are correct.
11. A portrait photographer produces output in packages of 100 photos each. If the output sold increases from 600 to 700 photos, total revenue increases from $1,200 to $1,400. The marginal revenue per photo is
    a. $200.
    b. $100.
    c. $20.
    d. $2.
    e. $1.
12. In the short run, a perfectly competitive firm is producing at a price below average total cost, its economic profit is
    a. positive.
    b. zero.
    c. negative.
    d. normal.

EXHIBIT 7-13 Total Revenue and Total Cost Graph

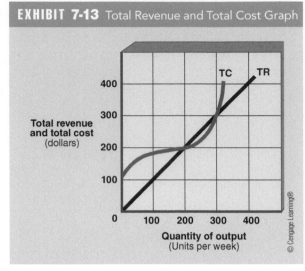

Total revenue and total cost (dollars)

Quantity of output (Units per week)

© Cengage Learning®

13. In Exhibit 7-13, if output is 200 units per week, economic profit for the firm is
   a. zero.
   b. at its minimum.
   c. at its maximum.
   d. None of the answers above are correct.

14. In Exhibit 7-13, economic profit for the firm is at a maximum when output per week equals
   a. zero units.
   b. 100 units.
   c. 200 units.
   d. 250 units.

15. The point of maximum profit for a business firm is where
   a. $P = AC$.
   b. $TR = TC$.
   c. $MR = AR$.
   d. $MR = MC$.

16. Above the shutdown point, a competitive firm's supply curve coincides with its
   a. marginal revenue curve.
   b. marginal cost curve.
   c. average variable cost curve.
   d. average total cost curve.

17. A perfectly competitive firm's short-run supply curve is the
   a. average total cost curve.
   b. demand curve above the marginal revenue curve.
   c. same as the market supply curve.
   d. marginal cost curve above the average variable cost curve.

18. A perfectly competitive firm's short-run supply curve is the
   a. segment of the marginal cost curve above average fixed cost.
   b. segment of the marginal cost curve above the minimum level of average variable cost.
   c. upward-sloping segment of the marginal cost curve.
   d. Both answers a. and b. are correct.

19. In long-run equilibrium, the perfectly competitive firm sets its price equal to which of the following?
   a. Short-run average total cost.
   b. Short-run marginal cost.
   c. Long-run average cost.
   d. All of the answers above are correct.

20. If there is a permanent increase in demand for the product of a perfectly competitive industry, the process of transition to a new long-run equilibrium will include
   a. the entry of new firms.
   b. temporarily higher profits.
   c. Both answers a. and b. are correct.
   d. Neither answer a. nor b. is correct.

Monopoly

In this chapter, you will learn to solve these economics puzzles:

* Why doesn't the monopolist gouge consumers by charging the highest possible price?

* How can price discrimination be fair?

* Are medallion cabs in New York City monopolists?

CHAPTER PREVIEW

Playing the popular board game of Monopoly teaches some of the characteristics of monopoly theory presented in this chapter. In the game version, players win by gaining as much economic power as possible. They strive to own railroads, utilities, Boardwalk, Park Place, and other valuable real estate. Then each player tries to bankrupt opponents by purchasing hotels that charge high prices. A player who rolls the dice and lands on another player's property has no choice—either pay the price or lose the game.

In the last chapter, we studied perfect competition, which may be viewed as the paragon of economic virtue. Why? Under perfect competition, there are many sellers, each lacking any power to influence price. Perfect competition and monopoly are polar extremes. The word *monopoly* is derived from two Greek words meaning "single seller." A monopoly has the market power to set its price and not worry about competitors. Perhaps your college or university has only one bookstore where you can buy textbooks. If so, students are likely to pay higher prices for textbooks than they would if many sellers competed in the campus textbook market.

This chapter explains why firms do not or cannot enter a particular market and compete with a monopolist. Then we explore some of the interesting monopolies around the world. We study how a monopolist determines what price to charge and how much to produce. The chapter ends with a discussion of the pros and cons of monopoly. Most of the analytical tools required here have been introduced in previous chapters.

8-1   THE MONOPOLY MARKET STRUCTURE

Monopoly A market structure characterized by (1) a single seller, (2) a unique product, and (3) impossible entry into the market.

The model at the opposite extreme from perfect competition is monopoly. Under **monopoly**, the consumer has a simple choice—either buy the monopolist's product or do without it. Monopoly is a market structure characterized by (1) a single seller, (2) a unique product, and (3) impossible entry into the market. Unlike perfect competition, there are no close substitutes for the monopolist's product. Monopoly, like perfect competition, corresponds only approximately to real-world industries, but it serves as a useful benchmark model. Following are brief descriptions of each monopoly characteristic.

8-1a   Single Seller

In perfect competition, many firms make up the industry. In contrast, a monopoly means that a single firm *is* the industry. One firm provides the total supply of a product in a given market. Local monopolies are more common real-world approximations of the model than national or world market monopolies. For example, a campus bookstore, cable television company, and electric power company may be local monopolies. The only gas station, drug store, or grocery store in Nowhere County, Utah, and a hotdog stand at a football game are also examples of monopolies. Nationally, the U.S. Postal Service monopolizes first-class mail.

8-1b   Unique Product

A unique product means there are *no close substitutes* for the monopolist's product. Thus, the monopolist faces little or no competition. In reality, however, there are few, if any, products that have no close substitutes. Students can buy used textbooks from sources other than the campus bookstore, and textbooks can be purchased over the Internet. Satellite television competes with cable television. Natural gas, oil furnaces, and solar energy are substitutes for electric heat. Similarly, the fax machine and email are substitutes for mail service.

8-1c   Impossible Entry

In perfect competition, there are no constraints to prevent new firms from entering an industry. In the case of monopoly, extremely high barriers make it very difficult or impossible for new firms to enter an industry. Following are the three major barriers that prevent new firms from entering a market and competing with a monopolist.

1.   Ownership of a Vital Resource

Sole control of the entire supply of a strategic input is one way a monopolist can prevent a newcomer from entering an industry. A famous historical example is Alcoa's monopoly of the U.S. aluminum market from the late 19th century until the end of World War II. The source of Alcoa's monopoly was its control of bauxite ore, which is necessary to produce aluminum. Today, it is very difficult for a new professional sports league to compete with the National Football League (NFL) and the National Basketball Association (NBA).

Why? NFL and NBA teams have contracts with the best players and leases for the best stadiums and arenas.

2. Legal Barriers

The oldest and most effective barriers protecting a firm from potential competitors are the result of government franchises and licenses. The government permits a single firm to provide a certain product and excludes competing firms by law. For example, water and sewer service, natural gas, and cable television operate under monopoly franchises established by state and local governments. In many states, the state government runs monopoly liquor stores and lotteries. The U.S. Postal Service has a government franchise to deliver first-class mail.

Government-granted licenses restrict entry into some industries and occupations. For example, the Federal Communications Commission (FCC) must license radio and television stations. In most states, physicians, lawyers, dentists, nurses, teachers, real estate agents, hair stylists, taxicabs, liquor stores, funeral homes, and other professions and businesses are required to have a license. Patents and copyrights are another form of government barrier to entry. The government grants patents to inventors, thereby legally prohibiting other firms from selling the patented product for 20 years. Copyrights give creators of literature, art, music, and movies exclusive rights to sell or license their works. The purpose behind granting patents and copyrights is to encourage innovation and new products by guaranteeing exclusive rights to profit from new ideas for a limited period.

3. Economies of Scale

Why might competition among firms be unsustainable so that one firm becomes a monopolist? Recall the concept of *economies of scale* from Chapter 6 on production costs. As a result of large-scale production, the long-run average cost (LRAC) of production falls. This means a monopoly can emerge in time *naturally* because of the relationship between average cost and the scale of an operation. As a firm becomes larger, its cost per unit of output is lower compared to a smaller competitor. In the long run, this "survival of the fittest" cost advantage forces smaller firms to leave the industry. Because new firms cannot hope to produce and sell output equal or close to that of the monopolist, thereby achieving the monopolist's low costs, they will not enter the industry. Thus, a monopoly can arise over time and remain dominant in an industry even though the monopolist does not own an essential resource or obtain legal barriers.

Natural monopoly An industry in which the long-run average cost of production declines throughout the entire market. As a result, a single firm can supply the entire market demand at a lower cost than two or more smaller firms.

Economists call the situation in which one seller emerges in an industry because of economies of scale a natural monopoly. A natural monopoly is an industry in which the long-run average cost of production declines throughout the entire market. As a result, a single firm can supply the entire market demand at a lower cost than two or more smaller firms. Public utilities, such as natural gas, water, and cable television, are examples of natural monopolies. The government grants these industries an exclusive franchise in a geographic area so consumers can benefit from the cost savings that occur when one firm in an industry with significant economies of scale sells a large output. The government then regulates these monopolies through a board of commissioners to prevent exploitation.

Exhibit 8-1 depicts the *LRAC* curve for a natural monopoly. A single firm can produce 100 units at an average cost of $15 and a total cost of $1,500. If two firms each produce 50 units, the total cost rises to $2,500. With five firms producing 20 units each, the total cost rises to $3,500.

CONCLUSION Because of economies of scale, a single firm in an industry will produce output at a lower per-unit cost than two or more firms.

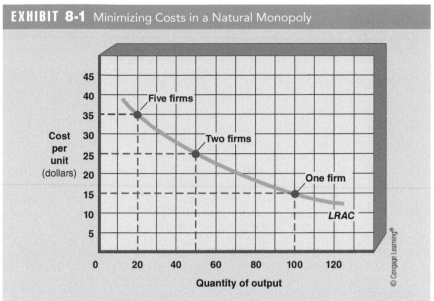

EXHIBIT 8-1 Minimizing Costs in a Natural Monopoly

In a natural monopoly, a single firm in an industry can produce at a lower cost than two or more firms. This condition occurs because the *LRAC* curve for any firm decreases over the relevant range. For example, one firm can produce 100 units at an average cost of $15 and a total cost of $1,500. Two firms in the industry can produce 100 units of output (50 units each) for a total cost of $2,500, and five firms can produce the same output for a total cost of $3,500.

8-1d Network Good

Network good A good that increases in value to each user as the total number of users increases. As a result, a firm can achieve economies of scale.

Economies of scale and monopoly power can exist because consumers choose a product that everyone else is using. A **network good** is a good that increases in value to each user as the total number of users increases. Examples include such internet products as Facebook and Match.com. People post on Facebook to belong to the same network where everyone posts their profile. Similarly, Match.com is the largest dating service with the largest selections of potential dates.

CONCLUSION The greater the number of people connected to a network goods system, the more benefits of the product to each person are increased.

Network goods can result in a firm increasing sales rapidly and thus achieving economies of scale, as illustrated in Exhibit 8-1. Smaller firms therefore have higher-cost products that cannot compete, and they go out of business.

8-2 PRICE AND OUTPUT DECISIONS FOR A MONOPOLIST

Price maker A firm that faces a downward-sloping demand curve and therefore it can choose among price and output combinations along the demand curve.

A major difference between perfect competition and monopoly is the shape of the demand curve, not the shapes of the cost curves. As explained in the previous chapter, a perfectly competitive firm is a *price taker*. In contrast, the next sections explain that a monopolist is a **price maker**. A price maker is a firm that faces a downward-sloping demand curve. This means a monopolist has the ability to select the product's price. In short, a monopolist can set the price with its corresponding level of output, rather than being a helpless pawn at the mercy of

GLOBAL ECONOMICS

Monopolies around the World

Applicable concept: monopoly

Interesting examples of monopolies can be found in other countries. Let's begin with a historical example. In the sixteenth through eighteenth centuries, monarchs granted monopoly rights for a variety of businesses. For example, in 1600 Queen Elizabeth I chartered the British East India Company and gave it a monopoly over England's trade with India. This company was even given the right to coin money and to make peace or war with non-Christian powers. As a result of its monopoly, the company made substantial profits from the trade in Indian cotton goods, silks, and spices. In the late 1700s, the growing power of the company and huge personal fortunes of its officers provoked more and more government control. Finally, in 1858, the company was abolished, ending its trade monopoly, great power, and patronage.

"Diamonds are forever," but will DeBeers be the diamond monopoly forever? DeBeers, a South African corporation, was close to being a world monopoly. It owns the world's largest diamond mine, which was discovered in 1866 on a farm in South Africa owned by Johannes DeBeer. Through its Central Selling Organization (CSO) headquartered in London, DeBeers controlled 80 percent of all the diamonds sold in the world. DeBeers controlled the price of jewelry-quality diamonds by requiring suppliers in Russia, Australia, Congo, Botswana, Namibia, and other countries to sell their rough diamonds through DeBeers's CSO. Why did suppliers of rough diamonds allow DeBeers to set the price and quantity of diamonds sold throughout the world? The answer was that the CSO could put any uncooperative seller out of business. All the CSO had to do was to reach into its huge stockpile of diamonds and flood the market with the type of diamonds

being sold by an independent seller. As a result, the price of diamonds would plummet in the competitor's market, and the independent seller would cease to sell diamonds.

In recent years, DeBeers lost some of its control of the market. Mines in Australia became more independent, diamonds were found in Canada, and Russian mines began selling to independents. To deal with the new conditions, DeBeers changed its policy in 2001 by closing the CSO and promoting DeBeers own brand of diamonds rather than trying to control the world diamond supply. DeBeers proclaimed its strategy to be "the diamond supplier of choice." Will this monopoly continue? It is an interesting question.

Genuine caviar, the salty black delicacy, is naturally scarce because it comes from the eggs of sturgeon harvested by fisheries from the Caspian Sea near the mouth of the Volga River. After the Bolshevik revolution in Russia in 1917, a caviar monopoly was established under the control of the Soviet Ministry of Fisheries and the Paris-based Petrosian Company. The Petrosian brothers limited exports of caviar and pushed prices up as high as $1,000 a pound for some varieties. As a result of this worldwide monopoly, both the Soviet government and the Petrosian Company earned handsome profits. It is interesting to note that the vast majority of the tons of caviar harvested each year was consumed at government banquets or sold at bargain prices to top Communist Party officials. With the fall of the Soviet Union, it was impossible for the Ministry of Fisheries to control all exports of caviar. Various former Soviet republics claimed jurisdiction and negotiated independent export contracts and caviar export prices dropped sharply.

the going industry price. To understand the monopolist, we again apply the marginal approach to our hypothetical electronics company—Computech.

8-2a Marginal Revenue, Total Revenue, and Price Elasticity of Demand

Suppose engineers at Computech discover an inexpensive miraculous electronic device called SAV-U-GAS that anyone can easily attach to a car's engine. Once installed, the device raises gasoline mileage to more than 100 miles per gallon. The government grants Computech a patent, and the company becomes a monopolist selling this gas-saver gizmo. Because of this barrier to entry, Computech is the only seller in the industry. Although other firms try to compete with this invention, they create poor substitutes. This means the downward-sloping demand curves for the industry and for the monopolist are identical.

Exhibit 8-2(a) illustrates the demand and the marginal revenue (*MR*) curves for a monopolist such as Computech. As the monopolist lowers its price to increase the quantity demanded, changes in both price and quantity affect the firm's

EXHIBIT 8-2 Demand, Marginal Revenue, and Total Revenue for a Monopolist

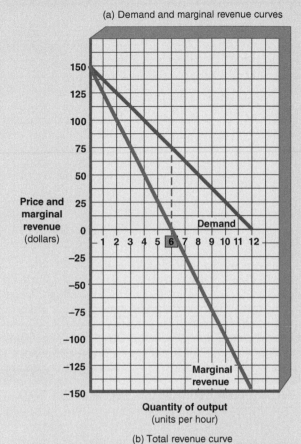

(a) Demand and marginal revenue curves

Part (a) shows the relationship between the demand and the marginal revenue curves. The *MR* curve is below the demand curve. Between 0 and 6 units of output, *MR* > 0; at 6 units of output, *MR* = 0; beyond 6 units of output, *MR* < 0.

The relationship between demand and total revenue is shown in part (b). When the price is $150, total revenue is zero. When the price is set at zero, total revenue is also zero. Between these two extreme prices, the price of $75 maximizes total revenue. This price corresponds to 6 units of output, which is where the *MR* curve intersects the quantity axis, halfway between the origin and the intercept of the demand curve.

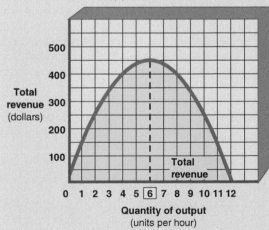

(b) Total revenue curve

Demand, Marginal Revenue, and Total Revenue for Computech as a Monopolist

Output per hour	Price	Total revenue	Marginal revenue
0	$150	$ 0	
			$138
1	138	138	
			112
2	125	250	
			89
3	113	339	
			61
4	100	400	
			40
5	88	440	
			10
6	75	450	
			0
			−9
7	63	441	
			−41
8	50	400	
			−58
9	38	342	
			−92
10	25	250	
			−107
11	13	143	
			−143
12	0	0	

© Cengage Learning®

total revenue (price times quantity), as shown graphically in Exhibit 8-2(b). If Computech charges $150, consumers purchase 0 units, and, therefore, total revenue is zero. To sell 1 unit, Computech must lower the price to $138, and total revenue rises from zero to $138. Because the marginal revenue is the increase in total revenue that results from a 1-unit change in output, the *MR* curve at the first unit of output is $138 ($138 − 0). Thus, the price and the marginal revenue from selling 1 unit are equal at $138. To sell 2 units, the monopolist must lower the price to $125, and total revenue rises to $250. The marginal revenue from selling the second unit is $112 ($250 − $138), which is $13 less than the price received.

As shown in Exhibit 8-2(a), as the monopolist lowers its price, price is greater than marginal revenue after the first unit of output. Like all marginal measurements, marginal revenue is plotted midway between the quantities.

> **CONCLUSION** The demand and marginal revenue curves of the monopolist are downward sloping, in contrast to the horizontal demand and corresponding marginal revenue curves facing the perfectly competitive firm. (Compare Exhibit 8-2(a) with Exhibit 7-1(b) of the previous chapter.)

Starting from zero output, as the price falls, total revenue rises until it reaches a maximum at 6 units, and then it falls, tracing the "revenue hill" drawn in part (b). The explanation was presented earlier in the discussion of price elasticity of demand in Chapter 5. Recall that a straight-line demand curve has an elastic ($E_d > 1$) segment along the upper half, a unit elastic ($E_d = 1$) at the midpoint, and an inelastic ($E_d < 1$) segment along the lower half (see Exhibit 5-4 in Chapter 5). Recall from Chapter 5 that when $E_d > 1$, total revenue rises as the price drops, and total revenue reaches a maximum where $E_d = 1$. When $E_d < 1$, total revenue falls as the price falls.

As shown in Exhibit 8-2(b), total revenue for a monopolist is related to marginal revenue. When the *MR* curve is above the quantity axis (elastic demand), total revenue is increasing. At the intersection of the *MR* curve and the quantity axis (unit elastic demand), total revenue is at its maximum. When the *MR* curve is below the quantity axis, total revenue is decreasing (inelastic demand). The monopolist will never operate on the inelastic range of its demand curve that corresponds to a negative marginal revenue. The reason is that, in this inelastic range, the monopolist can increase total revenue by cutting output and raising price. In our example, Computech would not charge a price lower than $75 or produce an output greater than 6 units per hour. Now we turn to the question of what price the monopolist will charge to maximize profit.

In Exhibit 8-2(a), observe that the *MR* curve cuts the quantity axis at 6 units, which is half of 12 units. Following an easy rule helps locate the point along the quantity axis where marginal revenue equals zero: *The marginal revenue curve for a straight-line demand curve intersects the quantity axis halfway between the origin and the quantity axis intercept of the demand curve.*

8-2b Short-Run Profit Maximization for a Monopolist Using the Total Revenue–Total Cost Method

Exhibit 8-3 reproduces the demand, total revenue, and marginal revenue data from Exhibit 8-2 and adds cost data from the previous two chapters. These data illustrate a situation in which Computech can earn monopoly economic profit in the short run. Subtracting total cost in column 6 from total revenue in column 3 gives the total profit or loss in column 8 that the firm earns at each level of output. From 0 to 1 unit, the monopolist incurs losses, and then a break-even point occurs before 2 units per hour. If the monopolist produces 5 units per hour, it earns the maximum profit of $190 per hour. As output expands between 5 and 8

EXHIBIT 8-3 Short-Run Profit Maximization Schedule for Computech as a Monopolist

(1) Output per Hour (Q)	(2) Price per Unit (P)	(3) Total Revenue (TR)	(4) Marginal Revenue (MR)	(5) Marginal Cost (MC)	(6) Total Cost (TC)	(7) Average Total Cost (ATC)	(8) Profit (+) or Loss (−)
0	$150	$ 0			$100	—	−$100
			$138	$50			
1	138	138			150	$150	−12
			112	34			
2	125	250			184	92	66
			89	24			
3	113	339			208	69	131
			61	19			
4	100	400			227	57	173
			40	23			
5	88	440			250	50	190
			25	25			
			10	30			
6	75	450			280	47	170
			−9	38			
7	63	441			318	45	123
			−41	48			
8	50	400			366	46	34
			−58	59			
9	38	342			425	47	−83
			−92	75			
10	25	250			500	50	−250
			−107	95			
11	13	143			595	54	−452
			−143	117			
12	0	0			712	59	−712

© Cengage Learning®

units of output, the monopolist's profit diminishes. After 8 units of output, there is a second break-even point, and losses increase as output expands. Exhibit 8-4 illustrates graphically that where the vertical distance between the total revenue and total cost curves is maximum corresponds to the profit-maximizing output. Note that the total revenue-maximizing output level of 6 units is greater than the profit-maximizing output at 5 units.

8-2c Short-Run Profit Maximization for a Monopolist Using the Marginal Revenue Equals Marginal Cost Method

Exhibit 8-5 reproduces the demand and cost curves from the table in Exhibit 8-3. Like the perfectly competitive firm, a monopolist maximizes profit by producing the quantity of output where $MR = MC$ and charging the corresponding price on its demand curve. In this case, 5 units is the quantity at which $MR = MC$. As represented by point *A* on the demand curve, the price at 5 units is $88. Point *B*

EXHIBIT 8-4 Short-Run Profit Maximization for a Monopolist Using the Total Revenue–Total Cost Method

The profit-maximizing level of output for Computech as a monopolist is shown in this exhibit. Part (a) shows that maximum profit is earned by producing 5 units per hour and charging a price of $88 per unit where the vertical distance between the total revenue and total cost curves is the greatest. In part (b), the maximum profit of $190 per hour corresponds to the profit-maximizing output of 5 units per hour illustrated in part (a). At output levels below 2 or above 8, the monopolist incurs losses.

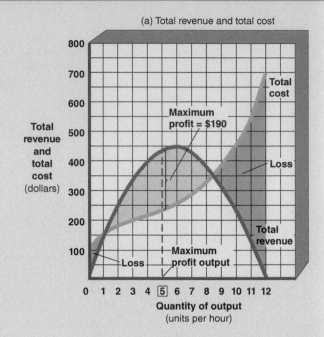

(a) Total revenue and total cost

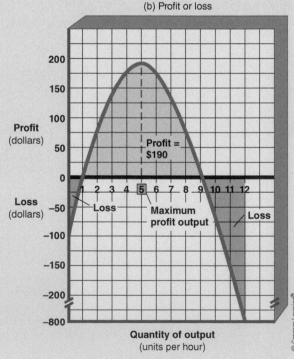

(b) Profit or loss

EXHIBIT 8-5 Short-Run Profit Maximization for a Monopolist Using the Marginal Revenue Equals Marginal Cost Method

Part (a) illustrates a monopolist electronics firm, Computech, maximizing profit by producing 5 units of output where the marginal revenue (*MR*) and the marginal cost (*MC*) curves intersect. The profit-maximizing price the monopolist charges at 5 units of output is $88, which is point *A* on the demand curve. Because $88 is above the average total cost (*ATC*) of $50 at point *B*, the monopolist earns a short-run profit of $190 per hour, represented by the shaded area ($38 profit per unit × 5 units).

At a price of $88 and output of 5 units per hour in part (a), the shaded area in part (b) shows that the profit curve is maximized at $190 per hour. At output levels below 2 or above 8, the monopolist incurs losses.

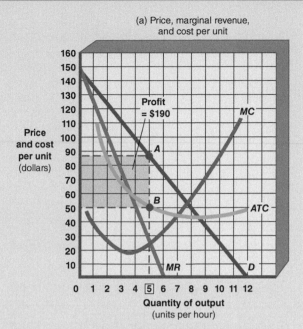

(a) Price, marginal revenue, and cost per unit

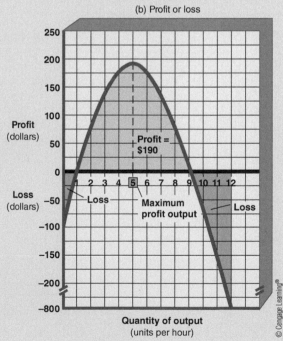

(b) Profit or loss

represents an average total cost (ATC) of $50 at 5 units. Because the price of $88 is above the *ATC* curve at the *MR* = *MC* output, the monopolist earns a profit of $38 per unit. At the hourly output of 5 units, total profit is $190 per hour, as shown by the shaded area ($38 per unit × 5 units).

Observe that a monopolist charges neither the highest possible price nor the total revenue-maximizing price. In Exhibit 8-5(a), $88 is not the highest possible price. Because Computech is a *price maker*, it could have set a price above $88 and sold less output than 5 units. However, the monopolist does not maximize profit by charging the highest possible price. Any price above $88 does not correspond to the intersection of the *MR* and *MC* curves. Now note that 5 units is below the output level where *MR* intersects the quantity axis and total revenue reaches its peak. Because $MR = 0$ and $E_d = 1$ when total revenue is maximum at 6 units of output, $MC = 0$ must also hold to maximize revenue and profit at the same time. A monopolist producing with zero marginal cost is an unlikely case. Hence, the price charged to maximize profit is higher on the demand curve than the price that maximizes total revenue.

> **CONCLUSION** The monopolist always maximizes profit by producing at a price on the elastic segment of its demand curve.

8-2d A Monopolist Facing a Short-Run Loss

Having a monopoly does not guarantee profits. A monopolist has no protection against changes in demand or cost conditions. Exhibit 8-6 shows a situation in which the demand curve is lower at any point than the *ATC* curve, and total cost therefore exceeds total revenue at any price charged. Because the point where *MR* = *MC* at a price of $50 (point *A*) on the demand curve is above the *AVC* curve, but below the *ATC* curve, the best Computech can do is to minimize its loss. This means the monopolist, like the perfectly competitive firm, produces in the short run at a quantity of 5 units per hour where *MR* = *MC*. At a price of $50 (point *A*), the ATC is $70 (point *B*), and Computech incurs a loss of $100 per hour, represented by the shaded area ($20 × 5 units).

What if *MR* = *MC* at a price on the demand curve that is below the *AVC* for a monopolist? As under perfect competition, the monopolist will shut down. To operate would only add further to its losses.

8-2e Monopoly in the Long Run

In perfect competition, economic profits are impossible in the long run. The entry of new firms into the industry drives the product's price down until profits reach zero. Extremely high barriers to entry, however, protect a monopolist.

> **CONCLUSION** If the positions of a monopolist's demand and cost curves give it a profit and nothing disturbs these curves, the monopolist will earn profit in the long run.

In the long run, the monopolist has great flexibility. The monopolist can alter its plant size to lower cost just as a perfectly competitive firm does. But firms such as Computech will not remain in business in the long run when losses persist—regardless of their monopoly status. Facing long-run losses, the monopolist will transfer its resources to a more profitable industry.

In reality, no monopolist can depend on barriers to protect it fully from competition in the long run. One threat is that entrepreneurs will find innovative ways to compete with a monopoly. For example, Computech must fear that firms will use their ingenuity and new electronic discoveries to develop a better and cheaper gasoline-saving device. To dampen the enthusiasm of potential rivals, one

EXHIBIT 8-6 Short-Run Loss Minimization for a Monopolist Using the Marginal Revenue Equals Marginal Cost Method

In part (a), all points along the demand curve lie below the *ATC* curve. If the market price charged corresponds to the output where the marginal revenue (*MR*) and marginal cost (*MC*) curves intersect, the firm will keep its loss to a minimum. At point *A*, the loss-minimizing price is $50 per unit, and marginal revenue equals marginal cost at an output of 5 units per hour with ATC equal to $70 per unit (point *B*). The short-run loss represented by the shaded area is $100 ($20 loss per unit × 5 units).

Part (b) shows that the firm's short-run loss will be greater at any output other than where the marginal revenue and the marginal cost curves intersect at an output of 5 units per hour. Because the price of $50 is above the average variable cost, each unit of output sold pays for the average variable cost and a portion of the average fixed cost.

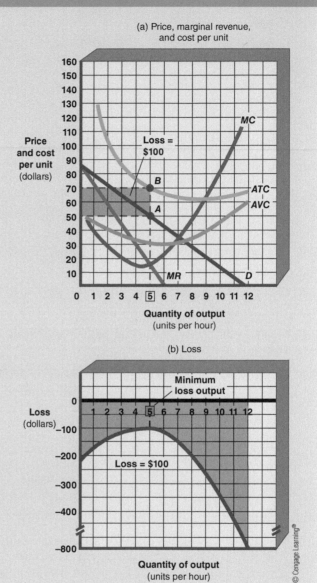

alternative for the monopolist is to sacrifice short-run profits to earn greater profits in the long run. Returning to part (a) of Exhibit 8-5, the monopolist might wish to charge a price below $88 and produce an output greater than 5 units per hour.

8-3 PRICE DISCRIMINATION

Price discrimination The practice of a seller charging different prices for the same product that are not justified by cost differences.

Our discussion so far has assumed the monopolist charges each customer the same price. What if Computech decides to sell identical SAV-U-GAS units for, say, $50 to truckers and $100 to everyone else? Under certain conditions, a monopolist may practice **price discrimination** to maximize profit. Price discrimination occurs when a seller charges different prices for the same product that are not justified by cost differences.

ECONOMICS IN PRACTICE

The Standard Oil Monopoly
Applicable concept: monopoly

Oil was discovered in western Pennsylvania by Colonel Edwin L. Drake in 1859, and after the Civil War, oil wells sprang up across the landscape. Because oil was plentiful, there was cutthroat competition, and the result was low prices and profits. At this time, John D. Rockefeller, who had grown up selling eggs, was a young Cleveland produce wholesaler in his early twenties. He was doing well in produce, but realized that greater profits could be made in refining oil, where there was less competition than in drilling for oil. So, in 1869, Rockefeller borrowed all the money he could and began with two small oil refineries.

To boost his market power, Rockefeller's Standard Oil of Ohio negotiated secret agreements with the railroads. In addition to information on his competitors' shipments, Rockefeller negotiated contracts with the railroads to pay rebates not only on Standard Oil's oil shipments, but also on its competitors' shipments. Soon Standard Oil was able to buy 21 of its 26 refining competitors in the Cleveland area. As its profits grew, Standard Oil expanded its refining

empire by acquiring its own oil fields, railroads, pipelines, and ships. The objective was to control oil from the oil well to the consumer. Over time, Rockefeller came to own a major part of the petroleum industry. Competitors found railroads and pipelines closed to their oil shipments. Rivals that could not be forced out of business were merged with Standard Oil.

In 1870, Standard Oil controlled only 10 percent of the oil industry in the United States. By 1880, Standard Oil controlled over 90 percent of the industry, and its oil was being shipped throughout the world. The more Standard Oil monopolized the petroleum industry, the higher its profits rose, and the greater its power to eliminate competition became. As competitors dropped out of the industry, Rockefeller became a price maker. He raised prices, and Standard Oil's profits soared. Finally, in 1911, Standard Oil was broken up under the Sherman Antitrust Act of 1890 into competing companies, including companies that eventually became Exxon and Mobil.

8-3a Conditions for Price Discrimination

All monopolists cannot engage in price discrimination. The following three conditions must exist before a seller can price discriminate:

1. The seller must be a price maker and therefore face a downward-sloping demand curve. This means that monopoly is not the only market structure in which price discrimination may occur.
2. The seller must be able to segment the market by distinguishing between consumers willing to pay different prices. Momentarily, this separation of buyers will be shown to be based on different price elasticities of demand.
3. It must be impossible or too costly for customers to engage in arbitrage. Arbitrage is the practice of earning a profit by buying a good at a low price and reselling the good at a higher price. For example, suppose your campus bookstore tried to boost profits by selling textbooks at a 50 percent discount to seniors. It would not take seniors long to cut the bookstore's profits by buying textbooks at the low price, selling these texts under the list price to all students who are not seniors, and pocketing the difference. In so doing, even without knowing the word *arbitrage*, the seniors would destroy the bookstore's price discrimination scheme.

Arbitrage The activity of earning a profit by buying a good at a low price and reselling the good at a higher price.

Although not monopolies, college and university tuition policies meet the conditions for price discrimination. First, lower tuition increases the quantity of openings demanded. Second, applicants' high school grades and SAT scores allow the admissions office to classify "consumers" with different price elasticities of demand. Students with lower grades and SAT scores have fewer substitutes, and their demand curve is less elastic than that of students with higher grades and SAT scores. If the tuition rises at University X, few students with lower grades will be lost because they have few offers of admission from other universities. On the other hand, the loss of students with higher grades and SAT scores is greater because they have more admissions opportunities. Third, the nature of the product prevents arbitrage. A student cannot buy University X admission at one price and sell it to another student for a higher price.

EXHIBIT 8-7 Price Discrimination

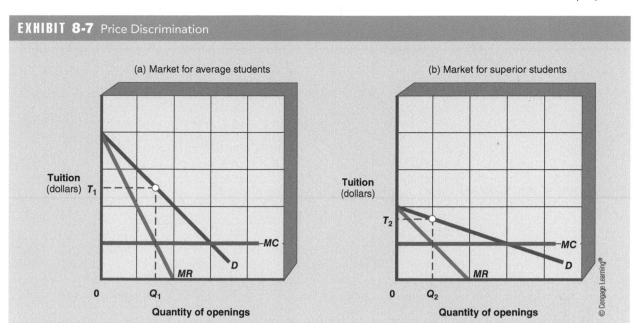

To maximize profit, University X separates students applying for admission into two markets. The demand curve for admission of average students in part (a) is less elastic than the demand curve for admission of superior students in part (b). Profit maximization occurs when $MR = MC$ in each market. Therefore, University X sets a tuition of T_1 for average students and gives scholarships to superior students, which lowers their tuition to T_2. Using price discrimination, University X earns a greater profit than it would by charging a single tuition to all students.

Exhibit 8-7 illustrates how University X price discriminates. For simplicity, assume the marginal cost of providing education to students is constant and therefore is represented by a horizontal MC curve. To maximize profit, University X follows the $MR = MC$ rule in each market. Given the different price elasticities of demand, the price at which $MR = MC$ differs for average and superior students. As a result, University X sets a higher tuition, T_1, in the average-student market, where demand is less responsive to the higher price. In the superior-student market, where demand is more responsive, these students receive scholarships, and their tuition is lower at T_2.

8-3b Is Price Discrimination Unfair?

Examples of price discrimination abound. Movie theaters offer lower prices for children than for adults. Electric utilities, which are monopolies, charge industrial users of electricity lower rates than residential users. Hotels and restaurants often give discounts to senior citizens, and airlines offer lower fares to groups of vacationers.

The typical reaction to price discrimination is that it is unfair. From the viewpoint of buyers who pay the higher prices, it is. But look at the other side of price discrimination. First, the seller is pleased because price discrimination increases profits. Second, many buyers benefit from price discrimination by not being excluded from purchasing the product. In Exhibit 8-7, price discrimination makes it possible for superior students who could not afford to pay a higher tuition to attend University X. Price discrimination also allows retired persons to enjoy hotels and restaurants they could not otherwise afford and enables more children to attend movies.

Why Don't Adults Pay More for Popcorn at the Movies?
At the movies, adults pay a higher ticket price than children, and each group gets a different-colored ticket. However, when adults and children go to the concession stand, both groups pay the same amount for popcorn and other snacks. Which of the following statements best explains why price discrimination stops at the ticket window? (1) The demand curve for popcorn is perfectly elastic. (2) The theater has no way to divide the buyers of popcorn based on different price elasticities of demand. (3) The theater cannot prevent resale.

8-4 COMPARING MONOPOLY AND PERFECT COMPETITION

Now that the basics of the two extremes of perfect competition and monopoly have been presented, we can compare and evaluate these market structures. This is an important assessment because the contrast between the disadvantages of monopoly and the advantages of perfect competition is the basis for many government policies, such as antitrust laws. To keep the analysis simple, we assume the monopolist charges a single price, rather than engaging in price discrimination.

8-4a The Monopolist as a Resource Misallocator

Recall the discussion of market efficiency in Chapter 4. This condition exists when a firm charging the equilibrium price uses neither too many nor too few resources to produce a product, so there is no *market failure*. Now you can state this definition of market efficiency in terms of price and marginal cost, as follows: *A perfectly competitive firm that produces the quantity of output at which* $P = MC$ *achieves an efficient allocation of resources.* This means production reaches the level of output where the price of the last unit produced matches the cost of producing it.

Exhibit 8-8(a) shows that a perfectly competitive firm produces the quantity of output at which $P = MC$. The price, P_c (marginal benefit), of the last unit produced equals the marginal cost of the resources used to produce it. In contrast, the monopolist shown in Exhibit 8-8(b) charges a price, P_m, greater than marginal cost, $P > MC$. Therefore, consumers are shortchanged because the marginal benefit of the last unit produced exceeds the marginal cost of producing it. Consumers want the monopolist to use more resources and produce additional units, but the monopolist restricts output to maximize profit.

> **CONCLUSION** A monopolist is characterized by inefficiency because resources are underallocated to the production of its product.

8-4b Perfect Competition Means More Output for Less

Exhibit 8-9 presents a comparison of perfect competition and monopoly in the same graph. Suppose the industry begins as perfectly competitive. The market demand curve, D (equal to MR), and the market supply curve, S, establish a perfectly competitive price, P_c, and output, Q_c. Recall from Exhibit 7-8 in the previous chapter that the competitive industry's supply curve, S, is the horizontal sum of the marginal cost (MC) curves of all the firms in the industry.

Now let's suppose the market structure changes when one firm buys out all the competing firms and the industry becomes a monopoly. Assume further that the demand and cost curves are unaffected by this dramatic change. In a monopoly, the industry demand curve *is* the monopolist's demand curve. Because the single firm is a price maker, the MR curve lies below the demand curve. The

EXHIBIT 8-8 Comparing a Perfectly Competitive Firm and a Monopolist

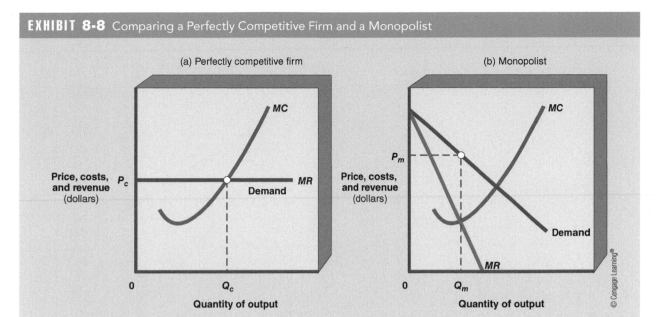

The perfectly competitive firm in part (a) sets $P = MC$ and produces Q_c output. Therefore, at the last unit of output, the marginal benefit is equal to the marginal cost of resources used to produce it. This condition means perfect competition achieves efficiency.

Part (b) shows that the monopolist produces output Q_m where $P > MC$. By so doing, consumers are shortchanged because the marginal benefit of the last unit produced exceeds the marginal cost of producing it. Under monopoly, inefficiency occurs because the monopolist underallocates resources to the production of its product. As a result, Q_m is less than Q_c.

industry supply curve now becomes the MC curve for the monopolist. To maximize profit, the monopolist sets $MR = MC$ by restricting the output to Q_m and raising the price to P_m.

CONCLUSION Monopoly harms consumers on two fronts. The monopolist charges a higher price and produces a lower output than would result under a perfectly competitive market structure.

8-5 THE CASE AGAINST AND FOR MONOPOLY

So far, a strong case has been made against monopoly and in favor of perfect competition. Now it is time to pause and summarize the economist's case against monopoly:

- A monopolist "gouges" consumers by charging a higher price than would be charged under perfect competition.

- Because a monopolist restricts output in order to maximize profit, too few resources are used to produce the product. Stated differently, the monopolist misallocates resources by charging a price greater than marginal cost. In perfectly competitive industries, price is set equal to marginal cost, and the result is an optimal allocation of resources.

- Long-run economic profit for a monopolist exceeds the zero economic profit earned in the long run by a perfectly competitive firm.

EXHIBIT 8-9 The Impact of Monopolizing an Industry

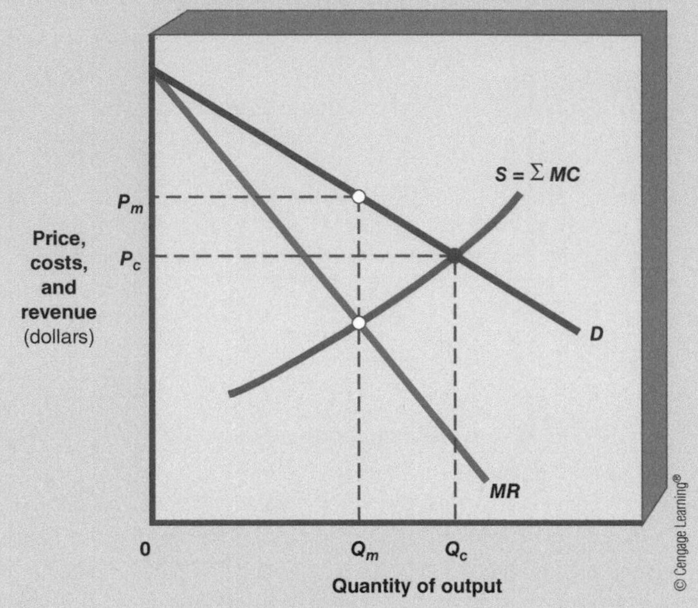

Assume an industry is perfectly competitive, with market demand curve D and market supply curve S. The market supply curve is the horizontal summation of all the individual firms' marginal cost curves above their minimum average variable costs. The intersection of market supply and market demand establishes the equilibrium price of P_c and the equilibrium quantity of Q_c. Now assume the industry suddenly changes to a monopoly. The monopolist produces the $MR = MC$ output of Q_m, which is less than Q_c. By restricting output to Q_m, the monopolist is able to charge the higher price of P_m.

- To the extent that the monopolist is a rich John D. Rockefeller, for example, and consumers of oil are poor, monopoly alters the distribution of income in favor of the monopolist.

Not all economists agree that monopoly is bad. Joseph Schumpeter and John Kenneth Galbraith praised monopoly power. They argued that the rate of technological change is likely to be greater under monopoly than under perfect competition. In their view, monopoly profits afford giant monopolies the financial strength to invest in the well-equipped laboratories and skilled labor necessary to create technological change.

The counterargument is that monopolists are slow to innovate. Freedom from direct competition means the monopolist is not motivated and therefore tends to stick to the "conventional wisdom." As Nobel laureate Sir John Hicks put it, "The best of all monopoly profit is a quiet life." In short, monopoly offers the opportunity to relax a bit and not worry about the rat race of technological change.

What does research on this issue suggest? Not surprisingly, many attempts have been made to verify or refute the effect of market structure on technological change. Unfortunately, the results to date have been inconclusive. For all we know, a mix of large and small firms in an industry may be the optimal mix to create technological change.

New York Taxicabs: Where Have All the Fare Flags Gone?

Applicable concept: perfect competition versus monopoly

©iStockphoto.com/JayLazarin

Yellow taxicabs in New York City, which are today one of the most famous icons of the city, are a love and hate relationship. The upside is that you can stick your arm in the sky to hail a cab that will take you to your destination. The downside is the traffic jams speckled with yellow cabs that service the city. Flashback to the 1920s, when New York taxicabs were competitive. There was no limit on the number of taxis, and hack licenses were only $10. In addition to a low barrier to entry, taxis engaged in price competition. Cabbies could choose among three different flags to attach to their cars. A red flag cab charged a surcharge for extra passengers. A white flag signaled no surcharge for extra passengers. A green flag meant the cabbie was offering a discount fare. Price wars often erupted, and the vast majority of cabbies flew green flags and charged bargain fares. One strategy was to fly the red flag (high rate) during rush hour and the green flag to offer discounts at off-peak times. Taxi companies also offered a variety of cabs—old, new, big, and small.[1]

As years passed, the system changed because of the concern that competition was causing an overabundance of taxis that congested city streets. The solution was to create a monopoly by law in 1937 designed to limit the number of cabs by requiring all cabs accepting street hails to be painted yellow and possess a medallion on the hood of the taxi. Currently, the Taxi and Limousine Commission (TLC) sets rates and imposes regulations. There are no price wars and the barrier to entry is high due to the high price of medallions. Today, the aluminum badges that give the rights to pick up passengers on the street cost more than $700,000, as determined at infrequent auctions. Because of their high prices, most cabs are owned by investment companies and are leased to the drivers. On the other hand, it is illegal for cabs without medallions to cruise and pick up passengers who hail them, although the law is often ignored. Nonmedallion cabs are authorized to respond only to customers who have ordered the cab in advance by phone or other means. There's no limit on the number of nonmedallion cabs or what the drivers may charge.

Now there is a "sharing economy" with unregulated rideshares provided by companies like Lyft sporting distinctive thick pink mustaches on the front grill of personal cars. Unlike traditional taxis, Lyft enables passengers to request rides from drivers who receive "donations" instead of fares from passengers. Lyft's slogan is "your friend with a car." Passengers are invited to sit in the front seat and give the driver a fist bump. Lyft estimates costs are 30 percent lower than cab fares. All drivers and passengers sign up on Facebook and rate each other on a 5-star scale. Cab companies have been up in arms, and the ridesharing business faces an uncertain regulatory landscape.

ANALYZE the ISSUE Use a graph to compare the price and output of medallion yellow cabs in New York City today with the taxi market before the 1920s.

[1]John Tierney, "You'll Wonder Where the Yellow Went," *The New York Times*, July 12, 1998, Section 6, p. 18.

Key Concepts

Monopoly	Network good	Price discrimination
Natural monopoly	Price maker	Arbitrage

Summary

- **Monopoly** is a single seller facing the entire industry demand curve because it is the industry. The monopolist sells a unique product and extremely high barriers to entry protect it from competition.

- **Barriers to entry** that prevent new firms from entering an industry are (1) ownership of an essential resource, (2) legal barriers, and (3) economies of scale. Government franchises, licenses, patents, and copyrights are the most obvious legal barriers to entry.

- A **natural monopoly** arises because of the existence of economies of scale in which the long-run average cost ($LRAC$) curve falls as production increases. Without government restrictions, economies of scale allow a single firm to produce at a lower cost than any firm producing a smaller output. Thus, smaller firms leave the industry, new firms fear competing with the monopolist, and the result is that a monopoly emerges *naturally*.

Natural Monopoly

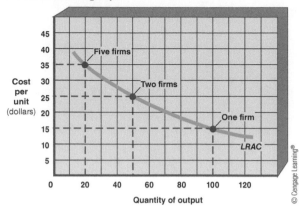

Quantity of output

- A **price-maker** firm faces a downward-sloping demand curve. It therefore searches its demand curve to find the price-output combination that maximizes its profit and minimizes its loss.

- The **marginal revenue** and demand curves are downward sloping for a monopolist. The marginal revenue curve for a monopolist is below the demand curve, and the total revenue curve reaches its maximum where marginal revenue equals zero.

- **Price elasticity of demand** corresponds to sections of the marginal revenue curve. When MR is positive, price elasticity of demand is elastic, $E_d > 1$. When MR is equal to zero, price elasticity of demand is unit elastic, $E_d = 1$. When MR is negative, price elasticity of demand is inelastic, $E_d < 1$.

- The **short-run profit-maximizing monopolist**, like the perfectly competitive firm, locates the profit-maximizing price by producing the output where the MR and MC curves intersect. If this price is less than the average variable cost (AVC) curve, the monopolist shuts down to minimize losses.

Short-Run Profit-Maximizing Monopolist

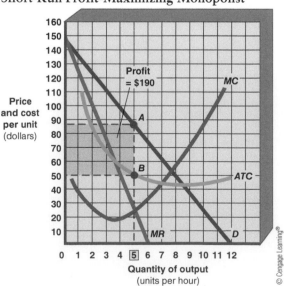

Short-Run Loss-Minimizing Monopolist

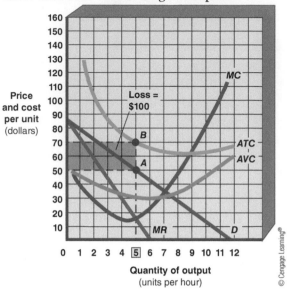

- The **long-run profit-maximizing monopolist** earns a profit because of barriers to entry. If demand and cost conditions prevent the monopolist from earning a profit, the monopolist will leave the industry.

- **Price discrimination** allows the monopolist to increase profits by charging buyers different prices rather than a single price. Three conditions are necessary for price discrimination: (1) the demand curve must be downward sloping, (2) buyers in different markets must have different price elasticities of demand, and (3) buyers must be prevented from reselling the product at a price higher than the purchase price.

Price Discrimination

(a) Market for average students

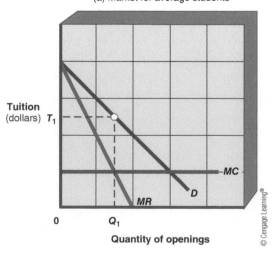

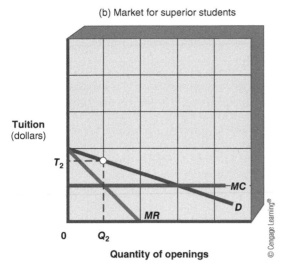

(b) Market for superior students

Tuition (dollars)

T_2

MC

D

MR

0   Q_2

Quantity of openings

© Cengage Learning®

- **Monopoly disadvantages** include the following: (1) a monopolist charges a higher price and produces less output than a perfectly competitive firm, (2) resource allocation is inefficient because the monopolist produces less than if competition existed, (3) monopoly produces higher long-run profits than if competition existed, and (4) monopoly transfers income from consumers to producers to a greater degree than under perfect competition.

Monopoly Disadvantages

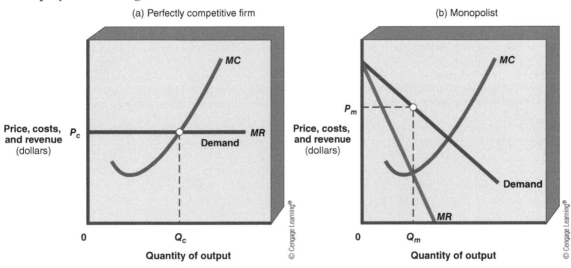

(a) Perfectly competitive firm

MC

Price, costs, and revenue (dollars)

P_c

MR

Demand

0   Q_c

Quantity of output

© Cengage Learning®

(b) Monopolist

MC

P_m

Price, costs, and revenue (dollars)

Demand

MR

0   Q_m

Quantity of output

© Cengage Learning®

Study Questions and Problems

1. Using the three characteristics of monopoly, explain why each of the following is a monopolist:
   a. Local water service
   b. San Francisco 49ers football team
   c. U.S. Postal Service
2. Why is the demand curve facing a monopolist downward sloping while the demand curve facing a perfectly competitive firm is horizontal?
3. Suppose an investigator finds that the prices charged for drugs at a hospital are higher than the prices charged for the same products at drugstores in the area served by the hospital. What might explain this situation?
4. Explain why you agree or disagree with the following statements:
   a. "All monopolies are created by the government."
   b. "The monopolist charges the highest possible price."
   c. "The monopolist never takes a loss."
5. Suppose the average cost of producing a kilowatt-hour of electricity is lower for one firm than for another firm serving the same market. Without the government granting a franchise to one of these competing power companies, explain why a single seller is likely to emerge in the long run.
6. Use the following demand schedule for a monopolist to calculate total revenue and marginal revenue. For each price, indicate whether demand is elastic, unit elastic, or inelastic. Using the data from the demand schedule, graph the demand curve, the marginal revenue curve, and the total revenue curve. Identify the elastic, unit elastic, and inelastic segments along the demand curve.

Price (P)	Quantity Demanded (Q)	Total Revenue (TR)	Marginal Revenue (MR)	Price Elasticity of Demand (E_d)
$5.00	0	$_____	$_____	_____
4.50	1	_____	_____	_____
4.00	2	_____	_____	_____
3.50	3	_____	_____	_____
3.00	4	_____	_____	_____
2.50	5	_____	_____	_____
2.00	6	_____	_____	_____
1.50	7	_____	_____	_____
1.00	8	_____	_____	_____
0.50	9	_____	_____	_____
0	10	_____	_____	_____

7. Make the unrealistic assumption that production is costless for the monopolist in question 6. Given the data from the above demand schedule, what price will the monopolist charge and how much output should the firm produce? How much profit will the firm earn? When marginal cost is above zero, what will be the effect on the price and output of the monopolist?
8. Explain why a monopolist would never produce in the inelastic range of the demand curve.
9. In each of the following cases, state whether the monopolist would increase or decrease output:
   a. Marginal revenue exceeds marginal cost at the output produced.
   b. Marginal cost exceeds marginal revenue at the output produced.
10. Suppose the demand and cost curves for a monopolist are as shown in Exhibit 8-10. Explain what price the monopolist should charge and how much output it should produce.
11. Which of the following constitute price discrimination and which does not?
    a. A department store has a 25 percent off sale.
    b. A publisher sells economics textbooks at a lower price in North Carolina than in New York.
    c. The Japanese sell cars at higher prices in the United States than in Japan.

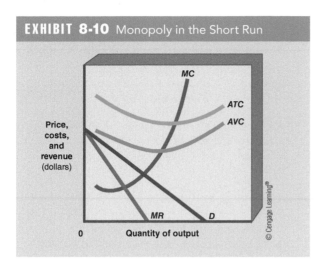

EXHIBIT 8-10 Monopoly in the Short Run

© Cengage Learning®

12. Suppose the candy bar industry approximates a perfectly competitive industry. Suppose also that a single firm buys all the assets of the candy bar firms and establishes a monopoly. Contrast these two market structures with respect to price, output, and allocation of resources. Draw a graph of the market demand and market supply for candy bars before and after the takeover.

13. Name three places you frequent that use price discrimination and explain the discrimination used.

Sample Quiz

1. The monopolist faces
   a. a perfectly inelastic demand curve.
   b. a perfectly elastic demand curve.
   c. the entire market demand curve.
   d. All of the answers above are correct.
2. To maximize its profit, a monopoly should choose a price where demand is
   a. elastic.
   b. inelastic.
   c. unitary elastic.
   d. vertical.
3. When marginal revenue is zero for a monopolist facing a downward-sloping straight-line demand curve, the price elasticity of demand is
   a. greater than 1.
   b. equal to 1.
   c. less than 2.
   d. equal to 0.
4. Both a perfectly competitive firm and a monopolist
   a. always earn an economic profit.
   b. maximize profit by setting marginal cost equal to marginal revenue.
   c. maximize profit by setting marginal cost equal to average total cost.
   d. are price takers.
5. Suppose a monopolist's demand curve lies below its average variable cost curve. The firm will

a. stay in operation in the short run.
b. earn an economic profit.
c. earn an economic profit in the long run.
d. shut down.

6. Which of the following statements *best* describes the price, output, and profit conditions of monopoly?
   a. Price will equal marginal cost at the profit-maximizing level of output and profits will be positive in the long run.
   b. Price will always equal average variable cost in the short run and either profits or losses may result in the long run.
   c. In the long run, positive economic profit will be earned.
   d. All of the answers above are correct.
7. Which of the following is *true* for the monopolist?
   a. Marginal revenue is less than the price charged.
   b. Economic profit is possible in the long run.
   c. Profit maximizing or loss minimizing occurs when marginal revenue equals marginal cost.
   d. All of the answers above are correct.
8. Although a monopoly can charge any price it wishes, it chooses
   a. the highest price.
   b. price equal to marginal cost.
   c. the price that maximizes profit.
   d. competitive prices.
   e. a fair price.

9. As shown in Exhibit 8-11, the profit-maximizing price for the monopolist is
    a. OP_1.
    b. OP_2.
    c. OP_3.
    d. OP_4.
    e. OP_5.

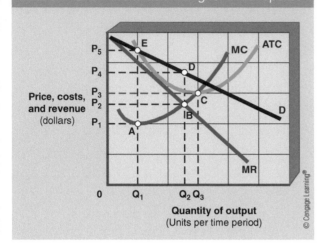

EXHIBIT 8-11 Profit Maximizing for a Monopolist

10. As shown in Exhibit 8-11, if the monopolist produces the profit-maximizing output, total revenue is the rectangular area
    a. OQ_1AP_1.
    b. OQ_2BP_2.
    c. OQ_3CP_3.
    d. OQ_2DP_4.
11. As shown in Exhibit 8-11, the monopolist's total cost is which of the following areas?
    a. P_1AEP_5.
    b. P_2BDP_4.
    c. P_3CDP_5.
    d. P_4DEP_5.
    e. None of the answers above are correct.
12. The profit-maximizing output for the monopolist in Exhibit 8-11 is
    a. zero.
    b. OQ_1.
    c. OQ_2
    d. OQ_3.

13. As shown in Exhibit 8-11, if the monopolist produces the profit-maximizing output, total revenue is the rectangular area
    a. $OQAP_1$.
    b. OQ_2BP_2.
    c. OQ_3CP_3.
    d. OQ_2DP_4.
14. As shown in Exhibit 8-11, the monopolist's profit maximizing price-quantity point is
    a. A.
    b. B.
    c. C.
    d. D.
    e. E.
15. Suppose a monopolist charges a price corresponding to the intersection of marginal cost and marginal revenue. If the price is between its average variable cost and average total cost curves, the firm will
    a. earn an economic profit.
    b. stay in operation in the short run, but shut down in the long run if demand remains the same.
    c. shut down.
    d. None of the answers above are correct.
16. The act of buying a commodity in one market at a lower price and selling it in another market at a higher price is known as
    a. buying long.
    b. selling short.
    c. a tariff.
    d. arbitrage.
17. One necessary condition for effective price discrimination is
    a. identical tastes among buyers.
    b. difference in the price elasticity of demand among buyers.
    c. a single, homogeneous market.
    d. two or more markets with easy resale of products between them.
18. An example of price discrimination is the price charged for
    a. an economics textbook at a campus bookstore.
    b. gasoline.
    c. theater tickets that offer lower prices for children.
    d. a postage stamp.

19. Suppose a monopolist and a perfectly competitive firm have the same cost curves. The monopolistic firm would
    a. charge a lower price than the perfectly competitive firm.
    b. charge a higher price than the perfectly competitive firm.
    c. charge the same price as the perfectly competitive firm.
    d. refuse to operate in the short run unless an economic profit could be made.

20. Suppose there are two markets for football games (1) rich alumni fully as committed as the lower-income students to their alma mater, and (2) students. Based on this information, which market will have the lower price elasticity of demand and pays the higher price if the university can price-discriminate?
    a. The student market.
    b. The alumni markets.

Monopolistic Competition and Oligopoly

In this chapter, you will learn to solve these economics puzzles:

- Why will Ivan's Oyster Bar make zero economic profit in the long run?
- Why do OPEC and other cartels tend to break down?
- Are Cheerios, Rice Krispies, and other brands sold by firms in the breakfast cereal industry produced under monopolistic competition or oligopoly?
- How does the NCAA Final Four basketball tournament involve imperfect competition?

CHAPTER PREVIEW

Suppose your favorite restaurant is Ivan's Oyster Bar. Ivan's does not fit either of the two extreme models studied in the previous two chapters. Instead, Ivan's characteristics are a blend of monopoly and perfect competition. For starters, like a monopolist, Ivan's demand curve is downward sloping. This means Ivan's is a *price maker* because it can charge a higher price for seafood and lose some customers, but many loyal customers will keep coming. The reason is that Ivan's distinguishes its product from the competition by advertising, first-rate service, a great salad bar, and other attributes. In short, like a monopolist, Ivan's has a degree of *market power*, which allows it to restrict output in order to maximize profit. But like a perfectly competitive firm and unlike a monopolist, Ivan's is not the only place to buy a seafood dinner in town. It must share the market with many other restaurants within an hour's drive.

The small Ivan's Oyster Bars and the gigantic Microsofts of the world represent most of the firms with which you deal. These firms compete in two different market structures: *monopolistic competition* or *oligopoly*.

Ivan's operates in the former, and Microsoft belongs to the latter. The theories of perfect competition and monopoly from the previous two chapters will help you understand the impact of monopolistic competition and oligopoly market structures on the price and output decisions of real-world firms.

9-1   THE MONOPOLISTIC COMPETITION MARKET STRUCTURE

Monopolistic competition A market structure characterized by (1) many small sellers, (2) a differentiated product, and (3) easy market entry and exit.

Economists define monopolistic competition as a market structure characterized by (1) many small sellers, (2) a differentiated product, and (3) easy market entry and exit. Monopolistic competition fits numerous real-world industries. The following is a brief explanation of each characteristic.

9-1a   Many Small Sellers

Under monopolistic competition, as under perfect competition, the exact number of firms cannot be stated. But in monopolistic competition, the number of sellers is smaller than in perfect competition. In this market structure, consumers have many different varieties of products from which to choose, and the prices are competitive. No single seller has a large enough share of the market to control prices. Ivan's Oyster Bar, described in the chapter preview, is an example of a monopolistic competitor. Ivan assumes that his restaurant can set prices slightly higher or improve service *independently* without fear that competitors will react by changing their prices or giving better service. Thus, if any single seafood restaurant raises its price, the going market price for seafood dinners increases by a very small amount.

> **CONCLUSION** The many-sellers condition is met when each firm is so small relative to the total market that its pricing decisions have a negligible effect on the market price.

9-1b   Differentiated Product

Product differentiation The process of creating real or apparent differences between goods and services.

The key feature of monopolistic competition is product differentiation. Product differentiation is the process of creating real or apparent differences between goods and services. A differentiated product has close, but not perfect, substitutes. Although the products of each firm are highly similar, the consumer views them as somewhat different or distinct. There may be 25 seafood restaurants in a given city, but they are not all the same. They differ in location, atmosphere, quality of food, quality of service, and so on.

Product differentiation can be real or imagined. It does not matter which is correct so long as consumers believe such differences exist. For example, many customers think Ivan's has the best seafood in town even though other restaurants offer a similar product. The importance of this viewpoint is consumers are willing to pay a slightly higher price for Ivan's seafood. This gives Ivan the incentive to appear on local TV cooking shows and to buy ads showing him personally catching the seafood he serves.

> **CONCLUSION** When a product is differentiated, buyers are not indifferent as to which seller's product they buy.

Nonprice competition The situation in which a firm competes using advertising, packaging, product development, better quality, and better service rather than lower prices.

The example of Ivan's restaurant makes it clear that under monopolistic competition rivalry centers on nonprice competition in addition to price competition. With nonprice competition, a firm competes using advertising, packaging, product development, better quality, and better service, rather than lower prices. Nonprice competition is an important characteristic of monopolistic competition that distinguishes it from perfect competition and monopoly. Under perfect competition, there is no nonprice competition because the product is identical for all firms. Likewise, the monopolist has little incentive to engage in nonprice competition because it sells a unique product.

9-1c Easy Entry and Exit

Unlike a monopoly, firms in a monopolistically competitive market face low barriers to entry. But entry into a monopolistically competitive market is not quite as easy as entry into a perfectly competitive market. Persons who want to enter the seafood restaurant business can get loans, lease space, and start serving seafood without too much trouble. However, these new seafood restaurants may at first have difficulty attracting consumers because of Ivan's established reputation as the best seafood restaurant in town. Ivan's product is therefore differentiated.

Monopolistic competition is by far the most common market structure in the United States. Examples include retail firms, such as grocery stores, hair salons, gas stations, stores, diet centers, and restaurants.

9-1d The Monopolistically Competitive Firm as a Price Maker

Given the characteristics of monopolistic competition, you might think the monopolistic competitor is a *price taker*, but it is not. The primary reason is that its product is differentiated. This gives the monopolistically competitive firm, like the monopolist, limited control over its price. When the price is raised, brand loyalty ensures some customers will remain steadfast. As for a monopolist, the demand curve and the corresponding marginal revenue curve for a monopolistically competitive firm are downward sloping. But the existence of close substitutes causes the demand curve for the monopolistically competitive firm to be more elastic than the demand curve for a monopolist. When Ivan's raises its prices 10 percent, the quantity of seafood dinners demanded declines, say, 30 percent. Instead, if Ivan's had a monopoly, no close substitutes would exist, and consumers would be less sensitive to price changes. As a monopolist, the same 10 percent price hike might lose Ivan's only, say, 15 percent of its quantity of seafood dinners demanded.

> **CONCLUSION** The demand curve for a monopolistically competitive firm is less elastic (steeper) than for a perfectly competitive firm and more elastic (flatter) than for a monopolist.

9-2 PRICE AND OUTPUT DECISIONS FOR A MONOPOLISTICALLY COMPETITIVE FIRM

Now we are prepared to develop the short-run and long-run graphical models for monopolistic competition. In the short run, you will see that monopolistic competition resembles monopoly. In the long run, however, entry by new firms leads to a more competitive market structure. This section presents a graphical analysis that shows why a monopolistically competitive firm is part perfectly competitive and part monopolistic.

9-2a Monopolistic Competition in the Short Run

Exhibit 9-1 shows the short-run equilibrium position for Ivan's Oyster Bar—a typical firm under monopolistic competition. As explained earlier, the demand curve slopes downward because customers believe, rightly or wrongly, that Ivan's product is a little better than its competitors' products. Customers like Ivan's family atmosphere, location, and quality of service. These nonprice factors differentiate Ivan's product and allow the restaurant to raise the price of sautéed alligator, shrimp, and oysters at least slightly without losing many sales.

Social Networking Sites: The New Advertising Game
Applicable concept: product differentiation

A key characteristic of the market structures discussed in this chapter is that they use advertising to promote product differentiation, which is a form of nonprice competition. The television commercial is considered the most effective method of mass-market advertising. This explains why TV networks charge such high prices for commercial airtime during prominent events, such as the Super Bowl game. However, the days when television commercials dominate the advertising world could be fading away. Don't want to be bothered by those advertisements? It's easy: Just press the fast-forward button on the remote of a digital video recorder (DVR). Advertisers are therefore competing to get the attention of consumers by tapping into the popularity of such social-networking sites as Facebook, Twitter, MySpace, and YouTube. These sites connect individuals who interact through personal profiles, games, video clips, and more. There are also niche sites focused on very specific activities for a hyper-targeted audience. For example, Dogster.com is a site for dog lovers, and Zappos.com is a popular site for women's and men's shoes. Product Wiki is a

resource for shoppers. It gives access to product reviews and lets you compare prices. Other new forms of advertisement include ads on apps, such as Pandora (music), used on iPhones, iPads, and other smartphones.

The challenge for Web economy entrepreneurs is to earn profits by differentiating their product and creating innovative ways to include advertising. The search engine is a highly successful business model. If someone Googles for golf clubs, sponsored links for golf clubs appear on the screen. Social networks provide the prospect of tailoring ads to people's specific interests. Now suppose a golf club company pays Facebook, the crown jewel of social networking, for a page where you and your friends can register and play a video game of golf. What does the company get out of it? A database of tens of thousands of names, all potential customers? Another form of advertising is called "retargeting" ads. Suppose you browse a swimsuit on Nordstrom.com and then an ad for this swimsuit shows up on your Facebook page. Do users enjoy personalized ads or are they alienated by such intrusive tracking?

Some ideas are not winners. Facebook implemented a new approach that informed friends whenever a member purchased something from online retailers. Consumers protested this was an invasion of privacy, and the program was abandoned. Now consider this idea: Imagine being at a concert and text messaging a shout-out to your friends. Your message appears during the concert next to the stage on a big screen with a large ad from a company. Is this imposing a negative externality that distracts others in the audience from the performance? And in 2012, GM decided to cancel its advertising because it thought Facebook ads had little effect on car purchases.

> **ANALYZE the ISSUE** Advertising is tasteless, offensive, and a nuisance that wastes resources. Give three arguments against this idea.

Like the monopolist, the monopolistically competitive firm maximizes short-run profit by following the $MR = MC$ rule. In this case, the marginal cost (MC) and marginal revenue (MR) curves intersect at an output of 600 seafood meals per week. The price per meal of $18 is the point on the demand curve corresponding to this level of output. Because the price exceeds the average total cost (ATC) of $15 per meal, Ivan's earns a short-run economic profit of $1,800 per week. As under monopoly, if the price equals the ATC curve, the firm earns a short-run normal profit. If the price is below the ATC curve, the firm suffers a short-run loss, and if the price is below the average variable cost (AVC) curve, the firm shuts down.

9-2b Monopolistic Competition in the Long Run

The monopolistically competitive firm, unlike a monopolist, will not earn an economic profit in the long run. Rather, like a perfect competitor, the monopolistically competitive firm earns only a normal profit (that is, zero economic profit) in the long run. Recall from Chapter 6 on production costs that *normal profit* is the minimum profit necessary to keep a firm in operation. The reason is that

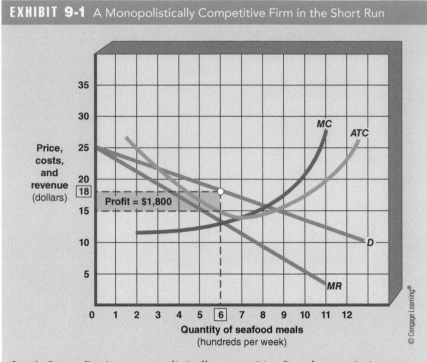

EXHIBIT 9-1 A Monopolistically Competitive Firm in the Short Run

Ivan's Oyster Bar is a monopolistically competitive firm that maximizes short-run profit by producing the output where marginal revenue equals marginal cost. At an output of 600 seafood dinners per week, the price of $18 per dinner is dictated by the firm's demand curve. Given the firm's costs, output, and prices, Ivan's will earn a short-run profit of $1,800 per week.

short-run profits and easy entry attract new firms into the industry. When Ivan's Oyster Bar earns a short-run profit, as shown in Exhibit 9-1, two things happen. First, Ivan's demand curve shifts downward as some of each seafood restaurant's market share is taken away by new firms seeking profit. Second, Ivan's, and other seafood restaurants as well, tries to recapture market share by advertising, improving its decor, and utilizing other forms of nonprice competition. As a result, long-run average costs increase, and the firm's *LRAC* curve shifts upward.

The combination of the leftward shift in the firm's demand curve and the upward shift in its *LRAC* curve continues in the long run until the monopolistic competitive firm earns zero or normal economic profit. The result is the long-run equilibrium condition shown in Exhibit 9-2. At a price of $17 per meal, the demand curve is tangent to the *LRAC* curve at the *MR = MC* output of 500 meals per week. Once long-run equilibrium is achieved in a monopolistically competitive industry, there is no incentive for new firms to enter or established firms to leave.

9-3 COMPARING MONOPOLISTIC COMPETITION AND PERFECT COMPETITION

Some economists argue that the long-run equilibrium condition for a monopolistically competitive firm, as shown in Exhibit 9-2, results in poor economic performance. Other economists contend that the benefits of a monopolistically competitive industry outweigh the costs. In this section, we again use the standard of perfect competition to understand both sides of this debate.

EXHIBIT 9-2 A Monopolistically Competitive Firm in the Long Run

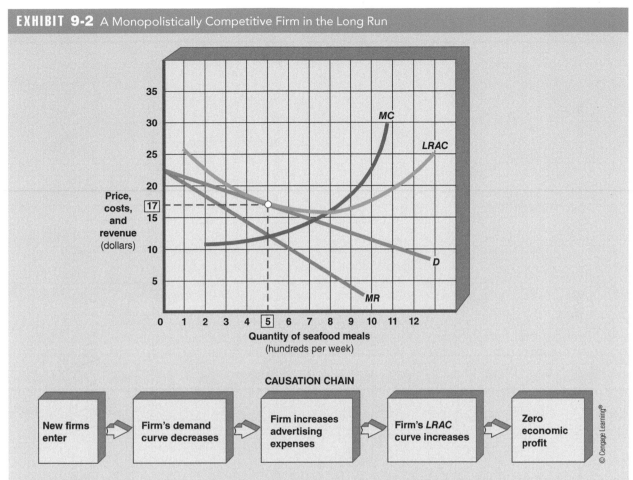

CAUSATION CHAIN

New firms enter → Firm's demand curve decreases → Firm increases advertising expenses → Firm's *LRAC* curve increases → Zero economic profit

In the long run, the entry of new seafood restaurants decreases the demand for Ivan's seafood. In addition, Ivan's shifts its average cost curve upward by increasing advertising and other expenses in order to compete against new entrants. In the long run, the firm earns zero economic profit at a price of $17 per seafood meal and produces an *MR = MC* output of 500 meals per week.

9-3a The Monopolistic Competitor as a Resource Misallocator

Like a monopolist, the monopolistically competitive firm fails the efficiency test. As shown in Exhibit 9-2, under monopolistic competition, Ivan's charges a price that exceeds the marginal cost. Thus, the value to consumers of the last meal produced is greater than the cost of producing it. Ivan's could devote more resources and produce more seafood dinners. To sell this additional output, Ivan's must move downward along its demand curve by reducing the $17 price per meal. As a result, customers would purchase the additional benefits of consuming more seafood meals. However, Ivan's uses less resources and restricts output to 500 seafood meals per week in order to maximize profits where *MR = MC*.

9-3b Monopolistic Competition Means Less Output for More

Exhibit 9-3(a) reproduces the long-run condition from Exhibit 9-2. Exhibit 9-3(b) assumes that the seafood restaurant market is perfectly competitive. Recall from Chapter 7 that the characteristics of perfect competition include the condition

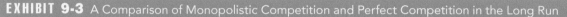

EXHIBIT 9-3 A Comparison of Monopolistic Competition and Perfect Competition in the Long Run

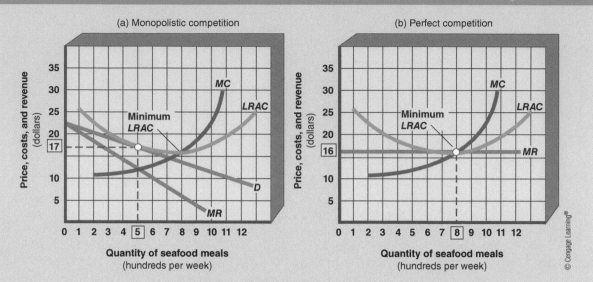

(a) Monopolistic competition

(b) Perfect competition

Quantity of seafood meals
(hundreds per week)

Quantity of seafood meals
(hundreds per week)

In part (a), Ivan's Oyster Bar is a monopolistically competitive firm that sets its price at $17 per seafood meal and produces 500 meals per week. As a monopolistic competitor, Ivan's earns zero economic profit in the long run and does not produce at the lowest point on its *LRAC* curve.

Under conditions of perfect competition in part (b), Ivan's becomes a price taker, rather than a price maker. Here the firm faces a flat demand curve at a price of $16 per seafood meal, which is the equilibrium price set by market demand and supply curves. The output is 800 meals per week, which corresponds to the lowest point on the *LRAC* curve. Therefore, the price is lower, and the excess capacity of 300 meals per week is utilized when Ivan's operates as a perfectly competitive firm, rather than as a monopolistically competitive firm.

that customers perceive seafood meals as *homogeneous* and, as a result, no firms engage in advertising. Because we now assume for the sake of argument that Ivan's product is identical to all other seafood restaurants, Ivan's becomes a *price taker*. In this case, the industry's long-run supply and demand curves set an equilibrium price of $16 per meal. Consequently, Ivan's faces a horizontal demand curve with the price equal to marginal revenue. Also recall from Chapter 7 that long-run equilibrium for a perfectly competitive firm is established by the entry of new firms until the minimum point of $16 per meal on the firm's *LRAC* curve equals the price, *MR* and *MC*. Stated as a formula:

$$P = MR = MC = LRAC$$

A comparison of parts (a) and (b) of Exhibit 9-3 reveals two important points. First, both the monopolistic competitor and the perfect competitor earn zero economic profit in the long run. Second, the long-run equilibrium output of the monopolistically competitive firm is to the left of the minimum point on the *LRAC* curve and the price exceeds *MC*. Like a monopolist, the monopolistically competitive firm therefore charges a higher price and produces less output than a perfectly competitive firm.

In our example, Ivan's would charge $1 less per meal and produce 300 more seafood meals per week in a perfectly competitive market. The extra 300 meals not produced are *excess capacity*, which represents underutilized resources. The criticism of monopolistic competition, then, is that there are too many firms producing too little output at inflated prices and wasting society's resources in the process. For example, on many nights, there are not enough customers for all the restaurants in town. Servers, cooks, tables, and other resources are therefore underutilized. With fewer firms, each would produce a greater output at a lower price and with a lower average cost.

Opinions vary concerning whether benefits of monopolistic competition exceed the costs. Having many seafood restaurants offers consumers more choice and variety of output. Having Ivan's Oyster Bar and many similar competitors gives consumers extra quality and service options. If you do not like Ivan's sautéed alligator, you may be able to find another restaurant that serves this dish. Also, having many restaurants in a market saves consumers' valuable time. Chances are that you will not shed crocodile tears because the travel time required to enjoy an alligator meal is lower.

9-4 OLIGOPOLY—COMPETITION AMONG A FEW

Now we turn to oligopoly, an imperfectly competitive market structure in which a few large firms dominate the market. Many manufacturing industries, such as steel, aluminum, automobiles, aircraft, drugs, and tobacco, are best described as oligopolistic. This is the "big business" market structure, in which firms aggressively compete by bombarding us with advertising on television and filling our mailboxes with junk mail.

Oligopoly A market structure characterized by (1) few large sellers, (2) either a homogeneous or a differentiated product, and (3) difficult market entry.

Economists define an oligopoly as a market structure characterized by (1) few large sellers, (2) either a homogeneous or a differentiated product, and (3) difficult market entry. Like monopolistic competition, oligopoly is found in real-world industries. Let's examine each characteristic.

9-4a Few Sellers

Oligopoly is competition "among the few." Here we use the "Big Three" or "Big Four" to mean that three or four firms dominate an industry. But what does "a few" firms really mean? Does this mean at least two, but less than ten? As with other market structures, there is no specific number of firms that must dominate an industry before it is an oligopoly. Basically, an oligopoly is a consequence of mutual interdependence. Mutual interdependence is a condition in which an action by one firm may cause a reaction from other firms. Stated another way, a market structure with a few powerful firms makes it easier for oligopolists to collude. The large number of firms under perfect competition or monopolistic competition and the absence of other firms in monopoly rule out mutual interdependence and collusion in these market structures.

Mutual interdependence A condition in which an action by one firm may cause a reaction from other firms.

When General Motors (GM) considers a price hike or a style change, it must predict how Ford, Chrysler, and Toyota will change their prices and styling in response. Therefore, the decisions under oligopoly are more complex than under perfect competition, monopoly, and monopolistic competition.

> **CONCLUSION** The few-sellers condition is met when these few firms are so large relative to the total market that they can affect the market price.

9-4b Homogeneous or Differentiated Product

Under oligopoly, firms can produce either a homogeneous (identical) or a differentiated product. The steel produced by USX is identical to the steel from Republic Steel. The oil sold by Saudi Arabia is identical to the oil from Iran. Similarly, zinc, copper, and aluminum are standardized or homogeneous products. But cars produced by the major automakers are differentiated products. Tires, detergents, and breakfast cereals are also differentiated products sold in oligopolies.

> **CONCLUSION** Buyers in an oligopoly may or may not be indifferent as to which seller's product they buy.

9-4c Difficult Entry

Similar to monopoly, formidable barriers to entry in an oligopoly protect firms from new entrants. These barriers include exclusive financial requirements, control over an essential resource, patent rights, and other legal barriers. But the most significant barrier to entry in an oligopoly is *economies of scale*. For example, larger automakers achieve lower average total costs than those incurred by smaller automakers. Consequently, the U.S. auto industry has moved over time from more than 60 firms to only three major U.S.-owned firms.

9-5 PRICE AND OUTPUT DECISIONS FOR AN OLIGOPOLIST

Mutual interdependence among firms in an oligopoly makes this market structure more difficult to analyze than perfect competition, monopoly, or monopolistic competition. The price–output decision of an oligopolist is not simply a matter of charging the price where $MR = MC$. Making price and output decisions in an oligopoly is like playing a game of chess. One player's move depends on the anticipated reactions of the opposing player. One player thinks, "If I move my rook here, my opponent might move her knight there." Likewise, a firm in an oligopoly can have many different possible reactions to the price, nonprice, and output changes of another firm. Consequently, there are different oligopoly models because no single model can cover all cases. The following is a discussion of four well-known oligopoly models: (1) nonprice competition, (2) price leadership, (3) the cartel, and (4) game theory.

9-5a Nonprice Competition

Major oligopolists often compete using advertising and product differentiation. Instead of "slugging it out" with price cuts, oligopolists may try to capture business from their rivals through better advertising campaigns and improved products. This model of behavior explains why advertising expenditures often are large in the cigarette, soft drink, athletic shoe, and automobile industries. It also explains why the research and development (R&D) function is so important to oligopolists. For example, much engineering effort is aimed largely at developing new products and improving existing products.

Why might oligopolists compete through nonprice competition, rather than price competition? The answer is that each oligopolist perceives that its rivals will easily and quickly match any price reduction. In contrast, it is much more difficult to combat a clever and/or important product improvement.

9-5b Price Leadership

Price leadership A pricing strategy in which a dominant firm sets the price for an industry and the other firms follow.

Without formal agreement, firms can play a game of follow-the-leader that economists call **price leadership**. Price leadership is a pricing strategy in which a dominant firm sets the price for an industry and the other firms follow. Following this tactic, firms in an industry simply match the price changes of perhaps, but not necessarily, the biggest firm. Price leadership is not uncommon. USX Corporation (steel), Alcoa (aluminum), DuPont (nylon), R. J. Reynolds (cigarettes), and Goodyear Tire and Rubber (tires) are other examples of price leaders in U.S. industries.

9-5c The Cartel

The price leadership model assumes that firms do not collude to avoid price competition. Instead, firms avoid price wars by informally playing by the established

GLOBAL ECONOMICS

Major Cartels in Global Markets

Applicable concept: cartel

Cartels flourished in Germany and other European countries in the first half of the twentieth century. Many had international memberships. After World War II, European countries passed laws against such restrictive trade practices. The following are some of the most important cartels today.

- **Organization of Petroleum Exporting Countries (OPEC).** OPEC was created by Iran, Iraq, Kuwait, Saudi Arabia, and Venezuela in Baghdad in 1960. Today, the Vienna-based OPEC's membership consists of 12 countries that control about 70 percent of the world's oil reserves. Cartels are anticonsumer. OPEC's objective is to set oil production quotas for its members and, in turn, influence global prices of oil and gasoline.
- **International Telecommunication Union (ITU).** Perhaps the world's least-known and most effective cartel

of about 193 member nations is based in Geneva, Switzerland. The ITU was founded in 1865 and became an agency of the United Nations in 1947. It is responsible for international regulations and standards governing global telecommunications, including satellite communication, Internet access, radio, and television broadcasting.
- **International Air Transport Association (IATA).** Originally founded in 1919, most of the world's international airlines belong to the IATA. This cartel headquartered in Montreal sets international airline ticket prices and safety and security standards for passenger and cargo shipping. It controls access to airports, and challenges rules and regulations considered to be unreasonable. The IATA also is concerned with minimizing the impact of air transport on the environment.

Cartel A group of firms that formally agree to reduce competition by coordinating control the price and output of a product.

GLOBAL ECONOMICS

pricing rules. Another way to avoid price wars is for oligopolists to agree to a peace treaty. Instead of allowing mutual interdependence to lead to rivalry, firms openly or secretly conspire to form a monopoly called a cartel. A cartel is a group of firms that formally agree to reduce competition by coordinating the price and output of a product. The goal of a cartel is to reap monopoly profits by replacing competition with cooperation. Cartels are illegal in the United States, but not in other nations. The best-known cartel is the Organization of Petroleum Exporting Countries (OPEC). The members of OPEC divide "black gold" output among themselves according to quotas openly agreed upon at meetings of the OPEC oil ministries. Saudi Arabia is the largest producer and has the largest quota. The Global Economics feature provides a brief summary of some of today's major global cartels.

Using Exhibit 9-4, we can demonstrate how a cartel works and why keeping members from cheating is a problem. Our analysis begins before oil-producing firms have formed a cartel. Assume each firm has the same cost curve shown in the exhibit. Price wars have driven each firm to charge \$75 a barrel, which is equal to the minimum point on its *LRAC* curve. Because oil is a standardized product, as under perfect competition, each firm fears raising its price because it will lose all its customers. Thus, the typical firm is in long-run competitive equilibrium at a price of \$75 per barrel (MR_1), producing 6 million barrels per day. In this condition, economic profits are zero, and the firms decide to organize a meeting of all oil producers to establish a cartel.

Now assume the cartel is formed and each firm agrees to reduce its output to 4 million barrels per day and charge \$120 per barrel. If no firms cheat, each firm faces a higher horizontal demand curve, represented by MR_2. At the cartel price, each firm earns an economic profit of \$120 million, rather than a normal profit. But what if one firm decides to cheat on the cartel agreement by stepping up its output while other firms stick to their quotas? Output corresponding to the point at which $MR_2 = MC$ is 8 million barrels per day. If a cheating firm expands output to this level, it can double its profit by earning an extra \$120 million. Of

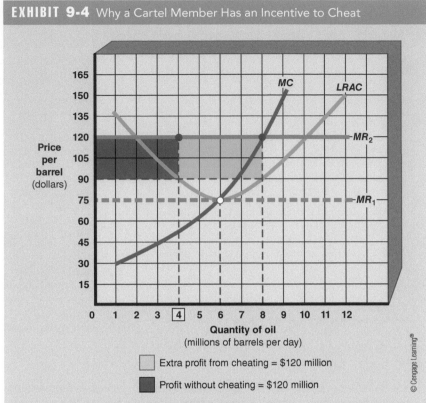

EXHIBIT 9-4 Why a Cartel Member Has an Incentive to Cheat

☐ Extra profit from cheating = $120 million

■ Profit without cheating = $120 million

A representative oil producer operating in a perfectly competitive industry would be in long-run equilibrium at a price of $75 per barrel, producing 6 million barrels per day and making zero economic profit. A cartel can agree to raise the price of oil from $75 to $120 per barrel by restricting the firm to 4 million barrels per day. As a result of this quota, the cartel price is above $90 on the *LRAC* curve, and the firm earns a daily profit of $80 million. However, if the firm cheats on the cartel agreement, it will set the cartel price equal to the *MC* curve and earn a total profit of $240 million by adding an additional $120 million. If all firms cheat, the original long-run equilibrium will be reestablished.

course, if all firms cheat and the cartel breaks up, the price and output of each firm returns to the initial levels, and economic profit again falls to zero.

9-5d Game Theory

Game theory A model of the strategic moves and countermoves of rivals.

Game theory is a model of the strategic moves and countermoves of rivals. To illustrate, let's use a noncollusive example of Delta Air Lines competing with American Airlines. Each airline independently sets its fare, and Exhibit 9-5 is a *payoff matrix* that shows profit outcomes for the two airlines resulting from charging either a high fare or a low fare. If both charge the high fare in cell A, they split the market, and each makes a profit of $8 billion. If both decide to charge the low fare in cell D, they also split the market, and the profit for each falls to $5 billion. If one charges the high fare and the other charges the low fare in cell B or cell C, then the low-fare airline attracts most of the customers and earns the maximum possible profit of $10 billion, while the high-fare airline loses $2 billion.

EXHIBIT 9-5 A Two-Firm Payoff Matrix

	US Airways' options	
American Airlines' options	**High fare**	**Low fare**
High fare	*A* Delta Air Lines' profit = $8 billion American Airlines' profit = $8 billion	*B* Delta Air Lines' profit = $10 billion American Airlines' loss = −$2 billion
Low fare	*C* Delta Air Lines' loss = −$2 billion American Airlines' profit = $10 billion	*D* Delta Air Lines' profit = $5 billion American Airlines' profit = $5 billion

© Cengage Learning®

Game theory is a method of analyzing the oligopoly puzzle. Two fare options of charging either a high fare or a low fare are given for Delta Air Lines and American Airlines. The profit or loss that each earns in cells A–D depends on the pricing decisions of these two rivals. Their collective interest is best served in cell A where each charges the high fare and each makes the maximum profit of $8 billion. But once either airline independently seeks the higher profit of $10 billion by using a low-fare strategy in cell B or C, the other airline counters with a low fare, and both end up charging the low fare in cell D. As a result, mutual profits are $5 billion, rather than $8 billion in cell A. Cell D is the equilibrium outcome because both airlines fear changing the price and causing the other to counter.

Both rivals in our example are clearly *mutually interdependent* because an action by one firm may cause a reaction from the other firm. Suppose both airlines initially select the most mutually profitable solution and both charge the high fare in cell A. This outcome creates an incentive for either airline to charge a lower fare in cell B or cell C and earn the highest possible profit by pulling customers away from its rival. Consequently, assume the next day one airline cuts its fare to gain higher profits. In order to avoid losing customers, this action causes the other airline to counter with an equally low fare. Price competition has therefore forced both airlines to charge the low fare in cell D and earn less than maximum joint profits. Once cell D is reached, neither airline has an incentive to alter the fare either higher or lower because both fear their rival's countermoves. Note that when both firms charge the low fare in equilibrium at cell D, consumers benefit from not paying high fares in the other cells.

CONCLUSION The payoff matrix demonstrates why a competitive oligopoly tends to result in both rivals using a low-price strategy that does not maximize profits.

How can these oligopolists avoid the low-fare outcome in cell D and instead stabilize the more jointly profitable high-fare payoffs in cell A? One possible strategy is called *tit-for-tat*. Under this approach, a player will do whatever the other player did the last time. If one airline defects from cell A by cutting its fare to gain a profit advantage, the other competitor will also cut its fare. After repeated trials, these price cutting responses serve as a signal that says, "You are not going to get the best of me so move your fare up!" Once the defector responds by moving back to the high fare, the other airline cooperates and also moves to the high fare. The result is that both players return to cell A without a formal agreement.

Another informal approach is for rivals to coordinate their pricing decisions based on price leadership, as discussed earlier in this chapter. For example, one airline may be much more established or dominant, and the other airline follows whatever price the leader sets. Another approach would be to informally rotate the leadership. Thus, without a formal agreement, the leader sets the profit-maximizing high price in cell A and the other competitor follows. However, this system does not eliminate the threat that the price follower will cheat.

Finally, if cartels were legal in the United States, the airlines could collude and make a formal agreement that each will charge the high fare. However, as explained in the previous section, there is always the incentive for one firm to cheat by moving from cell A to either cell B or cell C, and therefore cartels tend to break down. A remedy might be for the rivals to agree on a penalty for any party that reneges by lowering its fare.

> **CONCLUSION** As long as the benefits exceed the costs, cheating can threaten formal or informal agreements among oligopolists to maximize joint profits.

9-6 AN EVALUATION OF OLIGOPOLY

Oligopoly is much more difficult to evaluate than other market structures. None of the models just presented gives a definite answer to the question of efficiency under oligopoly. Depending on the assumptions made, an oligopolist can behave much like a perfectly competitive firm or more like a monopoly. Nevertheless, let's assume some likely changes that occur if a perfectly competitive industry is suddenly turned into an oligopoly selling a differentiated product.

First, the price charged for the product will be higher than under perfect competition. The smaller the number of firms in an oligopoly and the more difficult it is to enter the industry, the higher the oligopoly price will be in comparison to the perfectly competitive price.

Second, an oligopoly is likely to spend money on advertising, product differentiation, and other forms of nonprice competition. These expenditures can shift the demand curve to the right. As a result, both price and output may be higher under oligopoly than under perfect competition.

Third, in the long run, a perfectly competitive firm earns zero economic profit. The oligopolist, however, can earn a higher profit because it is more difficult for competitors to enter the industry.

CHECKPOINT

Which Model Fits the Cereal Aisle?
As you walk along the cereal aisle, notice the many different cereals on the shelf. For example, you will probably see General Mills' Wheaties, Total, and Cheerios; Kellogg's Corn Flakes, Cracklin' Oat Bran, Frosted Flakes, and Rice Krispies; Quaker Oats's Cap'n Crunch and 100% Natural; and Post's Super Golden Crisp, to name only a few. There are many different brands of the same-product cereal on the shelves. Each brand is slightly different from the others. Is the breakfast cereal industry's market structure monopolistic competition or oligopoly?

9-7 REVIEW OF THE FOUR MARKET STRUCTURES

Now that we have completed the discussion of perfect competition, monopoly, monopolistic competition, and oligopoly, you are prepared to compare these four market structures. Exhibit 9-6 summarizes the characteristics and gives examples of each market structure.

EXHIBIT 9-6 Comparison of Market Structures

Market structure	Number of sellers	Type of product	Entry condition	Control of Price	Examples
Perfect competition	Large	Homogeneous	Very easy	Price taker	Agriculture*
Monopoly	One	Unique	Impossible	Price maker	Public utilities*
Monopolistic competition	Many	Differentiated	Easy	Price maker	Retail trade*
Oligopoly	Few	Homogeneous or differentiated	Difficult	Price maker	Auto, steel, oil

© Cengage Learning®

*In the absence of government intervention.

ECONOMICS IN PRACTICE

How Oligopolists Compete at the Final Four
Applicable concept: oligopoly

Suppose March Madness included your basketball team making it all the way to the Final Four and you were going to be there. Before leaving, you checked the official Web site and noticed a Coke ad giving a prize to the person who submitted the best video commercial for a new Coke product. But this was only the beginning of the Great Cola Wars. Shortly after leaving the plane at the airport, you encountered a group of students who were giving away huge inflatable plastic hands with index fingers sticking up in the air signaling that your team is number one. The plastic hands were imprinted with the Pepsi-Cola logo and your choice of a Final Four team. And the group was also giving away free ice-cold cans of Pepsi. As you walked along the streets to your hotel, giant inflatable "cans" of Pepsi appeared all over the downtown area on the sidewalks, and on top of gas stations. And not to be outdone, the entire side of a prominent three-story building was painted Coca-Cola red and white with the 64 NCAA basketball finalists and all the winners listed, bracket by bracket. Following the first-round games, painters were three stories up on

scaffolding filling in the Coke sign's brackets for the final two teams, in school colors no less. Inside the arena, the colas continued their battle by scrolling cola ads with other ads under the press rows along either side of the basketball court. This was indeed competition between showboating industry giants worthy of the Final Four competition among the basketball teams.

Many fascinating markets function during the Final Four basketball tournament, including competitive markets that determine prices for parking lots, restaurants, and tickets. (Recall the Checkpoint in Chapter 4 on ticket scalping.) Then there were the hotels surrounding the arena, which joined a centralized booking service. Each hotel had raised its normal price by 75 percent for the weekend.

ANALYZE the ISSUE In this feature, two forms of oligopoly were observed. Identify each of these forms and explain why it is being used by the oligopolists.

Key Concepts

Monopolistic competition
Product differentiation
Nonprice competition

Oligopoly
Mutual interdependence
Price leadership

Cartel
Game theory

Summary

- **Monopolistic competition** is a market structure characterized by (1) many small sellers, (2) a differentiated product, and (3) easy market entry and exit. Given these characteristics, firms in monopolistic competition have a negligible effect on the market price.

- **Product differentiation** is a key characteristic of monopolistic competition. It is the process of creating real or apparent differences between products.

- **Nonprice competition** includes advertising, packaging, product development, better quality, and better service. Under monopolistic competition and oligopoly, firms may compete using nonprice competition, rather than price competition.

- **Short-run equilibrium for a monopolistic competitor** can yield economic losses, zero economic profits, or economic profits. In the long run, monopolistic competitors make zero economic profits.

Short-Run Equilibrium for a Monopolistic Competitor

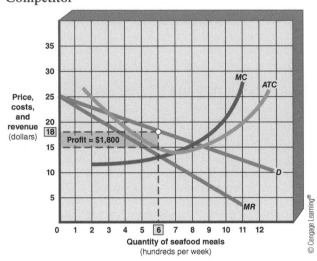

- **Comparing monopolistic competition with perfect competition,** we find that in the long run, the monopolistically competitive firm does not achieve allocative efficiency, charges a higher price, restricts output, and does not produce where average costs are at a minimum.

Comparison of Monopolistic Competition and Perfect Competition

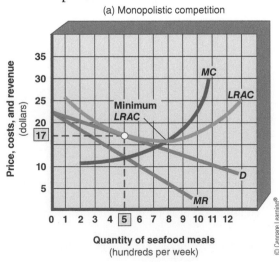

(a) Monopolistic competition

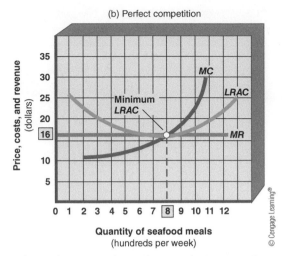

(b) Perfect competition

- **Oligopoly** is a market structure characterized by (1) few sellers, (2) either a homogeneous or a differentiated product, and (3) difficult market entry. Oligopolies are **mutually interdependent** because an action by one firm may cause a reaction from other firms.

- The **nonprice competition model** is a theory that might explain oligopolistic behavior. Under this theory, firms use advertising and product differentiation, rather than price reductions, to compete.

- **Price leadership** is another theory of pricing behavior under oligopoly. When a dominant firm in an industry raises or lowers its price, other firms follow suit.

- A **cartel** is a formal agreement among firms to set prices and output quotas. The goal is to maximize profits, but firms have an incentive to cheat, which is a constant threat to a cartel.

Cartel

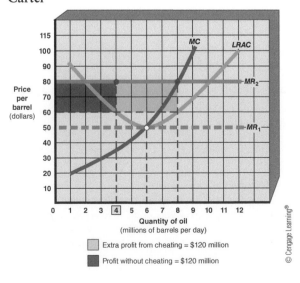

- **Game theory** reveals that (1) oligopolies are mutually interdependent in their pricing policies, (2) without collusion oligopoly prices and mutual profits are lower, and (3) oligopolists have a temptation to cheat on any collusive agreement.

- **Comparing oligopoly with perfect competition,** we find that the oligopolist allocates resources inefficiently, charges a higher price, and restricts output so that price may exceed average cost.

Study Questions and Problems

1. Compare the monopolistically competitive firm's demand curve to those of a perfect competitor and a monopolist.
2. Suppose the minimum point on the *LRAC* curve of a soft-drink firm's cola is $1 per liter. Under conditions of monopolistic competition, will the price of a liter bottle of cola in the long run be above $1, equal to $1, less than $1, or impossible to determine?
3. Exhibit 9-7 represents a monopolistically competitive firm in long-run equilibrium.

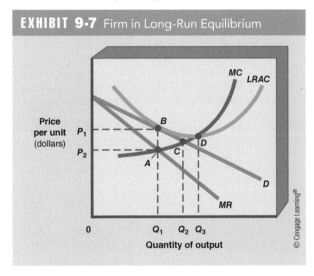

EXHIBIT 9-7 Firm in Long-Run Equilibrium

© Cengage Learning®

   a. Which price represents the long-run equilibrium price?
   b. Which quantity represents the long-run equilibrium output?
   c. At which quantity is the *LRAC* curve at its minimum?
   d. Is the long-run equilibrium price greater than, less than, or equal to the marginal cost of producing the equilibrium output?

4. Consider this statement: "Because price equals long-run average cost and profits are zero, a monopolistically competitive firm is efficient." Do you agree or disagree? Explain.

5. Assuming identical long-run cost curves, draw two graphs, and indicate the price and output that result in the long run under monopolistic competition and perfect competition. Evaluate the differences between these two market structures.
6. Draw a graph that shows how advertising affects a firm's *ATC* curve. Explain how advertising can lead to lower prices in a monopolistically competitive industry.
7. List four goods or services that you have purchased that were produced by an oligopolist. Why are these industries oligopolistic, rather than monopolistically competitive?
8. Why is mutual interdependence important under oligopoly, but not so important under perfect competition, monopoly, or monopolistic competition?
9. What might be a general distinction between oligopolists that advertise and those that do not?
10. Suppose Canon raised the price of its printers, but Hewlett-Packard (the largest seller) refused to follow. Two years later Canon cut its price, and Hewlett-Packard retaliated with an even deeper price cut, which Canon was forced to match. For the next five years, Hewlett-Packard raised its prices five times, and each time Canon followed suit within 24 hours. Does the pricing behavior of these computer industry firms follow the cartel model or the price leadership model? Why?
11. Evaluate the following statement: "A cartel will put an end to price war, which is a barbaric form of competition that benefits no one."
12. Assume the payoff matrix in Exhibit 9-5 applies to spending for advertising rather than airline fares. Substitute "Don't Advertise" for "High fare" and "Advertise" for "Low fare." Assume the same profit and loss figures in each cell, but substitute "Marlboro" for "Delta Air Lines," and "Camel's" for "American Airlines." Explain the dynamics of the model and why cigarette companies might be pleased with a government ban on all cigarette advertising.

Sample Quiz

1. Hair salons in cities are an illustration of
   a. perfect competition.
   b. monopoly.
   c. monopolistic competition.
   d. oligopoly.
2. Firms in a monopolistically competitive industry produce
   a. homogeneous goods and services.
   b. differentiated products.
   c. competitive goods only.
   d. consumption goods only.
3. Monopolistic competitive firms in the long run earn
   a. positive economic profits.
   b. zero pure economic profits.
   c. negative economic profits.
   d. None of the answers above are correct.
4. The theory of monopolistic competition predicts that in long-run equilibrium a monopolistically competitive firm will
   a. produce at the level in which price equals long-run average cost.
   b. operate at minimum long-run average cost.
   c. overutilize its insufficient capacity.
   d. None of the answers above are correct.
5. Which of the following statements *best* describes the price, output, and profit conditions of monopolistic competition?
   a. Price will equal marginal cost at the profit-maximizing level of output; profits will be positive in the long run.
   b. Price will always equal average variable cost in the short run and either profits or losses may result in the long run.
   c. Marginal revenue will equal marginal cost at the short run, profit-maximizing level of output; in the long run, economic profit will be zero.
   d. Marginal revenue will equal average total cost in the short run; long-run economic profits will be zero.
6. Entry of new firms will occur in a monopolistic competitive industry until
   a. marginal cost equals zero.
   b. marginal revenue equals zero.
   c. marginal revenue equals marginal cost.
   d. economic profit equals zero.
   e. economic profit is negative.

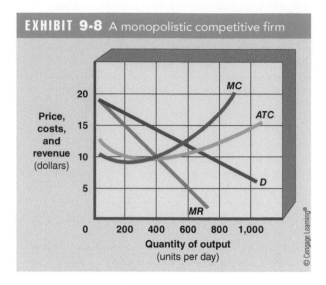

EXHIBIT 9-8 A monopolistic competitive firm

7. As presented in Exhibit 9-8, the short-run profit-maximizing output for the monopolistic competitive firm is
   a. zero units per day.
   b. 200 units per day.
   c. 400 units per day.
   d. 600 units per day.
8. As presented in Exhibit 9-8, the short-run profit per unit of output for the monopolistic competitive firm is
   a. zero.
   b. $5.
   c. $10.
   d. $15.
9. As represented in Exhibit 9-8, the maximum long-run economic profit earned by this monopolistic competitive firm is
   a. zero.
   b. $200 per day.
   c. $1,000 per day.
   d. $20,000 per day.
10. An oligopoly is a market structure in which
    a. one firm has 100 percent of a market.
    b. there are many small firms.
    c. there are many firms with no control over price.
    d. there are few firms selling either a homogeneous or differentiated product.
11. Mutual interdependence among firms in an oligopoly means that
    a. firms never practice price leadership.
    b. firms never form a cartel.
    c. it is difficult to know how firms will react to decisions of rivals.
    d. no formal agreement is possible among firms.

12. A common characteristic of oligopolies is
    a. interdependence in pricing decisions.
    b. independent pricing decisions.
    c. low industry concentration.
    d. few or no plant-level economies of scale.
13. Which of the following is an outcome of advertising for a monopolistically competitive firm?
    a. Long-run average costs shift downward.
    b. The firm's demand curve becomes flatter and shifts inward.
    c. The firm's demand curve keeps the same slope and shifts inward.
    d. Long-run average costs shift upward.
14. Which of the following is *true* about advertising?
    a. If monopolistically competitive firms compete through advertising, and if advertising requires sunk-cost investment and creates brand loyalty, then advertising can be an effective entry cost.
    b. Advertising may be the only way that a new entrant can penetrate a market dominated by long-established firms.
    c. Advertising has no impact on entry costs or market structure.
    d. Both a. and b. are correct.
15. Which of the following *best* describes a cartel?
    a. A group of monopolistically competitive firms that jointly reduce output and raise price in imitation of a monopolist. When entry is very costly, these high prices can persist.
    b. A group of cooperating oligopolists that jointly reduce output and raise price in imitation of a monopolist. When entry is very costly, these high prices can persist.
    c. A monopolist that reduces output and raises price. When entry is very costly, these high prices can persist.
    d. A group of identical noncooperative oligopolists that is able to reproduce a monopoly equilibrium through price rivalry.
16. Which of the following is *true* about an oligopoly equilibrium in comparison with equilibrium under similar circumstances but with perfect competition?
    a. Output is larger and price is lower than under perfect competition.
    b. Output is larger but price is higher than under perfect competition.
    c. Output is smaller and price is higher than under perfect competition.
    d. Output is smaller and price is lower than under perfect competition.
17. Which of the following market structures describes an industry in which a group of firms formally agree to control prices and output of a product?
    a. Perfect competition.
    b. Monopoly.
    c. Oligopoly.
    d. Cartel.
    e. Monopolistic competition.

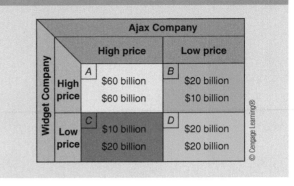

EXHIBIT 9-9 Two-Firm Payoff Matrix

		Ajax Company	
		High price	**Low price**
Widget Company **High price**	*A*	$60 billion $60 billion	*B* $20 billion $10 billion
Low price	*C*	$10 billion $20 billion	*D* $20 billion $20 billion

18. Assume costs are identical for the two firms in Exhibit 9-9. If both firms were allowed to form a cartel and agree on their prices, equilibrium would be established by
    a. Widget Co. charging the low price and Ajax Co. charging the high price.
    b. Widget Co. charging the high price and Ajax Co. charging the low price.
    c. Widget Co. charging the low price and Ajax Co. charging the low price.
    d. Widget Co. charging the high price and Ajax Co. charging the high price.
19. Suppose costs are identical for the two firms in Exhibit 9-9. If both firms assume the other will compete and charge a lower price, equilibrium will be established by
    a. Widget Co. charging the low price and Ajax Co. charging the low price.
    b. Widget Co. charging the high price and Ajax Co. charging the low price.
    c. Widget Co. charging the low price and Ajax Co. charging the high price.
    d. Widget Co. charging the high price and Ajax Co. charging the high price.
20. Suppose costs are identical for the two firms in Exhibit 9-9. Each firm assumes without formal agreement that if it sets the high price its rival will *not* charge a lower price. Under these "tit-for-tat" conditions, equilibrium will be established by
    a. Widget Co. charging the high price and Ajax Co. charging the low price.
    b. Widget Co. charging the high price and Ajax Co. charging the high price.
    c. Widget Co. charging the low price and Ajax Co. charging the low price.
    d. Widget Co. charging the low price and Ajax Co. charging the high price.

PART 3

The Macroeconomy and Fiscal Policy

The first three chapters in this part explain key measures of how well the macroeconomy is performing. These measures include GDP, business cycles, unemployment, and inflation. Chapter 14 presents an important theoretical macro model based on aggregate demand and supply, and Chapter 15 demonstrates its application to federal government taxing and spending policies. The part concludes with two chapters that provide actual data on such hotly debated topics as government spending and taxation, federal deficits, surpluses, and the national debt.

11

CHAPTER

Gross Domestic Product

© Florinikus/Shutterstock.com

In this chapter, you will learn to solve these economics puzzles:

- Why doesn't economic growth include increases in spending for welfare, Social Security, and unemployment programs?

- Can one newscaster report that the economy grew while another reports that for the same year the economy declined, and both reports be correct?

- How is the calculation of national output affected by environmental damage?

CHAPTER PREVIEW

Measuring the performance of the economy is an important part of life. Suppose one candidate for president of the United States proclaims that the economy's performance is the best in a generation, and an opposing presidential candidate argues that the economy is performing poorly. Which statistics would you seek to tell how well the economy is doing? The answer requires understanding some of the nuts and bolts of *national income accounting*. National income accounting is the system used to measure the aggregate income and expenditures for a nation. Despite certain limitations, the national income accounting system provides a valuable indicator of an economy's performance. For example, you can visit the Internet and check the annual *Economic Report of the President* to compare the size or growth of the U.S. economy between years.

Prior to the Great Depression, there were no national accounting procedures for estimating the data required to assess the economy's performance. In order to provide accounting methodologies for macro data, the late economist Simon Kuznets, the "father of GDP," published a small report in 1934 titled *National Income, 1929–32*. For his pioneering work, Kuznets earned the 1971 Nobel Prize in Economics. Today, thanks in large part to Kuznets, most countries use common national accounting methods. National income accounting serves a nation similar to the manner in which accounting serves a business or household. In each case, accounting methodology is vital for identifying economic problems and formulating plans for achieving goals.

11-1 GROSS DOMESTIC PRODUCT

Gross domestic product (GDP)
The market value of all final goods and services produced in a nation during a period of time, usually a year.

The most widely reported measure throughout the world of a nation's economic performance is **gross domestic product (GDP)**, which is the market value of all final goods and services produced in a nation during a period of time, usually a year. GDP therefore excludes production abroad by U.S. businesses. For example, GDP excludes Microsoft's earnings on its foreign operations. On the other hand, GDP includes Toyota's profits from its car plants in the United States. Why is GDP important? It tells a country how well its economy is doing. One advantage of GDP is that it avoids the "apples and oranges" measurement problem. If an economy produces 10 apples one year and 10 oranges the next, can we say that the value of output has changed in any way? To answer this question, we must attach price tags in order to evaluate the relative monetary value of apples and oranges to society. This is the reason GDP measures value using dollars, rather than listing the number of cars, heart transplants, legal cases, toothbrushes, and tanks produced. Instead, the market-determined dollar value establishes the monetary importance of production. In GDP calculations, "money talks." That is, GDP relies on markets to establish the relative value of goods and services.

GDP is compiled by the Bureau of Economic Analysis (BEA), which is an agency of the Department of Commerce. GDP requires that the following two points receive special attention: (1) GDP counts only new domestic production, and (2) it counts only final goods.

11-1a GDP Counts Only New Domestic Production

National income accountants calculating GDP carefully exclude transactions in two major areas: secondhand transactions and nonproductive financial transactions.

Secondhand Transactions

GDP includes only current transactions. It does not include the sale of a used car or the sale of a home constructed some years ago. Such transactions are merely exchanges of previously produced goods and not *current* production of new goods that add to the existing stock of cars and homes. Used items were counted previously in GDP for the year when they were newly produced. However, the sales commission on a used car or a home produced in another GDP period counts in current GDP because the salesperson performed a service during the present period of time.

Nonproductive Financial Transactions

Transfer payment A government payment to individuals not in exchange for goods or services currently produced.

GDP does not count purely private or public financial transactions, such as giving private gifts, buying and selling stocks and bonds, and making **transfer payments**. A transfer payment is a government payment to individuals not in exchange for goods or services currently produced. Welfare, Social Security, veterans' benefits, and unemployment benefits are transfer payments. These transactions are considered nonproductive because they do not represent production of any new or *current* output. Transfer payments are made to people who are entitled to them. The reason could be because of being poor or reaching a certain age. Similarly, stock market transactions represent only the exchange of certificates of ownership (stocks) or indebtedness (bonds) and not actual new production.

11-1b GDP Counts Only Final Goods

Final goods Finished goods and services produced for the ultimate user.

The popular press usually defines GDP as simply "the value of all goods and services produced." This is technically incorrect because GDP counts only **final goods**, which are finished goods and services produced for the ultimate user. Including all goods and services produced would inflate GDP by *double counting*

Intermediate goods Goods and services used as inputs for the production of final goods.

(counting many items more than once). In order to count only final goods and avoid overstating GDP, national income accountants must take care not to include **intermediate goods**. Intermediate goods are goods and services used as inputs for the production of final goods. Stated differently, intermediate goods are not produced for consumption by the ultimate user.

Suppose a wholesale distributor sells glass to an automaker. This transaction is not included in GDP. The glass is an intermediate good used in the production of cars. When a customer buys a new car from the car dealer, the value of the glass is included in the car's selling price, which is the value of a final good counted in GDP. Let's consider another example. A wholesale distributor sells glass to a hardware store. GDP does not include this transaction because the hardware store is not the final user. When a customer buys the glass from the hardware store to repair a broken window, the final purchase price of the glass is added to GDP as a consumer expenditure.

11-2 MEASURING GDP

GDP is like an enormous puzzle with many pieces to fit together, including markets for products, markets for resources, consumers spending and earning money, and businesses spending and earning money. How can one fit all these puzzle pieces together? One way to understand how all these concepts fit together is to use a simple macroeconomic model called the **circular flow model**. The circular flow model shows the exchange of money, and resources between households and businesses. In exchange for these resources, money payments flow between businesses and households. Exhibit 11-1 shows the circular flow in a hypothetical economy with no government, no financial markets, and no foreign trade. In this ultra-simple pure market economy, only the households and the businesses make decisions.

Circular flow model A diagram showing the exchange of money and resources between households and businesses.

11-2a The Circular Flow Model

The upper half of the diagram in Exhibit 11-1 represents *product markets* in which households exchange money for goods and services produced by firms. The red *supply* arrow in the top loop represents all finished products and the value of services produced, sold, and delivered to consumers. The blue *demand* arrow in the top loop shows why the businesses make this effort to satisfy the consuming households. When consumers decide to buy products, they are actually voting with their dollars. This flow of consumption expenditures from households is sales revenues to businesses and expenses from the viewpoint of households. Notice that the box labeled *product markets* contains a supply and demand graph. This means the forces of supply and demand in individual markets determine the price and quantity of each product exchanged without government intervention.

The bottom half of the circular flow diagram consists of the *factor markets*, in which firms *demand* the natural resources, labor, capital, and entrepreneurship needed to produce the goods and services sold in the product markets. Our hypothetical economy is capitalistic, and the model assumes for simplicity that households own the factors of production. Businesses therefore must purchase all their resources from the households. The red *supply* arrow in the bottom loop represents this flow of resources from households to firms, and the blue *demand* arrow is the flow of money payments to households for these resources. These payments are also income earned by households in the form of wages, rents, interest, and profits. As in the product markets, market supply and demand determine the price and quantity of factor payments.

This simple model also assumes all households live from hand to mouth. That is, households spend all the income they earn in the factor markets on

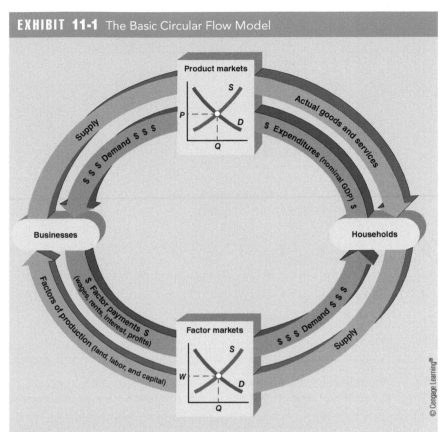

EXHIBIT 11-1 The Basic Circular Flow Model

In this simple economy, households spend all their income in the upper loop and demand consumer goods and services from businesses. Businesses seek profits by supplying goods and services to households through the product markets. Prices and quantities in individual markets are determined by the market supply and demand model. In the factor markets in the lower loop, resources (land, labor, and capital) are owned by households and supplied to businesses that demand these factors in return for money payments. The forces of supply and demand determine the returns to the factors, for example, wages and the quantity of labor supplied. Overall, goods and services flow clockwise, and the corresponding payments flow counterclockwise.

products. Households therefore do not save. Likewise, all firms spend all their income earned in the product markets on resources from the factor markets. The simple circular flow model therefore fails to mirror the real world. But it does aid your understanding of the relationships between product markets, factor markets, the flow of money, and the theory behind GDP measurement—to which we now turn our attention.

Expenditure approach The national income accounting method that measures GDP by adding all the spending for final goods during a period of time.

11-2b The Expenditure Approach

How does the government actually calculate GDP? One way national income accountants calculate GDP is to use the **expenditure approach** to measure total spending flowing through product markets in the circular flow diagram.[1]

---

[1] Another somewhat more complex method is called the *income approach*. This approach calculates GDP by summing the incomes earned by households for factors of production flowing through the factor markets in the circular flow diagram. The expenditure and income approaches yield the same GDP because the model assumes households spend all income earned.

EXHIBIT 11-2 Gross Domestic Product Using the Expenditure Approach, 2013

National income account		Amount (trillions of dollars)	Percentage of GDP
Personal consumption expenditures (**C**)		$11.5	69%
Durable goods	1.3		
Nondurable goods	2.6		
Services	7.6		
Gross private domestic investment (**I**)		2.7	16
Fixed investment	2.6		
Change in business inventories	0.11		
Government consumption expenditures and gross investment (**G**)		3.1	18
Federal	1.2		
State and local	1.9		
Net exports of goods and services (**X − M**)		−0.5	−3
Exports (**X**)	2.3		
Imports (**M**)	2.8		
Gross domestic product (**GDP**)		16.8	100%

Source: Bureau of Economic Analysis, *National Economic Accounts*, http://www.bea.gov/iTable/index_nipa.cfm, Table 1.1.5.

The expenditure approach measures GDP by adding all the spending for final goods during a period of time. Exhibit 11-2 shows 2013 GDP using the expenditure approach, which breaks down expenditures into four components. The data in this exhibit show that all production in the U.S. economy is ultimately purchased by spending from households, businesses, government, or foreigners. Let's discuss each of these expenditure categories.

11-2c Personal Consumption Expenditures (C)

The largest component of GDP in 2013 was $11.5 trillion for the category national income accountants call *personal consumption expenditures*, represented by the letter C. Personal consumption expenditures comprise total spending by households for durable goods, nondurable goods, and services. Durable goods include items such as automobiles, appliances, and furniture, because they last longer than three years. Food, clothing, soap, and gasoline are examples of nondurables, because they are considered used up or consumed in less than three years. Services, which is the largest category, include recreation, legal advice, medical treatment, education, and any transaction not in the form of a tangible object. This is why the U.S. economy is often referred to as a service economy.

11-2d Gross Private Domestic Investment (I)

In 2013, $2.7 trillion was spent for what is officially called *gross private domestic investment* (I). This national income account includes "gross" (all) "private" (not government) "domestic" (not foreign) spending by businesses for investment in capital assets that are expected to earn profits in the future. Gross private domestic investment is the sum of two components: (1) *fixed investment* expenditures for newly produced capital goods, such as commercial and residential structures, machinery, equipment, tools, and computers and (2) change in *business inventories*, which is the net change in spending for unsold finished goods. Note that gross private domestic investment is simply the national income accounting category for "investment," defined in Chapter 2. The only difference is that investment in Exhibit 2-5 of Chapter 2 was in physical capital, such as manufacturing plants, oil wells, or fast food restaurants, rather than the dollar value of capital used here.

Now we will take a closer look at gross private domestic investment. Note that national income accountants include the rental value of newly constructed residential housing in the $2.6 trillion spent for fixed investment. A new factory, warehouse, or robot is surely a form of investment, but why include residential housing as business investment rather than consumption by households? The debatable answer is that a new home is considered investment because it provides services in the future that the owner can rent for financial return. For this reason, all newly produced housing is considered investment whether the owner rents or occupies the property. Also note that starting from July 2013 intellectual property products that includes research and development (R&D) spending is added to gross domestic investment.

Finally, the $0.11 trillion change in business inventories means this amount of net dollar value of unsold finished goods and raw materials was added to the stock of inventories during 2013. A decline in inventories would reduce GDP because households consumed more output than firms produced during this year. When businesses have more on their shelves this year than last, more new production has taken place than has been consumed during this year.

11-2e Government Consumption Expenditures and Gross Investment (G)

This official category simply called *government spending* includes the value of goods and services government purchases at all levels measured by their costs. For example, spending for salaries for police and state university professors enters the GDP accounts at the prices the government pays for them. In addition, the government spends for investment additions to its stock of capital, such as tanks, schools, highways, bridges, and government buildings. In 2013, federal, state, and local government spending (G) totaled $3.1 trillion. As the figures in Exhibit 11-2 reveal, government spending by state and local governments far exceeded those of the federal government. It is important to understand that the government spending category of GDP excludes *transfer payments* because, as explained at the beginning of the chapter, they do not represent newly produced goods and services. Instead, transfer payments are paid to those entitled to Social Security benefits, veterans' benefits, welfare, unemployment compensation, and benefits from other programs.

11-2f Net Exports (X − M)

The last GDP account is net exports, expressed in the formula $(X - M)$. Exports (X) are spending by foreigners for U.S. domestically produced goods. Imports (M) are the dollar amount of U.S. purchases of Japanese automobiles, French wine, clothes from China, and other goods produced abroad. The positive sign $(+X)$ means that money flows into the United States from foreigners to pay for our exports. The negative sign $(-M)$ indicates dollars are flowing out of the United States to pay for imports. In 2013, export spending was $2.3 trillion and import spending was −$2.8 trillion. Net exports were therefore −$0.5 trillion. What is the effect of a negative sign for net exports? It means the United States is spending more dollars to purchase foreign products than it is receiving from abroad for U.S. goods. The effect of a negative net exports figure is to reduce U.S. GDP. Stated another way, higher exports (X) relative to imports (M) increases GDP. Prior to the early 1980s, the United States was a consistent net exporter, selling more goods and services to the rest of the world than we purchased from abroad. Since 1983, the United States has been a net importer. Chapter 21 discusses international trade in more detail.

11-2g A Formula for GDP

Using the expenditure approach, GDP is expressed mathematically in trillions of dollars as

$$GDP = C + I + G + (X - M)$$

For 2013 (see Exhibit 11-2),

$$\$14.6 = \$10.3 + \$1.8 + \$3.0 + (\$1.8 - \$2.3)$$

This simple equation plays a central role in macroeconomics. It is the basis for analyzing macro problems and formulating macro policy. When economists study the macro economy, they can apply this equation to predict the behavior of the major sectors of the economy: consumption (C) is spending by households, investment (I) is spending by firms, government spending (G) is spending by the government, and net exports (X − M) is net spending by foreigners.

CHECKPOINT

How Much Does Mario Add to GDP?
Mario works part-time at Pizza Hut and earns an annual wage plus tips of $15,000. He sold 4,000 pizzas at $15 per pizza during the year. He was unemployed part of the year, so he received unemployment compensation of $3,000. During the past year, Mario bought a used car for $5,000. Using the expenditure approach, how much has Mario contributed to GDP?

11-3 GDP IN OTHER COUNTRIES

GLOBAL ECONOMICS

Exhibit 11-3 compares GDP for selected countries in 2013. The United States had the world's highest GDP and China had the second largest GDP. U.S. GDP was about twice the size of China's GDP.

11-4 GDP SHORTCOMINGS

For various reasons, GDP omits certain measures of overall economic well-being. Because GDP is the basis of government economic policies, there is concern that GDP may be giving us a false impression of the nation's material well-being. GDP is a less-than-perfect measure of the nation's economic pulse because it excludes the following factors.

11-4a Nonmarket Transactions

Because GDP counts only market transactions, it excludes certain unpaid activities, such as homemaker production, child rearing, and do-it-yourself home repairs and services. For example, if you take your dirty clothes to the cleaners, GDP increases by the amount of the cleaning bill paid. But GDP ignores the value of cleaning these same clothes if you wash them yourself at home.

There are two reasons for excluding nonmarket activities from GDP. First, it would be extremely imprecise to attempt to collect data and assign a dollar value to services people provide for themselves or others without compensation. Second, it is difficult to decide which nonmarket activities to exclude and which ones to include. Perhaps repairing your own roof, painting your own house, and repairing your own car should be included. Now consider the value of washing

EXHIBIT 11-3 An International Comparison of GDPs, 2013 (trillions of dollars)

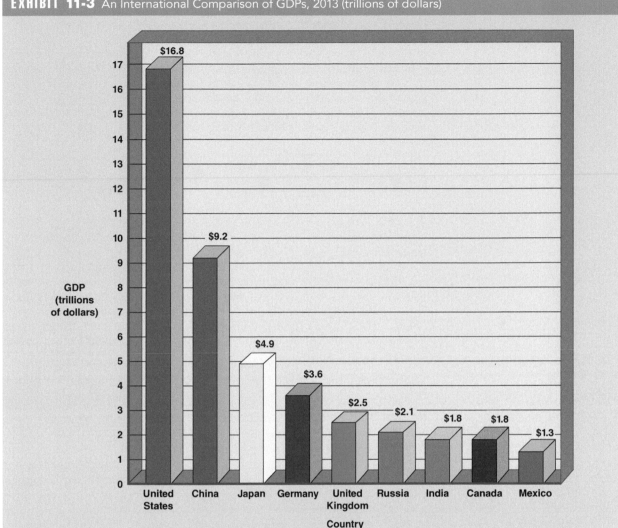

This exhibit shows GDPs in 2013 for selected countries. The United States has the world's highest GDP and China has the second largest GDP. U.S. GDP, for example, is about twice the size of China.

Source: International Monetary Fund, *World Economic Outlook Database*, http://www.imf.org/external/ns/cs.aspx?id=28.

your car. GDP does include the price of cleaning your car if you purchase that service at a car wash, so it could be argued that GDP should include the value of washing your car at home.

The issue of unpaid, do-it-yourself activities affects comparisons of the GDPs of different nations. One reason some less-developed nations have lower GDPs than major industrialized nations is that a greater proportion of people in less-developed nations farm, clean, make repairs, and perform other tasks for their families rather than hiring someone else to do the work.

11-4b Distribution, Kind, and Quality of Products

GDP is blind to whether a small fraction of the population consumes most of a country's GDP or consumption is evenly divided. GDP also wears a blind-fold with respect to the quality and kinds of goods and services that make up a nation's GDP. Consider the fictional economies of Zuba and Econa. Zuba has a GDP of $2,000 billion, and Econa has a GDP of $1,000 billion. At first glance, Zuba appears to possess superior economic well-being. However, Zuba's GDP consists of only military goods, and Econa's products include computers, cell phones, tractors, wheat, milk, houses, and other consumer items. Moreover, assume the majority of the people of Zuba could care less about the output of military goods and would be happier if the country produced more consumer goods. Now consider, for example, the difference in quality between a cell phone purchased today and a cell phone with only few capabilities purchased years ago. Such qualitative improvements are not reflected in GDP.

CONCLUSION GDP is a quantitative, rather than a qualitative, measure of the output of goods and services.

11-4c Neglect of Quality-of-Life

GDP does not directly measure quality-of-life or "happiness" variables such as leisure time.

In general, the wealthier a nation becomes, the more leisure time its citizens can afford. Rather than working longer hours, workers often choose to increase their time for recreation and travel. Since 1900, the length of the typical workweek in the United States declined steadily from about 50 hours in 1900 to about 34 hours in 2013.[2] Other quality-of-life indicators not included in GDP include life expectancy at birth, infant mortality rate, and the literacy rate. The last chapter discusses quality-of-life variables in more detail.

CONCLUSION It can be argued that GDP understates national well-being because no allowance is made for people working fewer hours than they once did.

11-4d The Underground Economy

Illegal gambling, prostitution, loan-sharking, illegal guns, and illegal drugs are goods and services that meet all the requirements for GDP. They are final goods with a value determined in "black" markets, but GDP does not include unreported criminal activities because no record is made of these transactions. The "underground" economy also includes tax evasion. One way to avoid paying taxes on a legal activity is to trade or barter goods and services rather than selling them. One person fixes a neighbor's car in return for babysitting services, and the value of the exchange is unreported. Other individuals and businesses make legal sales for cash and do not report the income earned to the Internal Revenue Service.

Estimates of the size of this subterranean economy vary. Some studies by economists estimate the size of the underground sector is about 9 percent of GDP. This range of estimates is slightly less than the estimated size of the underground economy in most European countries.

CONCLUSION If the underground economy is sizable, GDP will understate an economy's performance.

11-4e Economic Bads

More production means a larger GDP, regardless of the level of pollution created in the process. Recall from Chapter 4 the discussion of *negative externalities*, such as pollution caused by steel mills, chemical plants, and cigarettes. Air, water,

---

[2]*Economic Report of the President*, 2014, http://www.gpoaccess.gov/eop/, Table B-47.

Is GDP a False Beacon Steering Us into the Rocks?

Applicable concept: national income accounting "goods" and "bads"

Suppose a factory in your community has been dumping hazardous wastes into the local water supply, and people develop cancer and other illnesses from drinking polluted water. The Environmental Protection Agency (EPA) discovers this pollution and, under the federal "Superfund" law, orders a cleanup and imposes a fine for the damages. The company defends itself against the EPA by hiring lawyers and experts to take the case to court. After years of trial, the company loses the case and has to pay for the cleanup and damages.

In terms of GDP, an amazing "good" result occurs: The primary measure of national economic output, GDP, increases. GDP counts the millions of dollars spent to clean up the water supply. GDP even includes the health care expenses of anyone who develops cancer or other illnesses caused by drinking polluted water. GDP also includes the money spent by the company on lawyers and experts to defend itself against the EPA. And GDP includes the money spent by the EPA to regulate the polluting company.

Now consider what happens when trees are cut down and oil and minerals are used to produce houses, cars, and other goods. The value of the wood, oil, and minerals is an intermediate good implicitly computed in GDP because the value of the final goods is explicitly computed in GDP. Using scarce resources to produce goods and services therefore raises GDP and is considered a "good" result. On the other hand, don't we lose the value of trees, oil, and minerals in the production process, so isn't this a "bad" result?

The Bureau of Economic Analysis (BEA) is an agency of the U.S. Department of Commerce. The BEA is the nation's economic accountant, and it is the source of GDP data cited throughout this text. Critics have called for a new measure designed to estimate the kinds of damage described above. These new accounts would adjust for changes in air and water quality and depletion of oil and minerals. These accounts would also adjust for changes in the stock of renewable natural resources, such as forests and fish stocks. In addition, accounts should be created to measure global warming and destruction of the ozone layer.

As explained in this chapter, a dollar estimate of capital depreciation is subtracted from GDP to compute national income (NI). The argument here is that a dollar estimate of the damage to the environment should also be subtracted. To ignore measuring such environmental problems, critics argue, threatens future generations. In short, conventional GDP perpetuates a false dichotomy between economic growth and environmental protection.

Critics of this approach argue that assigning a dollar value to environmental damage and resource depletion requires a methodology that is extremely subjective and complex. Nevertheless, national income accountants have not ignored these criticisms and the National Academy of Sciences has reviewed BEA proposals for ways to account for interactions between the environment and the economy.

> **ANALYZE the ISSUE** Suppose a nuclear power plant disaster occurs. How could GDP be a "false beacon" in this case?

and noise pollution are *economic bads* that impose costs on society not reflected in private market prices and quantities bought and sold. When a polluting company sells its product, this transaction increases the GDP. However, critics of GDP argue that it fails to account for the diminished quality of life from the "bads" not reported in GDP.

Stated another way, if production results in pollution and environmental change, GDP overstates the nation's well-being.

> **CONCLUSION** Since the costs of negative by-products are not deducted, GDP overstates the national well-being.

11-4f GDP Alternatives

There are alternative measures for GDP that have been developed to value more diverse economic activities. The Measure of Economic Welfare (MEW) and the Genuine Progress Indicator (GPI) expand the range of economic activities counted, such as nonmarket work and leisure. MEW, for example, discounts spending on "wasteful" activities like the military and gives value to home production and inputs from the environment. The GPI puts weight on income distribution. Another measure is the Human Development Index (HDI) that includes life expectancy and education. However, the HDI does not include any measure of environmental sustainability. The Happy Planet Index (HPI) is distinctive because it provides no measure of market transactions. Instead the HDI places heavy weight on health systems, schools, and environmental sustainability. Using the HDI, Denmark, Finland, Norway, Sweden, and the Netherlands rank far above the United States.

11-5 OTHER NATIONAL INCOME ACCOUNTS

In addition to GDP, the media often report several other national income accounts because they are necessary for studying the macro economy. We now take a brief look at each.

11-5a National Income (NI)

It can be argued that depreciation should be subtracted from GDP. Recall that GDP is not entirely a measure of newly produced output because it includes an estimated value of capital goods required to replace those worn out in the production process. The measurement designed to correct this deficiency is national income (NI), which is the gross domestic product minus depreciation of the capital worn out in producing output. Stated as a formula:

National income (NI) The total income earned by resource owners, including wages, rents, interest, and profits. NI is calculated as gross domestic product minus depreciation of the capital worn out in producing output.

NI = GDP − depreciation (consumption of fixed capital)

In 2013, $2.3 trillion was the estimated amount of GDP attributable to depreciation during the year. Exhibit 11-4 shows the actual calculation of NI from GDP in 2013. NI measures how much income is *earned* by households that own and supply resources. It includes the total flow of payments to the owners of the factors of production including wages, rents, interest, and profits. Exhibit 11-5 illustrates the transition from GDP to NI and two other measures of the macro economy.[3]

11-5b Personal Income (PI)

Personal income (PI) The total income received by households that is available for consumption, saving, and payment of personal taxes.

National income measures the total amount of money *earned*, but determining the amount of income actually *received* by households (not businesses) requires a measurement of personal income (PI). Personal income is the total income received by households that is available for consumption, saving, and payment of personal taxes. Suppose we want to measure the total amount of money individuals receive that they can use to consume products, save, and pay taxes. National income is not the appropriate measure for two reasons. First, NI excludes transfer

EXHIBIT 11-4 National Income Calculated from Gross Domestic Product, 2013

	Amount (trillions of dollars)
Gross domestic product (GDP)	$16.8
Depreciation	−2.3
National income	$14.5

Source: Bureau of Economic Analysis, *National Economic Accounts*, http://www.bea.gov/iTable/index_nipa.cfm, Table 1.7.5.

---

[3]As a result of a revision in national income accounting, the only difference between net domestic product (NDP) and national income (NI) is a statistical discrepancy. Because NI is more widely reported in the media, and to simplify, NDP is not calculated here.

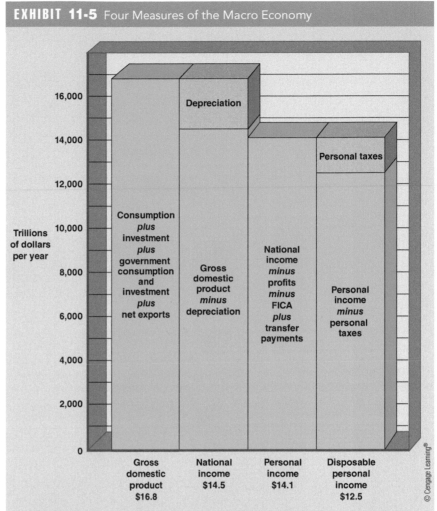

EXHIBIT 11-5 Four Measures of the Macro Economy

The four bars show four major measurements of the U.S. macro economy in 2013 in trillions of dollars. Beginning with gross domestic product, depreciation is subtracted to obtain national income. Next, personal income equals national income minus corporate profits and contributions for Social Security insurance (FICA payments) plus transfer payments and other income. Subtracting personal taxes from personal income yields disposable personal income.

payments, which constitute unearned income that can be spent, saved, or used to pay taxes. Second, NI includes corporate profits, but stockholders do not receive all these profits. A portion of corporate profits is paid in corporate taxes. Also, retained earnings are not distributed to stockholders, but are channeled back into business operations.

Exhibit 11-5 illustrates the relationship between personal income and national income, and Exhibit 11-6 gives the figures for 2013. National income accountants adjust national income by subtracting corporate profits and payroll taxes for Social Security (FICA deductions). Next, *transfer payments* and other income individuals receive from net interest and dividends are added. The net result is the personal income received by households, which in 2013 amounted to $14.1 trillion.

EXHIBIT 11-6 Personal Income Calculated from National Income, 2013

	Amount (trillions of dollars)
National income (NI)	$14.5
Corporate profits	−2.1
Contributions for Social Security (FICA)	−1.1
Transfer payments and other income	2.8
Personal income (PI)	$14.1

Source: Bureau of Economic Analysis, *National Economic Account,* http://www.bea.gov/iTable/index_nipa.cfm, Table 1.7.5.

EXHIBIT 11-7 Disposable Personal Income Calculated from Personal Income, 2013

	Amount (trillions of dollars)
Personal income (PI)	$14.1
Personal taxes	−1.6
Disposable personal income (DI)	$12.5

Source: Bureau of Economic Analysis, *National Economic Accounts,* http://www.bea.gov/iTable/index_nipa.cfm, Table 2.1.

11-5c Disposable Personal Income (DI)

Disposable personal income (DI) The amount of income that households actually have to spend or save after payment of personal taxes.

One final measure of national income is shown at the far right of Exhibit 11-5. **Disposable personal income (DI)** is the amount of income that households actually have to spend or save after payment of personal taxes. Disposable, or *after-tax* income, is equal to personal income minus personal taxes paid to federal, state, and local governments. Personal taxes consist of personal income taxes, personal property taxes, and inheritance taxes. As tabulated in Exhibit 11-7, disposable personal income in 2013 was $12.5 trillion.

11-6 CHANGING NOMINAL GDP TO REAL GDP

Nominal GDP The value of all final goods based on the prices existing during the time period of production.

So far, GDP has been expressed as **nominal GDP**. Nominal GDP is the value of all final goods based on the prices existing during the time period of production. Nominal GDP is also referred to as *current-dollar* or *money GDP*. Nominal GDP grows in three ways: First, output rises, and prices remain unchanged. Second, prices rise and output is constant. Third, in the typical case, both output and prices rise. The problem, then, is how to adjust GDP so it reflects only changes in output and not changes in prices. This adjusted GDP allows meaningful comparisons over time when prices are changing.

Changing prices can have a huge impact on how we compare dollar figures. Suppose a newspaper headline reports that a film entitled *The History of Economic Thought* is the biggest box-office sales movie of all time. You ask, How can this be? What about *Gone with the Wind*? Reading the article reveals that this claim is based on the nominal measure of gross box-office receipts. This gives a recent movie with higher ticket prices an advantage over a movie released in 1939 when the average ticket price was about $1. A better measure of popularity would be to compare "real" box-office receipts by multiplying actual attendance figures for each movie by a base-year movie price.

Measuring the difference between changes in output and changes in the price level involves making an important distinction between *nominal GDP* and **real GDP**. Real GDP is the value of all final goods produced during a given time period based on the prices existing in a selected base year. The U.S. Department of Commerce currently uses 2005 prices as the base year. Real GDP is also referred to as *constant dollar GDP*.

Real GDP The value of all final goods produced during a given time period based on the prices existing in a selected base year.

11-6a The GDP Chain Price Index

The most broadly based measure used to take the changes-in-the-price-level "air" out of the nominal GDP "balloon" and compute real GDP is officially called the **GDP chain price index**. The GDP chain price index is a measure that compares the prices of all final goods produced during a given time period to the prices of those goods in a base year. The GDP chain price index is a broad "deflator" index calculated by a complex chain-weighted geometric series (you are spared the details). It is highly inclusive because it measures not only price changes of consumer goods, but also price changes of business investment, government spending, exports, and imports. Do not confuse the GDP chain price index with the *consumer price index* (CPI), which is widely reported in the news media. The CPI is a different index, measuring only consumer prices, which we will discuss in Chapter 13.

GDP chain price index A measure that compares changes in the prices of all final goods during a given year to the prices of those goods in a base year.

Now it's time to see how the GDP chain price index works. We begin with the following conversion equation:

$$\text{real GDP} = \frac{\text{nominal GDP}}{\text{GDP chain price index}} \times 100$$

Using 2009 as the base year, suppose you are given the 2013 nominal GDP of $16,800 billion and the 2013 GDP chain price index of 106.59. To calculate 2013 real GDP, use the above formula as follows:

$$15,761 \text{ billion} = \frac{16,800 \text{ billion}}{106.59} \times 100$$

The table in Exhibit 11-8 shows actual U.S. nominal GDP, real GDP, and the GDP chain price index for selected years. Column 1 reports nominal GDP, column 2 gives real GDP figures for these years, and column 3 lists corresponding GDP chain price indexes. Notice that the GDP chain price index exceeds 100 in years beyond 2009. This means that prices, on average, have risen since 2009, causing the real purchasing power of the dollar to fall. In the years before 2009, the GDP chain price index is less than 100, which means the real purchasing power of the dollar was higher relative to the 2009 base year. At the base year of 2009, nominal and real GDP are identical, and the GDP chain price index equals 100.

The graph in Exhibit 11-8 traces real GDP and nominal GDP for the U.S. economy since 1970. Note that nominal GDP usually grows faster than real GDP because inflation is included in nominal GDP figures and not real GDP. For example, if we calculate the economy's growth rate in nominal GDP between 2009 and 2013, we find it was 16.5 percent. If instead we calculate the growth in real GDP between the same years, we find the growth rate was 9.3 percent. You must therefore pay attention to which GDP is being used in an analysis.

EXHIBIT 11-8 Nominal GDP, Real GDP, and the GDP Chain Price Index for Selected Years

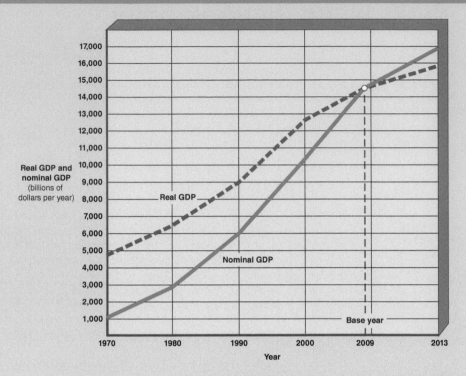

Year	(1) Nominal GDP (billions of dollars)	(2) Real GDP (billions of 2009 dollars)	(3) GDP chain price index (2009 = 100)
1970	1,076	4,718	22.8
1980	2,862	6,443	44.4
1990	5,980	8,945	66.8
2000	10,290	12,565	81.9
2009	14,418	14,418	100.0
2013	16,880	15,761	107.0

Real GDP reflects output valued at 2009 base-year prices, but nominal GDP is annual output valued at prices prevailing during the current year. The intersection of real and nominal GDP occurs in 2009 in the base year. Note that the nominal GDP curve has risen more sharply than the real GDP curve since 2009 as a result of inflation included in the nominal figures.

Sources: Bureau of Economic Analysis, *National Economic Accounts*, http://www.bea.gov/iTable/index_nipa.cfm, Tables 1.1.4, 1.1.5, and 1.1.6.

CHECKPOINT

Is the Economy Up or Down?
One person reports, "GDP rose this year by 8.5 percent." Another says, "GDP fell by 0.5 percent." Can both reports be right?

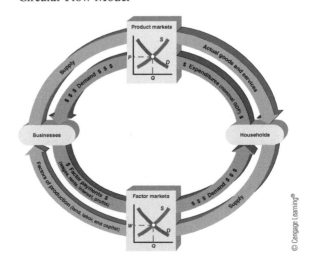

"And so, extrapolating from the best figures available, we see that current trends, unless dramatically reversed, will inevitably lead to a situation in which the sky will fall."

Key Concepts

Gross domestic product (GDP)	Circular flow model	Disposable personal income (DI)
Transfer payment	Expenditure approach	Nominal GDP
Final goods	National income (NI)	Real GDP
Intermediate goods	Personal income (PI)	GDP chain price index

Summary

- **Gross domestic product (GDP)** is the most widely used measure of a nation's economic performance. GDP is the market value of all **final goods** produced in the United States during a period of time, regardless of who owns the factors of production. Secondhand and financial transactions are not counted in GDP. To avoid double counting, GDP also does not include **intermediate goods** GDP is calculated by the expenditure approach.

- The **circular flow model** is a diagram representing the flow of products and resources between businesses and households in exchange for money payments.

- The **expenditure approach** sums the four major spending components of GDP: consumption, investment, government spending, and net exports. Algebraically, GDP = C + I + G + (X − M), where X equals foreign spending for domestic exports and M equals domestic spending for foreign products.

Circular Flow Model

- **National income (NI)** is total income *earned* by households that own and supply resources. It is calculated as GDP minus depreciation.

- **Personal income (PI)** is the total income *received* by households and is calculated as NI minus corporate taxes and Social Security taxes plus transfer payments and other income.

- **Disposable personal income (DI)** is personal income minus personal taxes. DI is the amount of income a household has available to consume or save.

- **Nominal GDP** measures all final goods and services produced in a given time period, valued at the prices existing during the time period of production.

- **Real GDP** measures all final goods and services produced in a given time period, valued at the prices existing in a base year.

- The **GDP chain price index** is a broad price index used to convert nominal GDP to real GDP. The GDP chain price index measures changes in prices of consumer goods, business investment, government spending, exports, and imports. Real GDP is computed by dividing nominal GDP for year *X* by year *X*'s GDP chain price index and then multiplying the result by 100.

Measures of the Macro Economy

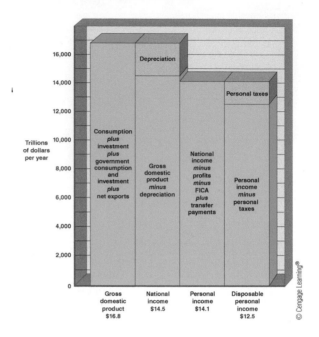

Study Questions and Problems

1. Which of the following are final goods or services, and which are intermediate goods or services?
   a. A haircut purchased from a hair salon.
   b. A new automobile.
   c. An oil filter purchased in a new automobile.
   d. Crude oil.

2. Using the basic circular flow model, explain why the value of businesses' output of goods and services equals the income of households.

3. A small economy produced the following final goods and services during a given month: 3 million pounds of food, 50,000 shirts, 20 houses, 50,000 hours of medical services, 1 automobile plant, and 2 tanks. Calculate the value of this output at the following market prices.
   a. $1 per pound of food.
   b. $20 per shirt.
   c. $50,000 per house.
   d. $20 per hour of medical services.
   e. $1 million per automobile plant.
   f. $500,000 per tank.

4. An economy produces final goods and services with a market value of $5,000 billion in a given year, but only $4,500 billion worth of goods and services is sold to domestic or foreign buyers. Is this nation's GDP $5,000 billion or $4,500 billion? Explain your answer.

5. Explain why a new forklift sold for use in a warehouse is a final good even though it is fixed investment (capital) used to produce other goods. Is there a double-counting problem if this sale is added to GDP?

6. Explain why the government spending (G) component of GDP falls short of actual government expenditures.

7. Explain how net exports affect the U.S. economy. Describe both positive and negative impacts on GDP. Why do national income accountants use net exports to compute GDP, rather than simply adding exports to the other expenditure components of GDP?

8. Suppose the data in Exhibit 11-9 are for a given year from the annual *Economic Report of the President*. Calculate GDP using the expenditure approach.

EXHIBIT 11-9 National Income Data

	Amount (billions of dollars)
Corporate profits	305
Depreciation	479
Gross private domestic investment	716
Personal taxes	565
Personal saving	120
Government spending	924
Imports	547
Net interest	337
Compensation of employees	2,648
Rental income	19
Exports	427
Personal consumption expenditures	2,966
Indirect business taxes	370
Contributions for social Security (FICA)	394
Transfer payments and other income	967
Proprietors' income	328

© Cengage Learning®

9. Using the data in Exhibit 11-9, compute national income (NI) by making the required subtraction from GDP. Explain why NI might be a better measure of economic performance than GDP.

10. Again using the data in Exhibit 11-9, derive personal income (PI) from national income (NI). Then, make the required adjustments from PI to obtain disposable personal income (DI).

11. Suppose U.S. nominal GDP increases from one year to the next year. Can you conclude that these figures present a misleading measure of economic growth? What alternative method would provide a more accurate measure of the rate of growth?

12. Which of the following are counted in this year's GDP? Explain your answer in each case.
    a. Flashy Car Company sold a used car.
    b. Juanita Jones cooked meals for her family.
    c. Microsoft paid interest on its bonds.
    d. Jose Suarez purchased 100 shares of Microsoft stock.
    e. Bob Smith received a welfare payment.
    f. Carriage Realty earned a brokerage commission for selling a previously owned house.
    g. The government makes interest payments to persons holding government bonds.
    h. Air and water pollution increase.
    i. Gambling is legalized in all states.
    j. A retired worker receives a Social Security payment.

13. Explain why comparing the GDPs of various nations might not tell you which nations are better off.

Sample Quiz

1. Gross domestic product is officially measured by adding together the
   a. quantity of each good and service produced by U.S. residents.
   b. market value of all final goods and services produced within the borders of a nation.
   c. quantity of goods and services produced by companies owned by U.S. citizens.
   d. None of the answers above are correct.

2. Which of the following items is included in the calculation of GDP?
   a. Purchase of 100 shares of Apple stock.
   b. Purchase of a used car.
   c. The value of a homemaker's services.
   d. Sale of Gulf War military surplus.
   e. e. None of the above would be included.

3. Which of the following expenditures would *not* be included in GDP?
   a. Purchase of a new lawnmower.
   b. Purchase of a silver cup previously sold new in 1950.
   c. Purchase of a ticket to the latest movie.
   d. All of the above would be counted in GDP.

4. Gross domestic product (GDP) includes
   a. intermediate as well as final goods.
   b. foreign goods as well as domestically produced goods.
   c. used goods sold in the current time period.
   d. only final goods and services.

5. GDP includes
   a. the negative attributes in our quest for more goods and services such as soil erosion and deforested landscape.
   b. all quality improvements resulting from higher quality goods replacing inferior goods.
   c. the cleaning-up expenses associated with pollution.
   d. the value of leisure time.

6. The largest component of GDP is
   a. personal consumption expenditures.
   b. government spending.
   c. durable goods.
   d. net exports.

7. The circular flow of economic activity is a model of the
   a. flow of goods, resources, payments, and expenditures between the sectors of the economy.
   b. influence of government on business behavior.
   c. influence of business on consumers.
   d. role of unions and government in the economy.

8. All final goods and services that make up GDP can be expressed in the form
   a. $GDP = C + I - G + (X + M)$.
   b. $GDP = C + I + G + (X + M)$.
   c. $GDP = C + I + G + (X - M)$.
   d. $GDP = C + I + (X - M)$.
   e. $GDP = C + I + G$.

9. The expenditure approach for the calculation of GDP includes spending on
   a. consumption, investment, durable goods, and exports.
   b. consumption, gross private domestic investment, government spending for goods and services, and exports.
   c. consumption, gross private domestic investment, government spending for goods and services, and net exports.
   d. consumption, net private domestic investment, government spending for goods and services, and net exports.
   e. consumption, gross private domestic investment, all government spending including transfer payments, and net exports.

10. Which of the following is a shortcoming of GDP?
    a. GDP excludes changes in inventories.
    b. GDP includes an estimate of illegal transactions.
    c. GDP excludes nonmarket transactions.
    d. GDP excludes business investment spending.

11. National income (NI) is calculated by adjusting GDP for
    a. depreciation.
    b. investment and net exports.
    c. Social Security insurance contributions and transfer payments.
    d. corporate and personal income taxes.

12. Which of the following is included in personal income but *not* in national income?
    a. Compensation for workers.
    b. Proprietors' income.
    c. Corporate profits.
    d. Social Security payments.

13. Which national income account should be examined to discover trends in the after-tax income that people have to save and spend?
    a. Gross domestic product (GDP).
    b. Gross national product (GNP).
    c. National income (NI).
    d. Disposable personal income (DI).

14. The equation for determining real GDP for year X is

   a. $\dfrac{\text{nominal GDP for year X}}{\text{average nominal GDP}}$.

   b. $\dfrac{\text{nominal GDP for year X}}{\text{GDP for year X}} \times 100$.

   c. $\dfrac{\text{nominal GDP for year X}}{\text{GDP chain price index for year X}} \times 100$.

   d. $\dfrac{\text{nominal GDP for year X}}{\text{average family income}} \times 100$.

15. The *most* broadly based price index is the
   a. real GDP price index.
   b. consumer price index.
   c. producer price index.
   d. GDP chain price index.
16. Which of the following would be counted as a final good for inclusion in GDP?
   a. A piece of glass bought this year by a consumer to fix a broken window.
   b. A sheet of glass produced this year by Ford for windows in a new car.
   c. A tire produced this year and sold to a car maker for a new car sold this year.
   d. None of the above would be counted in GDP.

17. Based on the circular flow model, money flows from households to businesses in
   a. factor markets.
   b. product markets.
   c. neither factor nor product markets.
   d. both factor and product markets.
18. If the underground economy is sizable, then GDP will
   a. understate the economy's performance.
   b. overstate the economy's performance.
   c. fluctuate unpredictably.
   d. accurately reflect this subterranean activity.
19. The income that people earn in resource or factor markets is called
   a. national income.
   b. personal income.
   c. disposable personal income.
   d. transfer payments.
   e. net national product.
20. Increased production, but *not* increased inflation, will result in higher
   a. nominal GDP.
   b. money GDP.
   c. real GDP.
   d. current dollar GDP.

Business Cycles and Unemployment

In this chapter, you will learn to solve these economics puzzles:

- What is the difference between a recession and a depression?
- Is a worker who has given up searching for work counted as unemployed?
- Can an economy produce more output than its potential?

CHAPTER PREVIEW

The headline in the morning newspaper reads, "The Economy Is in Deep Recession." Later in the day, a radio announcer begins the news by saying, "The unemployment rate increased for the tenth consecutive month." On television, the evening news broadcasts an interview with several economists who predict that the slump will last for years. Next, a presidential candidate appears on the screen and says, "It's time for change" and the media are abuzz with speculation on the potential political implications. The growth rate of the economy and the unemployment rate are headline-catching news. Indeed, these measures of macroeconomic instability are important because they affect your future. When real GDP rises and the economy "booms," jobs are more plentiful. A fall in real GDP means a "bust" because the economy forces some firms into bankruptcy and workers lose their jobs. Not being able to find a job when you want one is a painful experience not easily forgotten.

This chapter looks behind the macroeconomy at a story that touches each of us. It begins by discussing the business cycle. How are the expansions and contractions of business cycles measured? And what causes the business-cycle roller coaster? Finally, you will learn what the types of unemployment are, what "full employment" is, and what the monetary, nonmonetary, and demographic costs of unemployment are.

12-1 THE BUSINESS-CYCLE ROLLER COASTER

Business cycle Alternating periods of economic growth and contraction, which can be measured by changes in real GDP.

A central concern of macroeconomics is the upswings and downswings in the level of real output called the **business cycle**. The business cycle consists of alternating periods of economic growth and contraction. Business cycles are inherent in market economies. Market-based economies are driven by ever changing forces of supply and demand. A key measure of cycles is the rise and fall in real GDP, which mirrors changes in employment and other key measures of the macroeconomy. Recall from Chapter 11 that changes in real GDP measure changes in the value of national output, while ignoring changes in the price level.

12-1a The Four Phases of the Business Cycle

Exhibit 12-1(a) illustrates a theoretical business cycle. Although business cycles vary in duration and intensity, each cycle is divided into four phases: *peak, recession, trough,* and *expansion.* The business cycle looks like a roller coaster. It begins at a peak, drops to a bottom, climbs steeply, and then reaches another peak. Once the trough is reached, the upswing starts again. Although forecasters cannot precisely predict the phases of a cycle, the economy is always operating along one of these phases. Over time, there has been a long-term upward trend with shorter-term cyclical fluctuations around the long-run trend.

Peak The phase of the business cycle in which real GDP reaches its maximum after rising during a recovery.

Two **peaks** are illustrated in Exhibit 12-1(a). At each of these peaks, the economy is close to or at full employment. At a peak, real GDP reaches its maximum. That is, as explained in Chapter 2, the economy is operating near its production possibilities curve, and real GDP is at its highest level relative to recent years. However, a peak is a temporary high point. A macro setback called a **recession** or *contraction* follows each peak. A recession is a downturn in the business cycle during which real GDP declines, business profits fall, the percentage of the workforce without jobs rises, and production capacity is underutilized. A general rule is that a recession consists of at least two consecutive quarters (six months) in which there is a decline in real GDP. Stated differently, during a recession, the economy is functioning inside and farther away from its production possibilities curve.

Recession A downturn in the business cycle during which real GDP declines, and the unemployment rate rises. Also called a *contraction.*

What is the difference between a *recession* and a *depression*? According to the old saying: "A recession is when your neighbor loses his or her job, and a depression is when you also lose your job!" This one-liner is close to the true distinction between these two concepts. The answer is: Because no subsequent recession has approached the prolonged severity of the Great Depression from 1929 to 1933, the term *depression* is primarily a historical reference to this extremely deep and long recession. The Great Depression is discussed at the end of this chapter, Chapter 14, on aggregate demand and supply, and in Chapter 20, on monetary policy.

Trough The phase of the business cycle in which real GDP reaches its minimum after falling during a recession.

The **trough** is where the level of real GDP "bottoms out." The length of time between the peak and the trough is the duration of the recession. Since the end of World War II, recessions in the United States have averaged 11 months. As shown in Exhibit 12-2, the last recession called the Great Recession lasted 18 months, from December 2007 to June 2009. The percentage decline in real GDP was 4.1 percent, and the national unemployment rate hit a high of 9.7 percent. The Great Recession is the longest since the Great Depression, which lasted 43 months.

Expansion An upturn in the business cycle during which real GDP rises; also called a *recovery.*

The trough is both bad news and good news. It is simultaneously the bottom of the "valley" of the downturn and the foot of the "hill" of improving economic conditions called an **expansion** or *recovery.* An expansion is an upturn in the business cycle during which real GDP rises. During the expansion phase of the cycle, profits generally improve, real GDP increases, and employment moves toward full employment. The longest expansion in U.S. history occurred over 10 years from 1991 to 2001.

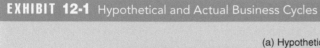

EXHIBIT 12-1 Hypothetical and Actual Business Cycles

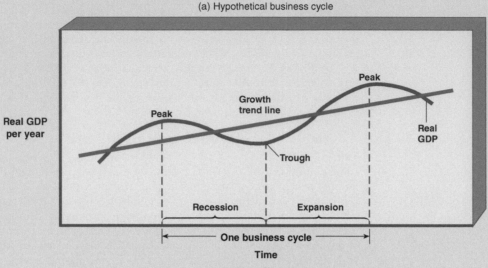

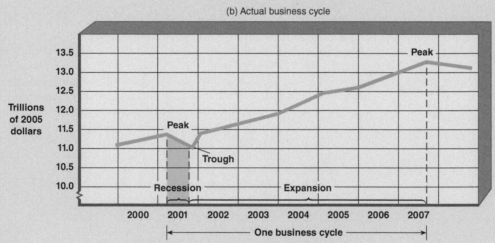

Part (a) illustrates a hypothetical business cycle consisting of four phases: peak, recession, trough, and recovery. These fluctuations of real GDP can be measured by a growth trend line, which shows that over time real GDP has trended upward. In reality, the fluctuations are not so clearly defined as those in this graph.

Part (b) illustrates actual ups and downs of the business cycle. After a recession in 2001, an upswing continued until the Great Recession began in 2007.

Source: Bureau of Economic Analysis, *National Economic Accounts*, http://www.bea.gov/iTable/index_nipa.cfm, Table 1.1.6.

Exhibit 12-1(b) illustrates an actual business cycle by plotting the movement of real GDP in the United States from 2000 to 2007. The economy's initial peak, recession, and trough occurred in 2001, and an expansion phase lasted until a second peak in 2007. The National Bureau of Economic Research's Business Cycle Dating Committee determines when the U.S. economy enters a recession and when a recession ends. This committee is composed of six economists who decide on the beginning and ending dates for a recession based on monthly data rather than real GDP because real GDP is measured quarterly and subject to

EXHIBIT 12-2 Severity of Post–World War II Recessions

Recession Dates	Duration (months)	Percentage decline in Real GDP	Peak Unemployment Rate
Nov. 1948–Oct. 1949	11	−1.7%	7.9%
July 1953–May 1954	10	−2.7	5.9
Aug. 1957–Apr. 1958	8	−1.2	7.4
Apr. 1960–Feb. 1961	10	−1.6	6.9
Dec. 1969–Nov. 1970	11	−0.6	5.9
Nov. 1973–Mar. 1975	16	−3.1	8.6
Jan. 1980–July 1980	6	−2.2	7.8
July 1981–Nov. 1982	16	−2.9	10.8
July 1990–Mar. 1991	8	−1.3	6.8
Mar. 2001–Nov. 2001	8	−0.5	5.6
Dec. 2007–June 2009	18	−4.1	9.7
Average	**11**	**−2.0**	**7.6**

Source: National Bureau of Economic Research, U.S. *Business Cycle Expansion and Contractions,* http://www.nber.org/cycles/cyclesmain.html. Real GDP and unemployment rate data added by author.

large revisions. Factors that the committee considers in defining a recession include decline in employment, industrial production, income, and sales.

12-1b Economic Growth

Economic growth An expansion in national output measured by the annual percentage increase in a nation's real GDP.

We will now expand the definition of **economic growth** given in Chapter 2. In this chapter, recall that an outward shift of the production possibilities curve illustrated economic growth. Also recall that factors such as increases in resources and technological advance were key reasons for economic growth. Here the discussion of economic growth is expanded. Economic growth is defined by economics as an expansion in national output measured by the annual percentage increase in a nation's real GDP. The growth trend line in the hypothetical model in Exhibit 12-1(a) illustrates that over time our real GDP tends to rise. This general, long-term upward trend in real GDP persists in spite of the peaks, recessions, troughs, and recoveries. As shown by the dashed line in Exhibit 12-3, since 1930 real GDP in the United States has grown at an average annual rate of 3.5 percent. This annual change may seem small, but about 3 percent annual growth will lead to a doubling of real GDP in only 24 years.

CONCLUSION We value economic growth as one of our nation's economic goals because it increases our standard of living—it creates a bigger "economic pie."

Closer examination of Exhibit 12-3 reveals that the growth path of the U.S. economy over time is not a smooth, rising trend, but instead a series of year-to-year variation in real GDP. Following the Great Recession beginning in 2007, the growth rate was a −2.8 percent in 2009 before rising to positive percentages since 2010. In 2013, the growth rate was a below average 1.9 percent.

EXHIBIT 12-3 A Historical Record of Business Cycles in the United States, 1929–2013

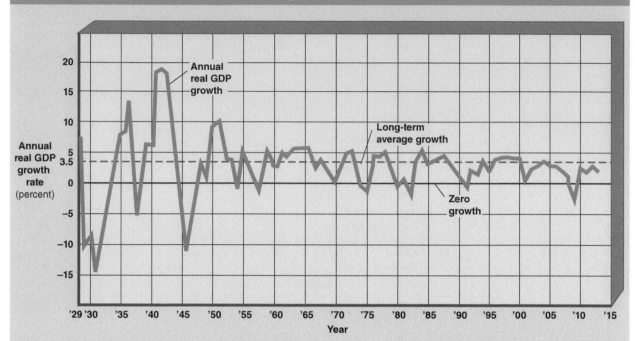

Real GDP has increased at an average annual growth rate of 3.5 percent since 1930. Above-average annual growth rates have alternated with below-average annual growth rates. Following the Great Recession of 2007, the annual growth rate was a negative 2.8 percent in 2009 before rising to positive percentages since 2010.

Source: Bureau of Economic Analysis, *National Economic Accounts*, http://www.bea.gov/iTable/index_nipa.cfm, Table 1.1.1.

CHECKPOINT

Where Are We on the Business-Cycle Roller Coaster?
Suppose the economy is in a recession and everyone is asking when the economy will recover. To find an answer to the state of the economy's health, a television reporter interviews Terrence Carter, a local car dealer. Carter says, "I do not see any recovery. The third quarter of this year we sold more cars than the second quarter, but sales in these two quarters were far below the first quarter." Is Mr. Carter correct? Are his observations consistent with the peak, recession, trough, or expansion phase of the business cycle?

GLOBAL
ECONOMICS

12-1c Real GDP Growth Rates in Other Countries

Exhibit 12-4 presents real GDP growth rates for selected countries in 2013. China and India had the largest rates of growth at 7.6 and 4.4 percent, respectively. The United States and other Western industrial countries in the exhibit had lower growth rates.

12-1d Business-Cycle Indicators

In addition to changes in real GDP, the media often report several other macro variables that measure business activity, which are published by the U.S. Department of Commerce in *Business Conditions Digest*. These economic *indicator* variables are classified in three categories: leading indicators, coincident indicators, and lagging indicators. Exhibit 12-5 lists the variables corresponding to each indicator series.

EXHIBIT 12-4 International Comparison of Real GDP Growth Rates, 2013

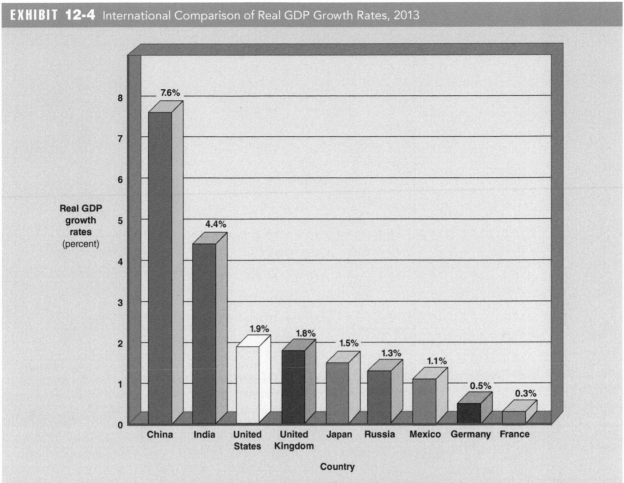

This exhibit shows that in 2013 China and India experienced the highest growth rates. In contrast, the United States and other Western industrial countries had lower growth rates for the year.

Source: International Monetary Fund, *World Outlook Database*, http://www.imf.org/external/ns/cs.aspx?id=28.

Leading indicators Variables that change before real GDP changes.

The government's chief forecasting gauge for business cycles is the index of **leading indicators**. Leading indicators are key variables that change before real GDP changes. This index captures the headlines when there is concern over swings in the economy. The first set of 10 variables in Exhibit 12-5 is used to forecast the business cycle months in advance. For example, a slump ahead is signaled when declines exceed advances in the components of the leading indicators data series. But beware! The leading indicators may rise for two consecutive months and then fall for the next three consecutive months. Economists are therefore cautious and wait for the leading indicators to move in a new direction for several months before forecasting a change in the cycle.

Is a recession near or when will a recession end? The Conference Board's Consumer Confidence Index is often reported in the news as a key measure of the economy's health. It is based on a survey of 5,000 households who are asked their expectations of how well the economy will perform over the next six months. Prolonged consumer pessimism can result in less consumer spending and contribute to slowing economic growth. Stated differently, persistent consumer pessimism can result in lower personal consumption expenditures (C) and

EXHIBIT 12-5 Business-Cycle Indicators

Leading Indicators	
Average workweek	New building permits
Unemployment claims	Stock prices
New consumer goods orders	Money supply
Delayed deliveries	Interest rates
New orders for plant and equipment	Consumer expectations
Coincident Indicators	**Lagging Indicators**
Nonagricultural payrolls	Unemployment rate
Personal income minus transfer payments	Duration of unemployment
Industrial production	Labor cost per unit of output
Manufacturing and trade sales	Consumer price index for services
	Commercial and industrial loans
	Commercial-credit-to-personal-income ratio
	Prime rate

© Cengage Learning®

business investment (I) because businesses reduce investment when consumers' purchases of their products fall.

The second data series of key variables listed in Exhibit 12-5 are four **coincident indicators**. Coincident indicators are variables that change at the same time that real GDP changes. For example, as real GDP rises, economists expect employment, personal income, industrial production, and sales to rise.

The third group of variables listed in Exhibit 12-5 are **lagging indicators**. Lagging indicators are seven variables that change after real GDP changes. For example, the duration of unemployment is a lagging indicator. As real GDP increases, the average time workers remain unemployed does not fall until months after the beginning of the expansion.

Coincident indicators Variables that change at the same time that real GDP changes.

Lagging indicators Variables that change after real GDP changes.

12-2 TOTAL SPENDING AND THE BUSINESS CYCLE

The uneven historical pattern of economic growth for the U.S. economy gives rise to the following question: What causes business cycles? The theory generally accepted by economists today is that changes in total or aggregate expenditures are the cause of variations in real GDP. Recall from the previous chapter that aggregate expenditures refer to total spending for *final goods* by households, businesses, government, and foreign buyers. Expressed as a formula:

Real GDP = C + I + G + (X − M) → Economic Growth

Why do changes in total spending cause the level of GDP to rise during an expansion? Suppose consumers are optimistic about the economic future. If consumer spending (C) increases, then businesses find it profitable to increase investment (I)

Does a Stock Market Crash Cause Recession?
Applicable concept: business cycles

The stock market soared during the "Roaring 20s." People bought fine clothes, had lavish parties, and danced the popular Charleston. Then, on October 29, 1929, Black Thursday, the stock market crashed. During the Great Depression, banks failed, businesses closed their doors, real GDP plummeted, and unemployment soared. Over the years, much debate has occurred over whether the 1929 stock market crash was merely a symptom or a major cause of the downturn. Evidence exists that the 1929 stock market crash only reflected an economic decline already in progress. For example, months before Black Thursday, industrial production had already fallen.

The National Association for Business Economics (NABE) was holding its annual meeting in the World Trade Center when disaster struck the building on September 11, 2001. "The chandeliers shook, we heard a concussive sound, and as we were herding out, we could see that one tower was burning," says Carl Tannenbaum, the chief economist of LaSalle Bank in Chicago, who was attending the meeting.[1] Just the day before a panel of NABE economists predicted slow growth for the economy but no recession. That forecast became obsolete the moment the first plane hit. Analysts predicted a recession and one reason was that the stock market would dive as profit expectations fell. Indeed, as a result of the 9/11 terrorist attacks, the stock market suffered its worst one-week loss since the Great Depression. In the immediate aftermath, equities losses were estimated to be a whopping $1.2 trillion in value.[2]

Prior to the September attacks, the Dow Jones Industrial Average reached a high of about 11,500 in May, but it had fallen almost 2,000 points to a low of 9,431 on September 10, 2001. During this period of time, the economy was plagued with the implosion of the dot.com companies and sharp declines in the high-tech stocks. After the attacks, the stock market closed for the remainder of the week and reopened the following Monday, September 17, 2001, with the famous statue of the Wall Street Bull decorated with American flags and the National Guard patrolling the streets. The result of trading was a huge sell-off and another loss of 1,371 points during the week. Throughout the remainder of the year, the Dow Jones Industrial Average gradually rose

toward pre–September 11 levels and closed at 10,022 on December 31, 2001. Real GDP contracted in the first three quarters of 2001, and then it rose in the final three months of 2001 by 2.7 percent, which was a surprisingly strong performance under the circumstances. The six-member panel at the National Bureau of Economic Research, which is considered the nation's arbiter of U.S. business cycles, declared in November 2001 that a recession had begun in March and ended in November of that year, eight months after it had begun.

Stock market plunges are widely reported headline news. One result of these plunges is that many Americans feel poorer because of the threat to their life's savings. In only a few hours, spectacular paper losses reduce the wealth that people are counting on to pay for homes, automobiles, college tuition, or retirement. Although not all U.S. households own stock, everyone fears a steep downhill ride on the Wall Street roller coaster. If a stock market crash leads to a recession, it would cause layoffs and cuts in profit sharing and pension funds. Businesses fear that many families will postpone buying major consumer items in case they need their cash to tide them over the difficult economic times ahead. Reluctance of consumers to spend lowers aggregate demand and, in turn, prices and profits fall. Falling sales and anxiety about a recession may lead many business executives to postpone modernization plans. Rather than buying new factories and equipment, businesses continue with used plants and machinery, which means lower private investment spending, employment, output, and income for the overall economy.

> **ANALYZE the ISSUE**
>
> 1. To see the effect of the 9/11 attack and accounting scandals on the stock market, visit Big Charts at http://bigcharts.marketwatch.com and click on DJIA graph. To see the changes in real GDP and its components, visit http://www.bea.gov/iTable/index_nipa.cfm.
>
> 2. Explain how a stock market crash could affect the economy. (Hint: Consider the effect on the attitudes of consumers and businesses.)
>
> 3. Research the 1987 stock market crash and its effect on the economy.

[1]"Worldwide, Hope for Recovery Dims," *Business Week*, Sept. 24, 2001, p. 42.
[2]"Economy under Siege," *Fortune*, Oct. 15, 2001, p. 86.

in plants and equipment. When firms become more productive, they use more land, labor, and capital. Such increased spending leads to economic growth in output, employment, and incomes. Economic growth occurs when government spending (G) increases. Growth also comes from increases in spending for exports (X) versus imports spending (M). A recession is the result of declines in sectors of real GDP. Now assume consumers become pessimistic about their economic future. If consumer spending (C) decreases, then business profits fall, and businesses decrease investment (I) in plants and equipment. Business becomes less productive and uses fewer resources. Economic growth can also fall if government spending (G) decreases or export spending (X) falls relative to import spending (M).

The situation just described assumes the economy is operating below full employment. Once the economy reaches full employment, increases in total spending have no impact on real GDP. Further spending in this case will simply pull up the price level and "inflate" nominal GDP.

In subsequent chapters, much more will be explained about the causes of business cycles. Using aggregate demand and supply curves, you will learn to analyze why changes occur in national output, unemployment, and the price level.

12-3 UNEMPLOYMENT

Since the abyss of the Great Depression, a major economic goal of the United States has been to achieve a high level of employment. The *Employment Act of 1946* declared it is the responsibility of the federal government to use all practical means consistent with free competitive enterprise to create conditions under which all able individuals who are willing to work and seeking work will be afforded useful employment opportunities. Later, Congress amended this act with the *Full Employment and Balanced Growth Act of 1978*, which established specific goals for unemployment and the level of prices.

Each month the Bureau of Labor Statistics (BLS) of the U.S. Department of Labor, in conjunction with the Bureau of the Census, conducts a survey of a random sample of about 60,000 households in the United States. Each member of the household who is 16 years of age or older is asked whether he or she is counted as employed or unemployed. If a person works at least 1 hour per week for pay or at least 15 hours per week as an unpaid worker in a family business, he or she is employed. If the person is not employed, the question then is whether he or she has looked for work in the last month. If so, the person is said to be unemployed. Based on its survey data, the BLS publishes the **unemployment rate** and other employment-related statistics monthly.

The unemployment rate is the percentage of people in the **civilian labor force** who are without jobs and are actively seeking jobs. But who is actually counted as an unemployed worker, and which people belong to the labor force? Certainly, all people without jobs are not classified as unemployed. Babies, full-time students, and retired persons are not counted as unemployed. Likewise, individuals who are ill or severely disabled are not included as unemployed. And there are other groups not counted. Turn to Exhibit 12-6. The *civilian labor force* is the number of people 16 years of age and over who are either employed or unemployed, excluding members of the armed forces and other groups listed in the "persons not in labor force" category. Based on survey data, the BLS computes the *civilian unemployment rate*, using the following formula:

$$\text{Unemployment rate} = \frac{\text{unemployed}}{\text{civilian labor force}} \times 100$$

In 2013, the unemployment rate was

$$7.4\% = \frac{11.5 \text{ million persons}}{155.4 \text{ million persons}} \times 100$$

Exhibit 12-7 charts a historical record of the U.S. unemployment rate since 1929. Note that the highest unemployment rate was 25 percent in 1933 during

Unemployment rate The percentage of people in the civilian labor force who are without jobs and are actively seeking jobs.

Civilian labor force The number of people 16 years of age and older who are employed, or who are actively seeking a job, excluding members of the armed forces, homemakers, discouraged workers, and other persons not in the labor force.

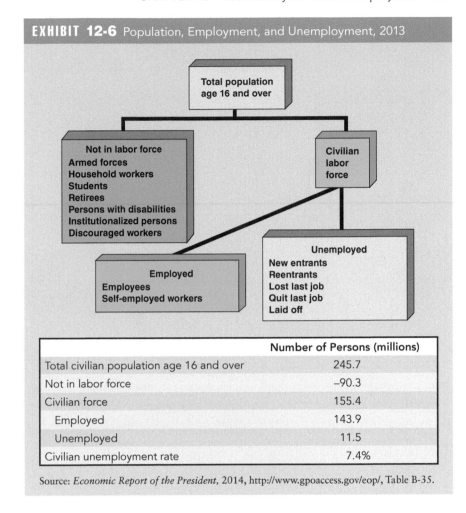

EXHIBIT 12-6 Population, Employment, and Unemployment, 2013

	Number of Persons (millions)
Total civilian population age 16 and over	245.7
Not in labor force	–90.3
Civilian force	155.4
Employed	143.9
Unemployed	11.5
Civilian unemployment rate	7.4%

Source: *Economic Report of the President*, 2014, http://www.gpoaccess.gov/eop/, Table B-35.

the Great Depression. At the other extreme, the lowest unemployment rate we have attained was 1.2 percent in 1944. Following the Great Recession of 2007–2009, the unemployment rate surged to 9.6 percent in 2010, which is the highest level since 1983. In 2013, the unemployment rate was 7.4 percent.

GLOBAL ECONOMICS

12-3a Unemployment in Other Countries

Exhibit 12-8 shows unemployment rates for selected countries in 2013. Most major industrial countries had unemployment rates lower than the United States. For example, the unemployment rate of Japan was 3.4 percent lower than the U.S. rate.

12-3b Unemployment Rate Criticisms

The unemployment rate is criticized for both understating and overstating the "true" unemployment rate. An example of *overstating* the unemployment rate occurs when respondents to the BLS survey report they are seeking employment. The motivation may be that their equilibrium for compensation or welfare benefits depends on actively pursuing a job. Or possibly an individual is "employed" in illegal activities.

EXHIBIT 12-7 The U.S. Unemployment Rate, 1929–2013

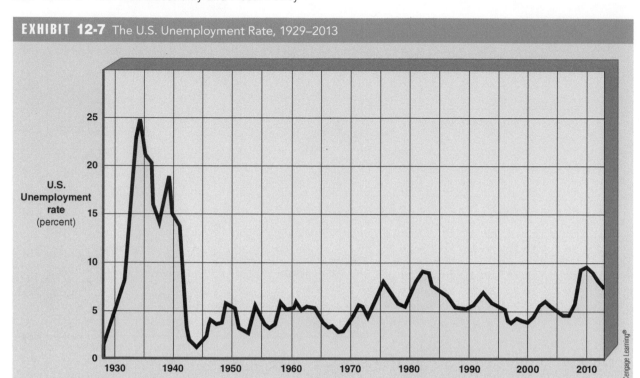

The figure shows fluctuations in the civilian unemployment rate since 1929. The unemployment rate reached a high point of 25 percent in 1933 during the Great Depression. The lowest unemployment rate of 1.2 percent was achieved during World War II in 1944. In 2013, the unemployment rate was 9.6 percent, which was the highest level since 1983. In 2013, the unemployment rate was 7.4 percent.

Source: *Economic Report of the President*, 2014, http://www.access.gpo.gov/eop/, Table B-35.

Discouraged worker A person who wants to work, but who has given up searching for work because he or she believes there will be no job offers.

The other side of the coin is that the official definition of unemployment *understates* the unemployment rate by not counting so-called discouraged workers. A discouraged worker is a person who wants to work but has given up searching for work because he or she believes there will be no job offers. After repeated rejections, discouraged workers often turn to their families, friends, and public welfare for support. The BLS counts a discouraged worker as anyone who has looked for work within the last 12 months, but is no longer actively looking. The BLS simply includes discouraged workers in the "not in labor force" category listed in Exhibit 12-6. Because the number of discouraged workers rises during a recession, the underestimation of the official unemployment rate increases during a downturn.

Another example of *understating* the unemployment rate occurs because the official BLS data include all part-time workers as fully employed. These workers are actually partially employed, and many would work full time if they could find full-time employment. The unemployment rate does not measure *underemployment*. If jobs are scarce and a college graduate takes a job not requiring his or her level of skills, a human resource is underutilized. Or suppose an employer cuts an employee's hours of work from 40 to 20 per week. Such losses of work potential are greater during a recession but are not reflected in the unemployment rate.

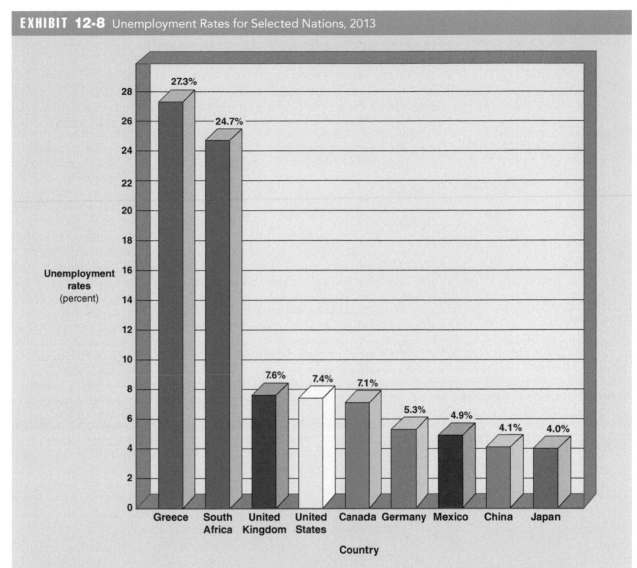

EXHIBIT 12-8 Unemployment Rates for Selected Nations, 2013

In 2013, other nations shown had a higher unemployment rate than the United States. For example, the unemployment rate of Greece was 19.9 percent higher than the U.S. rate. In 2013, the United States had an unemployment rate of 7.4 percent, while China and Japan had lower rates.

Source: International Monetary Fund, *World Economic Outlook Database,* http://www.imf.org/external/ns/cs.aspx?id=28.

12-4 TYPES OF UNEMPLOYMENT

The unemployment rate is determined by three different types of unemployment: *frictional, structural,* and *cyclical.* Understanding these conceptual categories of unemployment aids in understanding and formulating policies to ease the burden of unemployment. In fact, each type of unemployment requires a different policy prescription to reduce it.

12-4a Frictional Unemployment

For some unemployed workers, the absence of a job is only temporary. At any given time, some people with marketable skills are fired, and others voluntarily

Frictional unemployment
Temporary unemployment caused by the time required of workers to move from one job to another.

quit jobs to accept or look for new ones. And there are always young people who leave school and search for their first job. Workers in industries such as construction experience short periods of unemployment between projects, and temporary layoffs are common. Other workers are "seasonally unemployed." For example, ski resort workers will be employed in the winter but not in the summer, and certain crops are harvested "in season." Because jobs requiring the skills of these unemployed workers are available, these unemployed workers and the job vacancies are matched, and such workers are therefore considered "between jobs." This type of unemployment is called frictional unemployment, and it is not of great concern. Frictional unemployment is temporary unemployment caused by the time required for workers to move from one job to another. Frictional unemployment is unemployment caused by the normal search time required by workers with marketable skills who are changing jobs, initially entering the labor force, or reentering the labor force. The cause of frictional unemployment is either the transition time to a new job, or the lack of information required to match a job applicant immediately with a job vacancy. For this reason, frictional unemployment is sometimes called *transitional unemployment* or *search unemployment*.

The fact that job market information is imperfect and operates with "friction" causes frictional unemployment in the economy. Because it takes time to search for the information required to match employer and employees, some workers will always be frictionally unemployed. Frictional unemployment is therefore a normal condition in an economic system permitting freedom of job choice. Improved methods of distributing job information through job listings on the Internet help unemployed workers find jobs more quickly and reduce frictional unemployment.

12-4b Structural Unemployment

Structural unemployment
Unemployment caused by a mismatch of the skills of workers out of work and the skills required for existing job opportunities.

Unlike frictional unemployment, structural unemployment is not a short-term situation. Instead, it is long-term, or possibly permanent, unemployment. Structural unemployment is unemployment caused by a mismatch of the skills of workers who are out of work and the skills required for existing job opportunities. Note that changing jobs and lack of job information are *not* problems for structurally unemployed workers. Unlike frictionally unemployed workers who have marketable skills, structurally unemployed workers require additional education or retraining. The following are four causes of structural unemployment.

Lack of Education

Workers may face joblessness because they lack the education or the job-related skills to perform available jobs. This type of structural unemployment particularly affects teenagers and minority groups, but other groups of workers can be affected as well. For example, environmental concerns, such as protecting the spotted owl by restricting trees from being cut, cost some loggers their jobs. Reducing such structural unemployment requires retraining loggers for new jobs as, say, forest rangers.

Changes in Consumer Demand

The consuming public may decide to increase the demand for Porsches and decrease the demand for Chevrolet Corvettes. This shift in demand would cause U.S. auto workers who lose their jobs in Bowling Green, Kentucky, to become structurally unemployed. To regain employment, these unemployed auto workers must retrain and find job openings in other industries, for example, manufacturing printers in North Carolina. Another example involves the "peace dividend" from the reduction in defense spending after a war. This situation creates structural unemployment for discharged military personnel, who require retraining for, say, teaching, nursing, or police jobs.

Technological Advances

Implementation of the latest technology may also increase the pool of structural unemployment in a particular industry and region. For example, the U.S. textile industry, located primarily in the South, can fight less expensive foreign textile imports by installing modern machinery. This new capital may replace textile workers. But suppose these unemployed textile workers do not wish to move to a new location where new types of jobs are available. The costs of moving, fear of the unknown, and family ties are understandable reasons for being reluctant to move, and, instead, the workers become structurally unemployed until they are retrained for other jobs.

To summarize, there are many causes of structural unemployment, including poor schools, new products, new technology, foreign competition, geographic differences, restricted entry into jobs, and shifts in government priorities. Because of the numerous sources of mismatching between skills and jobs, economists consider a certain level of structural unemployment inevitable. Public and private programs that train employees to fill existing job openings decrease structural unemployment. Conversely, one of the concerns about the minimum wage is that it may contribute to structural unemployment. In Exhibit 4-5 of Chapter 4, we demonstrated that a minimum wage set by legislation above the equilibrium wage causes unemployment. One approach intended to offset such undesirable effects of the minimum wage is a subminimum wage paid during a training period to give employers an incentive to hire unskilled workers.

Globalization

Outsourcing The practice of a company having its work done by another company in another country.

Certain jobs can be globally resourced, which means they can be performed anywhere in the world. U.S. companies sometimes use outsourcing of U.S. jobs to India, China, and other countries. Outsourcing is the practice of a company having its work done by another company in another country. As a result, U.S. workers can lose their jobs and require retraining for other jobs. It can be argued that outsourcing allows U.S. companies to reduce their costs, lower the prices of U.S. goods, and therefore be more competitive in global markets. In short, jobs are saved from being lost to more efficient competitors, and consumers benefit from lower prices.

Offshoring The practice of having work for a company performed by the company's employees located in another country.

A company also has the choice of having a job performed by its own employees in the United States where the product is sold, or in another country. Offshoring occurs when a U.S. company hires employees from another country to perform jobs once done by the company's American employees. Suppose, for example, a U.S. company hires engineers in India to do jobs once done for this company in the United States. Assume the result is that the average salary paid by the company to these engineers drops $50,000 per year. A benefit is that the company reduces it costs although some Americans may lose their jobs and must find new jobs.

In conclusion, there will always be mismatching between skills and jobs. Economists therefore consider a certain level of structural unemployment inevitable.

12-4c Cyclical Unemployment

Cyclical unemployment Unemployment caused by the lack of jobs during a recession.

Cyclical unemployment is directly attributable to the lack of jobs caused by the business cycle. Cyclical unemployment is unemployment caused by the lack of jobs during a recession. When real GDP falls, companies close, jobs disappear, and workers scramble for fewer available jobs. Similar to the game of musical chairs, there are not enough chairs (jobs) for the number of players (workers) in the game.

The Great Depression is a dramatic example of cyclical unemployment. There was a sudden decline in consumption, investment, government spending, and net exports. As a result of this striking fall in real GDP, the unemployment rate rose to about 25 percent (see Exhibit 12-7). Now notice what happened to the unemployment rate when real GDP rose sharply during World War II. The Great Recession beginning in 2007 is another example of cyclical unemployment.

Falling home prices and a plunge in stock prices caused households to cut back on consumption spending and in combination with a fall in business investment spending caused a negative growth rate and sharp rise in the unemployment rate to a high of 9.7 percent at the end of the Great Recession in 2009. To smooth out these swings in unemployment, a focus of macroeconomic policy is to moderate cyclical unemployment.

CHECKPOINT

What Kind of Unemployment Did the Invention of the Wheel Cause?

But Egor, what about the effect on labor?

Did the invention of the wheel cause frictional, structural, or cyclical unemployment?

© 2013 Cengage Learning®

12-5 THE GOAL OF FULL EMPLOYMENT

Full employment The situation in which an economy operates at an unemployment rate equal to the sum of the frictional and structural unemployment rates. Also called the *natural rate of unemployment.*

In this section, we take a closer look at the meaning of **full employment**, also called *the natural rate of unemployment.* Because both frictional and structural unemployment are present in good and bad times, *full employment* does not mean "zero" percent unemployment. Full employment is the situation in which an economy operates at an unemployment rate equal to the sum of the frictional and structural unemployment rates. Full employment therefore is the rate of unemployment that exists without cyclical unemployment.

Unfortunately, economists cannot state with certainty what percentages of the labor force are frictionally and structurally unemployed at any particular point in time. In practice, therefore, full employment is difficult to define. Moreover, the full-employment rate of unemployment, or natural rate of unemployment, changes over time. In the 1960s, 4 percent unemployment was generally considered to represent full employment. In the 1980s, the accepted rate was 6 percent. Currently, the consensus among economists is that the natural rate is close to 5 with a frictional unemployment rate of 3 percent and a structural unemployment of 2 percent.

What Kind of Unemployment Do Robot Musicians Cause?

Applicable concept: types of unemployment

The following is a classic article from the late 1980s that illustrates the types of unemployment and describes a recurring labor market situation:

> People looking for job security have rarely chosen the music industry. But these days, musicians say, competition from machines has removed what little stability there was. Modern machines can effectively duplicate string sections, drummers, and even horn sections, so with the exception of concerts, the jobs available to live musicians are growing fewer by the day. . . .
>
> It is not the first time that technology has thrown a wrench into musical careers. When talking pictures helped usher in the death of vaudeville, and again, when recorded music replaced live music in radio station studios, the market for musicians took a beating from which it never fully recovered. . . . The musicians' plight is not getting universal sympathy. Some industry insiders say that the current job problems are an inevitable price of progress, and that musicians should update their skills to deal with the new instruments. . . .
>
> But others insist that more than musicians' livelihood is at stake. Mr. Glasel, [Musicians' Union] Local 802's president, warns that unbridled computerization of music could eventually threaten the quality of music. Jobs for trumpet players, for instance, have dropped precipitously since the synthesizer managed a fair approximation of the trumpet. And without trumpet players, he asked, "where is the next generation going to get its Dizzy Gillespie?"[1]

The threat to musicians' jobs continues: The Toyota Motor Corp. unveiled its instrument-playing humanoid robots at the 2005 World Exposition. The robots played drums and horn instruments, such as trumpets and tubas. And in 2008, a humanoid robot walked on the stage, said, "Hello, everyone," lifted the baton, and conducted the Detroit Symphony Orchestra. Its timing was judged to be impeccable, but the robot conductor lacked any spur-of-the-moment emotions. In 2011, Honda's humanoid robot named ASIMO was displayed at international events. ASIMO is the world's most advanced humanoid robot that can perform complicated tasks, such as playing soccer, dancing, and opening a sealed bottle and pouring a drink in a paper cup. And in 2012, robots played a soccer match at the RoboCup in Mexico City. Want a body double? A Japanese roboticist in 2013 displayed a striking breathing robotic lookalike of himself even down to its tiny movements and blinking eyes. In fact, someday robots may actually appear indistinguishable from humans.

1. Are the musicians experiencing frictional, structural, or cyclical unemployment? Explain.

2. What solution would you propose for the trumpet players mentioned above?

[1] James S. Newton, "A Death Knell Sounds for Musical Jobs," *The New York Times*, March 1, 1987, sec. 3, p. 9.

Several reasons are given for why full employment is not fixed. One reason is that between the early 1960s and the early 1980s, the participation of women and teenagers in the labor force increased. This change in the labor force composition increased the full-employment rate of unemployment because both women and young workers (under age 25) typically experience higher unemployment rates than men. Another frequently cited and controversial reason for the rise in the full-employment rate of unemployment is that larger unemployment compensation payments, food stamps, welfare, and Social Security benefits from the government make unemployment less painful. In the 1990s, the natural rate of unemployment declined somewhat because the entry of females and teenagers into the labor force slowed. Also, the baby boom generation has aged, and middle-aged workers have lower unemployment rates.

12-6 THE GDP GAP

GDP gap The difference between actual real GDP and potential or full-employment real GDP.

When people in an economy are unemployed, society forfeits the production of goods and services. To determine the dollar value of how much society loses if the economy fails to reach the natural rate of unemployment, economists estimate the **GDP gap**. The GDP gap is the difference between actual real GDP and full-employment real GDP. The level of GDP that could be

EXHIBIT 12-9 Actual and Potential GDP, 1998–2013

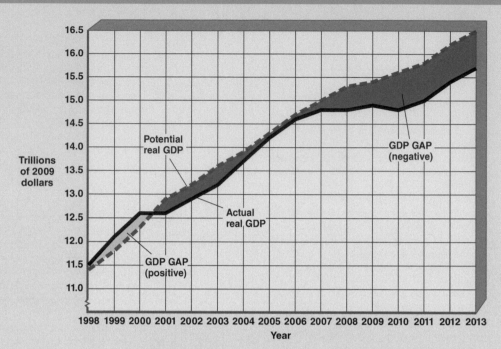

The GDP gap is the difference between actual real GDP and potential real GDP, which is based on the assumption that the economy operates at full employment. A positive GDP gap measures a boom in the economy when workers are employed overtime. Between 1998 and 2000, the U.S. economy experienced positive GDP gaps. The recession in 2001 reversed the GDP gap, and the economy has since operated with a negative GDP gap below its potential. Since the Great Recession beginning in 2007, the U.S. economy has experienced large negative GDP gaps.

Source: International Monetary Fund, *World Economic Outlook Database*, http://www.imf.org/external/ns/cs.aspx?id=28..

produced at full employment is also called *potential real GDP*. Expressed as a formula:

$$\text{GDP gap} = \text{actual real GDP} - \text{potential real GDP}$$

The GDP gap can be either positive if actual real GDP exceeds potential real GDP or negative if actual real GDP is less than potential real GDP. Because the GDP gap is calculated on the basis of the difference between GDP at the actual unemployment rate and estimated GDP at the full-employment rate of unemployment, the GDP gap measures the cost of cyclical unemployment. A positive GDP gap measures a boom in the economy when workers are employed overtime, and a negative GDP gap increases during a recession. Exhibit 12-9 shows the size of the GDP gap (in 2009 prices) from 1998 to 2013, based on potential real GDP and actual real GDP for each of these years. Prior to the 2001 recession, the economy operated above its potential (positive GDP gap). After the 2001 recession, the economy operated below its potential (negative gap). And since the Great Recession beginning in 2007, the U.S. economy has experienced large negative GDP gaps.

CONCLUSION The gap between actual and potential real GDP measures the monetary losses of real goods and services to the nation from operating at less than full employment.

12-6a Nonmonetary and Demographic Consequences of Unemployment

The burden of unemployment is more than the loss of potential output measured by the GDP gap. Unemployment also has nonmonetary costs. Some people endure unemployment pretty well because they have substantial savings to draw on, but others sink into despair. Without work, many people lose their feeling of worth. A person's self-image suffers when he or she cannot support a family and be a valuable member of society. Research has associated high unemployment with suicides, crime, mental illness, heart attacks, and other maladies. Moreover, severe unemployment causes despair, family breakups, and political unrest.

Various labor market groups share the impact of unemployment unequally. Exhibit 12-10 presents the unemployment rates experienced by selected demographic groups. In 2013, the overall unemployment rate was 7.4 percent, but the figures in the exhibit reveal the unequal burden by gender, race, age, and educational attainment. First, note that the unemployment rate for females was less than for males. Second, the unemployment rate for African Americans was more than twice the rate for whites and higher than the rate for Hispanics. Third, teenagers experienced a high unemployment rate because they are new entrants to the workforce who have little employment experience, high quit rates, and little job mobility. Again, race is a strong factor, and the unemployment rate for African-American teenagers was almost twice that for white teenagers. Among the explanations are discrimination; the concentration of African Americans in the inner city where job opportunities for less skilled (blue-collar) workers are inadequate; and the minimum-wage law.

EXHIBIT 12-10 Civilian Unemployment Rates by Selected Demographic Groups, 2013

Demographic Group	Unemployment Rate (percent)
Overall	7.4%
Sex	
Male	7.6
Female	7.1
Race	
White	6.5
Hispanics	9.1
African American	16.0
Teenagers (16–19 years old)	
All	22.9
White	20.3
Hispanics	27.5
African American	38.8
Education	
Less than high school diploma	11.0
High school graduates, no college	7.5
Bachelor's degree or higher	3.7

Source: Bureau of Labor Statistics, *Current Population Survey*, http://stats.bls.gov/cps/cpsatabs .htm, Table A1-A4.

Finally, comparison of the unemployment rates in 2013 by educational attainment reveals the importance of education as an insurance policy against unemployment. Firms are less likely to lay off a higher-skilled worker with a college education, in whom they have a greater investment in terms of training and salaries, than a worker with only a high school diploma.

Key Concepts

Business cycle	Coincident indicators	Outsourcing
Peak	Lagging indicators	Offshoring
Recession	Unemployment rate	Cyclical unemployment
Trough	Civilian labor force	Full unemployment
Expansion	Discouraged worker	GDP gap
Economic growth	Frictional unemployment	
Leading indicators	Structural unemployment	

Summary

- **Business cycles** are recurrent rises and falls in real GDP over a period of years. Business cycles vary greatly in duration and intensity. A cycle consists of four phases: peak, recession, trough, and recovery. The generally accepted theory today is that changes in the forces of demand and supply cause business cycles.

Hypothetical Business Cycle

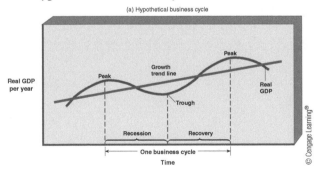

- A **recession** is generally defined as at least two consecutive quarters of real GDP decline. A **trough** is the turning point in national output between recession and recovery. During a **expansion**, there is an upturn in the business cycle during which real GDP rises.

- **Economic growth** is measured by the annual percentage change in real GDP in a nation. The long-term average annual growth rate since 1930 in the United States is 3.5 percent.

- **Leading, coincident,** and **lagging indicators** are economic variables that change before, at the same time as, and after changes in real GDP, respectively.

- The **unemployment rate** is the ratio of the number of unemployed to the number in the civilian labor force

multiplied by 100. The nation's **civilian labor force** consists of people who are employed plus those who are out of work, but seeking employment.

- **Discouraged workers** are a reason critics say the unemployment rate is *understated*. Discouraged workers are persons who want to work, but have given up searching for work. Another criticism of the unemployment rate is that it *overstates* unemployment because respondents can falsely report they are seeking a job.

- **Frictional, structural,** and **cyclical unemployment** are different types of unemployment. **Frictional unemployment,** including seasonal unemployment, results when workers are seeking new jobs that exist. The problem is that imperfect information prevents matching the applicants with the available jobs. **Structural unemployment** is long-term unemployment caused by factors in the economy, including lack of education, changes in consumer demand, technological change, and globalization. **Cyclical unemployment** is unemployment resulting from insufficient aggregate demand.

- **Full employment** occurs when the unemployment rate is equal to the total of the frictional and structural unemployment rates. Currently, the full-employment rate of unemployment (natural rate of unemployment) in the United States is considered to be close to 5 percent. At this rate of unemployment, the economy is producing at its maximum potential.

- The **GDP gap** is the difference between actual real GDP and full-employment real GDP, or potential real GDP. Therefore, the GDP gap measures the loss of output due to cyclical unemployment.

Study Questions and Problems

1. What is the basic cause of the business cycle?
2. Following are real GDP figures for 10 quarters:

Quarter	Real GDP (billions of dollars)	Quarter	Real GDP (billions of dollars)
1	$400	6	$ 500
2	500	7	800
3	300	8	900
4	200	9	1,000
5	300	10	500

© Cengage Learning®

Plot these data points, and identify the four phases of the business cycle. Give a theory that may explain the cause of the observed business cycle. What are some of the consequences of a prolonged decline in real GDP? Is the decline in real GDP from $1,000 billion to $500 billion a recession?

3. In a given year, there are 10 million unemployed workers and 120 million employed workers in the economy. Excluding members of the armed forces and persons in institutions and assuming these figures include only civilian workers, calculate the civilian unemployment rate.

4. Describe the relevant criteria that government statisticians use to determine whether a person is "unemployed."
5. How has the official unemployment rate been criticized for overestimating and underestimating unemployment?
6. Why is frictional unemployment inevitable in an economy characterized by imperfect job information?
7. How does structural unemployment differ from cyclical unemployment?
8. Is it reasonable to expect the unemployment rate to fall to zero for an economy? What is the relationship of frictional, structural, and cyclical unemployment to the full-employment rate of unemployment, or natural rate of unemployment?
9. In the 1960s, economists used 4 percent as their approximation for the natural rate of unemployment. Currently, full employment is on the order of 5 percent unemployment. What is the major factor accounting for this rise?
10. Speculate on why teenage unemployment rates exceed those for the overall labor force.
11. Explain the GDP gap.

Sample Quiz

1. A business cycle is
   a. the period of time in which expansion and contraction of economic activity are equal.
   b. the period of time in which there are three phases: peak, depression, and recovery.
   c. the recurring growth and decline in real GDP.
   d. the period of time in which a business is established and ceases operations.
2. A business cycle is the period of time in which
   a. a business is established and ceases operations.
   b. there are four phases: peak, recession, trough and recovery.
   c. the price level changes.
   d. expansion and contraction of economic activity are equal.
3. The _____ phase of the business cycle follows a recession.
   a. recovery
   b. recession
   c. peak
   d. trough

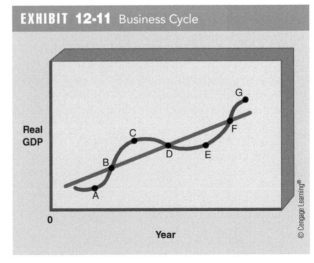

EXHIBIT 12-11 Business Cycle

© Cengage Learning®

4. In Exhibit 12-11, the expansion phase of the business cycle is represented by points
   a. A and C.
   b. B and F.
   c. B and D.
   d. C and G.

5. A general rule is that the economy is experiencing a recession when
   a. real GDP declines for at least three months.
   b. real GDP declines for at least nine months.
   c. nominal GDP declines for at least nine months.
   d. real GDP declines for at least six months.

6. A person who has given up searching for work is called
   a. frictionally unemployed.
   b. structurally unemployed.
   c. a discouraged worker.
   d. unemployed.

7. John Steinbeck's *Cannery Row* describes a character who takes his own life because of poor job prospects. If he was an unemployed person who gave up looking for work, he would be considered
   a. chronically unemployed.
   b. a discouraged worker.
   c. a member of the labor force.
   d. frictionally unemployed.

8. Unemployment that is of a short duration to allow time to find a new job is
   a. structural unemployment.
   b. cyclical unemployment.
   c. frictional unemployment.
   d. durational unemployment.

9. A person who voluntarily quits his/her job in New York and expects to get a similar job in Los Angeles is an example of
   a. structural unemployment.
   b. cyclical unemployment.
   c. durational unemployment.
   d. frictional unemployment.

10. Frictional unemployment refers to
    a. people who are out of work and have no job skills.
    b. short periods of unemployment needed to match jobs and job seekers.
    c. people who spend relatively long periods out of work.
    d. unemployment related to the ups and downs of the business cycle.

11. Sam is a musician who is out of work because electronic equipment replaced live musicians. This is an example of
    a. frictional unemployment.
    b. cyclical unemployment.
    c. structural unemployment.
    d. involuntary unemployment.

12. Louise is unemployed due to a decrease in the demand for workers with a knowledge of a certain word processing language. This is an example of
    a. cyclical unemployment.
    b. frictional unemployment.
    c. involuntary unemployment.
    d. structural unemployment.

13. Consider a broom factory that permanently closes because of foreign competition. If the broom factory's workers cannot find new jobs because their skills are no longer marketable, then they are classified as
    a. seasonally unemployed.
    b. frictionally unemployed.
    c. structurally unemployed.
    d. cyclically unemployed.

14. The increase in unemployment associated with a recession is called
    a. structural unemployment.
    b. frictional unemployment.
    c. discouraged unemployment.
    d. cyclical unemployment.

15. Which of the following is *true*?
    a. The GDP gap is the difference between full-employment real GDP and actual real GDP.
    b. We desire economic growth because it increases the nation's standard of living.
    c. Economic growth is measured by the annual percentage increase in a nation's real GDP.
    d. Discouraged workers are a reason critics say the unemployment rate is understated.
    e. All of the answers above are correct.

16. What stage of the business cycle immediately follows the trough?
    a. Peak.
    b. Recovery.
    c. Recession.
    d. Depression.

17. The government's chief forecasting gauge for business cycles is the
    a. unemployment rate.
    b. real GDP.
    c. personal income index.
    d. index of leading indicators.

18. Which of the following is *not* a lagging indicator?
    a. Duration of unemployment.
    b. Stock prices.
    c. Commercial and industrial loans.
    d. Prime rate.

19. Suppose the official unemployment rate is 10 percent. We can conclude without question that
    a. the same 10 percent of the people in the economy were out of work for the entire year.
    b. one of every 10 people in the civilian labor force is currently unemployed.
    c. the same 10 percent of the people in the civilian labor force were out of work for the entire year.
    d. every person in the civilian labor force was out of work for 10 percent of the year.

20. Sally lost her job when her company went out of business because of a recession. This is an example of
    a. frictional unemployment.
    b. structural unemployment.
    c. cyclical unemployment.
    d. technological unemployment.

Inflation

© Floronikus/Shutterstock.com

In this chapter, you will learn to solve these economics puzzles:

- What is the inflation rate of your college education?
- Can a person's income fall even though he or she received a raise?
- What is the real price of gasoline?
- What would Babe Ruth's salary be worth today?
- Can an interest rate be negative?
- Does inflation harm everyone equally?

CHAPTER PREVIEW

In addition to the goals of full employment and economic growth discussed in the previous chapter, keeping prices stable is one of the most important economic goals facing a nation. In the United States, the Great Depression of the 1930s produced profound changes in our lives. Similarly, the "Great Inflation" of the 1970s and early 1980s left memories of the miseries of inflation. In fact, every American president since Franklin Roosevelt has resolved to keep the price level stable. Politicians are aware that, as with high unemployment, voters are quick to blame any administration that fails to keep inflation rates under control.

This chapter explains what inflation is: What does it mean when a 50 percent hike in the price of gasoline causes pain at the pump, a gallon of milk is up 23 percent, a loaf of bread climbs 16 percent, and around the world others feel the pinch of higher prices? You will study how the government actually measures changes in the price level and computes the rate of inflation. The chapter concludes with a discussion of the consequences and root causes of inflation. It explains who the winners are and who the losers are. For example, you will see what happened in Zimbabwe when the inflation rate reached 231 million percent. After studying this chapter, you will have a much clearer understanding of why inflation is so feared.

13-1 MEANING AND MEASUREMENT OF INFLATION

Inflation An increase in the general (average) price level of goods and services in the economy.

Deflation A decrease in the general (average) price level of goods and services in the economy.

Consumer price index (CPI) An index that measures changes in the average prices of consumer goods and services.

After World War II, a 12-ounce bottle of Pepsi sold for 5 cents. Today, a 12-ounce can of Pepsi sells for more than 20 times that much. This is not **inflation**. Inflation is an increase in the *general* (average) price level of goods and services in the economy. Inflation's opposite is **deflation**. Deflation is a decrease in the *general* (average) price level of goods and services in the economy. Note that inflation does not mean that *all* prices of *all* products in the economy rise during a given period of time. For example, the annual percentage change in the average overall price level during the 1970s reached double digits, but the prices of calculators and digital watches actually declined. The reason that the average price level rose in the 1970s was that the rising prices of Pepsi, houses, and other goods outweighed the falling prices of calculators, digital watches, and other goods.

CONCLUSION Inflation is an increase in the overall average level of prices and not an increase in the price of any specific product.

13-1a The Consumer Price Index

The most widely reported measure of inflation is the **consumer price index (CPI)**, which measures changes in the average prices of consumer goods and services. The CPI is sometimes called the *cost-of-living index*. It includes only consumer goods and services in order to determine how rising prices affect the income of consumers. Unlike the *GDP chain price index* explained in Chapter 11, the CPI does not consider items purchased by businesses and government.

The Bureau of Labor Statistics (BLS) of the Department of Labor prepares the CPI. Each month the bureau's "price collectors" contact retail stores, homeowners, and tenants in selected cities throughout the United States. Based on these monthly inquiries, the BLS records average prices for a "market basket" of different items purchased by the typical family. These items are included under the following categories: food, housing, apparel and upkeep, transportation, medical care, entertainment, and other expenditures. Exhibit 13-1 presents a more detailed breakdown of these categories and shows the relative importance of each as a percentage of total expenditures. The survey reveals, for example, that 32 cents out of each consumer dollar are spent for housing and 18 cents for transportation. The composition of the market basket generally remains unchanged from one period to the next, so the CPI is called a *fixed-weight price index*. If 32 percent of consumer spending was on housing during a given base year, the assumption is that 32 percent of spending is still spent on housing in, say, 2013. Over time, particular items in the CPI change. For example, revisions have added personal computers, digital cameras, and cell phones. The base period is changed periodically.

13-1b How the CPI Is Computed

Exhibit 13-2 illustrates the basic idea behind the CPI using hypothetical data to show how this price index measures inflation. Suppose, in 1982, a typical family in the United States lived a very meager existence and purchased a market basket of only hamburgers, gasoline, and jeans. Column 1 shows the quantity

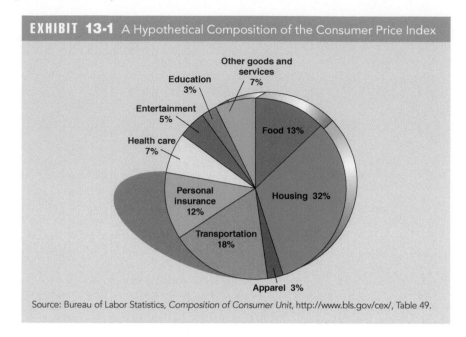

EXHIBIT 13-1 A Hypothetical Composition of the Consumer Price Index

Source: Bureau of Labor Statistics, *Composition of Consumer Unit*, http://www.bls.gov/cex/, Table 49.

purchased for each of these items, and column 2 lists the corresponding average selling price. Multiplying the price times the quantity gives the market basket cost in column 3 of each consumer product purchased in 1982. The total cost paid by our typical family for the market basket, based on 1982 prices and quantities purchased, is $245.

Twelve years later it is 1994, and we wish to know the impact of rising prices on consumer purchases. To calculate the CPI, we determine the cost of the *same* market basket, valued at 1994 *current-year prices*, and compare this to the cost at 1982 *base-year prices*. A **base year** is a year chosen as a reference point for comparison with some earlier or later year. Expressed as a general formula:

Base year A year chosen as a reference point for comparison with some earlier or later year.

$$CPI = \frac{\text{cost of market basket of products at current - year (1994) prices}}{\text{cost of same market basket of products at base - year (1982) prices}} \times 100$$

As shown in Exhibit 13-2, the 1994 cost for our market basket is calculated by multiplying the 1994 price for each item in column 4 times the 1982 quantity purchased in column 1. Column 5 lists the result for each item in the market basket, and the total market basket cost in 1994 is $335. The CPI value of 136.7 is computed in Exhibit 13-2 as the ratio of the current 1994 cost of the market basket ($335) to the cost of the same market basket in the 1982 base year ($245) multiplied by 100.

The value of the CPI in the base year is always 100 because the numerator and the denominator of the CPI formula are the same in the base year. Currently, the CPI uses 1982–1984 spending patterns as its base year. Once the BLS selects the base year and uses the market basket technique to generate the CPI numbers, the annual *inflation rate* is computed as the percentage change in the official CPI from one year to the next. Mathematically,

$$\text{Annual rate of inflation} = \frac{\text{CPI in given year} - \text{CPI in previous year}}{\text{CPI in previous year}} \times 100$$

Exhibit 13-3 lists actual CPI data for selected years. You can use the above formula and calculate the inflation rate for any given year using the base year

EXHIBIT 13-2 A Hypothetical Consumer Price Index for a Simple Economy

Products in Consumers Market Basket	(1) 1982 Quantity Purchased	(2) 1982 Price	(3) Market Basket Cost in 1982 [(1)×(2)]	(4) 1994 Price	(5) Market Basket Cost in 1994 [(1)×(4)]
Hamburgers	50	$ 0.80	$ 40	$ 1.00	$ 50
Gallons of gasoline	250	0.70	175	0.90	225
Jeans	2	15.00	30	30.00	60
			Total 1982 cost = $245		Total 1994 cost = $335

$$1994\,CPI = \frac{1994\,market\,basket\,cost}{1982\,market\,basket\,cost} \times 100$$

$$1994\,CPI = \frac{\$335}{\$245} \times 100 = 136.7$$

of 1982–1984 = 100. In 2013, for example, the CPI was 232.4, while in 2012 it was 228.9. The rate of inflation for 2013 is computed as follows:

$$1.5\% = \frac{232.4 - 228.9}{228.9} \times 100$$

The negative inflation rate of 9.9 percent for 1932 was deflation, and the 13.5 percent inflation rate for 1980 illustrates a relatively high rate in recent U.S. history. The fall in the inflation rate from 2.8 percent to 1.6 percent between 2001 and 2002 was disinflation. Disinflation is a reduction in the rate of inflation. Disinflation does not mean that prices are falling; rather, it means that the rate of increases in prices is falling. The negative inflation rate of −0.4 percent in 2009 was the first deflation since 1955.

Disinflation A reduction in the rate of inflation.

EXHIBIT 13-3 Consumer Price Indexes and Percentage Changes, Selected Years

Year	CPI	Percent Change
1931	15.2	–
1932	13.7	–9.9%
1979	72.6	–
1980	82.4	13.5
2000	172.2	–
2001	177.1	2.8
2002	179.9	1.6
2008	215.3	3.9
2009	214.5	–0.4
2012	228.9	–
2013	232.4	1.5

Source: Bureau of Labor Statistics, *Consumer Price Index*, http:///data.bls.gov/cgi-bin/surveymost?cu.

ECONOMICS IN PRACTICE

How Much More Does It Cost to Laugh?
Applicable concept: consumer price index

Are we paying bigger bucks for smaller yuks? Or is it a lower fee for more glee? Is there a bone to pick with the price of rubber chickens? Is the price of Groucho glasses raising eyebrows, the cost of *Mad* magazine driving you mad, and, well, you get the idea. Malcolm Kushner, an attorney-turned-humor consultant based in Santa Cruz, California, developed an index based on a compilation of leading humor indicators to measure price changes in things that make us laugh. Kushner created the cost-of-laughing index to track how trends in laughter affect the bottom line. He is a humor consultant who advises corporate leaders on making humor work for business professionals. For example, humor can make executives better public speakers, and laughter reduces stress and can even cure illnesses. Kushner believes humor is America's greatest asset, and his consulting business gets a lot of publicity from publication of the index. To combat rising humor costs, Kushner has established a Web site at http://www .kushnergroup.com. It organizes links to databases of funny quotes, anecdotes, one-liners, and other material for business speakers and writers.

The exhibit with the Groucho face traces annual percentage changes in the cost of laughing that Kushner has reported to the media. On an annual basis, the inflation rate for laughing remained almost flat as a pancake at about 3 percent from 2000 through 2005. Then, in 2006, the humor index took a slippery slide on a banana peel to a disinflation rate of only one-tenth of 1 percent. In 2007, the index rode a roller coaster ride up to 4.7 percent, which was the largest increase since 1999, and then down to −1.4 percent in 2009. This deflation was the first negative percent change in the index history that began in 1987. And since 2010 the index has fallen to a modest 1.7 percent in 2013.

Closer examination of the cost-of-laughing index over the years and some other items gives both smiley and sad faces. The good news in 2013 is that the price of the New York Comic Strip a whoopee cushion decreased, but the bad news is that the cost of rubber chickens flew up . The major reason for more expensive humor is the price of writing a half-hour television situation comedy. Just like the CPI, Kushner's index has been criticized. Note that the fee for writing a TV sitcom dominates the index. Kushner responds to this issue by saying, "Well, I wanted the index to be truly national. The fact that this price dominates the index reflects that TV comedy shows dominate our national culture. If you can laugh for free at a sitcom, you don't need to buy a rubber chicken or go to a comedy club."

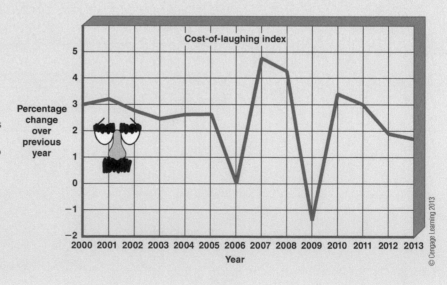

Cost of Laughing Index

Item	2010	2011	2012	2013
Rubber chicken[1]	$72.00	$78.00	$78.00	$84.00
Groucho glasses[1]	21.00	24.00	24.00	24.00
Whoopee Cushion[1]	3.00	1.20	4.50	5.00
Mad magazine	5.99	5.99	5.99	5.99
Singing telegrams[2]				
Pink gorilla	185.00	185.00	185.00	185.00
Dancing chicken	185.00	185.00	185.00	185.00
Fee for writing a TV sitcom[3]	15,946.00	16,437.00	16,752.00	17,045.00
Comedy clubs[4]				
Atlanta: The Punch Line	20.00	20.00	20.00	20.00
Chicago: Second City	27.00	27.00	28.00	28.00
Houston: Improv	15.00	15.00	17.00	20.80
Denver: Comedy Works	25.00	25.00	22.00	23.80
Indianapolis: Crackers Comedy	13.00	13.00	15.00	10.80
Los Angeles: Laugh Factory	20.00	20.00	20.00	23.00
New York: Comic Strip	25.00	25.00	20.00	16.26
Pittsburgh: Improv	15.00	15.00	20.00	20.00
San Francisco: Punch Line	21.00	21.00	21.00	23.50
Seattle: Comedy Underground	15.00	15.00	15.00	15.00
Total cost of humor basket	$16,613.99	$17,112.19	$17,432.49	$17,735.15
Annual inflation rate	**3.4%**	**3.0%**	**1.9%**	**1.7%**

[1] One dozen wholesale from Franco-American Novelty Company, Long Island City, New York.
[2] Available from International Singing Telegrams, Akron, Ohio.
[3] Minimum fee under Writers Guild of America Basic Agreement.
[4] Admission on Saturday night.

Source: Data provided by Malcolm Kushner.

ANALYZE the ISSUE No question here. This one is just for fun.

CHECKPOINT

The College Education Price Index

Suppose your market basket for a college education consisted of only the four items listed in the following table:

Item	2012	2013
Tuition and fees[1]	$4,500	$5,000
Room and board[2]	6,000	6,200
Books[3]	1,000	1,200
Soft drinks[4]	150	200

[1] Tuition for two semesters.
[2] Payment for nine months.
[3] Ten textbooks.
[4] Two hundred 12-ounce Coca-Colas.

Using 2012 as your base year, what is the percentage change in the college education price index in 2013?

13-1c History of U.S. Inflation Rates

Exhibit 13-4 shows how prices have changed in the United States since 1929, as measured by annual changes in the CPI. During the early years of the Great Depression, the nation experienced *deflation*, and the CPI declined at almost a double-digit rate. In contrast, the CPI reached a double-digit inflation rate during

EXHIBIT 13-4 The U.S. Inflation Rate, 1929–2013

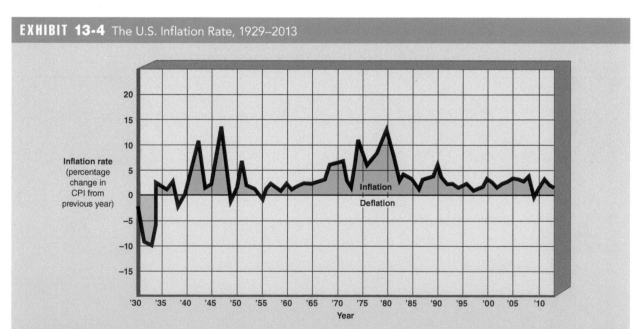

During the Great Depression, the economy experienced deflation as prices plunged. During and immediately after World War II, the annual rate of inflation reached the double-digit level. After 1950, the inflation rate was generally below 3 percent and until the inflationary pressures from the Vietnam War in the late 1960s. During the 1950–1968 period, the average inflation rate was only 2 percent. In contrast, the inflation rate climbed sharply to an average of 7.6 percent between 1969 and 1982. Between 1992 and 2009, inflation moderated and averaged 2.6 percent annually. In 2009, during the Great Recession, the deflation rate was –0.4 percent. In 2013, the inflation rate was a modest 1.5 percent.

Source: Economic Report of the President, 2011, http://www.gpoaccess.gov/eop/, Table B-64.

and immediately following World War II. After 1950, the inflation rate was generally below 3 percent until the inflationary pressures from the Vietnam War in the late 1960s. In fact the average inflation rate between 1950 and 1968 was only 2 percent. During the 1973–1982 period, the average annual inflation rate was 8.8 percent reaching a high of 13.5 percent in 1980. Following the 1990–1991 recession, the annual inflation rate moderated and it averaged 2.6 percent between 1992 and 2009. In 2009, during the Great Recession, the deflation rate was –0.4 percent. In 2013, the inflation rate was a modest 1.5 percent.

13-1d Consumer Price Index Criticisms

Just as there is criticism of the unemployment rate, the CPI is not a perfect measure of inflation, and it has been the subject of much public debate. There are three reasons for this criticism:

1. Changes in the CPI are based on a typical market basket of products purchased that does not match the actual market basket purchased by many consumers. Suppose you spend your nominal annual income entirely on lemonade, hot dogs, and jeans. During this year, the inflation rate is 5 percent, but assume the prices of lemonade, hot dogs, and jeans actually fall. In this case, your real income will rise, and the official inflation rate based on the CPI will *overstate* the impact of inflation on your standard of living. Retired persons, for example, buy a bundle of products that differs from that of the "typical" family. Because retired persons purchase proportionally more medical services than the typical family, the inflation rate may understate the impact of inflation on older persons.

2. The BLS has difficulty adjusting the CPI for changes in *quality*. Compare a TV made in the past with a new TV. The new TV may cost somewhat more, but it is much better than the old TV. A portion of the price increase therefore reflects better quality instead of simply a higher price for the same item. If the quality of items improves, increases in the CPI *overstate* inflation. Similarly, deteriorating quality *understates* inflation. The BLS attempts to make adjustments for quality changes in automobiles, electronic equipment, and other products in the market basket, but these adjustments are difficult to determine accurately.

3. The use of a single base-year market basket ignores the law of demand. If the price of a product rises, consumers purchase substitutes, and a smaller quantity is demanded. Suppose orange growers suffer from severe frosts and the supply of oranges decreases. Consequently, the price of oranges increases sharply. According to the *law of demand*, consumers will decrease the quantity demanded of oranges and substitute consumption of, say, apples for oranges. Because the market basket does not automatically change by reducing the percentage or weight of oranges and increasing the percentage of apples, the CPI will *overstate* the impact of higher prices for oranges on the price level. To deal with this *substitution* bias problem, the BLS takes annual surveys to keep up with changing consumption patterns and correct for the fixed market basket limitations of the CPI.

13-2 CONSEQUENCES OF INFLATION

We will now turn from measuring inflation to its effects on people's income and wealth. Why should inflation cause concern? You will learn in this section that inflation is feared because it can significantly alter one's standard of living. In this section, you will see that inflation can create winners, who enjoy a larger slice of the national income pie, and losers, who receive a smaller slice as a result of inflation.

13-2a Inflation Shrinks Income

Economist Arthur Okun once stated, "This society is built on implicit and explicit contracts. . . . They are linked to the idea that the dollar means something. If you cannot depend on the value of the dollar, this system is undermined. People will constantly feel they've been fooled and cheated." When prices rise, people worry whether the rise in their income will keep pace with inflation. And the more quickly prices rise, the more people suffer from the stresses of inflation and its uncertainties.

Inflation tends to reduce your standard of living through declines in the purchasing power of money. The greater the rate of inflation, the greater the decline in the quantity of goods we can purchase with a given nominal income or *money income*. Nominal income is the actual number of dollars received over a period of time. The source of income can be wages, salary, rent, dividends, interest, or pensions.

Nominal income does not measure your real purchasing power. Finding out if you are better or worse off over time requires converting nominal income to real income. Real income is the actual number of dollars received (nominal income) adjusted for changes in the CPI. Real income measures the amount of goods and services that can be purchased with one's nominal income. If the CPI increases and your nominal income remains the same, your real income (purchasing power) falls. In short, if your nominal income fails to keep pace with inflation, your standard of living falls. Suppose your nominal income in 2012 is $50,000 and the 2012 CPI value is 228.9. Your real income relative to a base year is

$$\text{Real income} = \frac{\text{nominal income}}{\text{CPI (as decimal, or CPI/100)}}$$

$$2012 \text{ real income} = \frac{\$50,000}{2.289} = \$21,844$$

Now assume your nominal income rises in 2013 by 10 percent, from $50,000 to $55,000, and the CPI increases by 1.5 percent, from 228.9 to 232.4. Thus, you earn more money, but how much better off are you? To answer this question, you must compute your 2013 real income as follows:

$$2013 \text{ real income} = \frac{\$55,000}{2.324} = \$23,666$$

Using the real-income figures we computed, the percentage change in your real income between 2012 and 2013 was 8.3 percent ($1,822/$21,844 × 100). This means that your standard of living has risen because you have an extra $1,822 to spend on movies, clothes, or travel. Even though the general price level has risen, your purchasing power has increased because the percentage rise in nominal income more than offsets the rate of inflation. Instead of precisely calculating this relationship, a good approximation can be obtained through the following simple formula:

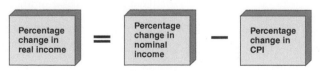

It should be noted that workers with union contracts are largely unaffected by inflation because their wages automatically increase with increases in the CPI, which is called a *cost-of-living adjustment* (COLA). For example, under union contracts with a COLA provision, an inflation rate of 3 percent in a given year would automatically increase wages by 3 percent.

Nominal income The actual number of dollars received over a period of time.

Real income The actual number of dollars received (nominal income) adjusted for changes in the CPI.

Library of Congress Prints and Photographs Division(LC-US262-98072)

CONCLUSION People whose nominal incomes rise faster than the rate of inflation gain purchasing power, while people whose nominal incomes do not keep pace with inflation lose purchasing power.

Now suppose someone asks you the following question: In 1932, Babe Ruth, the New York Yankee's home run slugger, earned $80,000. How much did he earn in 2013 dollars? Economists convert a past salary into a salary today by using this formula:

$$\text{Salary in given year} = \text{Salary in previous year} \times \frac{\text{CPI given year}}{\text{CPI previous year}}$$

$$\text{Salary in 2013 dollars} = \$80,000 \times \frac{232.4}{13.7} = \$1,357,080$$

In other words, a salary of $80,000 in 1932 is the same as earning a salary of about 1.3 million today.

CHECKPOINT

What Is the Real Price of Gasoline?

In 1981, consumers were shocked when the average price for gasoline reached $1.35 per gallon because only a few years previously gasoline was selling for one half this price. If the CPI in 1981 was 90.9 and the CPI in 2013 was 232.4, what is the average inflation adjusted price in 2013 dollars?

"I've called the family together to announce that, because of inflation, I'm going to have to let two of you go."

Joseph Farris/Condé Nast Publications/www.cartoonbank.com

13-2b Inflation and Wealth

Wealth The value of the stock of assets owned at some point in time.

Income is one measure of economic wellbeing, and **wealth** is another. Income is a flow of money earned by selling factors of production. Wealth is the value of the stock of assets owned at some point in time. Wealth includes real estate, stocks, bonds, bank accounts, life insurance policies, cash, and automobiles.

A person can have a high income and little wealth, or great wealth and little income.

Inflation can benefit holders of wealth because the value of assets tends to increase as prices rise. Consider a home purchased for $200,000 that sells ten years later for $300,000. This 50 percent increase can be largely as a result of inflation. People who own forms of wealth that increase in value faster than the inflation rate, such as real estate or stocks are winners. On the other hand, the impact of inflation on wealth penalizes people without it. Consider younger couples wishing to purchase a home. As prices rise, it becomes more difficult for them to buy a home or acquire other assets.

13-2c Inflation and the Real Interest Rate

Nominal interest rate The actual rate of interest without adjustment for the inflation rate.

Real interest rate The nominal rate of interest minus the inflation rate.

Borrowers and savers may be winners or losers, depending on the rate of inflation. Understanding how this might happen requires making a distinction between the nominal interest rate and the real interest rate. The nominal interest rate is the actual rate of interest earned over a period of time. The nominal interest rate, for example, is the interest rate specified on a loan or savings account. If you borrow $10,000 from a bank at a 5 percent annual interest rate for five years, this is more accurately called a 5 percent annual nominal interest rate. Similarly, a $10,000 certificate of deposit that yields 5 percent annual interest is said to have a 5 percent annual nominal interest rate.

The real interest rate is the nominal interest rate minus the inflation rate. The occurrence of inflation means that the real rate of interest will be less than the nominal rate. Suppose the inflation rate during the year is 2 percent. This means that a 5 percent annual nominal interest rate paid on a $10,000 loan amounts to a 3 percent *real interest rate*, and a certificate of deposit that yields 5 percent annual nominal interest also earns 3 percent *real interest*.

To understand how inflation can make those who borrow winners, suppose you receive a one-year loan from your parents to start a business. Earning a profit is not your parents' motive, and they know you will repay the loan. Their only concern is that you replace the decline in purchasing power of the money they loaned you. Both you and your parents anticipate the inflation rate will be 2 percent during the year, so the loan is made and you agree to repay the principal plus the 2 percent to offset inflation. In short, both parties assume payment of a zero real interest rate (the 2 percent nominal interest rate minus the 2 percent rate of inflation). Now consider what happens if the inflation rate is actually 5 percent during the year of the loan. The clear unintentional winner is you, the debtor, because your creditor parents are paid the principal plus 2 percent interest, but their purchasing power still falls by 3 percent because the actual inflation rate is 5 percent. Stated differently, instead of zero, the real interest rate paid on the loan was −3 percent (the 2 percent nominal interest rate minus the 5 percent rate of inflation). In real terms, your parents paid you to borrow from them.

Adjustable-rate mortgage (ARM) A home loan that adjusts the nominal interest rate to changes in an index rate, such as rates on Treasury securities.

During the late 1970s, the rate of inflation rose frequently. This forced mortgage lenders to protect themselves against declining real interest rates on their loans by offering adjustable-rate mortgages (ARMs) in addition to conventional fixed-rate mortgages. ARMs are home loans that adjust the nominal interest rate to changes in an index rate, such as rates on Treasury securities. A *subprime loan crisis* associated with the Great Recession of 2007 resulted from homeowners who were unable to make payments as the interest rate rose on their ARMs. This subject is discussed in more detail in the chapter on monetary policy.

A nest egg in the form of a savings account set aside for a rainy day is also affected by inflation. For example, if the interest rate on a one-year $10,000 certificate of deposit is 5 percent and the inflation rate is zero (5 percent real interest rate), the certificate holder will earn a 5 percent return on his or her savings. If the inflation rate exceeds the nominal rate of interest, the real interest rate is negative, and the saver is hurt because the interest earned does not keep pace with the inflation rate. This is the reason: Suppose, after one year, the saver withdraws the original $10,000 plus the $500 interest earned and the inflation rate during the year has been 10 percent. The real value of $10,500 adjusted for loss of purchasing power is only $9,500 [$10,000 + ($10,000 × −0.05)].

Finally, it is important to note that the nominal interest rate is never negative, but the real interest rate can be either positive or negative.

> **CONCLUSION** When the real rate of interest is negative, lenders and savers lose because interest earned does not keep up with the inflation rate.

13-3 DEMAND-PULL AND COST-PUSH INFLATION

Economists distinguish between two basic types of inflation, depending on whether it originates from the buyers' or the sellers' side of the market. The analysis presented in this section returns to the cause-and-effect relationship between total spending and the business cycle discussed in the previous chapter.

13-3a Demand-Pull Inflation

Demand-pull inflation A rise in the general price level resulting from an excess of total spending (demand).

Perhaps the most familiar type of inflation is demand-pull inflation, which is a rise in the general price level resulting from an excess of total spending (demand). Demand-pull inflation is often expressed as "too much money chasing too few goods." When sellers are unable to supply all the goods and services buyers demand, sellers respond by raising prices. In short, the general price level in the economy is "pulled up" by the pressure from buyers' total expenditures.

Demand-pull inflation occurs at or close to full employment, when the economy is operating at or near full capacity. Recall that at full employment all but the frictionally and structurally unemployed are working and earning income. Therefore, total, or aggregate, demand for goods and services is high. Businesses find it profitable to expand their plants and production to meet the buyers' demand, but cannot in the short run. As a result, national output remains fixed, and prices rise as buyers try to outbid one another for the available supply of goods and services. If total spending subsides, so will the pressure on the available supply of products and prices will not rise as rapidly or may even fall.

A word of caution: The only culprit in the demand-pull story may not be consumers. Recall that total aggregate spending includes consumer spending (C), business investment (I), government spending (G), and net exports (X − M). Even foreigners may contribute to inflation by bidding up the price of U.S. exports.

13-3b Cost-Push Inflation

Cost-push inflation An increase in the general price level resulting from an increase in the cost of production.

An excess of total spending is not the only possible explanation for rising prices. For example, suppose the Organization of Petroleum Exporting Countries (OPEC) sharply increased the price of oil. This action means a significant increase in the cost of producing goods and services. The result could be cost-push inflation. Cost-push inflation is a rise in the general price level resulting from an increase in the cost of production.

The source of cost-push inflation is not always such a dramatic event as an OPEC price hike. Any sharp increase in costs to businesses can be a potential source of cost-push inflation. This means that upward pressure on prices can be caused by cost increases for labor, raw materials, construction, equipment, borrowing, and so on. Businesses can also contribute to cost-push inflation by raising prices to increase profits.

The influence of *expectations* on both demand-pull and cost-push inflation is an important consideration. Suppose buyers see prices rise and believe they should purchase that new house or car today before these items cost much more tomorrow. At or near full employment, this demand-pull results in a rise in prices. On the suppliers' side, firms might expect their production costs to rise in the future, so they raise prices in anticipation of the higher costs. The result is cost-push inflation.

Here you should take note of coming attractions. The next chapter develops aggregate demand and supply. Using this modern macro model, you will learn to analyze with more precision factors that determine national output, employment, and the price level. In particular, the last section of Chapter 14 applies the aggregate demand and supply model to the concepts of demand-pull and cost-push inflation. Also, Chapter 20 on monetary policy will discuss the theory that inflation is the result of increases in the money supply in excess of increases in the production of goods and services.

13-4 INFLATION IN OTHER COUNTRIES

Exhibit 13-5 reveals that inflation rates vary widely among nations. In 2013, Venezuela and Sudan experienced very high rates of inflation. In contrast, the United States had a low inflation rate of 1.5 percent, while Japan had only a 0.4 percent rate.

13-4a Inflation on a Rampage

Hyperinflation An extremely rapid rise in the general price level.

Some people must carry a large stack of money to pay for a chocolate bar because of the disastrous consequences of **hyperinflation**. Hyperinflation is an extremely rapid rise in the general price level. There is no consensus on when a

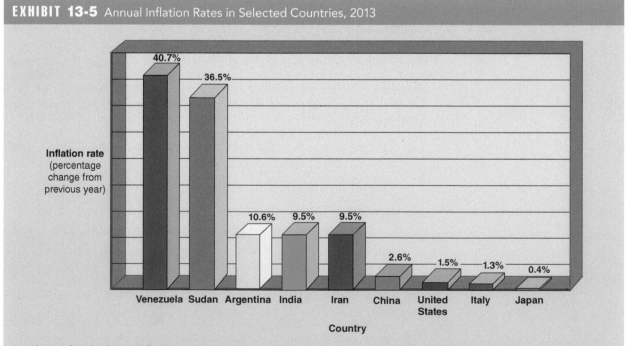

EXHIBIT 13-5 Annual Inflation Rates in Selected Countries, 2013

Inflation rate (percentage change from previous year)

- Venezuela 40.7%
- Sudan 36.5%
- Argentina 10.6%
- India 9.5%
- Iran 9.5%
- China 2.6%
- United States 1.5%
- Italy 1.3%
- Japan 0.4%

Country

As shown by the bars, inflation was a serious problem in 2013 for Venezuela, and Sudan. The United States experienced a low inflation rate of 1.5 percent, while Japan had only a 0.4 percent rate.

Source: International Monetary Fund, *World Economic Outlook Database*, http://www.imf.org/external/ns/cs.aspx?id=28.

particular rate of inflation becomes "hyper." However, most economists would agree that an inflation rate of about 100 percent per year or more is hyperinflation. Runaway inflation is conducive to rapid and violent social and political change stemming from four causes.

GLOBAL ECONOMICS

When the Inflation Rate Is 116,000 Percent, Prices Change by the Hour

Applicable concept: hyperinflation

The following are two historical examples of hyperinflation:

A *Wall Street Journal* 1985 article described hyperinflation in La Paz, Bolivia:

A courier stumbles into Banco Boliviano Americano, struggling under the weight of a huge bag of money he is carrying on his back. He announces that the sack contains 32 million pesos, and a teller slaps on a notation to that effect. The courier pitches the bag into a corner. "We don't bother counting the money anymore," explains Max Lowes Stah, a loan officer standing nearby. "We take the client's word for what's in the bag." Pointing to the courier's load, he says, "That's a small deposit." At that moment the 32 million pesos—enough bills to stuff a mail sack—were worth only $500. Today, less than two weeks later, they are worth at least $180 less. Life's like that with quadruple-digit inflation. . . .

Prices go up by the day, the hour or the customer. If the pace continues all year, it would mean an annual rate of 116,000 percent. The 1,000-peso bill, the most commonly used, costs more to print than it purchases. To purchase an average-size television set with 1,000-peso bills, customers have to haul money weighing more than 68 pounds into the showroom. Inflation makes use of credit cards impossible here, and merchants generally can't take checks, either. Restaurant owners often covered their menus with cellophane and changed prices several times daily using a dry-erase marker.[1]

A *San Francisco Chronicle* article reported on hyperinflation in Zimbabwe:

What is happening is no laughing matter. (In 2008, the annual inflation rate was 231 million percent.) For untold numbers of Zimbabweans, bread, margarine, meat, and even the morning cup of tea have become unimaginable luxuries. The city suffers rolling electrical blackouts because the state cannot afford parts or technicians to fix broken down power turbines. Mounds of uncollected garbage pile up on the streets

of slums. Public-school fees and other ever-rising government surcharges have begun to exceed the monthly incomes of many urban families lucky enough to work. Those with spare cash put it not in banks, but in gilt-edged investments like bags of cornmeal and sugar, guaranteed not to lose their value.[2] In 2010, Zimbabwe's central bank announced the introduction of new 100 trillion, 50 trillion, and 10 trillion notes. Want to be a trillionaire? Buy Zimbabwe notes.

A *Newsweek* article made the following thoughtful observation:

Hyperinflation is the worst economic malady that can befall a nation, wiping out the value of money, savings, assets, and thus work. It is worse even than a deep recession. Hyperinflation robs you of what you have now (savings), whereas a recession robs you of what you might have had (higher standards of living if the economy had grown). That's why it so often toppled governments and produced revolution. Recall that it was not the Great Depression that brought the Nazis to power in Germany but rather hyperinflation, which destroyed the middle class of that country by making its savings worthless.[3]

ANALYZE the ISSUE

1. Can you relate inflation psychosis to these excerpts? Give an example of a debtor–lender relationship that is jeopardized by hyperinflation.
2. Explain why the workers in Bolivia were striking even though wages rose at an annual rate of 1,500 percent. Do you see any connection between hyperinflation and the political system?

[1] Sonia L. Nazario, "When Inflation Rate Is 116,000 Percent, Prices Change by the Hour," *The Wall Street Journal*, Feb. 7, 1985, p. 1.
[2] Michale Wines, "Zimbabwe: Inflation Capitol," *San Francisco Chronicle*, May 2, 2006, p. A-2.
[3] Fareed Zakaria, "Is This the End of Inflation? Turkey's Currency Crisis May Be the Last Battle in the Global War against Hyperinflation," *Newsweek*, Mar. 19, 2001, p. 38.

First, individuals and businesses develop an *inflation psychosis*, causing them to buy quickly today in order to avoid paying even more tomorrow. Everyone feels pressure to spend their earnings before their purchasing power deteriorates. No matter whether you are paid once, twice, or any number of times per day, you will be eager to spend it immediately.

Second, huge unanticipated inflation jeopardizes debtor–lender contracts, such as credit cards, home mortgages, life insurance policies, pensions, bonds, and other forms of savings. For example, if nominal interest rates rise unexpectedly in response to higher inflation, borrowers find it more difficult to make their monthly payments.

Wage–price spiral A situation that occurs when increases in nominal wage rates are passed on in higher prices, which, in turn, result in even higher nominal wage rates and prices.

Third, hyperinflation sets a wage–price spiral in motion. A wage–price spiral occurs in a series of steps when increases in nominal wage rates are passed on in higher prices, which, in turn, result in even higher nominal wage rates and prices. A wage–price spiral continues when management believes it can boost prices faster than the rise in labor costs. As the cost of living moves higher, however, labor must again demand even higher wage increases. Each round yields higher and higher prices as wages and prices chase each other in an upward spiral.

Fourth, because the future rate of inflation is difficult or impossible to anticipate, people turn to more speculative investments that might yield higher financial returns. To hedge against the high losses of purchasing power from hyperinflation, funds flow into gold, silver, stamps, jewels, art, antiques, and other currencies, rather than into new factories, machinery, and technological research, which expand an economy's production possibilities curve.

History reveals numerous hyperinflation examples. One of the most famous occurred during the 1920s in the German Weimar Republic. Faced with huge World War I reparations payments, the Weimar government simply printed money to pay its bills. By late 1923, the annual inflation rate in Germany had reached 35,000 percent per month. Prices rose frequently, sometimes increasing in minutes, and German currency became so worthless that it was used as kindling for stoves. No one was willing to make new loans, and credit markets collapsed. Wealth was redistributed because those who were heavily in debt easily paid their debts, and people's savings were wiped out.

Finally, hyperinflation is invariably the result of a government's ill-advised decision to increase a country's money supply. Moreover, hyperinflation is not a historical relic, as illustrated in the Global Economics article.

Key Concepts

Inflation

Deflation

Consumer price index (CPI)

Base year

Disinflation

Nominal income

Real income

Wealth

Nominal interest rate

Real interest rate

Adjustable-rate mortgage (ARM)

Demand-pull inflation

Cost-push inflation

Hyperinflation

Wage-price spiral

Summary

- **Inflation** is an increase in the general (average) price level of goods and services in the economy.

- **Deflation** is a decrease in the general level of prices. During the early years of the Great Depression, there was deflation, and the CPI declined at about a double-digit rate.

- The **consumer price index (CPI)** is the most widely known price-level index. It measures the cost of purchasing a market basket of goods and services by a typical household during a time period relative to the cost of the same bundle during a base year. The annual rate of inflation is computed using the following formula:

$$\frac{\text{annual rate}}{\text{of inflation}} = \frac{\text{CPI in given year} - \text{CPI in previous year}}{\text{CPI in previous year}} \times 100$$

- **Disinflation** is a reduction in the inflation rate. Between 1980 and 1986, there was disinflation. This does not mean that prices were falling, only that the inflation rate fell.

- The **inflation rate** determined by the CPI is criticized because (1) it is not representative, (2) it has difficulty adjusting for quality changes, and (3) it ignores the relationship between price changes and the importance of items in the market basket.

- **Nominal income** is income measured in actual money amounts. Measuring your purchasing power requires converting nominal income into **real income**, which is nominal income adjusted for inflation.

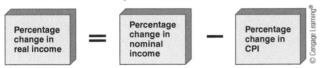

- The **real interest rate** is the *nominal interest rate* adjusted for inflation. If real interest rates are negative, lenders incur losses.

- An **adjustable-rate mortgage** is a home loan that adjusts the nominal interest rate to changes in an index rate, such as rates on Treasury securities.

- **Demand-pull inflation** is caused by pressure on prices originating from the buyers' side of the market. In contrast, **cost-push inflation** is caused by pressure on prices originating from the sellers' side of the market.

- **Hyperinflation** can seriously disrupt an economy by causing inflation psychosis, credit market collapses, a wage–price spiral, and speculation. A **wage–price spiral** occurs when increases in nominal wages cause higher prices, which, in turn, cause higher wages and prices.

Study Questions and Problems

1. Consider this statement: "When the price of a good or service rises, the inflation rate rises." Do you agree or disagree? Explain.

2. Suppose in the base year, a typical market basket purchased by an urban family cost $250. In Year 1, the same market basket cost $950. What is the consumer price index (CPI) for Year 1? If the same market basket cost $1,000 in Year 2, what is the CPI for Year 2? What was the annual rate of inflation for Year 2?

3. What are three criticisms of the CPI?

4. Suppose you earned $100,000 in a given year. Calculate your real income, assuming the CPI is 200 for this year.

5. Explain how a person's purchasing power can decline in a given year even though he or she received a salary increase.

6. Who loses from inflation? Who wins from inflation?

7. Suppose you borrow $100 from a bank at 5 percent interest for one year and the inflation rate that year is 10 percent. Was this loan advantageous to you or to the bank?

8. Suppose the annual nominal rate of interest on a bank certificate of deposit is 12 percent. What would be the effect of an inflation rate of 13 percent?

9. When the economy approaches full employment, why does demand-pull inflation become a problem?

10. How does demand-pull inflation differ from cost-push inflation?

11. Explain this statement: "If everyone expects inflation to occur, it will."

Sample Quiz

1. Inflation is defined as an increase in
   a. real wages of workers.
   b. real GDP.
   c. the average price level.
   d. all consumer products.

2. Inflation is measured by an increase in
   a. homes, autos, and basic resources.
   b. prices of all products in the economy.
   c. the consumer price index (CPI).
   d. None of the answers above are correct.

3. Which one of the following groups benefits from inflation?
   a. Borrowers.
   b. Savers.
   c. Landlords.
   d. Lenders.

4. Price indexes like the CPI are calculated using a base year. The term base year refers to
   a. the first year that price data are available.
   b. any year in which inflation was higher than 5 percent.
   c. the most recent year in which the business cycle hit the trough.
   d. an arbitrarily chosen reference year.

5. If the consumer price index (CPI) in Year 1 was 200 and in Year 2 was 215, the rate of inflation was
   a. 215 percent.
   b. 15 percent.
   c. 5 percent.
   d. 7.5 percent.
   e. 8 percent.

6. Which of the following statements is *true*?
   a. Deflation is an increase in the general level of prices.
   b. The consumer price index (CPI) measures changes in the average prices of consumer goods and services.
   c. Disinflation is an increase in the rate of inflation.
   d. Real income is the actual number of dollars received over a period of time.

7. Suppose the price of bananas rises over time and consumers respond by buying fewer bananas. This situation contributes to which bias in the consumer price index?
   a. Substitution bias.
   b. Transportation bias.
   c. Quality bias.
   d. Indexing bias.

8. Deflation means a decrease in
   a. the rate of inflation.
   b. the prices of all products in the economy.
   c. homes, autos, and basic resources.
   d. the general level of prices in the economy.

9. Real income in Year X is equal to
   a. $\dfrac{\text{Year X nominal income}}{\text{Year X real GDP}} \times 100$
   b. $\dfrac{\text{Year X nominal income}}{\text{Year X real output}} \times 100$
   c. $\dfrac{\text{Year X nominal income}}{\text{CPI}/100}$
   d. Year X nominal income $\times$ CPI

10. The real interest rate is defined as the
    a. actual interest rate.
    b. fixed-rate on consumer loans.
    c. nominal interest rate minus the inflation rate.
    d. expected interest rate minus the inflation rate.

11. If the inflation rate exceeds the nominal rate of interest,
    a. the real interest rate is negative.
    b. lenders lose.
    c. savers lose.
    d. All of the answers above are correct.

12. Suppose you place $10,000 in a retirement fund that earns a nominal interest rate of 8 percent. If you expect inflation to be 5 percent or lower, then you are expecting to earn a real interest rate of at least
    a. 1.6 percent.
    b. 3 percent.
    c. 4 percent.
    d. 5 percent.

13. Which of the following can create demand-pull inflation?
    a. Excessive aggregate spending.
    b. Sharply rising oil prices.
    c. Higher labor costs.
    d. Recessions and depressions.

14. Which of the following statements is *true*?
    a. Demand-pull inflation is caused by excess total spending.
    b. Cost-push inflation is caused by an increase in resource costs.
    c. If nominal interest rates remain the same and the inflation rate falls, real interest rates increase.
    d. If real interest rates are negative, lenders incur losses.
    e. All of the answers above are correct.

15. Cost-push inflation is due to
    a. labor cost increases.
    b. energy cost increases.
    c. raw material cost increases.
    d. All of the answers above are correct.

16. During periods of hyperinflation, which of the following is the *most* likely response of consumers?
    a. Save as much as possible.
    b. Spend money as fast as possible.
    c. Invest as much as possible.
    d. Lend money.

17. The base year in the consumer price index (CPI) is
    a. given a value of zero.
    b. a year chosen as a reference for prices in all other years.
    c. always the first year in the current decade.
    d. established by law.

18. Deflation
    a. was prevalent during the oil shocks of the 1970s.
    b. under the current trends will cause consumers' purchasing power to shrink.
    c. has been persistent in the U.S. economy since the Great Depression.
    d. None of the answers above are correct.
19. As the price of gasoline rose during the 1970s, consumers cut back on their use of gasoline relative to other consumer goods. This situation contributed to which bias in the consumer price index?
    a. Substitution bias.
    b. Transportation bias.
    c. Quality bias.
    d. Indexing bias.
20. If the rate of inflation in a given time period turns out to be lower than lenders and borrowers anticipated, then the effect will be a
    a. redistribution of wealth from borrowers to lenders.
    b. redistribution of wealth from lenders to borrowers.
    c. net loss in purchasing power for lenders relative to borrowers.
    d. net gain in purchasing power for borrowers relative to lenders.

PART 4

Money, Banking, and Monetary Policy

Students often find the material in these chapters the most interesting in their principles course because the topic is *money*. Chapter 18 begins the discussion of money with basic definitions and a description of the Federal Reserve System. Of special interest is a feature on the history of money in the colonies. Chapter 19 explains how the banking system and the Federal Reserve influence the supply of money. Chapter 20 compares different macroeconomic theories and concludes with a discussion of monetary policy in the Great Depression and the Great Recession.

Money and the Federal Reserve System

In this chapter, you will learn to solve these economics puzzles:

- Why do nations use money?
- Is "plastic money" really money?
- What does a Federal Reserve Bank do?

CHAPTER PREVIEW

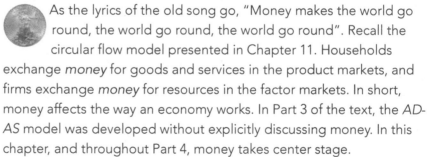

As the lyrics of the old song go, "Money makes the world go round, the world go round, the world go round". Recall the circular flow model presented in Chapter 11. Households exchange *money* for goods and services in the product markets, and firms exchange *money* for resources in the factor markets. In short, money affects the way an economy works. In Part 3 of the text, the *AD-AS* model was developed without explicitly discussing money. In this chapter, and throughout Part 4, money takes center stage.

Exactly what is money? The answer may surprise you. Imagine yourself on the small South Pacific island of Yap. You are surrounded by exotic fowl, crystal-clear lagoons, delicious fruits, and sunny skies. Now suppose while leisurely strolling along the beach one evening, you suddenly discover a beautiful bamboo hut for sale. As you will discover in this chapter, to pay for your dream hut, you must roll a 5-foot-diameter stone to the area of the island designated as the "bank."

We begin our discussion of money with the three functions money serves. Next, we identify the components of three different definitions of the money supply used in the United States. The remainder of the chapter describes the organization and services of the Federal Reserve System, our nation's central bank. Also, we discuss the Monetary

Control Act of 1980 and its relationship to the savings and loan crisis of the 1980s and early 1990s that predated the banking crisis and Great Recession of 2007–2009. Beginning in this chapter and in the next three chapters, you will learn how the Federal Reserve System controls the stock of money in the economy. Then, using the *AD-AS* model, you will learn how variations in the stock of money in the economy affect total spending, unemployment, and prices.

18-1 WHAT MAKES MONEY *MONEY?*

Barter The direct exchange of one good or service for another good or service rather than for money.

Can exchange occur in an economy without money? It certainly can, using a trading system called barter. Barter is the direct exchange of one good or service for another good or service, rather than for money. The problem with barter is that it requires a *coincidence of wants*. Imagine for a moment that dollars and coins are worthless. Farmer Brown needs shoes, so he takes his bushels of wheat to the shoe store and offers to barter wheat for shoes. Unfortunately, the store owner refuses to barter because she wants to trade shoes for pencils, toothpaste, and coffee. Undaunted, Farmer Brown spends more time and effort to find Mr. Jones, who has pencils, toothpaste, and coffee; he will trade for bushels of wheat. Although Farmer Brown's luck has improved, he and Mr. Jones must agree on the terms of exchange. Exactly how many pounds of coffee, for example, is a bushel of wheat worth? Assuming this exchange is worked out, Farmer Brown must spend more time returning to the shoe store and negotiating the terms of an exchange of pencils, coffee, and toothpaste for shoes.

CONCLUSION The use of money simplifies and therefore increases market transactions. Money also prevents wasting time that can be devoted to production, thereby promoting economic growth by increasing a nation's production possibilities.

18-1a The Three Functions of Money

Money Anything that serves as a medium of exchange, unit of account, and store of value.

Suppose citizens of the planet of Starcom want to replace their barter system and must decide what to use for money. Assuming this planet is fortunate enough to have economists, they would explain that anything, regardless of its value, can serve as money if it conforms to the following definition. Money is anything that serves as a medium of exchange, unit of account, and store of value. Money is not limited to dimes, quarters, and dollar bills. Notice that "anything" meeting the three tests is a candidate to serve as money. This explains why precious metals, beaver skins, wampum (shells strung in belts), and cigarettes have all served as money. Let's discuss each of the three functions money serves.

18-1b Money as a Medium of Exchange

Medium of exchange The primary function of money to be widely accepted in exchange for goods and services.

In a simple society, barter is a way for participants to exchange goods and services in order to satisfy wants. Barter, however, requires wasting time in the process of exchange that people could use for productive work. If the goal is to increase the volume of transactions and live in a modern economy, the most important function of money is to serve as a medium of exchange. Medium of exchange is the primary function of money to be widely accepted in exchange for goods and services. Money removes the problem of coincidence of wants because everyone is willing to accept money in payment, rather than haggling over goods and services. You give up two $20 bills in exchange for a ticket to a rock concert. Because money serves as generalized purchasing power, all in society know that no one will refuse to trade their products for money. In short, money increases trade by providing a much more convenient method of exchange than a cumbersome barter system.

A fascinating question is whether people will find digital cash a more convenient means of payment. Each year more people avoid using checks, paper currency, or coins by transferring funds electronically from their accounts via debit cards and various Internet-based and other systems. In fact, it is possible that widespread adoption of privately issued digital cash will ultimately replace government-issued currency. Vending and copy machines on many college campuses already accept plastic stored-value cards. Someday vending machines everywhere are likely to have smart card readers that accept electronic money.

18-1c Money as a Unit of Account

How does a wheat farmer know whether a bushel of wheat is worth one, two, or more pairs of shoes? How does a family compare its income to expenses or a business know whether it is making a profit? Government must be able to measure tax revenues collected and program expenditures made. And GDP is the *money* value of final goods and services used to compare the national output of the United States to, say, Japan's output. In each of these examples, money serves as a **unit of account**. Unit of account is the function of money to provide a common measurement of the relative value of goods and services. Without dollars, there is no common denominator. We must therefore decide if one pizza equals a box of pencils, 20 oranges equals one quart of milk, and so forth. Now let's compare the value of two items using money. If the price of one pizza is $10 and the price of a movie ticket is $5, then the value of one pizza equals two movie tickets. In the United States, the monetary unit is the dollar; in Japan, it is the yen; Mexico has its peso; and so on.

18-1d Money as a Store of Value

Can you put shrimp under your mattress for months and then exchange them for some product? No! Money, on the other hand, serves as a **store of value** in exchange for some item in the future. Store of value is the ability of money to hold value over time. You can bury money in your backyard or store it under your mattress for months or years and not worry about it spoiling. This also means you can save money and be confident that you can spend it in the future. However, recall from Chapter 13 that hyperinflation can destroy money's store-of-value function and, in turn, its medium-of-exchange function.

> **CONCLUSION** Money is a useful mechanism for transforming income in the present into future purchases.

The key property of money is that it is completely *liquid*. This means that money is immediately available to spend in exchange for goods and services without any additional expense. Money is more liquid than real assets (real estate or gold) or paper assets (stocks or bonds). These assets also serve as stores of value, but liquidating (selling) them often involves expenses, such as brokerage fees, and time delays.

> **CONCLUSION** Money is the most liquid form of wealth because it can be spent directly in the marketplace.

18-1e Are Credit Cards Money?

Credit cards, such as Visa, MasterCard, and American Express, are often called "plastic money," but are these cards really money? Let's test credit cards for the three functions of money. First, because credit cards are widely accepted, they serve as a means of payment in an exchange for goods or services.

Second, the credit card statement, and not the card itself, serves as a unit of account. One of the advantages of credit cards is that you receive a statement listing

---

Unit of account The function of money to provide a common measurement of the relative value of goods and services.

Store of value The ability of money to hold value over time.

GLOBAL ECONOMICS

Why a Loan in Yap Is Hard to Roll Over

Applicable concept: functions of money

David Fleetham/Alamy

On the tiny South Pacific island of Yap, life is easy and the currency is hard as a rock. In fact, it is a rock. For nearly 2,000 years, the Yapese have used large stone wheels to pay for major purchases, such as land, canoes, and permission to marry. The people of Yap have been using stone money ever since a Yapese warrior named Anagumang first brought the huge stones over from limestone caverns on neighboring Palau, some 1,500 to 2,000 years ago. Inspired by the moon, he fashioned the stone into large circles and the rest is history.

Yap is a U.S. trust territory, and the dollar is used in grocery stores and gas stations, but reliance on stone money continues. Buying property with stones is "much easier than buying it with U.S. dollars," says John Chodad, who purchased a building lot with a 30-inch stone wheel. "We don't know the value of the U.S. dollar." However, stone wheels don't make good pocket money, so Yapese use other forms of currency, such as beer for small transactions. Besides stone wheels and beer, the Yapese sometimes spend gaw, consisting of necklaces of stone beads strung together around a whale's tooth. They also buy things with yar, a currency made from large seashells, but these are small change.

Yapese lean the stone wheels against their houses or prop up rows of them in village "banks." Most of the stones are 2 1/2 to 5 feet in diameter, but some are as much as 12 feet across. Each has a hole in the center so that it can be slipped onto the trunk of a fallen betel-nut tree and carried. It takes 20 men to lift some wheels. By custom, the stones are worthless when broken. Rather than risk a broken stone—or their backs—Yapese tend to leave the larger stones where they are and make a mental accounting that the ownership has been transferred. The worth of stone money doesn't depend on size. Instead, the pieces are valued by how hard it was to get them there. There are some decided advantages to using massive stones for money. They are immune to black-market trading, for one thing, and they pose formidable obstacles to pickpockets.

ANALYZE the ISSUE

1. Explain how Yap's large stones pass the three tests in the definition of money.

2. Briefly discuss Yap's large stones in terms of other desirable properties of money.

the exact price in dollars paid for each item you charged. Your credit card statement clearly records the dollar amount you spent for gasoline, a dinner, or a trip.

But credit cards clearly fail to meet the store-of-value criterion and are therefore *not* money. The word *credit* means receiving money today to buy products in return for a promise to pay in the future. A credit card represents only a prearranged short-term loan up to a certain limit. If the credit card company goes out of business or for any reason decides not to honor your card, it is worthless. Hence, credit cards do not store value and are *not* money.

CHECKPOINT

Are Debit Cards Money?
Debit cards are used to pay for purchases, and the money is automatically deducted from the user's bank account. Are debit cards money?

18-2 OTHER DESIRABLE PROPERTIES OF MONEY

Once something has passed the three basic requirements to serve as money, there are additional hurdles to clear. First, an important consideration is *scarcity*. Money must be scarce, but not too scarce. Sand, for example, could theoretically

History of Money in the Colonies

© Gregory James Van Raalte/Shutterstock.Com

The early colonists left behind their well-developed money system in Europe. North American Indians accepted wampum as money which are beads of polished shells strung in belts. Soon, a group of settlers learned to counterfeit wampum, and it lost its value. As a result, the main method of trading with the Indians was to barter. Later, trade developed with the West Indies, and Spanish coins called "pieces of eight" were circulated widely. Colonists often cut these coins into pieces to make change. Half of a coin became known as "four bits." A quarter part of the coin was referred to as "two bits." The first English colony to mint its own coins was Massachusetts in 1652. A striking pine tree was engraved on these coins called shillings. Other coins such as a six-pence and three-pence were also produced at a mint in Boston. Several other colonies followed by authorizing their own coin issues.

The first national coin of the United States was issued in 1787 when Congress approved a one-cent copper coin.

serve as money, but sand is a poor choice because people can easily gather a bucketful to pay their bills. A Picasso painting would also be undesirable as money. Because there are so few for circulation, people would have to resort to barter.

Counterfeiting threatens the scarcity of money. Advances in computer graphics, scanners, and color copiers were allowing counterfeiters to win their ongoing battle with the U.S. Secret Service. In response, new bills were issued with a polymer security thread running through them. The larger off-center portraits on the bills allow for a watermark next to the portrait that is visible from both sides against a light.

> **CONCLUSION** The supply of money must be great enough to meet ordinary transaction needs, but not be so plentiful that it becomes worthless.

Second, money should be *portable* and *divisible*. That is, people should be able to reach into their pockets and make change to buy items at various prices. Statues of George Washington might be attractive money, but they would be difficult to carry and make change. Finally, money must be *uniform*. An ounce of gold is an ounce of gold. The quality differences of beaver skins and seashells, on the other hand, complicate using these items for money. Each exchange would involve the extra trouble of buyers and sellers arguing over which skins or shells are better or worse.

18-3 WHAT STANDS BEHIND OUR MONEY?

Commodity money Anything that serves as money while having market value in other uses.

Historically, early forms of money played two roles. If, for example, a ruler declared beans as money, you could spend them or sell them in the marketplace. Precious metals, tobacco, cows, and other tangible goods are examples of **commodity money**. Commodity money is anything that serves as money while having market value based on the material from which it is made. This means that money itself has intrinsic worth (the market value of the material). For example, money can be pure gold or silver, both of which are valuable for non-money uses, such as making jewelry and serving other industrial purposes.

One side was decorated with a chain of 13 links encircling the words, "We Are One." The other side had a sundial, the noonday sun, and the Latin word "fugo," meaning "time flies." Later, this coin became known as the Franklin cent, although there is no evidence that Benjamin Franklin played any role in its design.

In 1792, Congress established a mint in Philadelphia. It manufactured copper cents and half-cents about the size of today's quarters and nickels. In 1794, silver half dimes and half dollars increased the variety of available coins. The next year gold eagles ($10) and half eagles ($5) appeared. The motto "E Pluribus Unum" ("out of many, one") was first used on the half eagle in 1795. The next year America's first quarters and dimes were issued.

The first paper money in the Americas was printed in 1690. Massachusetts soldiers returned to the colony from fighting the French in Quebec, where they had unsuccessfully laid siege to the city. The colony had no precious metal to pay the soldiers. Hundreds of soldiers threatened mutiny, and the colony decided it must issue bills of credit, which were simply pieces of paper promising to pay the soldiers. Other colonies followed this example and printed their own paper money. Soon paper money was being widely circulated.

In 1775, the need to finance the American Revolution forced the Continental Congress to issue paper money "continentals," but so much was issued that it rapidly lost its value. George Washington complained, "A wagon load of money will scarcely purchase a wagon load of provisions." This statement is today shortened to the phrase "not worth a continental."

Today, U.S. paper money and coins are no longer backed by gold or silver. Our paper money was exchangeable for gold or silver until 1934. As a result of the Great Depression, people rapidly tried to get rid of their paper money. The U.S. Treasury's stock of gold dropped so low that Congress passed a law in 1934 that prevented anyone from exchanging gold for $5 and larger bills. Later, in 1963, Congress removed the right to exchange $1 bills for silver. And in the mid-1960s, zinc, copper, and nickel replaced silver in coins.

The important consideration for money is acceptability. The acceptability of a dollar is due in no small degree to the fact that Uncle Sam decrees it to be **fiat money**. Fiat money is money accepted by law and not because of its tangible value. A dollar bill contains only about 3 cents worth of paper, printing inks, and other materials. A quarter contains maybe 10 cents worth of nickel and copper. Pull out a dollar bill and look at it closely. In the upper left corner on the front side is small print that proclaims, "THIS NOTE IS LEGAL TENDER FOR ALL DEBTS, PUBLIC AND PRIVATE." This means that your paper money is fiat money. Also notice that nowhere on the note is there any promise to redeem it for gold, silver, or anything else.

Fiat money Money accepted by law and not because of its tangible value.

CONCLUSION An item's ability to serve as money does not depend on its own market value or the backing of precious metal.

18-4 MONEY SUPPLY DEFINITIONS

Now that you understand the basic definition of money, we turn to exactly what constitutes the money supply of the U.S. economy. The following sections examine the two basic methods used to measure the money supply, officially called M1 and M2.

18-4a M1: The Most Narrowly Defined Money Supply

M1 The narrowest definition of the money supply. It includes currency and checkable deposits.

M1 is the narrowest definition of the money supply. This money supply definition measures purchasing power immediately available to the public without borrowing or having to give notice. Specifically, M1 measures the currency, and checkable deposits held by the public at a given time, such as a given day, month, or year. Expressed as a formula:

$$M1 = \text{currency} + \text{checkable deposits}$$

Exhibit 18-1 shows the components of M1 and M2 money supply definitions based on daily averages during 2013.

18-4b Currency

Currency Money, including coins and paper money.

Currency includes coins and paper money, officially called Federal Reserve notes, that the public holds for spending. The purpose of currency is to enable us to make small purchases. Currency represents 44 percent of M1.

18-4c Checkable Deposits

Checkable deposits The total of checking account balances in financial institutions convertible to currency "on demand" by writing a check without advance notice.

Most "big ticket" purchases are paid for with checks or credit cards (which are not money), rather than currency. Checks eliminate trips to the bank, and they are safer than cash. If lost or stolen, checks and credit cards can be replaced at little cost—money cannot. Exhibit 18-1 shows that a major share of M1 consists of **checkable deposits**. Checkable deposits are the total in financial institutions that can be withdrawn by writing a check. A checking account balance is a book-keeping entry, often called a *demand deposit* because it can be converted into cash "on demand." Before the 1980s, only commercial banks could legally provide demand deposits. However, the law changed with the passage of the Depository Institutions Deregulation and Monetary Control Act of 1980. (This act will be discussed later in the chapter.) Today, checking accounts are available from many different financial institutions, such as savings and loan associations, credit unions, and mutual savings banks. For example, many people hold deposits in negotiable order of withdrawal (NOW) accounts or automatic transfer of savings (ATS) accounts, which serve as interest-bearing checking accounts. NOW and ATS accounts permit depositors to spend their deposits without a trip to the bank to withdraw funds. In December 2013, 56 percent of M1 was checkable deposits.

EXHIBIT 18-1 Definitions of the Money Supply, 2013

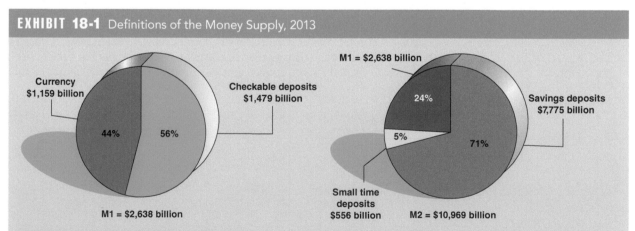

Each of the two pie charts represents the money supply for 2013. M1, the most narrowly defined money supply, is equal to currency (coins and paper money) in circulation plus checkable deposits in financial institutions. M2 is a more broadly defined money supply, equal to M1 plus savings deposits and small time deposits of less than $100,000.

Source: *Economic Report of the President*, 2013, http://www.gpoaccess.gov/eop/, Tables B-69 and B-70.: *Federal Reserve Board*, http://www.federalreserve.gov/releases/h6/Curent/, Tables 1, 2, and 3.

18-4d M2: Adding Near Monies to M1

M2 is a broader measure of the money supply because it equals M1 plus *near monies*. Many economists consider M1 to be too narrow a measure because it does not include near money accounts that can be used to purchase goods and services. These include passbook savings accounts, money market accounts, mutual fund accounts, and time deposits of less than $100,000. Near monies are interest-bearing deposits easily converted into spendable funds. Written as a formula:

$$M2 = M1 + \text{near monies}$$

rewritten as

$$M2 = M1 + \text{savings deposits} + \text{small time deposits of less than } \$100{,}000$$

Savings Deposits As shown in Exhibit 18-1, M1 was 71 percent of M2 in 2013, with savings deposits and small time deposits constituting the remainder of M2. Savings deposits are interest-bearing accounts that can be easily withdrawn. These deposits include passbook savings accounts, money market accounts, mutual fund accounts, and other types of interest-bearing deposits with commercial banks, mutual savings banks, savings and loan associations, and credit unions.

Small Time Deposits There is a distinction between a *checkable deposit* and a *time deposit*. A time deposit is an account in a financial institution with guaranteed interest for a period of time. Certificates of deposit (CDs), for example, are deposits for a specified time, with a penalty charged for early withdrawal. Where is the line drawn between a small and a large time deposit? The answer is that time deposits of less than $100,000 are "small" and therefore are included in M2. In 2013, 5 percent of M2 was small time deposits.

> **CONCLUSION** M1 is more liquid than M2.

To simplify the discussion throughout the remainder of this text, we will be referring to M1 when we discuss the money supply. However, one can argue that M2, or another measurement of the money supply, may be the best definition. Actually, the boundary lines for any definition of money are somewhat arbitrary.

18-5 THE FEDERAL RESERVE SYSTEM

What controls the money supply in the United States? The answer is the **Federal Reserve System**, popularly called the "Fed." The Fed is the central banker for the nation and provides banking services to commercial banks, other financial institutions, and the federal government. The Fed regulates, supervises, and is responsible for policies concerning money. Congress and the president consult with the Fed to control the size of the money supply and thereby influence the economy's performance.

Other major nations have central banks, such as the Bank of England, the Bank of Japan, and the European Central Bank. The movement in the United States to establish a central banking system gained strength early in the twentieth century as a series of bank failures resulted in the Panic of 1907. In that year, stock prices fell, many businesses and banks failed, and millions of depositors lost their savings. The prescription for preventing financial panic was for the government to establish more centralized control over banks. This desire for more safety in banking led to the creation of the Federal Reserve System by the Federal Reserve Act of 1913 during the administration of President Woodrow Wilson. No longer would the supply of money in the economy be determined by individual banks.

18-5a The Fed's Organizational Chart

The *Federal Reserve System* is an independent agency of the federal government. Congress is responsible for overseeing the Fed but does not interfere with its day-to-day decisions. The chair of the Fed reports to Congress twice each year and often coordinates its actions with the U.S. Treasury and the president. Although the Fed enjoys independent status, its independence can be revoked. If the Fed were to pursue policies contrary to the interests of the nation, Congress could abolish the Fed.

The Federal Reserve System consists of 12 central banks that service banks and other financial institutions within each of the Federal Reserve districts. Each Federal Reserve bank serves as a central banker for the private banks in its region. The United States is the only nation in the world to have 12 separate regional banks instead of a single central bank. In fact, the Fed's structure is the result of a compromise between the traditionalists, who favored a single central bank, and the populists, who distrusted concentration of financial power in the hands of a few. In addition, 25 Federal Reserve branch banks are located throughout the country. The map in Exhibit 18-2 shows the 12 Federal Reserve districts.

The organizational chart of the Federal Reserve System, given in Exhibit 18-3, shows that the Board of Governors, located in Washington, D.C., administers the system. The Board of Governors, appointed by the president and confirmed by the U.S. Senate, is made up of seven members, who serve for one nonrenewable 14-year term. Their responsibility is to supervise and control the money supply and the banking system of the United States. Fourteen-year terms for Fed governors create autonomy and insulate the Fed from short-term politics. These terms are staggered so one term expires every two years. This staggering of terms prevents a president from stacking the board with members favoring the incumbent party's political interests. A president usually makes two appointments in a one-term presidency and four appointments in a two-term presidency. The president designates one member of the Board of Governors to serve as chair for a four-year term. The chair is the principal spokesperson for the Fed and has considerable power over policy decisions. In fact, it is often argued that the Fed's chair is the most powerful individual in the United States next to the

Board of Governors of the Federal Reserve System The seven members appointed by the president and confirmed by the U.S. Senate who serve for one nonrenewable 14-year term. Their responsibility is to supervise and control the money supply and the banking system of the United States.

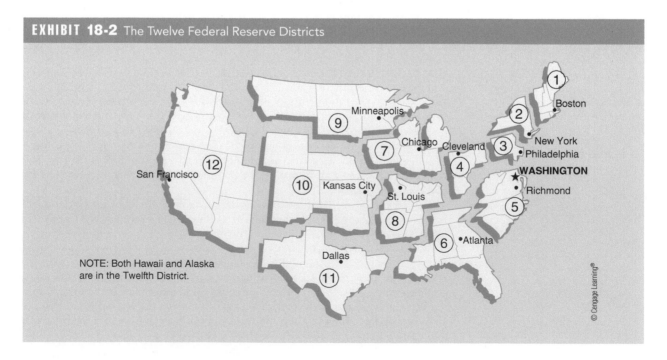

EXHIBIT 18-2 The Twelve Federal Reserve Districts

NOTE: Both Hawaii and Alaska are in the Twelfth District.

© Cengage Learning®

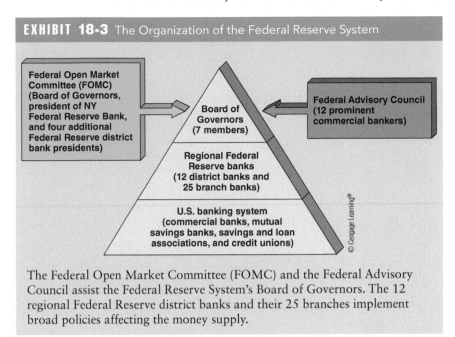

EXHIBIT 18-3 The Organization of the Federal Reserve System

The Federal Open Market Committee (FOMC) and the Federal Advisory Council assist the Federal Reserve System's Board of Governors. The 12 regional Federal Reserve district banks and their 25 branches implement broad policies affecting the money supply.

Janet Yellen, Chairman of the Board of Governors of the Federal Reserve System.

Federal Open Market Committee (FOMC) The Federal Reserve's committee that directs the buying and selling of U.S. government securities, which are major instruments for controlling the money supply. The FOMC consists of the seven members of the Federal Reserve's Board of Governors, the president of the New York Federal Reserve Bank, and the presidents of four other Federal Reserve district banks.

president. The current chair is Janet Yellen, who was appointed by President Obama in 2013.

The Federal Reserve System receives no funding from Congress. This creates financial autonomy for the Fed by removing the fear of congressional review of its budget. Then where does the Fed get funds to operate? Recall from Exhibit 17-7 of the previous chapter that the Fed holds government securities issued by the U.S. Treasury. The Fed earns interest income from the government securities it holds and the loans it makes to depository institutions. Because the Fed returns any profits to the Treasury, it is motivated to adopt policies to promote the economy's well-being, rather than earning a profit. Moreover, the Board of Governors does not take orders from the president or any other politician. Thus, the Board of Governors is the independent, self-supporting authority of the Federal Reserve System.

On the left side of the organizational chart in Exhibit 18-3 is the very important **Federal Open Market Committee (FOMC)**. The FOMC directs the buying and selling of U.S. government securities, which are major instruments for controlling the money supply. The FOMC consists of the seven members of the Board of Governors, the president of the New York Federal Reserve Bank, and the presidents of four other Federal Reserve district banks. The FOMC meets to discuss trends in inflation, unemployment, growth rates, and other macro data. FOMC members express their opinions on implementing various monetary policies and then issue policy statements known as *FOMC directives*. A directive, for example, might set the operation of the Fed to stimulate or restrain M1 in order to influence the economy. The next two chapters explain the tools of monetary policy in more detail.

As shown on the right side of the chart, the *Federal Advisory Council* consists of 12 prominent commercial bankers. Each of the 12 Federal Reserve district banks selects one member each year. The council meets periodically to advise the Board of Governors.

Finally, at the bottom of the organizational chart is the remainder of the Federal Reserve System, consisting of about 3,000 member banks of the approximately 7,000 commercial banks in the United States. Although these 3,000 Fed member banks represent only about 40 percent of U.S. banks, they have about 70 percent of all U.S. bank deposits. A sure sign of Fed membership is the word *National* in a bank's name. The U.S. comptroller of the currency charters national banks, and they are required to be Fed members. Banks that do not have "National" in their title can also be Fed members. States can also charter banks, and these state banks have the option of joining the Federal Reserve. Less than 20 percent of state banks choose to join the Fed. Exhibit 18-4 shows the top 10 U.S. banks based on their total assets.

Nonmember depository institutions, including many commercial banks, savings and loan associations (S&Ls), savings banks, and credit unions, are not official members of the Fed team. They are, however, influenced by and depend on the Fed for a variety of services, which we will now discuss.

18-6 WHAT A FEDERAL RESERVE BANK DOES

The typical bank customer never enters the doors of a Federal Reserve district bank or one of its branch banks. The reason is that the Fed does not offer the public checking accounts, savings accounts, or any of the services provided by

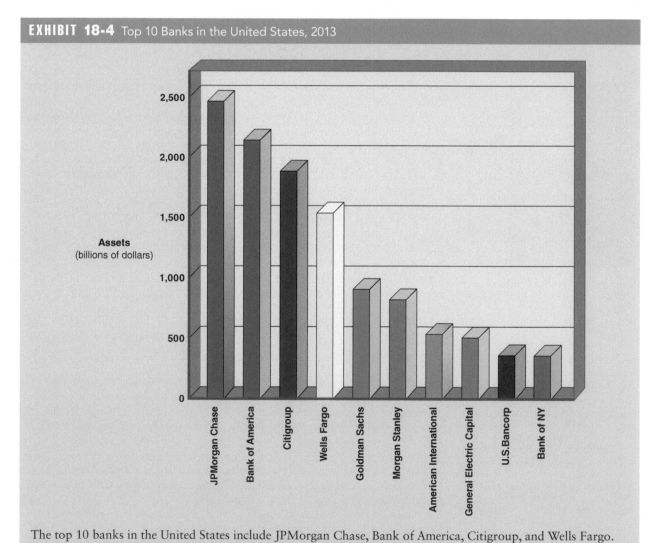

EXHIBIT 18-4 Top 10 Banks in the United States, 2013

The top 10 banks in the United States include JPMorgan Chase, Bank of America, Citigroup, and Wells Fargo.

Source: http://www.ffiec.gov/nicpubweb/nicweb/Top50Form.aspx.

commercial banks. Instead, the Federal Reserve serves as a "banker's bank." Following are brief descriptions of some of the principal functions of the Federal Reserve.

18-6a Controlling the Money Supply

The primary role of the Fed is to control the nation's money supply. The mechanics of Fed control over the money supply are explained in the next two chapters. To most people, this is a wondrously mysterious process. So that you do not suffer in complete suspense, here is a sneak preview: The Fed has three policy tools, or levers, it can use to change the stock of money in the banking system. The potential macro outcome of changes in the money supply is to affect total spending and therefore real GDP, employment, and the price level.

18-6b Clearing Checks

Because people and businesses use checks to pay for goods and services, check clearing is an important function. Suppose you live in Virginia and have a checking account with a bank in that state. While on vacation in California, you purchase tickets to Disneyland with a check for $200. Disneyland accepts your check and then deposits it in its business checking account in a California bank. This bank must collect payment for your check and does so by sending an electronic copy of your check to the Federal Reserve bank in San Francisco. From there, your check is sent to the Federal Reserve bank in Richmond. Finally, the process ends when $200 is subtracted from your personal checking account. Banks in which checks are deposited have their Fed accounts credited, and banks on which checks are written have their accounts debited. The Fed clearinghouse process is much speedier than depending on the movement of a check between commercial banks.

18-6c Supervising and Regulating Banks

Federal Deposit Insurance Corporation (FDIC) A government agency established in 1933 to insure commercial bank deposits up to a specified limit.

The Fed examines banks' books, sets limits for loans, approves bank mergers, and works with the **Federal Deposit Insurance Corporation (FDIC)**. The FDIC is a government agency that insures customer deposits up to a limit if a bank fails. Congress created the FDIC in 1933 in response to the huge number of bank failures during the Great Depression and set the insurance limit at $25,000. If the government provides a safety net, people are less likely to panic and withdraw their funds from banks during a period of economic uncertainty. When deposits are insured and a bank fails, the government stands ready to pay depositors or transfer their deposits to a solvent bank. Banks that are members of the Fed are members of the FDIC. State agencies supervise state-chartered banks that are not members of either the Federal Reserve System or the FDIC. However, most state banks are members of the FDIC and are audited by their state agency and the FDIC. The banks pay for deposit insurance through premiums charged by the FDIC. To shore up confidence in the U.S. banking system in the wake of bank failures in 2008, the $700 billion U.S. financial industry rescue law raised the FDIC coverage of bank deposits to $250,000 per customer.

The 1946 film *It's a Wonderful Life* is based on a fractional reserve banking system without the FDIC.

18-6d Maintaining and Circulating Currency

Recall that the M1 money supply consists of currency (coins and Federal Reserve notes) and checkable deposits. Note that the Fed does *not* print currency—it *maintains* and *circulates* money. All Federal Reserve notes are printed at the Bureau of Engraving and Printing's facilities in Washington, D.C., and Fort Worth, Texas. The Treasury mints and issues all coins. Coins are made at U.S. mints located in Philadelphia and Denver. The bureau and the mints ship new notes and coins to the Federal Reserve banks for circulation. Much of this money is printed or minted simply to replace worn-out bills and coins. Another use of new currency is to meet public demand. Suppose it's the holiday season and banks need more paper money and coins to meet their customers' shopping needs. The Federal Reserve must be ready to ship extra money from its large vaults by armored truck.

18-6e Protecting Consumers

Since 1968, the Federal Reserve has played a role in protecting consumers by enforcing statues enacted by Congress. Perhaps the most important is the *Equal Credit Opportunity Act*, which prohibits discrimination based on race, color, gender, marital status, religion, or national origin in the extension of credit. It also gives married women the right to establish credit histories in their own names. The Federal Reserve receives and tries to resolve consumer complaints against banks.

In 2010, the **Consumer Financial Protection Bureau (CFPB)** was established. This is an independent bureau within the Federal Reserve that helps consumers make financial decisions. The goal of the CFPB is to promote fairness and make mortgages, credit cards, and other consumer financial services understandable. The objective is to let consumers see clearly the costs and features of loans. As a result, consumers will not be caught by hidden fees or sign loans they cannot afford.

Consumer Financial Protection Bureau (CFPB) An independent bureau within the Federal Reserve that helps consumers make their financial decisions.

18-6f Maintaining Federal Government Checking Accounts and Gold

The Fed is also Uncle Sam's bank. The U.S. Treasury has the Fed handle its checking account. From this account, the federal government pays for such expenses as federal employees' salaries, Social Security, tax refunds, veterans' benefits, defense, and highways.

Finally, it is interesting to note that the New York Federal Reserve District Bank holds one of the oldest forms of money—*gold*. This gold belongs mainly to foreign governments and is one of the largest accumulations of this precious metal in the world. Viewing a Federal Reserve Bank's vault is not something that most tourists typically have on their list of things to do, but I strongly recommend this tour.

The gold vault at the New York Federal Reserve bank is nearly half the length of a football field and filled with steel and concrete walls several yards thick. Most cells contain the gold of only one nation, and only a few bank employees know the identities of the owners. When trade occurs between two countries, payment between the parties can be made by transferring gold bars from one compartment to another. Note that the Fed and the monetary system of the Yapese are similar. Recall from the Global Economics box that in Yap large stone wheels are not moved; rather they just change ownership.

18-6g Lender of Last Resort

The Fed acts as the lender of last resort to prevent a banking crisis. For example, after the terrorist attacks in 2001, the Fed issued billions in loans to banks throughout the United States. And in 2008, several large banks collapsed and others were on the verge. The Fed lent banks enough required reserve balances to meet their obligation to depositors.

18-7 THE U.S. BANKING REVOLUTION

Prior to the 1980s, the U.S. banking system was simpler. It consisted of many commercial banks authorized by law to offer checking accounts. Then there were the other financial institutions, the so-called thrifts, which included S&Ls, mutual savings banks, and credit unions. The thrifts by law were permitted to accept only savings deposits with no checking privileges. The commercial banks, on the other hand, could not pay interest on checkable deposits. Moreover, a "maximum interest rate allowed by law" limited competition among commercial banks and other financial institutions. As will be explained momentarily, this relatively tranquil U.S. banking structure changed dramatically, and the stage was set for a fascinating banking "horror story."

18-8 THE MONETARY CONTROL ACT OF 1980

Monetary Control Act A law, formally titled the Depository Institutions Deregulation and Monetary Control Act of 1980, that gave the Federal Reserve System greater control over nonmember banks and made all financial institutions more competitive.

A significant law affecting the U.S. banking system is the Depository Institutions Deregulation and Monetary Control Act of 1980, commonly called the **Monetary Control Act**. This law gave the Federal Reserve System greater control over nonmember banks and made all financial institutions more competitive. The act's four major provisions are the following:

1. **The authority of the Fed over nonmember depository institutions was increased.** Before the Monetary Control Act, less than half of the banks in the United States were members of the Fed and subject to its direct control. Under the act's provisions, the Federal Reserve sets uniform reserve requirements for *all* commercial banks, including state and national banks, S&Ls, and credit unions with checking accounts.
2. **All depository institutions are able to borrow loan reserves from Federal Reserve banks.** This practice, called *discounting*, will be explained in the next chapter. Banks also have access to check clearing and other services of the Fed.
3. **The act allowed commercial banks, thrifts, money market mutual funds, stock brokerage firms, and retailers to offer a wide variety of banking services.** For example, commercial banks and other financial institutions can pay unrestricted interest rates on checking accounts. Also, S&Ls and other financial institutions can offer checking accounts. Federal credit unions are authorized to make residential real estate loans and other major corporations can offer traditional banking services.
4. **The act eliminated all interest rate ceilings.** Before this act, S&Ls were allowed to pay depositors a slightly higher interest rate on passbook savings deposits than those paid by commercial banks. The Monetary Control Act removed this advantage of S&Ls over other financial institutions competing for depositors.

Finally, the movement toward deregulation, which blurred the distinctions between financial institutions, continued in 1999 when the *Financial Services Modernization Act* was signed into law. This sweeping measure lifted Depression-era barriers and allows banks, securities firms, and insurance companies to merge and sell each other's products.

18-8a The Savings and Loan Crisis

In 2013, Cyprus experienced a financial crisis and closed its banks. After the banks opened, depositors stood in long lines day after day hoping to be able to withdraw a limited amount from their accounts. Could this happen in the United States? In fact it has happened. Before the recent financial crisis discussed in Chapter 20 on monetary policy, the savings and loan crisis of the 1980s and early 1990s was one of the worst U.S. financial crisis since the Great Depression and a classic case of the unintended consequences of legislation. After the Monetary Control Act removed interest rate ceilings on deposits, competition for customers forced S&Ls to pay higher interest rates on short-term deposits. Unlike the banks, however, S&Ls were earning their income from long-term mortgages at fixed interest rates below the rate required to keep or attract new deposits. The resulting losses enticed the S&Ls to forsake home mortgage loans, which they knew best, and seek high-interest, but riskier, commercial and consumer loans. Unfortunately, these risky higher-interest loans resulted in defaults and more losses. If conditions were not bad enough, lower oil prices depressed the oil-based state economies in Texas, Louisiana, and Oklahoma.

ECONOMICS IN PRACTICE

The Wreck of Lincoln Savings and Loan
Applicable concept: deposit insurance

The case of Lincoln Savings and Loan is a classic example of what went wrong during one of the worst financial crisis in U.S. history prior to the financial crisis and Great Recession of 2007–2009. In 1984, the Securities and Exchange Commission charged Charles Keating, Jr., with fraud in an Ohio loan scam, but regulators later allowed him to buy Lincoln Savings and Loan in California. Keating hired a staff to carry out his wishes and paid them and his relatives millions. Keating was also generous with politicians in Washington, D.C. Allegedly, five U.S. senators received $1.5 million in campaign contributions from Keating to influence regulators.

Where did Keating's money come from? It came from Lincoln Savings depositors and, ultimately, from taxpayers because the federal government insures deposits of failed S&Ls. When Keating took over Lincoln, it was a healthy S&L with assets of $1.1 billion. But because of deregulation mandated by the Monetary Control Act and other legislation and the lack of enforcement of regulations under the new laws, many S&Ls plunged into high-risk, but potentially highly profitable, ventures. Keating therefore took Lincoln out of sound home mortgage loans and into speculation in Arizona hotels costing $500,000 per room to build, raw land for golf courses, shopping centers, junk bonds, and currency futures.

In 1987, after it was already too late, California regulators became alarmed at the way Lincoln operated and asked the FBI and the FSLIC to take over Lincoln. Keating responded by contacting his friends in Washington, and the regulatory process moved at a snail's pace. Years passed before the government finally closed Lincoln and informed the public that their deposits were not safe in this S&L. During the time

regulators were deciding what action to take, it is estimated that Lincoln cost taxpayers another $1 billion. Ultimately, the collapse of Lincoln cost U.S. taxpayers about $3 billion, making it the most expensive S&L failure of all.

Keating and other S&L entrepreneurs say they did nothing wrong. After all, Congress and federal regulators encouraged, or did not discourage, S&Ls to compete by borrowing funds at high interest rates and making risky, but potentially highly profitable, investments. If oil prices and land values fall unexpectedly and loans fail, this is simply the way a market economy works and not the fault of risk-prone wheeler-dealers like Keating.

In 1993, a federal judge sentenced Keating to 12 1/2 years in prison for swindling small investors. The sentence ran concurrently with a 10-year state prison sentence. The judge also ordered Keating to pay $122.4 million in restitution to the government for losses caused by sham property sales. However, the government was unable to locate any significant assets. Keating served four years and nine months.

ANALYZE the ISSUE Critics of federal banking policy argue that deposit insurance is a key reason for banking failures. The banks enjoy a "heads I win, tails the government loses" proposition. Several possible reforms of deposit insurance have been suggested. For example, the limit on insured deposits can be raised, reduced, or eliminated. Do you think a change in deposit insurance would prevent bank failures?

The Federal Savings and Loan Insurance Corporation (FSLIC) was the agency that insured deposits in S&Ls, similar to how the FDIC insures banks deposits. The magnitude of the losses exceeded the insurance fund's ability to pay depositors, and Congress placed the FSLIC's deposit insurance fund under the FDIC's control. To close or sell ailing S&Ls and protect depositors, Congress enacted the Thrift Bailout Bill in 1989. One provision of this act created the Resolution Trust Corporation (RTC) to carry out a massive federal bailout of failed institutions. The RTC bought the assets and deposits of failed S&Ls and sold them to offset the cost borne by taxpayers. The RTC closed in 1995, and the ultimate cost to taxpayers totaled over $125 billion.

Key Concepts

Barter

Money

Medium of exchange

Unit of account

Store of value

Commodity money

Fiat money

M1, M2

Currency

Checkable deposits

Federal Reserve System

Board of Governors

Federal Open Market Committee (FOMC)

Federal Deposit Insurance Corporation (FDIC)

Consumer Financial Protection Bureau (CFPB)

Monetary Control Act

Summary

- **Money** can be anything that meets these three tests. Money must serve as (1) a medium of exchange, (2) a unit of account, and (3) a store of value. Money facilitates more efficient exchange than barter. Other desirable properties of money include scarcity, portability, divisibility, and uniformity.

- **Medium of exchange** is the most important function of money. This means that money is widely accepted in payment for goods and services.

- **Unit of account** is another important function of money. Money is used to measure relative values by serving as a common yardstick for valuing goods and services.

- **Store of value** is the ability of money to hold its value over time. Money is said to be highly *liquid*, which means it is readily usable in exchange.

- **Credit cards** are not money. Credit cards represent a short-term loan and therefore fail as a store of value.

- **Commodity money** is money that has a marketable value, such as gold and silver. Today, the United States uses *fiat money*, which must be accepted by law, but is not convertible into gold, silver, or any commodity.

- **M1** is the narrowest definition of the money supply, which equals currency plus checkable deposits. **M2** is a broader definition of the money supply, which equals M1 plus *near monies*, such as savings deposits and small time deposits.

Definitions of Money (M1 and M2)

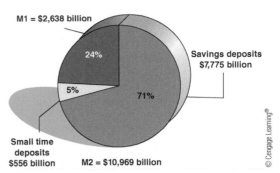

M1 = $2,638 billion · Savings deposits $7,775 billion · 24% · 5% · 71% · Small time deposits $556 billion · M2 = $10,969 billion

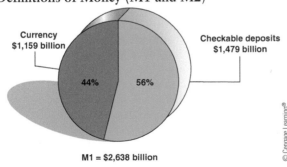

Currency $1,159 billion · Checkable deposits $1,479 billion · 44% · 56%

M1 = $2,638 billion

- The **Federal Reserve System**, our central bank, was established in 1913. The Fed consists of 12 Federal Reserve district banks with 25 branches. The **Board of Governors** is the Fed's governing body. The **Federal Open Market Committee (FOMC)** directs the buying and selling of U.S. government securities, which is a key method of controlling the money supply.

- **Basic Federal Reserve bank functions** are (1) controlling the money supply, (2) clearing checks, (3) supervising and regulating banking, (4) maintaining and circulating currency, (5) protecting consumers, and (6) maintaining the federal government's checking accounts and gold.

- The **Monetary Control Act of 1980** revolutionized U.S. banking by expanding the authority of the Federal Reserve System to all financial institutions. In addition, this law increased competition by blurring the distinctions between commercial banks, thrift institutions, and even nonfinancial institutions.

Study Questions and Problems

1. Discuss this statement: "A man with a million dollars who is lost in the desert learns the meaning of money."

2. Could each of the following items potentially serve as money? Consider each as (1) a medium of exchange, (2) a unit of account, and (3) a store of value.
   a. Visa credit card
   b. Federal Reserve note
   c. Dog
   d. Beer mug

3. Consider each of the items in Question 2 in terms of scarcity, portability, divisibility, and uniformity.

4. What backs the U.S. dollar? Include the distinction between commodity money and fiat money in your answer.

5. What are the components of the most narrowly defined money supply in the United States?

6. Distinguish between M1 and M2. What are near monies?

7. What is the major purpose of the Federal Reserve System? What is the major responsibility of the Board of Governors and the Federal Open Market Committee?

8. Should the Fed be independent or a government agency subordinate to Congress and the President?

9. Which banks must be insured by the FDIC? Which banks can choose not to be insured by the FDIC?

10. Briefly discuss the importance of the Depository Institutions Deregulation and Monetary Control Act of 1980.

Sample Quiz

1. Buying a cup of coffee with a dollar bill represents the use of money as a
   a. medium of exchange.
   b. unit of account.
   c. store of value.
   d. All of the answers above are correct.

2. Comparing how many dollars it takes to attend college each year to annual earnings on a job represents the use of money as a
   a. medium of exchange.
   b. unit of account.
   c. store of value.
   d. store of coincidence.

3. Which of the following items does *not* provide a store of value?
   a. Currency.
   b. Checkable deposits.
   c. Credit cards.
   d. All of the answers above are correct.

4. Anything can be money if it acts as a
   a. unit of account.
   b. store of value.
   c. medium of exchange.
   d. All of the answers above must be correct.

5. The ease with which an asset can be converted into a medium of exchange is known as
   a. volatility.
   b. liquidity.
   c. currency.
   d. speculative exchange.

6. Which of the following items is included when computing M1?
   a. Coins in circulation.
   b. Currency in circulation.
   c. Checking accounting entries.
   d. All of the answers above are correct.

7. Which of the following statements is *true*?
   a. Money must be relatively "scarce" if it is to have value.
   b. Money must be divisible and portable.
   c. M1 is the narrowest definition of money.
   d. All of the answers above are correct.

8. M1 money includes all *but* which one of the following?
   a. Checkable deposits.
   b. Savings accounts.
   c. Paper money.
   d. Coins.

9. Which of the following is counted as part of M2?
   a. Currency.
   b. Checkable deposits at commercial banks.
   c. Money market funds.
   d. All of the answers above are correct.

10. Which definition of the money supply includes credit cards?
    a. M1.
    b. M2.
    c. Each of the answers includes credit card balances.
    d. None of the answers include credit card balances.

11. With respect to controlling the money supply, the law requires the Fed to take orders from
    a. the president.
    b. the Speaker of the House.
    c. the Secretary of the Treasury.
    d. No one—the Fed is an independent agency.

12. Which of the following is *not* part of the Federal Reserve System?
    a. Council of Economic Advisors.
    b. Board of Governors.
    c. Federal Open Market Committee.
    d. 12 Federal Reserve district banks.

13. The Fed's principal decision-making body, which directs buying and selling U.S. government securities, is known as the
    a. Federal Deposit Insurance Corporation.
    b. District Board of Governors.
    c. Federal Open Market Committee.
    d. Reserve Requirement Regulation Conference.

14. The major protection against sudden mass attempt to withdraw cash from banks is the
    a. Federal Reserve.
    b. Consumer Protection Act.
    c. Deposit insurance provided by the FDIC.
    d. Gold and silver backing the dollar.

15. The Monetary Control Act of 1980
    a. created less competition among various financial institutions.
    b. allowed fewer institutions to offer checking account services.
    c. restricted savings and loan associations to long-term loans.
    d. None of the answers above are correct.
16. Which of the following is a store of value?
    a. Federal Reserve notes.
    b. Debit card.
    c. Passbook savings deposit.
    d. Each of the answers is a store of value.
17. The difference between M1 and M2 is given by which of the following?
    a. M1 includes currency, coins, gold, and silver, whereas M2 does not contain gold and silver.
    b. M1 is made up of currency and checkable deposits, whereas M2 contains M1 plus savings deposits and small time deposits.
    c. M1 is limited to checkable deposits, whereas M2 contains currency.
    d. M1 includes only currency, whereas M2 contains M1 plus checkable deposits.

18. Which of the following is a desirable property of money?
    a. Scarcity.
    b. Portability.
    c. Divisibility.
    d. All of the answers above are correct.
19. The Federal Reserve System was founded in
    a. 1913.
    b. 1929.
    c. 1933.
    d. 1935.
20. The Monetary Control Act of 1980 extended the Fed's authority to
    a. impose required-reserve ratios on all depository institutions.
    b. control the discount rate.
    c. control the federal funds rate.
    d. All of the answers above are correct.

PART 5

The International Economy

The final part of this text is devoted to global topics. Chapter 21 explains the importance of free trade and the mechanics of trade bookkeeping and exchange rates. Here you will find a feature on the birth of the euro. Chapter 22 takes a historical look at the theoretical debate over capitalism and the transition of Cuba, Russia, and China toward this system. In the opposite direction, there is a discussion of nationalization in the United States. Chapter 23 provides comparisons of advanced and developing countries. The chapter concludes with the fascinating success of Hong Kong.

International Trade and Finance

In this chapter, you will learn to solve these economics puzzles:

- How does Babe Ruth's decision not to remain a pitcher illustrate an important principle in international trade?

- Is there a valid argument for trade protectionism?

- Should the United States return to the gold standard?

CHAPTER PREVIEW

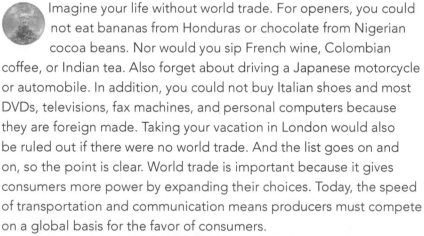

Imagine your life without world trade. For openers, you could not eat bananas from Honduras or chocolate from Nigerian cocoa beans. Nor would you sip French wine, Colombian coffee, or Indian tea. Also forget about driving a Japanese motorcycle or automobile. In addition, you could not buy Italian shoes and most DVDs, televisions, fax machines, and personal computers because they are foreign made. Taking your vacation in London would also be ruled out if there were no world trade. And the list goes on and on, so the point is clear. World trade is important because it gives consumers more power by expanding their choices. Today, the speed of transportation and communication means producers must compete on a global basis for the favor of consumers.

Trade is often highly controversial. Regardless of whether it is a World Trade Organization (WTO) meeting, or a G8 summit meeting, global trade talks face protesters in the streets complaining that globalization has triggered a crisis in the world, such as global warming, poverty, soaring oil prices, or food shortages. And in the United States outsourcing jobs to lower paid workers overseas has continued to be a debated issue.

The first part of this chapter explains the theoretical reason for why countries should specialize in producing certain goods and then trade them for imports. Also, you will study arguments for and against the United States protecting itself from "unfair" trade practices by other countries. In the second part of the chapter, you will learn how nations pay each other for world trade. Here you will explore international bookkeeping and discover how supply and demand forces determine that, for example, 1 dollar is worth 100 yen.

21-1 WHY NATIONS NEED TRADE

The United States leads the world in imports while also being one of the top exporters in the world. Exhibit 21-1 reveals which regions are our major trading partners (exports plus imports). Leading the list of nations is Canada, our largest trading partner, followed by China, Mexico, and Japan. Leading U.S. exports are chemicals, machinery, agricultural products, airplanes, computers, and automobiles. Major imports include cars, trucks, petroleum, electronics, and clothing. Why does a nation even bother to trade with the rest of the world? Does it seem strange for the United States to import goods it could produce for itself? Indeed, why doesn't the United States become self-sufficient by growing all its own food, including bananas, sugar, and coffee, making all its own cars, and prohibiting sales of all foreign goods? This section explains why specialization and trade are a nation's keys to a higher standard of living.

EXHIBIT 21-1 U.S. Trading Partners, 2013

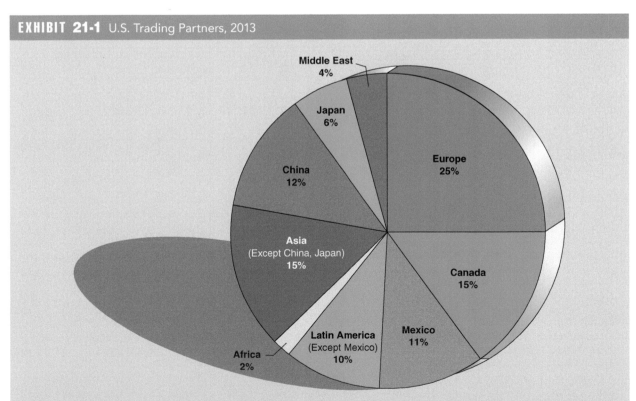

In 2013, Canada, China, Mexico, and Japan accounted for over 40 percent of U.S. trade (exports plus imports).

Source: Bureau of Economic Analysis, *U.S. International Transactions by Area*, http://www.bea.gov/international/index.htm, Table 12.

21-1a The Production Possibilities Curve Revisited

Consider a world with only two countries—the United States and Japan. To keep the illustration simple, also assume both countries produce only two goods—grain and steel. Accordingly, we can construct in Exhibit 21-2 a *production possibilities curve* for each country. We will also set aside the *law of increasing opportunity costs*, explained in Chapter 2, and assume workers are equally suited to producing grain or steel. This assumption transforms the bowed-out shape of the production possibilities curve into a straight line.

Comparing parts (a) and (b) of Exhibit 21-2 shows that the United States can produce more grain than Japan. If the United States devotes all its resources to this purpose, 100 tons of grain are produced per day, represented by point *A* in Exhibit 21-2(a). The maximum grain production of Japan, on the other hand, is only 40 tons per day because Japan has less labor, land, and other factors of production than the United States. This capability is represented by point *D* in Exhibit 21-2(b).

Now consider the capacities of the two countries for producing steel. If all their respective resources are devoted to this output, the United States produces 50 tons per day (point *C*), and Japan produces only 40 tons per day (point *F*). Again, the greater potential maximum steel output of the United States reflects its greater resources. Both countries are also capable of producing other combinations of grain and steel along their respective production possibilities curves, such as point *B* for the United States and point *E* for Japan.

EXHIBIT 21-2 The Benefits of Specialization and Trade

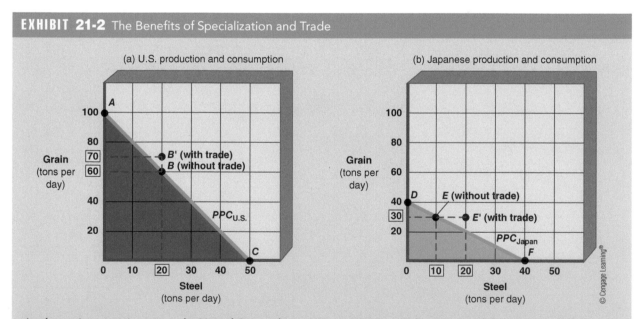

As shown in part (a), assume the United States chooses point *B* on its production possibilities curve, *PPC*$_{U.S.}$. Without trade, the United States produces and consumes 60 tons of grain and 20 tons of steel. In part (b), assume Japan also operates along its production possibilities curve, *PPC*$_{Japan}$, at point *E*. Without trade, Japan produces and consumes 30 tons of grain and 10 tons of steel.

Now assume the United States specializes in producing grain at point *A* and imports 20 tons of Japanese steel in exchange for 30 tons of grain. Through specialization and trade, the United States moves to consumption possibility point *B'*, outside its production possibilities curve. Japan also moves to a higher standard of living at consumption possibility point *E'*, outside its production possibilities curve.

21-1b Specialization without Trade

Assuming no world trade, the production possibilities curve for each country also defines its *consumption possibilities*. Stated another way, we assume that both countries are *self-sufficient* because without imports they must consume only the combination chosen along their production possibilities curve. Under the assumption of self-sufficiency, suppose the United States prefers to produce and consume 60 tons of grain and 20 tons of steel per day (point *B*). Also assume Japan chooses to produce and consume 30 tons of grain and 10 tons of steel (point *E*). Exhibit 21-3 lists data corresponding to points *B* and *E* and shows that the total world output is 90 tons of grain and 30 tons of steel.

Now suppose the United States specializes by producing and consuming at point *A*, rather than point *B*. Suppose also that Japan specializes by producing and consuming at point *F*, rather than point *E*. As shown in Exhibit 21-3, specialization in each country increases total world output per day by 10 tons of grain and 10 tons of steel. Because this extra world output has the potential for making both countries better off, why wouldn't the United States and Japan specialize and produce at points *A* and *F*, respectively? The reason is that although production at these points is clearly possible, neither country wants to consume these combinations of output. The United States prefers to consume less grain and more steel at point *B* compared to point *A*. Japan, on the other hand, prefers to consume more grain and less steel at point *E*, rather than point *F*.

> **CONCLUSION** When countries specialize, total world output increases, and therefore, the potential for greater total world consumption also increases.

21-1c Specialization with Trade

Now let's return to Exhibit 21-2 and demonstrate how world trade benefits countries. Suppose the United States agrees to specialize in grain production at point *A* and to import 20 tons of Japanese steel in exchange for 30 tons of its grain output. Does the United States gain from trade? The answer is Yes. At point *A*, the United States produces 100 tons of grain per day. Subtracting the 30 tons of grain traded to Japan leaves the United States with 70 tons of its own grain production to consume. In return for grain, Japan unloads 20 tons of steel on U.S. shores. Hence, specialization and trade allow the United States to move from point *A* to point *B'*, which is a consumption possibility *outside* its production possibilities curve in Exhibit 21-2(a). At point *B'*, the United States consumes the

EXHIBIT 21-3 Effect of Specialization without Trade on World Output

	Grain Production (tons per day)	Steel Production (tons per day)
Before specialization		
United States (at point *B*)	60	20
Japan (at point *E*)	30	10
Total world output	90	30
After specialization		
United States (at point *A*)	100	0
Japan (at point *F*)	0	40
Total world output	100	40

© Cengage Learning®

same amount of steel and 10 more tons of grain compared to point *B* (without trade).

Japan also has an incentive to specialize by moving its production mix from point *E* to point *F*. With trade, Japan's consumption will be at point *E'*. At point *E'*, Japan has as much grain to consume as it had at point *E*, plus 10 more tons of steel. After trading 20 tons of the 40 tons of steel produced at point *F* for grain, Japan can still consume 20 tons of steel from its production, rather than only 10 tons of steel at point *E*. Thus, point *E'* is a consumption possibility that lies *outside* Japan's production possibilities curve.

> **CONCLUSION** International trade allows a country to consume a combination of goods that exceeds its production possibilities curve.

21-2 ABSOLUTE AND COMPARATIVE ADVANTAGE

Absolute advantage The ability of a country to produce a good using the same or fewer resources than another country.

Comparative advantage The ability of a country to produce a good at a lower opportunity cost than another country.

Why did the United States decide to produce and export grain instead of steel? Why did Japan choose to produce and export steel rather than grain? Here you study the economic principles that determine specialization and trade. These concepts are absolute advantage and comparative advantage. **Absolute advantage** is the ability of a country to produce more of a good using the same or fewer resources as another country. **Comparative advantage** is the ability of a country to produce a good at a lower opportunity cost than another country.

Perhaps a noneconomic example will clarify the difference between absolute advantage and comparative advantage. When Babe Ruth played for the New York Yankees, he was the best hitter and the best pitcher not only on the team but also in all of Major League Baseball. In fact, before Ruth was traded to the Yankees and switched to the outfield, he was the best left-handed pitcher in the American League for a few seasons with the Boston Red Sox. His final record was 94–46. In other words, he had an *absolute advantage* in both hitting and throwing the baseball. Stated differently, Babe Ruth could produce the same home runs as any other teammate with fewer times at bat. The problem was that if he pitched, he would bat fewer times because pitchers need rest after pitching. The coaches decided that the Babe had a *comparative advantage* in hitting. A few pitchers on the team could pitch almost as well as the Babe, but no one could touch his hitting. In terms of opportunity costs, the Yankees would lose fewer games if the Babe specialized in hitting.

21-2a Absolute Advantage

So far in our grain versus steel example, a country's production and trade decisions have not considered how much labor, land, or capital either the United States or Japan uses to produce a ton of grain or steel. For example, Japan might have an absolute advantage in producing *both* grain and steel. In our example, compared to the United States Japan might use fewer resources per ton to produce grain and steel. Maybe the Japanese work harder or are more skilled. In short, the Japanese may be more productive producers, but their absolute advantage does not matter in specialization and world trade decisions. If Japan has a comparative advantage in steel, it should specialize in steel even if compared to the United States Japan can produce both grain and steel with fewer resources.

> **CONCLUSION** Specialization and trade are based on opportunity costs (comparative advantage) and not an absolute advantage.

21-2b Comparative Advantage

Engaging in world trade permits countries to escape the prison of their own production possibilities curves by producing bread, cars, or whatever goods they make best. The decision of the United States to specialize in and export grain and the decision of Japan to specialize in and export steel are based on comparative advantage. Continuing our example from Exhibit 21-2, we can calculate opportunity costs for the two countries and use comparative advantage to determine which country should specialize in grain and which should specialize in steel. For the United States, the opportunity cost of producing 50 tons of steel is 100 tons of grain not produced, so 1 ton of steel costs 2 tons of grain. For Japan, the opportunity cost of producing 40 tons of steel is 40 tons of grain, so 1 ton of steel costs 1 ton of grain. Japan's steel is therefore cheaper in terms of grain forgone. This means Japan has a comparative advantage in steel production because it must give up less grain to produce steel than the United States. Stated differently, the opportunity cost of steel production is lower in Japan than in the United States.

The other side of the coin is to measure the cost of grain in terms of steel. For the United States, the opportunity cost of producing 100 tons of grain is 50 tons of steel not produced. This means 1 ton of grain costs 1/2 ton of steel. For Japan, the opportunity cost of producing 40 tons of grain is 40 tons of steel so 1 ton of grain costs 1 ton of steel. The United States has a comparative advantage in grain because its opportunity cost in terms of steel forgone is lower. Thus, the United States should specialize in grain because it is more efficient in grain production. Japan, on the other hand, is relatively more efficient at producing steel and should specialize in this product.

> **CONCLUSION** Comparative advantage refers to the relative opportunity costs between different countries of producing the same goods. World output and consumption are maximized when each country specializes in producing and trading goods for which it has a comparative advantage.

CHECKPOINT

Do Nations with an Advantage Always Trade?
Comparing labor productivity, suppose the United States has an absolute advantage over Costa Rica in the production of calculators and towels. In the United States, a worker can produce 4 calculators or 400 towels in 10 hours. In Costa Rica, a worker can produce 1 calculator or 100 towels in the same amount of time. Under these conditions, are specialization and trade advantageous?

21-3 FREE TRADE VERSUS PROTECTIONISM

Free trade The flow of goods between countries without restrictions or special taxes.

Protectionism The government's use of embargoes, tariffs, quotas, and other restrictions to protect domestic producers from foreign competition.

Embargo A law that bars trade with another country.

In theory, international trade should be based on comparative advantage and free trade. Free trade is the flow of goods between countries without restrictions or special taxes. In practice, despite the advice of economists, to some degree every nation protects its own domestic producers from foreign competition. Behind these barriers to trade are special interest groups whose jobs and incomes are threatened, so they clamor to the government for protectionism. Protectionism is the government's use of embargoes, tariffs, quotas, and other restrictions to protect domestic producers from foreign competition.

21-3a Embargo

Embargoes are the strongest limit on trade. An embargo is a law that bars trade with another country. For example, the United States and other nations in the world imposed an arms embargo on Iraq in response to its invasion of Kuwait in 1990. The United States also maintains embargoes against Iran, Cuba, and North Korea.

21-3b Tariff

Tariff A tax on an import.

Tariffs are the most popular and visible measures used to discourage trade. A tariff is a tax on an import. Tariffs are also called customs duties. Suppose the United States imposes a tariff of 2.9 percent on autos. If a foreign car costs $40,000, the amount of the tariff equals $1,160 ($40,000 × 0.029) and the U.S. price, including the tariff, is $41,160. The current U.S. tariff code specifies tariffs on nearly 70 percent of U.S. imports. A tariff can be based on weight, volume, or number of units, or it can be *ad valorem* (figured as a percentage of the price). The average U.S. tariff is less than 5 percent, but individual tariffs vary widely. Tariffs are imposed to reduce imports by raising import prices and to generate revenues for the U.S. Treasury. Exhibit 21-4 shows the trend of the average tariff rate since 1930.

During the worldwide depression of the 1930s, when one nation raised its tariffs to protect its industries, other nations retaliated by raising their tariffs. Under the Smoot-Hawley tariffs of the 1930s, the average tariff in the United States reached a peak of 20 percent. Durable imports, which were one-third of imports, were subject to an unbelievable tariff rate of 60 percent. In 1947, most of the world's industrialized nations mutually agreed to end the tariff wars by signing the *General Agreement on Tariffs and Trade (GATT)*. Since then, GATT nations have met periodically to negotiate lower tariff rates. GATT agreements

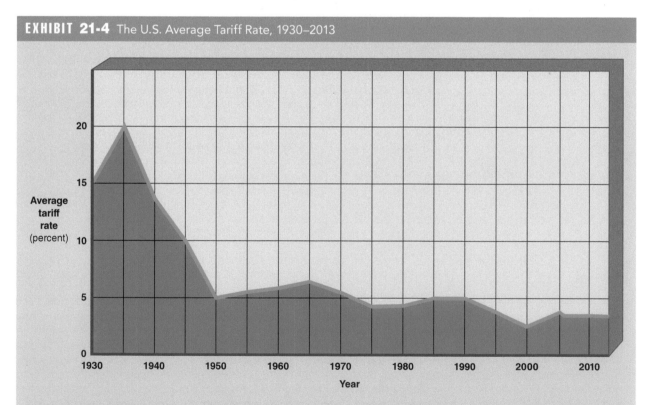

EXHIBIT 21-4 The U.S. Average Tariff Rate, 1930–2013

Under the Smoot-Hawley Act of 1930, the average tariff rate peaked at 20 percent. Since the GATT in 1947 and other trade agreements, tariffs have declined to less than 5 percent.

Sources: *Economic Report of the President 1989*, http://www.gpoaccess.gov/eop/, p. 151; United States International Trade Commission, *The Economic Effect of Significant U.S. Import Restraints*, June 2002, p. 146, http://www.usitc.gov/; and Trade Profiles, http://stat.wto.org /CountryProfiles/US_e.htm.

World Trade Organization (WTO) An international organization of member countries that oversees international trade agreements and rules on trade disputes.

have significantly reduced tariffs over the years among member nations. In the 1994 *Uruguay round*, member nations signed a GATT agreement that decreased tariffs and reduced other trade barriers. The most divisive element of this agreement was the creation in 1995 of the Geneva-based World Trade Organization (WTO) to enforce rulings in global trade disputes. The WTO has 160 members and a standing appellate body to render final decisions regarding disputes between WTO members. Critics fear that the WTO might be far more likely to rule in favor of other countries in their trade disputes with the United States. Some people argue that the WTO is unaccountable, and these critics reject free trade and globalization.

To illustrate an interesting WTO case, the United States imposed tariffs in 2002 on steel imports to protect jobs in the struggling U.S. steel industry against foreign competition. The WTO ruled these tariffs were illegal, and countries in Europe and Asia prepared a list of retaliatory tariffs. These levies targeted products such as citrus fruit grown in Florida and apparel produced in southern states crucial to President Bush's reelection. Meanwhile, U.S. automakers and other steel-consuming industries complained because the tariffs increased their costs. Facing these threats, the United States removed the tariffs on steel imports in 2003. It is interesting to compare this case to the Global Economics feature titled World Trade Slips on Banana Peel.

21-3c Quota

Quota A limit on the quantity of a good that may be imported in a given time period.

Another way to limit foreign competition is to impose a quota. A quota is a limit on the quantity of a good that may be imported in a given time period. For example, the United States may allow 10 million tons of sugar to be imported over a one-year period. Once this quantity is reached, no more sugar can be imported for the year. About 12 percent of U.S. imports are subject to import quotas. Examples include import quotas on sugar, dairy products, textiles, steel, and even ice cream. Quotas can limit imports from all foreign suppliers or from specific countries. In 2005, for example, global quotas were lifted from Chinese imports. The United States and the European countries demanded quotas to protect their countries from Chinese textiles. Critics argued that, like all barriers to trade, quotas invite nations to retaliate with more measures to restrict trade, and consumers are harmed by higher prices because of the lack of competition from lower-priced imports. In addition to embargoes, tariffs, and quotas, some nations use subtler measures to discourage trade, such as setting up an overwhelming number of bureaucratic steps that must be taken in order to import a product.

21-4 ARGUMENTS FOR PROTECTION

Free trade provides consumers with lower prices and larger quantities of goods from which to choose. Thus, removing import barriers might save each family a few hundred dollars a year. The problem, however, is that imports could cost some workers their jobs and thousands of dollars per year from lost income. Thus, it is no wonder that in spite of the greater total benefits from free trade to consumers, trade barriers exist. The reason is primarily because workers and owners from import-competing firms have more at stake than consumers, so they go to Washington and lobby for protection. The following are some of the most popular arguments for protection. These arguments have strong political or emotional appeal but weak support from economists.

21-4a Infant Industry Argument

As the name suggests, the *infant industry argument* is that a new domestic industry needs protection because it is not yet ready to compete with established foreign competitors. An infant industry is in a formative stage and must bear high start-up costs to train an entire workforce, develop new technology, establish marketing channels, and reach economies of scale. With time to grow and protection, an infant industry can reduce costs and "catch up" with established foreign firms.

Economists ask where one draws the arbitrary line between an "infant" and a "grown-up" industry. It is also difficult to make a convincing case for protecting an infant industry in a developed country, such as the United States, where industries are well established. The infant industry argument, however, may have some validity for less-developed countries. Yet, even for these countries, there is a danger. Once protection is granted, the new industry will not experience the competitive pressures necessary to encourage reasonably quick growth and participation in world trade. Also, once an industry is given protection, it is difficult to take it away.

21-4b National Security Argument

Another common argument is that defense-related industries must be protected with embargoes, tariffs, and quotas to ensure national security. By protecting critical defense industries, a nation will not be dependent on foreign countries for the essential defense-related goods it needs to defend itself in wartime. The *national defense argument* has been used to protect a long list of industries, including petrochemicals, munitions, steel, and rubber.

This argument gained validity during the War of 1812. Great Britain, the main trading partner of the United States, became an enemy that blockaded our coast. Today, this argument makes less sense for the United States. The government stockpiles missiles, sophisticated electronics, petroleum, and most goods needed in wartime.

21-4c Employment Argument

The *employment argument* suggests that restricting imports increases domestic jobs in protected industries. According to this protectionist argument, the sale of an imported good comes at the expense of its domestically produced counterpart. Lower domestic output therefore leads to higher domestic unemployment than would otherwise be the case.

It is true that protectionism can increase output and save jobs in some industries at home. Ignored, however, are the higher prices paid by consumers because protectionism reduces competition between domestic goods and imported goods. In addition, there are employment reduction effects to consider. For example, suppose a strict quota is imposed on steel imported into our nation. Reduced foreign competition allows U.S. steelmakers to charge higher prices for their steel. As a result, prices rise and sales fall for cars and other products using steel, causing production and employment to fall in these industries. Thus, the import quota on steel may save jobs in the steel industry but at the expense of more jobs lost in the steel-consuming industries. Also, by selling U.S. imports, foreigners earn dollars that they can use to buy U.S. exports. Import quotas cause foreigners to have fewer dollars to spend on U.S. exports, resulting in a decrease in employment in U.S. export industries. In short, protectionism may cause a net reduction in the nation's total employment.

21-4d Cheap Foreign Labor Argument

Another popular claim is the *cheap labor argument*. It goes something like this: "How can we compete with such unfair competition? Labor costs $10 an hour in the United States, and firms in many developing countries pay only $1 an hour. Without protection, U.S. wages will be driven down, and our standard of living will fall."

GLOBAL ECONOMICS

World Trade Slips on Banana Peel

Applicable concept: protectionism

© iStockphoto.com/RedHelga

Growing bananas for European markets was a multibillion-dollar bright spot for Latin America's struggling economies. In fact, about half of this region's banana exports traditionally were sold to Europe. Then, in 1993, the European Union (EU) adopted a package of quotas and tariffs aimed at cutting Europe's banana imports from Latin America. The purpose of these restrictions was to give trade preference to 66 banana-growing former colonies of European nations in Africa, the Caribbean, and the Pacific. Ignored was the fact that growers in Latin America grow higher-quality bananas at half the cost of EU-favored growers because of their low labor costs and flat tropical land near port cities.

In 1999, the World Trade Organization (WTO) ruled that the EU was discriminating in favor of European companies importing the fruit and the WTO imposed $191.4 million per year in punitive tariffs on European goods. This was the first time in the four years the WTO had been in existence that such retaliation had been approved, and only the second time going back to its predecessor, the General Agreement on Tariffs and Trade. When the EU failed to comply with the WTO findings, the United States enforced its WTO rights by imposing increased duties on EU imports, including goods ranging from cashmere sweaters and Italian handbags to sheep's milk cheese, British biscuits, and German coffeemakers. The effect of the U.S. sanctions was to double the wholesale prices of these items. Denmark and the Netherlands were exempt from the U.S. tariffs because they were the only nations that voted against the EU banana rules.

Critics charged that the United States was pushing the case for political reasons. American companies, including Chiquita Brands International and Dole Food Company, grow most of their bananas in Latin America. With America's trade deficit running at a record level, U.S. trade experts also argued that the United States had little choice but to act against the EU for failing to abide by the WTO's ruling. Moreover, with increasing voices in the United States questioning the wisdom of international trade and globalization, it was important that the WTO prove that it could arbitrate these disputes.

In 2001, it appeared that the banana dispute might be resolved. The EU agreed to increase market access for U.S. banana distributors, and the United States lifted its retaliatory duties on EU products. The agreement also provided that the United States could reimpose the duties if the EU did not complete its phased-in reductions in restrictions on banana imports.

But the banana story just kept "slipping along."

European Union anti-fraud officials say that illegal banana trafficking (2002) is proving more lucrative than that in cocaine. A recently exposed scheme saw Italian banana importers use false licenses to pay greatly reduced customs duties on non-quota fruit. The fraud netted smugglers hundreds of millions of euros over a two-year period. Italian public prosecutor Fabio Scavone says more is being made from simple customs fraud than from serious crimes such as narcotics trafficking.[1]

In 2004, Latin American growers again complained that the EU was discriminating against their bananas in favor of producers from African, Caribbean, and Pacific countries. Under the 2001 WTO ruling, the EU was compelled to replace its complex quota and tariff system on bananas with a tariff-only regime. So the EU placed a 176 euro tariff per ton on Latin American suppliers to get into the EU market, while bananas from African and Caribbean countries could export up to 775,000 tons duty-free. The banana war continued in 2008 when a WTO dispute panel ruled for the third time that the EU tariff/quota banana regime was unfair. Finally, the EU initiated a deal agreed to in 2009 that might end this longest trade battle in history. The EU will gradually cut the import tariff on bananas from Latin America in stages until 2017. Also, the banana-producing countries from African, Caribbean, and Pacific countries will receive financial aid to help them adjust to stiffer competition.

ANALYZE *the* ISSUE   Make an argument in favor of the European import restrictions. Make an argument against this plan.

[1] "Banana Scam Beats Cocaine," *Australian Business Intelligence*, July 24, 2002.

Birth of the Euro

In 1958, several European nations formed a Common Market to eliminate trade restrictions among member countries. The Common Market called for gradual removal of tariffs and import quotas on goods traded among member nations. Later, the name was changed to the *Euro Economic Community (EEC)*, and it is now called the *European Union*. This organization established a common system of tariffs for imports from nonmember nations and created common policies for economic matters of joint concern, such as agriculture and transportation. The EU now comprises the 28 nations listed in the following table.

In 1999, 11 European countries, joined later by Greece, followed the United States as an example and united in the *European Economic and Monetary Union (EMU)*. In the United States, 50 states are linked with a common currency, and the Federal Reserve serves as the central bank by conducting monetary policy for the nation. Among the states, trade, labor, and investment enjoy freedom of movement. In 2002, the EMU members replaced their national currencies with a single currency, the euro. The objective was to remove exchange rate fluctuations that impede crossborder transactions. This is why the U.S. Congress

A major flaw in this argument is that it neglects the reason for the difference in the wage rates between countries. A U.S. worker has more education, training, capital, and access to advanced technology. Therefore, if U.S. workers produce more output per hour than workers in another country, U.S. workers will earn higher wages without a competitive disadvantage. Suppose textile workers in the United States are paid $10 per hour. If a U.S. worker takes 1 hour to produce a rug, the labor cost per rug is $10. Now suppose a worker in India earns $1 per hour, but requires 20 hours to produce a rug on a handloom. In this case, the labor cost per rug is $20. Although the wage rate is 10 times higher in the United States, U.S. productivity is 20 times higher because a U.S. worker can produce 20 rugs in 20 hours, while the worker in India produces only 1 rug in the same amount of time.

Sometimes U.S. companies move their operations to foreign countries where labor is cheaper. Such moves are not always successful because the savings from paying foreign workers a lower wage rate are offset by lower productivity. Other disadvantages of foreign operations include greater transportation costs to U.S. markets and political instability.

21-5 FREE TRADE AGREEMENTS

The trend in recent years has been for nations to negotiate a reduction in trade barriers. In 1993, Congress approved the *North American Free Trade Agreement (NAFTA)*, which linked the United States to two of its largest trading partners, Canada and Mexico. Under NAFTA, which became effective January 1, 1994, tariffs were phased out, and other impediments to trade and investment were eliminated among the three nations. For example, elimination of trade restrictions allows the United States to supply Mexico with more U.S. goods and to boost created a national currency in 1863 to replace state and private bank currencies.

The EU faces many unanswered questions. Unlike the states of the United States, the EU's member nations do not share a common language or governments. This makes maintaining common macropolicies difficult. France, for example, might seek to control inflation, while Germany has reducing unemployment as its highest priority. Coordinating monetary policy among EU nations is also difficult and in recent years several members have experienced

financial crisis. Although the EU has established the *European Central Bank* headquartered in Frankfurt, Germany, with sole authority over the supply of euros, the central banks of member nations still function. But these national central banks operate similar to the district banks of the Federal Reserve System in the United States. Only time will tell whether EU nations will perform better with a single currency than with separate national currencies. Currently, the United Kingdom, Denmark, and Sweden still use their own currencies.

European Union (EU) Members			
Austria	Estonia	Italy	Portugal
Belgium	Finland	Latvia	Romania
Bulgaria	France	Lithuania	Slovakia
Croatia	Germany	Luxembourg	Slovenia
Cyprus	Greece	Malta	Spain
Czech Republic	Hungary	Netherlands	Sweden
Denmark	Ireland	Poland	United Kingdom

U.S. jobs. On the other hand, NAFTA was expected to raise Mexico's wages and standard of living by increasing Mexican exports to the United States. Note that NAFTA made no changes in restrictions on labor movements and workers must enter the United States under a limited immigration quota or illegally. The success of NAFTA remains controversial. At the conclusion of this chapter, we will use data to examine its impact.

The United States and other countries are considering other free trade agreements. In Europe, 28 nations have joined the *European Union (EU)*, which is dedicated to removing all trade barriers within Europe, thereby creating a single European economy almost as large as the U.S. economy. See the Birth of the Euro boxed feature in this chapter.

The *Asian-Pacific Economic Cooperation (APEC)* was formed in 1989 and today has 21 member nations, including China, Hong Kong, Russia, Japan, and Mexico. This organization is based on a nonbinding agreement to reduce trade barriers between member nations.

In 2003, trade ministers from 34 nations met in Miami to create a plan for the world's largest free trade area that would tear down trade barriers from Alaska to Argentina. The *Free Trade Area of the Americas (FTAA)* would span the Western Hemisphere except Cuba.

In 2005, the *Central American Free Trade Agreement (CAFTA)* extended the free trade zone to six Central American countries that signed, including Costa Rica, Guatemala, El Salvador, Honduras, Nicaragua, and Dominican Republic. The success or failure of CAFTA will have an impact on future negotiation for FTAA.

Critics are concerned that regional free trade accords will make global agreements increasingly difficult to achieve. Some fear that trading blocs may erect new barriers, creating "Fortress North America," "Fortress Europe," and similar impediments to the worldwide reduction of trade barriers.

21-6 THE BALANCE OF PAYMENTS

Balance of payments A bookkeeping record of all the international transactions between a country and other countries during a given period of time.

When trade occurs between the United States and other nations, many types of financial transactions are recorded in a summary called the balance of payments. The balance of payments is a bookkeeping record of all the international transactions between a country and other countries during a given period of time. This summary is the best way to understand interactions between economies because it records the value of a nation's spending inflows and outflows made by individuals, firms, and governments. Exhibit 21-5 presents a simplified U.S. balance of payments for 2013.

Note the pluses and minuses in the table. A transaction that is a payment to the United States is entered as a positive amount. A payment by the United States to another country is entered with a minus sign. As our discussion unfolds, you will learn that the balance of payments provides much useful information.

21-6a Current Account

Balance of trade The value of a nation's imports subtracted from its exports. Balance of trade can be expressed in terms of goods, services, or goods and services.

The first section of the balance of payments is the *current account*, which includes trade in goods and services and income receipts and payments. The most widely reported part of the current account is the balance of trade, also called the trade balance. The balance of trade is the value of a nation's imports subtracted from its exports, and it can be expressed in terms of goods, services, or goods and services. The balance of trade most often reported is in terms of goods and services. As shown in lines 1–4, the United States had a *balance of trade deficit* of −$416 billion in 2013. A trade deficit occurs when the value of a country's imports exceeds the value of its exports. When a nation has a trade deficit, it is called an *unfavorable balance of trade* because more is spent for imports than is earned from exports. Recall that net exports can have a positive (favorable) or negative (unfavorable) effect on GDP = C + I + G + (X − M).

EXHIBIT 21-5 U.S. Balance of Payments, 2013 (billions of dollars)

Type of Transaction	
Current account	
1. Goods exports	$+1,593
2. Goods imports	−2,294
3. Service exports	+687
4. Service imports	−462
Trade balance (lines 1–4)	−476
5. Income (net)	+76
Current account balance (lines 1–5)	−400
Capital account	
6. U.S. capital inflow	+1,018
7. U.S. capital outflow	−645
Capital account balance (lines 6–7)	+373
8. Statistical discrepancy	+27
Net balance (lines 1–8)	0

Source: Bureau of Economic Analysis, *U.S. International Transactions*, http://www.bea.gov /international/index.htm, Table 1.1.

Exhibit 21-6 charts the annual balance of trade for the United States from 1975 through 2013. Observe that the United States experienced a *balance of trade surplus* in 1975. A trade surplus arises when the value of a country's exports is greater than the value of its imports. This is called a *favorable balance of trade* because the United States earned more from exports than it spent for imports. Since 1975, however, growing sizable trade deficits have occurred. These trade deficits have attracted much attention because in part they reflect the popularity of foreign goods and the lack of competitiveness of goods "Made in U.S.A." Between 2005 and 2008, the U.S. trade deficits reached record breaking levels of about $700 billion due in part to the rising price of oil imports. During this period, the price per barrel grew steadily until reaching a peak in 2008, and the U.S. trade deficit with OPEC countries doubled while our trade deficit with China tripled. After 2008, oil import prices decreased from a high of $134 per barrel in 2008 to $92 per barrel in 2013, and U.S. trade deficits with OPEC countries fell while U.S. trade deficits with China increased slightly. These factors contributed to the fall in the U.S. balance of trade deficits after 2008.

Lines 3–5 of the current account in Exhibit 21-5 list ways other than trade of goods that move dollars back and forth between the United States and other

EXHIBIT 21-6 U.S. Balance of Trade, 1975–2013

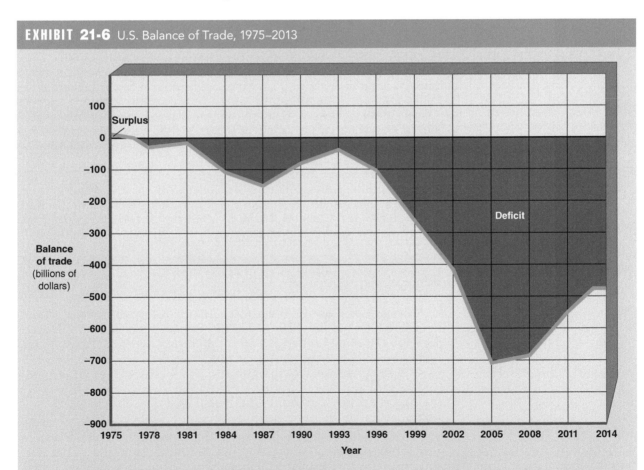

Since 1975, the United States has experienced trade deficits in which the value of goods and services imports has exceeded the value of exports and imports. These trade deficits attract much attention because in part they reflect the popularity of foreign goods in the United States. The deficit grew to an all-time high of about $700 billion between 2005 and 2008 before declining to $476 billion in 2013.

Source: Bureau of Economic Analysis, *U.S. International Transactions*, http://www.bea.gov/international/index.htm, Tables 1.1 and 12.

countries. Services include insurance, banking, transportation, and tourism. For example, a Japanese tourist who pays a hotel bill in Hawaii buys an export of services, which is a plus or credit to our current account (line 3). Similarly, an American visitor to foreign lands buys an import of services, which is a minus or debit to our services and therefore a minus to our current account (line 4). As shown on line 5, income flowing back from U.S. investments abroad, such as plants, real estate, and securities, is a payment for use of the services of U.S. capital. Foreign countries also receive income receipts flowing from the services of their capital owned in the United States. This category includes gifts made by our government, charitable organizations, or private individuals to other governments or private parties elsewhere in the world. For example, this item includes U.S. foreign aid to other nations. Similar unilateral transfers into the United States must be subtracted to determine net income transfers. In 2013, line 5 of the table reports a net income flow of $76 billion to the United States.

Adding lines 1–5 gives the current account balance deficit of −$400 billion in 2013. This deficit means that foreigners sent us more goods, services, and income than we sent them. Because the current account balance includes more than goods and services, it is a broader measure than the trade balance. Since 1982, the trend in the current account balance has followed the swing into the red shown by the trade balance in Exhibit 21-6.

21-6b Capital Account

The second section of the balance of payments is the *capital account*, which records payment flows for financial capital, such as real estate, corporate stocks, bonds, government securities, and other debt instruments. For example, when Chinese investors buy U.S. Treasury bills or Japanese investors purchase farmland in Hawaii, there is an inflow of dollars into the United States. As Exhibit 21-5 shows, foreigners made payments of $1,018 billion to our capital account (line 6). This exceeded the −645 billion (line 7) outflow from the United States to purchase foreign-owned financial capital.

An important feature of the capital account is that the United States finances any deficit in its current account through this account. The capital account balance in 2013 was $373 billion. This surplus indicates that there was more foreign investment in U.S. assets than U.S. investment in foreign assets during this year.

> **CONCLUSION** A current account deficit is financed by a capital account surplus.

The current account deficit should equal the capital account surplus, but line 8 in the exhibit reveals that the balance of payments is not perfect. The capital account balance does not exactly offset the current account balance. Hence, a credit amount is simply recorded as a statistical discrepancy; therefore, the balance of payments always balances, or equals zero.

21-6c The International Debt of the United States

If each nation's balance of payments is always zero, why is there so much talk about a U.S. balance of payments problem? The problem is with the *composition* of the balance of payments. Suppose the United States runs a $500 billion deficit in its current account. This means that the current account deficit must be financed by a net annual capital inflow in the capital account of $500 billion. That is, foreign lenders, such as banks and businesses, must purchase U.S. assets and grant loans to the United States that on balance equal $500 billion. For example, a Chinese bank could buy U.S. Treasury bonds. Recall from Exhibit 17-7 in Chapter 17 on federal deficits and the national debt that this portion of the national debt owed to lenders outside the United States is called *external debt*.

In 1984, the United States became a net debtor for the first time in about 70 years. This means that investments in the United States accumulated by foreigners—stocks, bonds, real estate, and so forth—exceeded the stock of foreign assets owned by the United States. In fact, during the decade of the 1980s, the United States moved from being the world's largest creditor nation in the world to being the largest debtor nation.

Exhibit 21-7 shows that the United States has its largest trade deficits with China, Germany, Japan, and Mexico respectively. The concern over continuing trade deficits and the rising international debt that accompanies them is that the United States is artificially enjoying a higher standard of living. When the United States continues to purchase more goods and services abroad than it exports, it could find itself "enjoying now and paying later." Suppose the Chinese and other foreigners decide not to make new U.S. investments and loans. In this case, the United States will be forced to eliminate its trade deficit by bringing exports and imports into balance. In fact, if other countries not only refuse to provide new capital inflows, but also decide to liquidate their investments, the United States

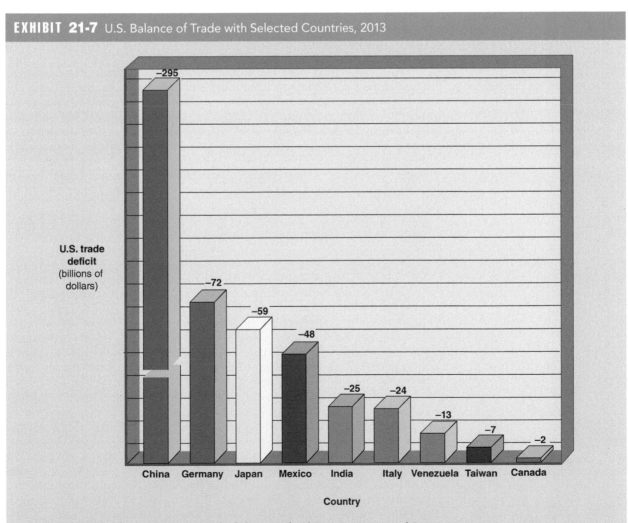

EXHIBIT 21-7 U.S. Balance of Trade with Selected Countries, 2013

The United States has its greatest trade deficits with China, Germany and Japan.

Source: Bureau of Economic Analysis, *U.S. International Transactions by Area*, http://www.bea.gov/international/index.htm, Table 12.

would be forced to run a trade surplus. Stated differently, we would be forced to tighten our belts and accept a lower standard of living. How a change in foreign willingness to purchase U.S. assets also affects the international value of the dollar is the topic to which we now turn.

CHECKPOINT

> **Should Everyone Keep a Balance of Payments?**
> Nations keep balances of payments and calculate accounts such as their trade deficit or surplus. If nations need these accounts, the 50 states should also maintain balances of payments to manage their economies. Or should they? What about cities?

21-7 EXCHANGE RATES

Each transaction recorded in the balance of payments requires an exchange of one country's currency for that of another. Suppose you buy a Japanese car made in Japan, say, a Mazda. Mazda wants to be paid in yen and not dollars, so dollars must be traded for yen. On the other hand, suppose Pink Panther Airline Company in France purchases an airplane from Boeing in the United States. Pink Panther has euros to pay the bill, but Boeing wants dollars. Consequently, euros must be exchanged for dollars.

Exchange rate The number of units of one nation's currency that equals one unit of another nation's currency.

The critical question for Mazda, Pink Panther, Boeing, and everyone involved in world trade is, "What is the exchange rate?" The exchange rate is the number of units of one nation's currency that equals one unit of another nation's currency. For example, assume 1.81 dollars can be exchanged for 1 British pound. This means the exchange rate is 1.81 dollars = 1 pound. Alternatively, the exchange rate can be expressed as a reciprocal. Dividing 1 British pound by 1.81 dollars gives 0.552 pounds per dollar. Now suppose you are visiting England and want to buy a T-shirt with a price tag of 10 pounds. Knowing the exchange rate tells you the T-shirt costs $18.10 (10 pounds × $1.81/pound).

> **CONCLUSION** An exchange rate can be expressed as a reciprocal.

21-7a Supply and Demand for Foreign Exchange

The exchange rate for dollars, or any nation's currency floats, which means it is determined by international forces of supply and demand. For example, consider the exchange rate of yen to dollars, shown in Exhibit 21-8. Like the price and the quantity of any good traded in markets, the quantity of dollars exchanged is measured on the horizontal axis, and the price per unit is measured on the vertical axis. In this case, the price per unit is the value of the U.S. dollar expressed as the number of yen per dollar.

The demand for dollars in the world currency market comes from Japanese individuals, corporations, and governments that want to buy U.S. exports. Because the Japanese buyers must pay for U.S. exports with dollars, they *demand* to exchange their yen for dollars. As expected, the demand curve for dollars or any foreign currency is downward sloping. A decline in the number of yen per dollar means that one yen buys a larger portion of a dollar. This means U.S. goods and investment opportunities are less expensive to Japanese buyers because they must pay fewer yen for each dollar. Thus, as the yen price of dollars decreases, the quantity of dollars demanded by the Japanese to purchase Fords, stocks, land, and other U.S. products and investments increases. For example, suppose a CD recording of the hottest rock group has a $20 price tag. If the exchange rate is 200 yen to the dollar, a Japanese importer would pay 4,000 yen. If the price

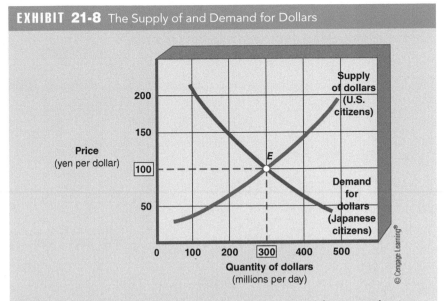

EXHIBIT 21-8 The Supply of and Demand for Dollars

The number of Japanese yen per dollar in the foreign exchange market is determined by the demand for dollars by Japanese citizens and the supply of dollars by U.S. citizens. The equilibrium exchange rate is 100 yen per dollar, and the equilibrium quantity is $300 million per day.

of dollars to Japanese buyers falls to 100 yen each, the same $20 CD will cost Japanese importers only 2,000 yen. This lower price causes Japanese buyers to increase their orders, which, in turn, increases the quantity of dollars demanded.

The supply curve of dollars is upward sloping. This curve shows the amount of dollars offered for exchange at various yen prices per dollar in the world currency exchange market. Similar to the demand for dollars, the supply of dollars in this market flows from individuals, corporations, and governments in the United States that want to buy Mazdas, stocks, land, and other products and investments from Japan. Because U.S. citizens must pay for the Japanese goods and services in yen, they must exchange dollars for yen. An example will illustrate why the supply curve of dollars slopes upward. Suppose a Nikon camera sells for 100,000 yen in Tokyo and the exchange rate is 100 yen per dollar or 0.01 dollar per yen ($1/100 yen). Therefore, the camera costs an American tourist $1,000. Now assume the exchange rate rises to 250 yen per dollar or 0.004 dollar per yen ($1/250 yen). The camera will now cost the American buyer only $400. Because the prices of the Nikon camera and other Japanese products fall when the number of yen per dollar rises, Americans respond by purchasing more Japanese imports, which, in turn, increases the quantity of dollars supplied.

The foreign exchange market in Exhibit 21-8 is in equilibrium at an exchange rate of 100 yen for $1. As you learned in Chapter 3, if the exchange rate is above equilibrium, there will be a surplus of dollars in the world currency market. Citizens of the United States are supplying more dollars than the Japanese demand, and the exchange rate falls. On the other hand, below equilibrium, there will be a shortage of dollars in the world currency market. In this case, the Japanese are demanding more dollars than Americans supply, and the exchange rate rises.

21-7b Shifts in Supply and Demand for Foreign Exchange

For most of the years between World War II and 1971, currency exchange rates were *fixed*. Exchange rates were based primarily on gold. For example, the German

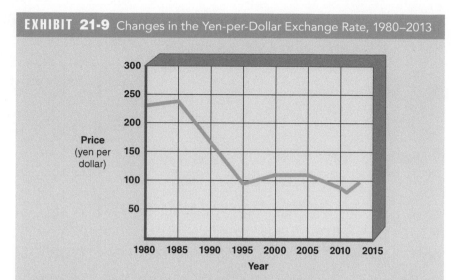

EXHIBIT 21-9 Changes in the Yen-per-Dollar Exchange Rate, 1980–2013

Today, most economies are on a system of flexible exchange rates. As the demand and supply curves for currencies change, exchange rates change. In 1980, 1 dollar was worth about 230 Japanese yen. By 2011, the exchange rate had dropped to a postwar low of 80 yen per dollar. In 2013, a dollar was worth 98 Japanese yen.

Source: Foreign Exchange Rates, http://www.federalreserve.gov/releases/G5A/current/.

mark was fixed at about 25 cents. The dollar was worth 1/35 of an ounce of gold, and 4 German marks were worth 1/35 of an ounce of gold. Therefore, 1 dollar equaled 4 marks, or 25 cents equaled 1 mark. In 1971, Western nations agreed to stop fixing their exchange rates and to allow their currencies to *float* according to the forces of supply and demand. Exhibit 21-9 illustrates that these rates can fluctuate widely. For example, in 1980, 1 dollar was worth about 230 Japanese yen. After gyrating up and down over the years, the exchange rate hit a postwar low of 80 yen per dollar in 2011. In 2013, the rate rose to 98 yen per dollar.

Recall from Chapter 3 that the equilibrium price for products changes in response to shifts in the supply and demand curves. The same supply and demand analysis applies to equilibrium exchange rates for foreign currency. There are four important sources of shifts in the supply and demand curves for foreign exchange. Let's consider each in turn.

21-7c Tastes and Preferences

Exhibit 21-10(a) illustrates one important factor that causes the demand for foreign currencies to shift. Suppose the Japanese lose their "taste" for tobacco, U.S. government bonds, and other U.S. products and investment opportunities. This decline in the popularity of U.S. products in Japan decreases the demand for dollars at each possible exchange rate, and the demand curve shifts leftward from D_1 to D_2. This change causes the equilibrium exchange rate to fall from 150 yen to the dollar at E_1 to 100 yen to the dollar at E_2. Because the number of yen to the dollar declines, the dollar is said to *depreciate* or become *weaker*. **Depreciation of currency** is a fall in the price of one currency relative to another.

Depreciation of currency A fall in the price of one currency relative to another.

What happens to the exchange rate if the "Buy American" idea changes our tastes and the demand for Japanese imports decreases? In this case, U.S. citizens supply fewer dollars at any possible exchange rate, and the supply curve in Exhibit 21-10(b) shifts leftward from S_1 to S_2. As a result, the equilibrium

EXHIBIT 21-10 Changes in the Supply and Demand Curves for Dollars

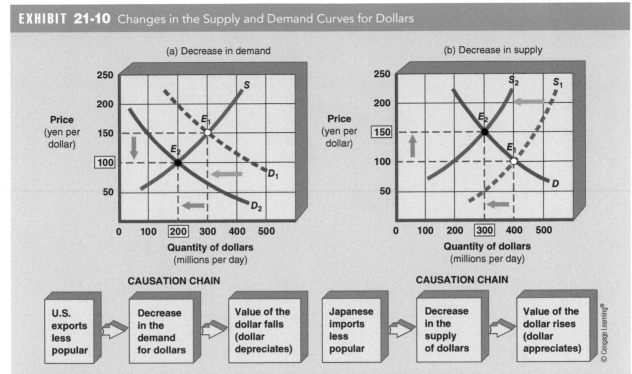

In part (a), U.S. exports become less popular in Japan. This change in tastes for U.S. products and investments decreases the demand for dollars, and the demand curve shifts leftward from D_1 to D_2. As a result, the equilibrium exchange rate falls from 150 yen to the dollar at E_1 to 100 yen to the dollar at E_2.

Part (b) assumes U.S. citizens are influenced by the "Buy American" idea. In this case, our demand for Japanese imports decreases, and U.S. citizens supply fewer dollars to the foreign currency market. The result is that the supply curve shifts leftward from S_1 to S_2, and the equilibrium exchange rate rises from 100 yen per dollar at E_1 to 150 yen per dollar at E_2.

Appreciation of currency A rise in the price of one currency relative to another.

exchange rate rises from 100 yen to the dollar at E_1 to 150 yen to the dollar at E_2. Because the number of yen per dollar rises, the dollar is said to *appreciate* or become *stronger*. **Appreciation of currency** is a rise in the price of one currency relative to another.

21-7d Relative Incomes

Assume income in the United States rises, while income in Japan remains unchanged. As a result, U.S. citizens buy more domestic products and more Japanese imports. The results are a rightward shift in the supply curve for dollars and a decrease in the equilibrium exchange rate. Paradoxically, growth of U.S. income leads to the dollar depreciating, or becoming weaker, against the Japanese yen.

CONCLUSION An expansion in relative U.S. income causes a depreciation of the dollar.

21-7e Relative Price Levels

Now we consider a more complex case in which a change in a factor causes a change in both the supply and demand curves for dollars. Assume the foreign exchange rate begins in equilibrium at 100 yen per dollar, as shown at point E_1 in

EXHIBIT 21-11 The Impact of Relative Price Level Changes on Exchange Rates

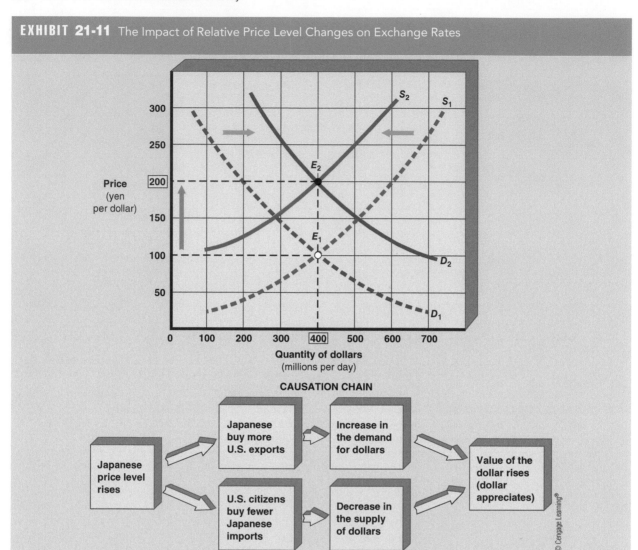

Begin at E_1, with the exchange rate equal to 100 yen per dollar. Assume prices in Japan rise relative to those in the United States. As a result, the demand for dollars increases, and the supply of dollars decreases. The new equilibrium is at E_2 when the dollar appreciates (rises in value) to 200 yen per dollar.

Exhibit 21-11. Now assume the price level increases in Japan, but remains constant in the United States. The Japanese therefore want to buy more U.S. exports because they have become cheaper relative to Japanese products. This willingness of the Japanese to buy U.S. goods and services shifts the demand curve for dollars rightward from D_1 to D_2. In addition, U.S. products are cheaper for U.S. citizens compared to Japanese imports. As a result, the willingness to import from Japan is reduced at each exchange rate, which means the supply curve of dollars decreases from S_1 to S_2. The result of the shifts in both the demand and supply curves for dollars is to establish a new equilibrium at point E_2, and the exchange rate reaches 200 yen per dollar.

CONCLUSION A rise in a trading partner's relative price level causes the dollar to appreciate.

21-7f Relative Real Interest Rates

Changes in relative real (inflation-adjusted) interest rates can have an important effect on the exchange rate. Suppose real interest rates in the United States rise, while those in Japan remain constant. To take advantage of more attractive yields, Japanese investors buy an increased amount of bonds and other interest-bearing securities issued by private and government borrowers in the United States. This change increases the demand for dollars, which increases the equilibrium exchange rate of yen to the dollar, causing the dollar to appreciate (or the yen to depreciate).

There can also be an effect on the supply of dollars. When real interest rates rise in the United States, our citizens purchase fewer Japanese securities. Hence, they offer fewer dollars at each possible exchange rate, and the supply curve for dollars shifts leftward. As a result, the equilibrium exchange rate increases, and the dollar appreciates from changes in both the demand for and supply of dollars.

21-7g The Impact of Exchange Rate Fluctuations

Now it is time to stop for a minute and draw some important conclusions. As you have just learned, exchange rates between most major currencies are flexible. Instead of being pegged to gold or another fixed standard, their value floats as determined by the laws of supply and demand. Consequently, shifts in supply and demand create a weaker or a stronger dollar. But it should be noted that exchange rates do not fluctuate with total freedom. Governments often buy and sell currencies to prevent wide swings in exchange rates. In summary, the strength or weakness of any nation's currency has a profound impact on its economy.

A weak dollar is a "mixed blessing." Ironically, a weak dollar makes U.S. producers happy. Because foreigners pay less of their currency for dollars, this means U.S. producers can sell their less expensive exports to foreign buyers. As export sales rise, jobs are created in the United States. On the other hand, a weak dollar makes foreign producers and domestic consumers unhappy because the prices of Japanese cars, French wine, and Italian shoes are higher. As U.S. imports fall, jobs in foreign countries are lost.

CONCLUSION When the dollar is weak or depreciates, U.S. goods and services cost foreign consumers less, so they buy more U.S. exports. At the same time, a weak dollar means foreign goods and services cost U.S. consumers more, so they buy fewer imports.

A strong dollar is also a "mixed blessing." A strong dollar therefore makes our major trading partners happy. U.S. buyers pay fewer dollars for foreign currency, which means the prices of Japanese cars, French wine, and Italian shoes are lower. A strong dollar, contrary to the implication of the term, makes U.S. producers unhappy because their exports are more expensive and related jobs decline. Conversely, a strong dollar makes foreign producers happy because the prices of their goods and services are lower, causing U.S. imports to rise. Exhibit 21-12 summarizes weak versus strong dollar effects.

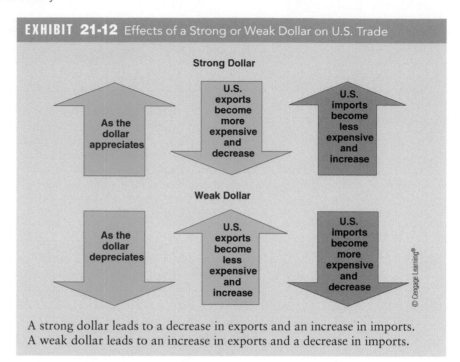

EXHIBIT 21-12 Effects of a Strong or Weak Dollar on U.S. Trade

A strong dollar leads to a decrease in exports and an increase in imports. A weak dollar leads to an increase in exports and a decrease in imports.

CONCLUSION When the dollar is strong or appreciates, U.S. goods and services cost foreign consumers more, so they buy fewer U.S. exports. At the same time, a strong dollar means foreign goods and services cost U.S. consumers less, so they buy more foreign imports.

Finally, as promised earlier in this chapter, we return to the discussion of NAFTA in order to illustrate the impact of this free trade agreement and the effect of a strong dollar. Recall that in January 1994, NAFTA began a gradual phaseout of tariffs and other trade barriers. Exhibit 21-13 provides trade data for the United States and Mexico for the years surrounding NAFTA. As the exhibit shows, both exports and imports of goods increased sharply after NAFTA.

EXHIBIT 21-13 U.S. Trade Balances with Mexico, 1993–2013

Year	U.S. Exports to Mexico (billions of dollars)	U.S. Imports from Mexico (billions of dollars)	Exchange Rate (pesos per dollar)	U.S. Trade Surplus (+) or Deficit (−) (billions of dollars)
1993	$52	$48	3.12	$ +4
1995	55	71	6.45	−16
1997	82	97	7.92	−15
1999	101	120	9.55	−19
2001	118	143	9.34	−25
2005	143	188	10.89	−45
2012	244	298	13.15	−54
2013	256	304	12.75	−48

Sources: Bureau of Economic Analysis, *U.S. International Transactions by Area*, http://www.bea.gov/international.index.htm, Table 12 and Foreign Exchange Rates, http://www.federalreserve.gov/releases/G5A/current/.

GLOBAL ECONOMICS

Return to the Yellow Brick Road?

Applicable concept: exchange rates

Gold is always a fascinating story: *The Wonderful Wizard of Oz* was first published in 1900, and this children's tale has been interpreted as an allegory for political and economic events of the 1890s. For example, the Yellow Brick Road represents the gold standard, Oz in the title is an abbreviation for ounce, Dorothy is the naive public, Emerald City symbolizes Washington, D.C., the Tin Woodman represents the industrial worker, the Scarecrow is the farmer, and the Cyclone is a metaphor for a political revolution. In the end, Dorothy discovers magical powers in her *silver* shoes (changed to ruby in the 1939 film) to find her way home and not the fallacy of the Yellow Brick Road. Although the author of the story, L. Frank Baum, never stated it was his intention, it can be argued that the issue of the story concerns the election of 1896. Democratic presidential nominee William Jennings Bryan (the Cowardly Lion) supported fixing the value of the dollar to both gold and silver (bimetallism), but Republican William McKinley (the Wicked Witch) advocated using only the gold standard. Since McKinley won, the United States remained on the Yellow Brick Road.[1]

The United States adopted the gold standard in 1873, and until the 1930s, most industrial countries were on the gold standard. The gold standard served as an international monetary system in which currencies were defined or pegged in terms of gold. Under the gold standard, a nation with a balance of payments deficit was required to ship gold to other nations to finance the deficit. Hence, a large excess of imports over exports meant a corresponding outflow of gold from a nation. As a result, that nation's money supply decreased, which, in turn, reduced the aggregate demand for goods and services. Lower domestic demand led to falling prices, lower production, and fewer jobs. In contrast, a nation with a balance of payments surplus would experience an inflow of gold and the opposite effects. In this case, the nation's money supply increased, and its aggregate demand for goods and services rose. Higher aggregate spending, in turn, boosted employment and the price level. In short, the gold standard meant that governments could not control their money supplies and thereby conduct monetary policy.

The gold standard worked fairly well as a fixed exchange rate system so long as nations did not face sudden or severe swings in flows from their stocks of gold. The Great Depression marked the beginning of the end of the gold standard. Nations faced with trade deficits and high unemployment began going off the gold standard, rather than contracting their money supplies by following the gold standard.

In 1933, President Franklin D. Roosevelt took the United States off the gold standard and ordered all 1933 gold double eagle coins already manufactured to be melted down and not circulated. Through a long twisted story worthy of a Sherlock Holmes mystery novel involving the Smithsonian Institution, the former king of Egypt, the Treasury Department, the Justice Department, the U.S. Mint, and a long list of intriguing supporting characters, one 1933 double eagle surfaced and was sold for $7.59 million in 2002. This was double the previous record for a coin.

Once the Allies felt certain they would win World War II, the finance ministers of Western nations met in 1944 at Bretton Woods, New Hampshire, to establish a new international monetary system. The new system was based on fixed exchange rates and an international central bank called the International Monetary Fund (IMF). The IMF makes loans to countries faced with short-term balance of payments problems. Under this system, nations were expected to maintain fixed exchange rates within a narrow range. In the 1960s and early 1970s, the Bretton Woods system became strained as conditions changed. In the 1960s, inflation rates in the United States rose relative to those in other countries, causing U.S. exports to become more expensive and U.S. imports to become less expensive. This situation increased the supply of dollars abroad and caused an increasing surplus of dollars, thus putting downward pressure on the exchange rate. Monetary authorities in the United States worried that central banks would demand gold for their dollars, the U.S. gold stock would diminish sharply, and the declining money supply would adversely affect the economy.

Something had to give, and it did. In August 1971, President Richard Nixon announced that the United States would no longer honor its obligation to sell gold at $35 an ounce. By 1973, the gold standard was dead, and most of our trading partners were letting the forces of supply and demand determine exchange rates.

Today, some people advocate returning to the gold standard. These gold buffs do not trust the government to control the money supply without the discipline of a gold standard. They argue that if governments have the freedom to print money, political pressures will sooner or later cause them to increase the money supply too much and let inflation rage.

One argument against the gold standard is that no one can control the supply of gold. Big gold discoveries can cause inflation and have done so in the past. On the other hand, slow growth in the stock of mined gold can lead to slow economic growth and a loss of jobs. Governments therefore are unlikely to return to the gold standard because it would mean turning monetary policy over to uncontrollable swings in the stock of gold.

 Return to Exhibit 21-8, and assume the equilibrium exchange rate is 150 yen per dollar and the equilibrium quantity is $300 million. Redraw this figure, and place a horizontal line through the equilibrium exchange rate to represent a fixed exchange rate. Now use this figure to explain why a country would abandon the gold standard.

[1] Bradley A. Hansen, "The Fable of the Allegory," *Journal of Economic Education*, Summer 2002, pp. 254–264.

On the other hand, a small U.S. trade surplus of $4 billion with Mexico in 1993 turned into a large trade deficit of −$48 billion in 2013.

Before blaming this trade deficit entirely on NAFTA, you must note that the exchange rate rose from 3.12 to 12.75 pesos per dollar in 2013. Since 1995, the peso was devalued and the stronger dollar has put the price of U.S. goods out of reach for many Mexican consumers. This is one reason U.S. exports to Mexico have been lower than they would have been otherwise. At the same time, Mexican goods became less expensive for U.S. consumers, so U.S. imports from Mexico have risen. Conversely, the exchange rate fell in 2013, and the deficit decreased.

Key Concepts

Absolute advantage	Tariff	Exchange rate
Comparative advantage	World Trade Organization (WTO)	Depreciation of currency
Free trade	Quota	Appreciation of currency
Protectionism	Balance of payments	
Embargo	Balance of trade	

Summary

- **Comparative advantage** is a principle that allows nations to gain from trade. Comparative advantage means that each nation *specializes* in a product for which its opportunity cost is lower in terms of the production of another product, and then nations trade. When nations follow this principle, they gain. The reason is that world output increases, and each nation ends up with a higher standard of living by consuming more goods and services than would be possible without specialization and trade.

Comparative Advantage

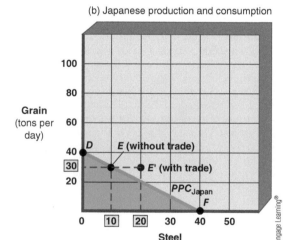

(b) Japanese production and consumption

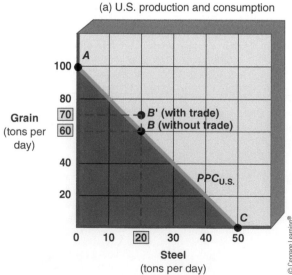

(a) U.S. production and consumption

- **Free trade** benefits a nation as a whole, but individuals may lose jobs and incomes because of the competition from foreign goods and services.

- **Protectionism** is a government's use of embargoes, tariffs, quotas, and other methods to impose barriers intended to both reduce imports and protect particular domestic industries.

- **Embargoes** prohibit the import or export of particular goods. **Tariffs** discourage imports by making them more expensive. **Quotas** limit the quantity of imports or exports of certain goods. These trade barriers often result primarily from domestic groups that exert political pressure on government in order to gain from these barriers.

- The **balance of payments** is a summary bookkeeping record of all the international transactions a country makes during a year. It is divided into different accounts, including the *current account*, the *capital account*, and the *statistical discrepancy*. The current account summarizes all transactions in currently produced goods and services. The overall balance of payments is always zero after an adjustment for the statistical discrepancy.

- The **balance of trade** measures only goods (not services) that a nation exports and imports. A balance of trade can be in deficit or in surplus. The balance of trade is the most widely reported and largest part of the current account. Since 1975, the United States has experienced balance of trade deficits.

Balance of Trade

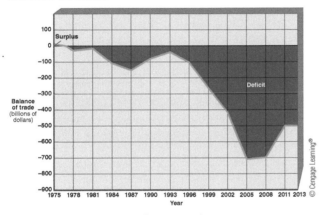

- An **exchange rate** is the price of one nation's currency in terms of another nation's currency. Foreigners who wish to purchase U.S. goods,

services, and financial assets demand dollars. The supply of dollars reflects the desire of U.S. citizens to purchase foreign goods, services, and financial assets. The intersection of the supply and demand curves for dollars determines the number of units of a foreign currency per dollar.

Exchange Rate

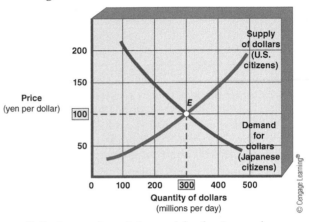

- **Shifts in supply and demand for foreign exchange** result from changes in such factors as tastes, relative price levels, relative real interest rates, and relative income levels.

- **Depreciation of currency** occurs when one currency becomes worth fewer units of another currency. If a currency depreciates, it becomes weaker. Depreciation of a nation's currency increases its exports and decreases its imports.

- **Appreciation of currency** occurs when one currency becomes worth more units of another currency. If a currency appreciates, it becomes stronger. Appreciation of a nation's currency decreases its exports and increases its imports.

Study Questions and Problems

1. The countries of Alpha and Beta produce diamonds and pearls. The production possibilities schedule below describes their potential output in tons per year.

Points on Production Possibilities Curve	Alpha		Beta	
	Diamonds	Pearls	Diamonds	Pearls
A	150	0	90	0
B	100	25	60	60
C	50	50	30	120
D	0	75	0	180

Using the data in the table, answer the following questions.

a. What is the opportunity cost of diamonds for each country?

b. What is the opportunity cost of pearls for each country?

c. In which good does Alpha have a comparative advantage?

d. In which good does Beta have a comparative advantage?

e. Suppose Alpha is producing and consuming at point *B* on its production possibilities curve and Beta is producing and consuming at point *C* on its production possibilities curve. Use a table such as Exhibit 21-3 to explain why both nations would benefit if they specialize.

f. Draw a graph, and use it to explain how Alpha and Beta benefit if they specialize and Alpha agrees to trade 50 tons of diamonds to Beta and Alpha receives 50 tons of pearls in exchange.

2. Bill can paint either two walls or one window frame in one hour. In the same time, Frank can paint either three walls or two window frames. To minimize the time spent painting, who should specialize in painting walls, and who should specialize in painting window frames?

3. Consider this statement: "The principles of specialization and trade according to comparative advantage among nations also apply to states in the United States." Do you agree or disagree? Explain.

4. Would the U.S. government gain any advantage from using tariffs or quotas to restrict imports?

5. Suppose the United States passed a law stating that we would not purchase imports from any country that imposed any trade restrictions on our exports. Who would benefit and who would lose from such retaliation?

6. Now consider Question 5 in terms of the law's impact on domestic producers that export goods. Does this policy adversely affect domestic producers that export goods?

7. Consider this statement: "Unrestricted foreign trade costs domestic jobs." Do you agree or disagree? Explain.

8. Do you support a constitutional amendment to prohibit the federal government from imposing any trade barriers, such as tariffs and quotas, except in case of war or national emergency? Why or why not?

9. Discuss this statement: "Because each nation's balance of payments equals zero, it follows that there is actually no significance to a balance of payments deficit or surplus."

10. For each of the following situations, indicate the direction of the shift in the supply curve or the demand curve for dollars, the factor causing the change, and the resulting movement of the equilibrium exchange rate for the dollar in terms of foreign currency:

a. American-made cars become more popular overseas.

b. The United States experiences a recession, while other nations enjoy economic growth.

c. Inflation rates accelerate in the United States, while inflation rates remain constant in other nations.

d. Real interest rates in the United States rise, while real interest rates abroad remain constant.

e. The Japanese put quotas and high tariffs on all imports from the United States.

f. Tourism from the United States increases sharply because of a fare war among airlines.

11. The following table summarizes the supply and the demand for euros.

	U.S. Dollars per Euro				
	$0.05	$0.10	$0.15	$0.20	$0.25
Quantity demanded (per day)	500	400	300	200	100
Quantity supplied (per day)	100	200	300	400	500

Using the above table,
a. graph the supply and demand curves for euros.
b. determine the equilibrium exchange rate.
c. determine what the effect of a fixed exchange rate at $0.10 per euros would be.

Sample Quiz

1. The theory of comparative advantage suggests that a(an)
   a. industrialized country should not import.
   b. country that is not competitive should import everything.
   c. country that specializes in producing goods or services for which it has a lower opportunity cost.
   d. None of the answers above are correct.

2. Assume the United States can use a given amount of its resources to produce either 20 airplanes or 8 automobiles and Japan can employ the same amount of its resources to produce either 20 airplanes or 10 automobiles. The U.S. should specialize in
   a. airplanes.
   b. automobiles.
   c. both goods a. and b.
   d. neither good a. nor b.

EXHIBIT 21-14 Potatoes and Wheat Output (tons per day)

Country	Potatoes	Wheat
United States	4	2
Ireland	3	1

© Cengage Learning®

3. In Exhibit 21-14, the United States has an absolute advantage in producing
   a. potatoes.
   b. wheat.
   c. Both answers a. and b. are correct.
   d. Neither answer a. nor b. is correct.

4. In Exhibit 21-14, Ireland's opportunity cost of producing one unit of wheat is
   a. 1/3 ton of potatoes.
   b. 3 tons of potatoes.
   c. Either answer a. or b. is correct.
   d. Neither answer a. nor b. is correct.

5. In Exhibit 21-14, the United States has a comparative advantage in producing
   a. potatoes.
   b. wheat.
   c. Both answers a. and b. are correct.
   d. Neither answer a. nor b. is correct.

6. If each nation in Exhibit 21-14 specializes in producing the good for which it has a comparative advantage, then
   a. Ireland would produce neither potatoes nor wheat.
   b. the United States would produce both potatoes and wheat.
   c. the United States would produce potatoes.
   d. Ireland would produce potatoes.

7. A tariff is a
   a. tax on an exported product.
   b. limit on the number of goods that can be exported.
   c. limit on the number of goods that can be imported.
   d. tax on an imported product.

8. The principal objective of WTO is to
   a. reduce the level of all tariffs.
   b. establish fair prices for all goods traded internationally.
   c. prevent the trading of services across nations' borders.
   d. encourage countries to establish quotas.

9. Which of the following is *not* an argument used in favor of protectionism?
   a. To protect an "infant" industry.
   b. To protect domestic jobs.
   c. To preserve national security.
   d. To protect against "unfair" competition because of cheap foreign labor.
   e. To reduce prices paid by domestic consumers.

10. The main explanation for why the cheap foreign labor argument is a poor reason for restricting international trade is that
    a. workers who get paid less tend to have lower productivity than those who get paid more.
    b. all firms and workers gain when there are no restrictions on international trade.
    c. infant industries such as steel and automobiles need to be protected.
    d. specialization and free trade usually raise the prices of all the traded goods, so that the workers can get paid more.

11. The account that records a nation's foreign economic transactions is called the
    a. trade account.
    b. T account.
    c. exchange market.
    d. balance of payments.

12. Expenditures for services such as tourism, income for foreign investment, and foreign gifts are tabulated in the
    a. current account.
    b. capital account.
    c. official reserve account.
    d. goods account.
13. Suppose a German bank purchases a U.S. Treasury bond. This transaction would be recorded in the
    a. capital account.
    b. current account.
    c. goods trade balance.
    d. unilateral transfers.

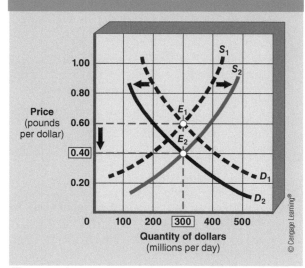

EXHIBIT 21-15 Foreign Exchange Market for U.S. Dollars and British Pounds

14. Exhibit 21-15 shows a situation in which
    a. both the dollar and the pound have depreciated.
    b. both the dollar and the pound have appreciated.
    c. the dollar has depreciated and the pound has appreciated.
    d. the dollar has appreciated and the pound has depreciated.
15. Which of the following could cause the dollar–pound exchange rate to change as shown in Exhibit 21-15?
    a. American goods become more popular in Great Britain.

b. British incomes rise, while U.S. incomes remain unchanged.
    c. The U.S. price level rises, while the British price level remains unchanged.
    d. The U.S. real interest rate rises, while the British real interest rate remains unchanged.
16. A country that has a lower opportunity cost of producing a good
    a. has a comparative advantage.
    b. can produce the good using fewer resources than another country.
    c. requires fewer labor hours to produce the good.
    d. All of the answers above are correct.
17. If one country can produce a good with fewer resources than another country, this is called
    a. specialization.
    b. geographic advantage.
    c. comparative advantage.
    d. absolute advantage.
18. One big difference between tariffs and quotas is that tariffs
    a. raise the price of a good while quotas lower it.
    b. generate tax revenues while quotas do not.
    c. stimulate international trade while quotas inhibit it.
    d. hurt domestic producers while quotas help them.
19. Which of the following is *not* included in the current account?
    a. Exports of goods.
    b. Imports of goods.
    c. U.S. capital inflow and outflow.
    d. Unilateral transfers.
20. A shift of the U.S. demand curve for Mexican pesos to the left and a decrease in the pesos price per dollar would likely result from
    a. an increase in the U.S. inflation rate relative to the rate in Mexico.
    b. a change in U.S. consumers' tastes away from Mexican products and toward products made in South Korea, India, and Taiwan.
    c. U.S. buyers perceiving that domestically produced products are of a lower quality than products made in Mexico.
    d. All of the answers above are correct.

APPENDIX A

Answers to Odd-Numbered Study Questions and Problems

CHAPTER 1
INTRODUCING THE ECONOMIC WAY OF THINKING

1. A poor nation with people who lack food, clothing, and shelter, certainly experiences wants beyond the availability of goods and services to satisfy these unfulfilled wants. On the other hand, no wealthy nation has all the resources necessary to produce everything everyone in the nation wishes to have. Even if you had $1 million and were completely satisfied with your share of goods and services, other desires would be unfulfilled. There is never enough time to accomplish all the things that you can imagine would be worthwhile.

3. Macroeconomics applies an overview perspective to an economy by examining economy-wide variables, such as inflation, unemployment, and growth of the economy. Microeconomics examines individual economic units, such as the market for corn, gasoline, or ostrich eggs.

5. The real world is full of complexities that make it difficult to understand and predict the relationships between variables. For example, the relationship between changes in the price of gasoline and changes in consumption of gasoline requires abstraction from the reality that such variables as the fuel economy of cars and weather conditions often change at the same time as the price of gasoline.

7. The two events are associated because the first event (cut in military spending) is followed by the second event (higher unemployment in the defense industry). The point is that association does not necessarily mean causation, but it might. For example, the economy could be in recession.

APPENDIX 1
APPLYING GRAPHS TO ECONOMICS

1. a. The probability of living is *inversely* related to age. This model could be affected by improvements in diet, better health care, reductions in hazards to health in the workplace, or changes in the speed limit.

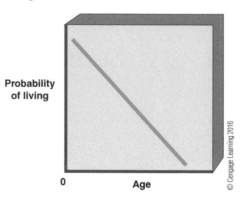

b. Annual income and years of formal education are *directly* related. This relationship might be influenced by changes in such human characteristics as intelligence, motivation, ability, and family background. An example of an institutional change that could affect this relationship over a number of years is the draft.

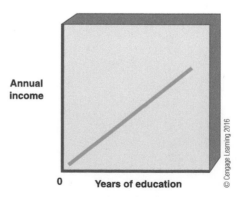

c. Inches of snow and sales of bathing suits are *inversely* related. The weather forecast and the price of travel to sunny vacation spots can affect this relationship.

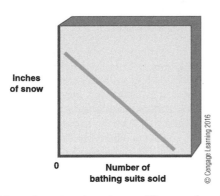

d. Most alumni and students will argue that the number of football games won is *directly* related to the athletic budget. They reason that winning football games is great advertising and results in increased attendance, contributions, and enrollment that, in turn, increase the athletic budget. Success in football can also be related to other factors, such as school size, age and type of institution, number and income of alumni, and quality of the faculty and administrators.

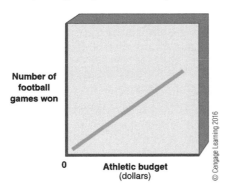

CHAPTER 2
PRODUCTION POSSIBILITIES, OPPORTUNITY COST, AND ECONOMIC GROWTH

1. Because the wants of individuals and society exceed the goods and services available to satisfy these desires, choices must be made. The consumption possibilities of an individual with a fixed income are limited, and as a result, additional consumption of one item necessarily precludes an expenditure on another next-best choice. The forgone alternative is called the opportunity cost, and this concept also applies to societal decisions. If society allocates resources to the production of guns, then those same resources cannot be used at the same time to make butter.

3. Regardless of the price of a lunch, economic resources—land, labor, and capital—are used to produce the lunch. These scarce resources are no longer available to produce other goods and services.

5. Using marginal analysis, students weigh the benefits of attending college against the costs. There is an incentive to attend college when the benefits (improved

job opportunities, income, intellectual improvement, social life, and so on) outweigh the opportunity costs.

7.

Flower Boxes	Opportunity Cost (pies foregone)
0	–
1	4 (30–26)
2	5 (26–21)
3	6 (21–15)
4	7 (15–8)
5	8 (8–0)

9. Movements along the curve are efficient points and conform to the well-known "free lunch" statement. However, inefficient points are exceptions because it is possible to produce more of one output without producing less of another output.

11. c. The curve is not bowed outward and instead is a downward-sloping straight line reflecting constant opportunity costs. Selecting any of the output combinations requires shifting 3 hours of study time from one subject to another. Each 3-hour change in study time reflects a constant slope of one letter grade gain for one letter grade loss.

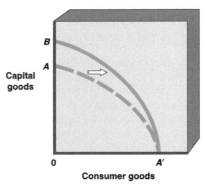

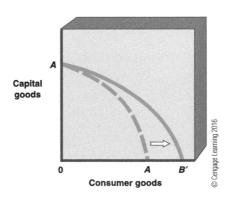

CHAPTER 3
MARKET DEMAND AND SUPPLY

1. If people buy a good or service because they associate higher quality with higher price, this is a violation

of the ceteris paribus assumption. An increase in the quantity demanded results only from a decrease in price. Quality and other nonprice determinants of demand, such as tastes and preferences and the price of related goods, are held constant in the model.

3. a. Demand for cars decreases; oil and cars are *complements*.
   b. Demand for insulation increases; oil and home insulation are *substitutes*.
   c. Demand for coal increases; oil and coal are *substitutes*.
   d. Demand for tires decreases; oil and tires are *complements*.

5. One reason that the demand curve for word processing software shifted to the right might be that people desire new, higher quality output features. The supply curve can shift to the right when new technology makes it possible to offer more software for sale at different prices.

7. a. Demand shifts to the right.
   b. Supply shifts to the left.
   c. Supply shifts to the right.
   d. Supply shifts to the right.
   e. Demand shifts to the right.
   f. Supply of corn shifts to the left.

9. a. The supply of CD players shifts rightward.
   b. The demand for CD players is unaffected.
   c. The equilibrium price falls and the equilibrium quantity increases.
   d. The demand for CDs increases because of the fall in the price of CD players (a complementary good).

11. The number of seats (quantity supplied) remains constant, but the demand curve shifts because tastes and preferences change according to the importance of each game. Although demand changes, the price is a fixed amount, and to manage a shortage, colleges and universities use amount of contributions, number of years as a contributor, or some other rationing device.

CHAPTER 4
MARKETS IN ACTION

1.

a. The equilibrium price is $6.00 per gallon, and the equilibrium quantity is 300 million gallons per month. The price system will restore the market's $6.00 per gallon price because either a surplus will drive prices down or a shortage will drive prices up.

b. The support price results in a persistent surplus of 200 million gallons of milk per month, which the government purchases with taxpayers' money. Consequently, taxpayers who do not drink milk are still paying for milk. The purpose of the support price is to bolster the incomes of dairy farmers.

c. The ceiling price will result in a persistent shortage of 200 million gallons of milk per month, but 200 million gallons are purchased by consumers at the low price of $4.00 per gallon. The shortage places a burden on the government to ration milk in order to be fair and to prevent black markets. The government's goal is to keep the price of milk below the equilibrium price of $6.00 per gallon, which would be set by a free market.

3. Labor markets can be divided into two separate markets, one for skilled union workers and one for unskilled workers. If the minimum wage is above the equilibrium wage rate and is raised, the effect will be to increase the demand for, and the wage of, skilled union workers because the two groups are substitutes.

5. The equilibrium price rises.

7. The government can reduce emissions by (a) regulations that require smoke-abatement equipment or (b) pollution taxes that shift supply leftward.

9. Pure public goods are not produced in sufficient quantities by private markets because there is no feasible method to exclude free riders.

CHAPTER 5
PRICE ELASTICITY OF DEMAND

1. Demand is elastic because the percentage change in quantity is greater than the percentage change in price.

3. If the price of used cars is raised 1 percent, the quantity demanded will fall 3 percent. If the price is raised 10 percent, the quantity demanded will fall 30 percent.

5.
$$E_d = \frac{\%\Delta Q}{\%\Delta P} = \frac{\dfrac{4{,}500 - 5{,}000}{5{,}000 + 4{,}500}}{\dfrac{3{,}500 - 3{,}000}{3{,}000 + 3{,}000}} = \frac{\dfrac{1}{19}}{\dfrac{1}{13}} = 0.68$$

The price elasticity of demand for the university is inelastic.

7. Demand for popcorn is perfectly inelastic, and total revenue will increase.

9. a. Sunkist oranges
   b. Cars
   c. Foreign travel in the long run

CHAPTER 6
PRODUCTION COSTS

1. a. explicit cost
   b. explicit cost
   c. implicit cost
   d. implicit cost
   e. explicit cost
   f. implicit cost

3. a.

Labor	Marginal Product
1	8
2	10
3	12
4	13
5	12
6	10
7	8
8	6
9	3
10	−2

b.

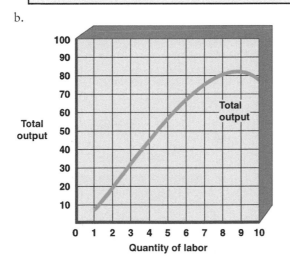

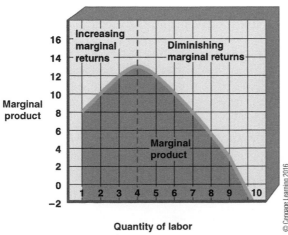

5. None. The position of a firm's short-run average total cost curve is not related to the demand curve.

7. The *ATC* and *AVC* curves converge as output expands because *ATC* = *AVC* + *AFC*. As output increases, *AFC* declines, so most of *ATC* is therefore *AVC*.

9. The average total cost–marginal cost rule states that when the marginal cost is below the average total cost, the addition to total cost is below the average total cost, and the average total cost falls. When the marginal cost is greater than the average total cost, the average total cost rises. In this case, the average total cost is at a minimum because it is equal to the marginal cost.

11. The marginal product for any number of workers is the slope of the total output curve. The marginal product is the derivative of the total output curve dTO/dQ, where *TO* is the total output and *Q* is the number of workers.

CHAPTER 7
PERFECT COMPETITION

1. A perfectly competitive firm will not advertise. Because all firms in the industry sell the same product, there is no reason for customers to be influenced by ads into buying one firm's product rather than another firm's product.

3.

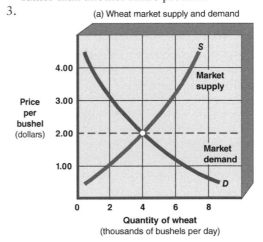

(a) Wheat market supply and demand

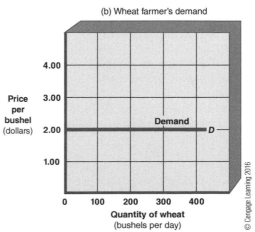

(b) Wheat farmer's demand

A single wheat farmer is a price taker facing a perfectly elastic demand curve because in perfect competition, one seller has no control over its price. The reason is that each wheat farmer is one among many, sells a homogeneous product, and must compete with any new farmer entering the wheat market.

5. At a price of $150, the firm produces 4 units and earns an economic profit of $70 ($TR - TC = \$600 - \$530$). The firm breaks even at an output of 2 units.

7. This statement is incorrect. A firm can earn maximum profit (or minimum loss) when marginal revenue equals marginal cost. The confusion is between the "marginal" and the "total" concepts. Marginal cost is the change in total cost from one additional unit of output, and marginal revenue is the change in total revenue from one additional unit of output.

9. The statement is incorrect. The perfectly competitive firm must consider both its marginal revenue and its marginal cost. Instead of trying to sell all the quantity of output possible, the firm will sell the quantity where $MR = MC$ because beyond this level of output the firm earns less profit.

11. Advise the residential contractor to shut down because the market price exceeds the average variable cost and the firm cannot cover its operating costs.

CHAPTER 8
MONOPOLY

1. Each market is served by a single firm providing a unique product. There are no close substitutes for local water service, professional football in San Francisco, and first-class mail service. A government franchise imposes a legal barrier to potential competitors in the water and first-class mail services. An NFL franchise grants monopoly power to its members in most geographic areas.

3. The reason may be that the hospital has monopoly power because it is the only hospital in the area and patients have no choice. On the other hand, there may be many drugstores competing to sell drugs and this keeps prices lower than those charged by the hospital.

5. In a natural monopoly, a single seller can produce electricity at a lower cost because the $LRAC$ curve declines. One firm can therefore sell electricity at a cheaper price and drive its competitor out of business over time. Another possibility would be for two competing firms to merge and earn greater profit by lowering cost further.

7. In this special case, sales maximization and profit maximization are the same. The monopolist should charge $2.50 per unit, produce 5 units of output, and earn $12.50 in profit. When the marginal cost curve is not equal to zero, the monopolist's $MR = MC$ output is less than 5 units, the price is higher than $2.50 per unit, and profit is below $12.50.

9. a. increase output
   b. decrease output
11. a. not price discrimination
    b. price discrimination
    c. not price discrimination if justified by a transportation cost difference
13. Answer will vary with students.

CHAPTER 9
MONOPOLISTIC COMPETITION AND OLIGOPOLY

1. The monopolistically competitive firm's demand curve is less elastic (steeper) than a perfectly competitive firm's demand curve, but more elastic (flatter) than a monopolist's demand curve.

3. a. P_1
   b. Q_1
   c. Q_3
   d. greater than the marginal cost ($B > A$)

5.

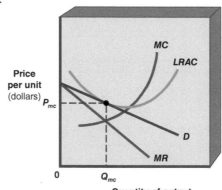

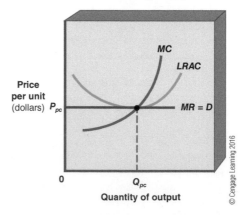

Because $P_{mc} > MC$, the monopolistically competitive firm fails to achieve allocative efficiency. The monopolistically competitive firm is also inefficient because it charges a higher price and produces less output than under perfect competition. The perfectly competitive firm sets P_{pc} equal to MC and produces a level of output corresponding to the minimum point on the *LRAC* curve.

7. Answers might include automobiles, airline travel, personal computers, and cigarettes. An oligopoly differs from monopolistic competition by having few sellers, rather than many sellers; either a homogeneous or a differentiated product; rather than all differentiated products, and difficult entry, rather than easy entry.

9. In general, the nonadvertising oligopolist produces intermediate goods, such as steel, rather than final consumer goods, such as beer and automobiles.

11. The cartel model is highly desirable from the oligopolist's viewpoint. If successful, the cartel allows each firm to maximize profits as a monopolist by setting the price and using quotas to restrict output. From the viewpoint of the consumer, a cartel has no economic desirability because its purpose is to raise prices.

CHAPTER 10
LABOR MARKETS AND INCOME DISTRIBUTION

1. This statement is incorrect. Workers supply their labor to employers. Demand refers to the quantity of labor employers hire at various wage rates based on the marginal revenue product of labor.

3. The *MRP* of the second worker is this person's contribution to total revenue, which is $50 ($150 − $100). Because *MRP* = *P* × *MP* and *MP* = *MRP/P*, the second worker's marginal product (*MP*) is 10 ($50/$5).

5. The firm in a perfectly competitive labor market is a price taker. Because a single firm buys the labor of a relatively small portion of workers in an industry, it can hire additional workers and not drive up the wage rate. For the industry, however, all firms must offer higher wages to attract workers from other industries.

7. Students investing in education are increasing their human capital. A student with greater human capital increases his or her marginal product. At a given product price, the *MRP* is higher, and firms find it profitable to hire the better educated worker and pay higher wages.

9. At a wage rate of $90 per day, Zippy Paper Company hires 3 workers because each worker's *MRP* exceeds or equals the wage rate. Setting the wage rate at $100 per day causes Zippy Paper Company to cut employment from 3 to 2 workers because the third worker's *MRP* is $10 below the union-caused wage rate of $100 per day.

11. This is an opinion question. To agree, you assume markets are perfectly competitive and discrimination is therefore unprofitable. To disagree, you can argue that in reality labor markets will never be perfectly competitive and the government must therefore address the institutional causes of poverty.

CHAPTER 11
GROSS DOMESTIC PRODUCT

1. a. final service
   b. final good
   c. intermediate good
   d. intermediate good

3.

3 million pounds of food × $1 per pound	= $3 million
50,000 shirts × $20 per shirt	= 1 million
20 houses × $50,000 per house	= 1 million
50,000 hours of medical services × $20 per hour	= 1 million
1 automobile plant × $1 million per plant	= 1 million
2 tanks × $500,000 per tank	= 1 million
Total value of output	= $8 million

5. Capital is not excluded from being a final good. A final good is a finished good purchased by an ultimate user and not for resale. The ultimate user is the warehouse, so the sale would be included in GDP and there would be no double-counting problem.

7. Using the expenditure approach, net exports are exports minus imports. If the expenditures by foreigners for U.S. products exceed the expenditures by U.S. citizens for foreign products, net exports will be a positive contribution to GDP. If foreigners spend less for U.S. products than U.S. citizens spend for foreign products, GDP is reduced. Net exports are used by national income accountants because actual consumption, investment, and government figures reported to the U.S. Department of Commerce do not exclude the amount of expenditures for imports.

9. *NI* = *GDP* − Depreciation
   $4,007 = $4,486 − $479
   The depreciation charge is not a measure of newly produced output. It is an estimate, subject to error, of the value of capital worn out in the production of final goods and services. Errors in the capital consumption allowance overstate or understate GDP.

11. When the price level is rising, nominal GDP overstates the rate of change between years. Dividing nominal GDP by the GDP chain price index results in real GDP by removing the distortion from inflation. Comparison of the changes in real GDP between years reflects only changes in the market value of all final products and not changes in the price level.

13. GDP does not tell the mix of output in two nations, say, between military and consumer goods. GDP also does not reveal whether GDP is more equally distributed in one nation compared to another.

CHAPTER 12
BUSINESS CYCLES AND UNEMPLOYMENT

1. The generally accepted theory of business cycles is that they are the result of changes in the level of total spending, or aggregate demand. Total spending includes spending for final goods by households, businesses, government, and foreign buyers. Expressed as a formula, $GDP = C + I + G + (X - M)$.

3. Civilian unemployment rate

$$\frac{unemployed}{civilian\ labor\ force} \times 100$$

where the civilian labor force = unemployed + employed. Therefore,

$$8.3\% = \frac{10\ million\ persons}{120\ million\ persons} \times 100$$

5. The official unemployment rate is overstated when respondents to the BLS falsely report that they are seeking employment. The unemployment rate is understated when *discouraged workers* who want to work have given up searching for a job.

7. Structural unemployment occurs when those seeking jobs do not possess the skills necessary to fill the available jobs. Cyclical unemployment is caused by a recession (deficient total spending). In this case, there are not enough available jobs.

9. The increasing participation of women and teenagers in the labor force has increased the rate of unemployment. Women take more time out of the labor force than do men for childbearing and child rearing.

11. The GDP gap is the difference between potential real GDP and actual real GDP. Because potential real GDP is estimated on the basis of the full-employment rate of unemployment, the GDP gap measures the cost of *cyclical* unemployment in terms of real GDP.

CHAPTER 13
INFLATION

1. This statement is incorrect. The price of a single good or service can rise while the average price of all goods and services falls. In short, the inflation rate rises when the average price of consumer goods and services rises.

3. First, the CPI is based on a typical market basket purchased by the urban family. Any group not buying the same market basket, such as retired persons, is not experiencing the price changes measured by

changes in the CPI. Second, the CPI fails to adjust for quality changes. Third, the CPI ignores the law of demand and the substitution effect as prices of products change.

5. If the percentage increase in the CPI exceeds the salary increase, a person's purchasing power declines in a given year.

7. The loan is advantageous to you because the real interest rate is −5 percent (5 percent nominal interest rate minus 10 percent inflation). In one year, you must repay $105. If prices rise by 10 percent during the year, the real value of the $105 will be only $95. Therefore, you have borrowed $100 worth of purchasing power and are repaying $95 worth of purchasing power.

9. At full employment, the economy operates at full capacity and produces the maximum output of goods and services. As buyers try to outbid one another for the fixed supply of goods and services, prices rise rapidly.

11. If buyers think prices will be higher tomorrow, they may buy products today and cause demand-pull inflation. If businesses believe prices for inputs will be higher in the future, many will raise prices today and cause cost-push inflation.

CHAPTER 14
AGGREGATE DEMAND AND SUPPLY

1. There are three reasons why the aggregate demand curve is downward sloping.
   a. The *real balances* means that a lower price level increases the purchasing power of money and other financial assets. The result is an increase in consumption, which increases the quantity of real GDP demanded.
   b. The *interest-rate effect* assumes a fixed money supply, and, therefore, a lower price level reduces the demand for borrowing and the interest rate. The lower rate of interest increases spending for consumption and investment.
   c. The *net exports effect* encourages foreign customers to buy more of an economy's domestic exports relative to its domestic purchases of imports when the price level falls. An increase in net exports increases aggregate expenditures. Rationales for the downward-sloping demand curve for an individual market are the income effect, the substitution effect, and the law of diminishing marginal utility, which are quite different from the three effects that determine the aggregate demand curve.

3. a. A leftward shift occurs because of a decrease in the consumption schedule.
   b. A rightward shift occurs because of an increase in autonomous investment spending.

c. A rightward shift occurs because of an increase in government spending.

d. A rightward shift occurs because of an increase in net exports.

5. This statement may not be correct. The equilibrium GDP is not necessarily the same as the full-employment GDP. Equilibrium GDP refers to the equality between the aggregate demand and the aggregate supply curves, which does not necessarily equal the full capacity of the economy to produce goods and services.

7. a. leftward because of an increase in response
   b. rightward because of a decrease in resource prices
   c. rightward because technological change reduces the cost of production
   d. leftward because of an increase in taxes means the price must cover the tax at each possible quantity supplied

9. a. Aggregate demand increases.
   b. Aggregate supply increases.
   c. Aggregate demand decreases.
   d. Aggregate supply decreases.
   e. Aggregate demand decreases along the classical range.
   f. Aggregate demand increases along the Keynesian range.

11. Assuming the aggregate supply curve remains constant, a rightward shift of the aggregate demand curve from AD_1 to AD_2 in the upward-sloping or the vertical range of the aggregate supply curve causes the price level to rise from P_1 to P_2. In addition to demand-pull inflation, the level of real GDP increases from Q_1 to Q_2 and provides the economy with new jobs. In the classical range, inflation is the only undesirable result, and real GDP remains unaffected at Q_2.

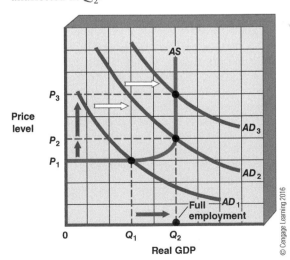

CHAPTER 14

APPENDIX: THE SELF-CORRECTING AGGREGATE DEMAND AND SUPPLY MODEL

1. There are three reasons why the aggregate demand curve is downward sloping.
   a. The *real balances* means that a lower price level increases the purchasing power of money and other financial assets. The result is an increase in consumption, which increases the quantity of real GDP demanded.
   b. The *interest-rate effect* assumes a fixed money supply, and, therefore, a lower price level reduces the demand for borrowing and the interest rate. The lower rate of interest increases spending for consumption and investment.
   c. The *net exports effect* encourages foreign customers to buy more of an economy's domestic exports relative to its domestic purchases of imports when the price level falls. An increase in net exports increases aggregate expenditures.

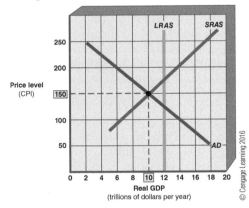

3. Beginning at long-run equilibrium E_1, the aggregate demand curve increases from AD_1 to AD_2. Since nominal incomes are fixed in the short run, firms raise product prices, earn higher profits, and expand output to short-run equilibrium point E_2 with a price level of 175 and real GDP of $12 trillion. This macro equilibrium corresponds to full-employment or potential real GDP at LRAS.

5.

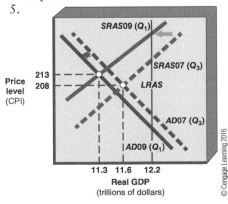

CHAPTER 15
FISCAL POLICY

1. *Expansionary* fiscal policy refers to increasing government spending and/or decreasing taxes in order to increase aggregate demand and eliminate a GDP gap. *Contractionary* fiscal policy is designed to cool inflation by decreasing aggregate demand. This result is accomplished by decreasing government spending and/or increasing taxes.
3. a. contractionary fiscal policy
   b. contractionary fiscal policy
   c. expansionary fiscal policy
5. The spending multiplier is

$$\frac{1}{1 - \text{MPC}} = \frac{1}{0.25} = \frac{1}{1/4} = 4$$

The spending multiplier (*M*) times the change in government spending (Δ*G*) equals the change in aggregate demand (Δ*AD*). Therefore,

Δ*G* × M = Δ*AD*
Δ*G* × 4 = $500 billion
Δ*G*   = $125 billion

The government must increase government spending by $125 billion in order to eliminate the GDP gap.
7. The tax multiplier equals 1 minus the spending multiplier. Thus, the impact of the expansion in government spending exceeds the impact of an equal amount of tax cut.
9. As a supply-side economist, you would argue that the location of the aggregate supply curve is related to the tax rates. Ceteris paribus, if the tax rates are cut, there will be strong incentives for workers to supply more work, households to save more, and businesses to invest more in capital goods. Thus, cutting tax rates shifts the aggregate supply curve rightward, the level of real GDP rises, and the price level falls.
11. a. rightward shift in the aggregate demand curve
    b. leftward shift in the aggregate demand curve
    c. rightward shift in the aggregate supply curve
    d. rightward shift in the aggregate demand curve
    e. leftward shift in the aggregate supply curve

CHAPTER 16
THE PUBLIC SECTOR

1. Transfer payments account for the difference between total government expenditures, or outlays, and total government spending. Transfers do not "use up" resources; they reallocate purchasing power by collecting taxes from one group and paying benefits to other groups.
3. The primary sources are individual income taxes at the federal level, sales and excise taxes at the state level, and property taxes at the local level.

5. The marginal tax rate is the percentage of additional income paid in taxes. The average tax rate is the amount of taxes paid as a percentage of income.
7. a. more than $6,000
   b. less than $6,000
   c. $6,000
9. Sales tax paid as a percentage of income
   10%
    7%
    6%
    4%
   Because the sales tax paid as a percentage of income falls as income rises, the tax is regressive.
11. A profit-maximizing firm follows the marginal rule that units will be produced so long as the marginal benefit exceeds or equals the marginal cost. Dollars can measure the intensity of benefits in relation to costs. A "one-person, one-vote" system does not necessarily measure benefits in proportion to the dollar value of benefits among individual voters. Thus, a majority of voters can approve projects for which costs exceed benefits and reject projects for which benefits exceed costs.

CHAPTER 17
FEDERAL DEFICITS, SURPLUSES, AND THE NATIONAL DEBT

1. The national debt is the sum of past federal budget deficits. When budget deficits are large, the national debt increases at a rapid rate. When budget deficits are small, the national debt increases at a lower rate.
3. The statement makes the argument that most of the debt is internal national debt that one U.S. citizen owes to another U.S. citizen. Suppose the federal government finances a deficit by having the Treasury sell government bonds to one group of U.S. citizens, thereby increasing the national debt. When the bonds mature, the government can pay the interest and principal by issuing new government bonds (rolling over the debt) to another group of U.S. citizens. This argument ignores the income distribution problem that results because interest payments go largely to those who are better off financially.
5. When the government makes interest payments on internally held debt, the money remains in the hands of U.S. citizens. External debt is very different. Repayment of interest and principal to foreigners withdraws purchasing power from U.S. citizens in favor of citizens abroad.
7. a. In year one, the federal deficit begins at $50 billion, and the U.S. Treasury issues $50 billion worth of bonds to finance the deficit.
   b. The next year the federal government must pay interest of $5 billion to service the debt ($50 billion bonds × 0.10 interest rate). Adding the

interest payment to the $100 billion spent for goods and services yields a $105 billion expenditure in year two.

    c. For the second year, the deficit is $55 billion ($105 billion in expenditures – $50 billion in taxes), and the U.S. Treasury borrows this amount by issuing new bonds. The new national debt is $105 billion, consisting of the $50 billion in bonds issued in the first year and the $55 billion in bonds issued in the second year.

9. During a depression, tax hikes and/or expenditure cuts would only reduce aggregate demand and, in turn, real GDP, jobs, and income. Because the economy is operating in the Keynesian segment of the aggregate demand curve, this fiscal policy would have no impact on the price level.

11. This answer should be logical and supported by a thoughtful explanation. For example, the federal deficit might be the result of a recession and you could argue that the deficit is correct fiscal policy. When the recession ends, the deficit will decline. Other arguments include some combinations of cutting spending or increasing taxes.

CHAPTER 18
MONEY AND THE FEDERAL RESERVE SYSTEM

1. Money is worthless in and of itself. The value of money is to serve as a medium of exchange, a unit of account, and a store of value.

3. a. The quantity of credit cards can be controlled. Credit cards are portable, divisible, and uniform in quality.

    b. The quantity of Federal Reserve notes is controlled by the U.S. government. These notes are portable, divisible, and uniform in quality.

    c. The quantity of dogs is difficult to control. Dogs are not very portable or divisible, and they are certainly not uniform.

    d. The quantity of beer mugs can be controlled. Beer mugs are not very portable or divisible, but they could be made fairly uniform.

5. The narrowest definition of money in the United States is M1. M1 = currency (coins + paper bills) + checkable deposits.

7. The Fed's most important function is to regulate the U.S. money supply. The *Board of Governors* is composed of seven persons who have the responsibility to supervise and control the money supply and the U.S. banking system. The *Federal Open Market Committee (FOMC)* controls the money supply by directing the buying and selling of U.S. government securities.

9. Banks that belong to the Fed must join the FDIC. Banks chartered by the states may affiliate with the FDIC. There are relatively few nonmember, noninsured state banks.

CHAPTER 19
MONEY CREATION

1. At first, the goldsmiths followed Shakespeare's advice and gave receipts only for gold on deposit in their vaults. They then realized that at any given time new deposits were coming in that could offset old deposits people were drawing down. The conclusion is that banking does not require a 100 percent required reserve ratio. Therefore, loans can be made, which stimulate the economy.

3. Banks can and do create money by granting loans to borrowers. These loans are deposited in customers' checking accounts, and, therefore, banks are participants in the money supply creation process.

5. There is no impact on the money supply. A check deposited in bank *A*, drawn on bank *B*, increases deposits, reserves, and lending at bank *A*. However, bank *B* experiences an equal reduction in deposits, reserves, and lending.

7.

First National Bank Balance Sheet			
Assets		Liabilities	
Reserves	–$1,000	Checkable deposits	–$1,000
Required	–$100		
Excess	–$900		
Total assets	–$1,000	Total liabilities	–$1,000

Negative excess reserves mean that loans must be reduced by $1,000.

9. Some customers may hold cash, rather than writing a check for the full amount of the loan. Some banks may hold excess reserves, rather than using these funds to make loans.

11. The decision of the public to hold cash and the willingness of banks to use excess reserves for loans affect the money multiplier. Variations in the money multiplier can cause unexpected changes in the money supply. Nonbanks can make loans and offer other financial services that are not under the direct control of the Federal Reserve. Finally, the public can decide to transfer funds from M1 to M2 or other definitions of the money supply.

CHAPTER 20
MONETARY POLICY

1. a. Transactions and precautionary balances increase.
    b. Speculative balances decrease.

c. Transactions and precautionary balances decrease.

d. Speculative balances increase.

e. Transactions and precautionary balances decrease.

3.

Bond Price ($)	Interest Rate (%)
800	10
1,000	8
2,000	4

There is an inverse relationship between the price of a bond and the interest rate.

5. a. The price level declines slightly. Real GDP and employment fall substantially.

b. The price level, real GDP, and employment rise.

c. The price level declines slightly. Real GDP and employment fall substantially.

7. In the monetarist view, the velocity of money, V, and the output, Q, variables in the equation of exchange are constant. Therefore, the quantity theory of money is stated as $M \times V = P \times Q$.

Given this equation, changes in the money supply, M1, yield proportionate changes in the price level, P.

9. In the Keynesian view, an increase in the money supply decreases the interest rate and causes investment spending, which increases aggregate demand through the multiplier effect and causes demand-pull inflation. In the monetarist view, money supply growth gives people more money to spend. This direct increase in aggregate demand causes demand-pull inflation.

11. Under such conditions, the Keynesian view is correct. The Fed would have no influence on investment because changes in the interest rate failed to alter the quantity of investment goods demanded.

CHAPTER 21
INTERNATIONAL TRADE AND FINANCE

1. a. In Alpha, the opportunity cost of producing 1 ton of diamonds is 1/2 ton of pearls. In Beta, the opportunity cost of producing 1 ton of diamonds is 2 tons of pearls.

b. In Alpha, the opportunity cost of producing 1 ton of pearls is 2 tons of diamonds. In Beta, the opportunity cost of producing 1 ton of pearls is 1/2 ton of diamonds.

c. Because Alpha can produce diamonds at a lower opportunity cost than Beta can, Alpha has a comparative advantage in the production of diamonds.

d. Because Beta can produce pearls at a lower opportunity cost than Alpha can, Beta has a comparative advantage in the production of pearls.

e.

	Diamonds (tons per year)	Pearls (tons per year)
Before specialization		
Alpha (at point B)	100	25
Beta (at point C)	30	120
Total output	130	145
After specialization		
Alpha (at point A)	150	0
Beta (at point D)	0	180
Total output	150	180

As shown in the above table, specialization in each country increases total world output per year by 20 tons of diamonds and 35 tons of pearls.

f.

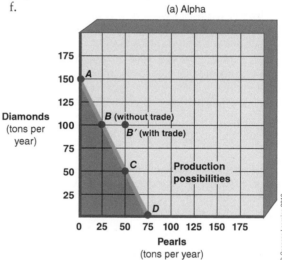

(a) Alpha

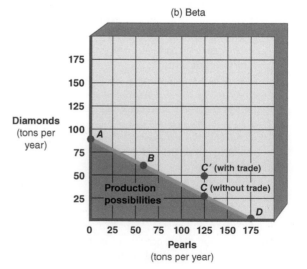

(b) Beta

© Cengage Learning 2016

Without trade, Alpha produces and consumes 100 tons of diamonds and 25 tons of pearls at point *B* on its production possibilities curve. Without trade, Beta produces and consumes 30 tons of diamonds and 120 tons of pearls (point *C*). Now assume Alpha specializes in producing diamonds at point *A* and imports 50 tons of pearls in exchange for 50 tons of diamonds. Through specialization and trade, Alpha moves its consumption possibility to point *B'*, outside its production possibilities curve.

3. The principle of specialization and trade according to comparative advantage applies to both nations and states in the United States. For example, Florida grows oranges, and Idaho grows potatoes. Trade between these states, just like trade between nations, increases the consumption possibilities.

5. U.S. industries (and their workers) that compete with restricted imports would benefit. Consumers would lose from the reduced supply of imported goods from which to choose and from higher prices for domestic products, resulting from lack of competition from imports.

7. Although some domestic jobs may be lost, new ones are created by international trade. Stated differently, the economy as a whole gains when nations specialize and trade according to the law of comparative advantage, but imports will cost jobs in some specific industries.

9. Although each nation's balance of payments equals zero, its current and capital account balances usually do not equal zero. For example, a current account deficit means a nation purchased more in imports than it sold in exports. On the other hand, this nation's capital account must have a surplus to offset the current account deficit. This means that foreigners are buying more domestic capital (capital inflow) than domestic citizens are buying foreign capital (capital outflow). Thus, net ownership of domestic capital stock is in favor of foreigners.

11. a.

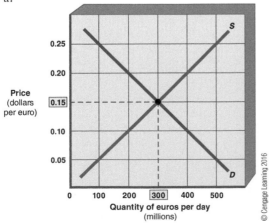

b. $0.15 per euro
c. An excess quantity of 200 million euros would be demanded.

CHAPTER 22
ECONOMIES IN TRANSITION

1. Americans prefer large cars and canned soup. Europeans predominantly buy small cars and dry soup. The role of women and minorities in the workplace is an excellent example of how culture relates to the labor factor of production.

3. Such a program would provide additional economic security for the elderly, but higher taxes could reduce the incentive to work, and economic efficiency might be reduced.

5. In a traditional agricultural system, a benefit would be that members of society would cooperate by helping to build barns, harvest, and so on. Under the command system, worrying about errors and crop failures would be minimized because the state makes the decisions and everyone in society has a basic income. In a market economy, a bumper crop would mean large profits and the capacity to improve one's standard of living.

7. Because most economies are mixed systems, this term is too broad to be very descriptive. The terms *capitalism* and *communism* are more definitive concerning the role of private ownership, market allocations, and decentralized decision making. Embracing a market-oriented system means a transfer of power from the command bureaucracy to consumers. Markets are incompatible with the principle that socialist citizens are supposed to be concerned with the collective interest.

CHAPTER 23
GROWTH AND THE LESS-DEVELOPED COUNTRIES

1. The difference between IACs and LDCs is based on GDP per capita. This classification is somewhat arbitrary. A country with a high GDP per capita and narrow industrial development based on oil, such as the United Arab Emirates, is excluded from the IAC list. There are 27 economies listed in the text as IACs, including Switzerland, Japan, the United States, Singapore, and Hong Kong. The following countries are considered to be LDCs: Argentina, Mexico, South Africa, Jordan, and Bangladesh.

3. a. Based only on GDP per capita, you would conclude that Alpha is a better place to live because this country produces a greater output of goods and services per person.

b. Based on the additional evidence, you would change your mind and prefer to live in Beta because the quality-of-life data indicate a higher standard of living in this country.

5. The average growth rate of GDP per capita for IACs exceeds the GDP per capita growth rate for LDCs. This evidence is consistent with the argument. The argument is oversimplified because there is considerable diversity among the LDCs. In a given year, a LDC may have a GDP per capita growth rate greater than many IACs.

7. Economic growth and development are complicated because there is no single prescription that a country can follow. The chapter presents a multidimensional model with five basic categories: natural resources, human resources, capital, technological progress, and political environment. Because an LDC is weak in one or more of the key factors, such as natural resources, does not necessarily mean that the LDC cannot achieve economic success.

9. Because they are poor countries with low GDP per capita, they lack domestic savings to invest in capital; and lacking investment, they remain poor. The rich in these poor countries often put their savings abroad because of the fear of political instability. An inflow of external funds from abroad permits the LDC to increase its capital without reducing its consumption and to shift its production possibilities curve outward.

11. Poor countries are too poor to save enough to finance domestic capital formation. International trade is a way LDCs can generate savings from abroad. Exports provide the LDCs with foreign exchange to pay for imports of capital stock that is necessary for economic growth and development.

Answers to Sample Quizzes

Chapter 1 **Introducing the Economic Way of Thinking**

1. d 2. c 3. a 4. c 5. b 6. d 7. d 8. d 9. b
10. d 11. a 12. c 13. a 14. b 15. c 16. d
17. d 18. b 19. a 20. d

Appendix 1 **Applying Graphs to Economics**

1. d 2. d 3. b 4. c 5. a 6. a 7. d 8. c 9. a
10. c 11. d 12. a. 13. b 14. d 15. d 16. c
17. c 18. c 19. d 20. c

Chapter 2 **Production Possibilities, Opportunity Cost, and Economic Growth**

1. d 2. b 3. a 4. c 5. c 6. e 7. b 8. a 9. c
10. d 11. d 12. b 13. a 14. b 15. a 16. a
17. d 18. e 19. c 20. a

Chapter 3 **Market Demand and Supply**

1. b 2. a 3. d 4. c 5. d 6. c 7. c 8. d
9. b 10. a 11. b 12. e 13. d 14. a 15. b
16. c 17. b 18. a 19. a 20. b 21. c 22. e
23. d 24. a 25. e

Chapter 4 **Markets in Action**

1. b 2. a 3. d 4. b 5. a 6. b 7. b 8. b 9. c
10. a 11. a 12. b 13. c 14. d 15. c 16. c
17. b 18. c 19. e 20. a

Chapter 5 **Price Elasticity of Demand**

1. d. 2. b 3. a 4. c 5. b 6. a 7. b 8. b 9. b
10. c 11. c 12. a 13. c 14. a 15. d 16. a
17. a 18. b 19. a 20. a

Chapter 6 **Production Costs**

1. d 2. a 3. c 4. c 5. c 6. d 7. b 8. e 9. b
10. b 11. c 12. d 13. e 14. c 15. b 16. c 17. c
18. b. 19. a 20. a 21. c 22. c 23. b 24. a 25. c

Chapter 7 **Perfect Competition**

1. e 2. d 3. c 4. c 5. a 6. e 7. c 8. d 9. d
10. b 11. d 12. c 13. a 14. d 15. d 16. b
17. d 18. b 19. d 20. c

Chapter 8 **Monopoly**

1. c 2. a 3. b 4. b 5. d 6. c 7. d 8. c 9. d
10. d 11. e 12. c 13. d 14. d 15. b 16. d
17. b 18. c 19. b 20. b

Chapter 9 **Monopolistic Competition and Oligopoly**

1. c 2. b 3. b 4. a 5. c 6. d 7. c 8. b 9. a
10. d 11. c 12. a 13. d 14. d 15. b 16. c
17. d 18. d 19. a 20. b

Chapter 10 **Labor Markets and Income Distribution**

1. b 2. a 3. c 4. d 5. d 6. a 7. c 8. c 9. c
10. d 11. d 12. c 13. d 14. b 15. a 16. c
17. a 18. d 19. b 20. d 21. b 22. c 23. d
24. d 25. a

Chapter 11 **Gross Domestic Product**

1. b 2. e 3. b 4. d 5. c 6. a 7. a 8. c 9. c
10. c 11. a 12. d 13. d 14. c 15. d 16. a
17. b 18. a 19. a 20. c

Chapter 12 **Business Cycles and Unemployment**

1. c 2. b 3. d 4. b 5. d 6. c 7. b 8. c 9. d
10. b 11. c 12. d 13. c 14. d 15. e 16. b
17. d 18. b 19. b 20. c

Chapter 13 **Inflation**

1. c 2. c 3. a 4. d 5. d 6. b 7. a 8. d 9. c
10. c 11. d 12. b 13. a 14. e 15. d 16. b
17. b 18. d 19. a 20. a

Chapter 14 **Aggregate Demand and Supply**

1. c 2. e 3. a 4. b 5. a 6. a 7. d 8. a 9. c
10. b 11. c 12. c 13. d 14. b 15. b 16. a
17. a 18. e 19. c 20. c

Appendix 14 **The Self-Correcting Aggregate Demand and Supply Model**

1. c 2. e 3. a 4. d 5. b 6. a 7. d 8. d 9. b
10. b 11. b 12. a 13. b 14. b 15. b 16. a
17. a 18. c 19. d 20. c

Chapter 15 **Fiscal Policy**

1. c 2. c 3. d 4. a 5. d 6. d 7. d 8. a 9. c
10. c 11. b 12. a 13. d 14. d 15. d 16. b
17. a 18. c 19. b 20. a

Chapter 16 **The Public Sector**

1. a 2. a 3. a 4. a 5. b 6. d 7. c 8. a 9. a
10. b 11. c 12. c 13. b 14. d 15. b 16. d
17. a 18. c 19. d 20. b

Chapter 17 **Federal Deficits, Surpluses, and the National Debt**

1. a 2. d 3. c 4. c 5. d 6. b 7. d 8. d 9. c
10. d 11. a 12. d 13. a 14. d 15. a 16. d
17. d 18. a 19. a 20. e

Chapter 18 **Money and the Federal Reserve System**

1. a 2. b 3. c 4. d 5. b 6. d 7. d 8. b 9. d
10. d 11. d 12. a 13. c 14. c 15. d 16. d
17. b 18. d 19. a 20. a

Chapter **19 Money Creation**
1. c 2. b 3. a 4. b 5. e 6. b 7. a 8. b 9. a
10. c 11. c 12. c 13. b 14. a 15. d 16. e
17. b 18. b 19. b 20. a

Chapter **20 Monetary Policy**
1. a 2. c 3. e 4. b 5. b 6. b 7. d 8. a 9. b
10. d 11. a 12. c 13. d 14. b 15. a 16. b
17. d 18. e 19. d 20. e

Appendix **20 Policy Disputes Using the Self-Correcting Aggregate Demand and Supply Model**
1. a 2. d 3. a 4. c 5. b 6. b 7. a 8. b 9. a
10. d 11. a 12. c 13. b 14. c 15. d

Chapter **21 International Trade and Finance**
1. c 2. a 3. c 4. b 5. b 6. d 7. d 8. a 9. e
10. a 11. d 12. a 13. a 14. c 15. c 16. a
17. d 18. b 19. c 20. b

Chapter **22 Economies in Transition**
1. d 2. a 3. c 4. a 5. c 6. d 7. d 8. a 9. c
10. a 11. a 12. d 13. a 14. b 15. d 16. b
17. d 18. c 19. d 20. c

Chapter **23 Growth and the Less Developed Countries**
1. d 2. d 3. c 4. b 5. e 6. d 7. b 8. d 9. d
10. d 11. e 12. a 13. e 14. a 15. b 16. b
17. c 18. a 19. c 20. b

GLOSSARY

A

Ability-to-pay principle The concept that those who have higher incomes can afford to pay a greater proportion of their income in taxes, regardless of benefits received.

Absolute advantage The ability of a country to produce a good using the same or fewer resources than another country.

Adjustable-rate mortgage (ARM) A home loan that adjusts the nominal interest rate to changes in an index rate, such as rates on Treasury securities.

Agency for International Development (AID) The agency of the U.S. State Department that is in charge of U.S. aid to foreign countries.

Aggregate demand curve (AD) The curve that shows the level of real GDP purchased by households, businesses, government, and foreigners (net exports) at different possible price levels during a time period, ceteris paribus.

Aggregate supply curve (AS) The curve that shows the level of real GDP produced at different possible price levels during a time period, ceteris paribus.

Appreciation of currency A rise in the price of one currency relative to another.

Arbitrage The activity of earning a profit by buying a good at a low price and reselling the good at a higher price.

Automatic stabilizers Federal expenditures and tax revenues that automatically change levels in order to stabilize an economic expansion or contraction; sometimes referred to as nondiscretionary fiscal policy.

Average fixed cost (AFC) Total fixed cost divided by the quantity of output produced.

Average tax rate The tax divided by the income.

Average total cost (ATC) Total cost divided by the quantity of output produced.

Average variable cost (AVC) Total variable cost divided by the quantity of output produced.

B

Balance of payments A bookkeeping record of all the international transactions between a country and other countries during a given period of time.

Balance of trade The value of a nation's imports subtracted from its exports. Balance of trade can be expressed in terms of goods, services, or goods and services.

Barrier to entry Any obstacle that makes it difficult for a new firm to enter a market.

Barter The direct exchange of one good or service for another good or service rather than for money.

Base year A year chosen as a reference point for comparison with some earlier or later year.

Benefit-cost analysis The comparison of the additional rewards and costs of an economic alternative.

Benefits-received principle The concept that those who benefit from government expenditures should pay the taxes that finance their benefits.

Board of Governors of the Federal Reserve System The seven members appointed by the president and confirmed by the U.S. Senate who serve for one nonrenewable 14-year term. Their responsibility is to supervise and control the money supply and the banking system of the United States.

Budget deficit A budget in which government expenditures exceed government revenues in a given time period.

Budget surplus A budget in which government revenues exceed government expenditures in a given time period.

Business cycle Alternating periods of economic growth and contraction, which can be measured by changes in real GDP.

C

Capital Human-made goods used to produce other goods and services.

Capitalism An economic system characterized by private ownership of resources and markets.

Cartel A group of firms that formally agree to reduce competition by coordinating control the price and output of a product.

Ceteris paribus A Latin phrase that means while certain variables change, "all other things remain unchanged."

Change in demand An increase or a decrease in the quantity demanded at each possible price. An increase in demand is a rightward shift in the entire demand curve. A decrease in demand is a leftward shift in the entire demand curve.

Change in quantity demanded A movement between points along a stationary demand curve, ceteris paribus.

Change in quantity supplied A movement between points along a stationary supply curve, ceteris paribus.

Change in supply An increase or a decrease in the quantity supplied at each possible price. An increase in supply is a rightward shift in the entire supply curve. A decrease in supply is a leftward shift in the entire supply curve.

Checkable deposits The total of checking account balances in financial institutions convertible to currency "on demand" by writing a check without advance notice.

Circular flow model A diagram showing the exchange of money and resources between households and businesses.

Civilian labor force The number of people 16 years of age and older who are employed, or who are actively seeking a job, excluding members of the armed forces, homemakers, discouraged workers, and other persons not in the labor force.

Classical economics The theory that free markets will restore full employment without government intervention.

Classical economists A group of economists whose theory dominated economic thinking from the 1770s to the Great Depression. They believed recessions would naturally cure themselves because the price system would automatically restore full employment.

Classical range The vertical segment of the aggregate supply curve, which represents an economy at full-employment output.

Coincident indicators Variables that change at the same time that real GDP changes.

Collective bargaining The process of negotiating labor contracts between the union and management concerning wages and working conditions.

Combating recession and inflation It can be accomplished by changing government spending or taxes.

Command economy An economic system that answers the *What*, *How*, and *For Whom* questions by a dictator or central authority.

Commodity money Anything that serves as money while having market value in other uses.

Communism A stateless, classless economic system in which all the factors of production are owned by the workers, and people share in production according to their needs. In Marx's view, this is the highest form of socialism toward which the revolution should strive.

Comparative advantage The ability of a country to produce a good at a lower opportunity cost than another country.

Complementary goods A good that is jointly consumed with another good. As a result, there is an inverse relationship between a price change for one good and the demand for its "go together" good.

Constant returns to scale A situation in which the long-run average cost curve does not change as the firm increases output.

Consumer Financial Protection Bureau (CFPB) An independent bureau within the Federal Reserve that helps consumers make their financial decisions.

Consumer price index (CPI) An index that measures changes in the average prices of consumer goods and services.

Consumer sovereignty The freedom of consumers to cast their dollar votes to buy, or not to buy, at prices determined in competitive markets.

Contractionary fiscal policy A deliberate decrease in government spending, a deliberate increase in taxes, or some combination of these two options.

Cost-push inflation An increase in the general price level resulting from an increase in the cost of production.

Crowding-in effect An increase in private-sector spending as a result of federal budget deficits financed by U.S. Treasury borrowing. At less than full employment, consumers hold more Treasury securities and this additional wealth causes them to spend more. Business investment spending increases because of optimistic profit expectations.

Crowding-out effect A reduction in private-sector spending as a result of federal budget deficits financed by U.S. Treasury borrowing. When federal government borrowing increases interest rates, the result is lower consumption by households and lower investment spending by businesses.

Currency Money, including coins and paper money.

Cyclical unemployment Unemployment caused by the lack of jobs during a recession.

D

Debt ceiling A legislated legal limit on the national debt.

Deflation A decrease in the general (average) price level of goods and services in the economy.

Demand A curve or schedule showing the various quantities of product consumers are willing to purchase at possible prices during a specified period of time, ceteris paribus.

Demand curve for labor A curve showing the different quantities of labor employers are willing to hire at different wage rates in a given time period, ceteris paribus. It is equal to the marginal revenue product of labor.

Demand for money curve A curve representing the quantity of money that people hold at different possible interest rates, ceteris paribus.

Demand-pull inflation A rise in the general price level resulting from an excess of total spending (demand).

Depreciation of currency A fall in the price of one currency relative to another.

Derived demand The demand for labor and other factors of production that depends on the consumer demand for the final goods and services the factors produce.

Direct relationship A positive association between two variables. When one variable increases, the other variable increases, and when one variable decreases, the other variable decreases.

Discount rate The interest rate the Fed charges on loans of reserves to banks.

Discouraged worker A person who wants to work, but who has given up searching for work because he or she believes there will be no job offers.

Discretionary fiscal policy The deliberate use of changes in government spending or taxes to alter aggregate demand and stabilize the economy.

Diseconomies of scale A situation in which the long-run average cost curve rises as the firm increases output.

Disinflation A reduction in the rate of inflation.

Disposable personal income (DI) The amount of income that households actually have to spend or save after payment of personal taxes.

E

Earned Income Tax Credit (EITC) Comparable worth The principle that employees who work for the same employer must be paid the same wage when their jobs, even if different, require similar levels of education, training, experience, and responsibility. A non-market wage-setting process is used to evaluate and compensate jobs according to point scores assigned to different jobs.

Economic growth The ability of an economy to produce greater levels of output, represented by an outward shift of its production possibilities curve.

Economic growth and economic development Both are related, but somewhat different, concepts. Economic growth is measured quantitatively by GDP per capita, while economic development is a broader concept. In addition to GDP per capita, economic development includes quality-of-life measures, such as life expectancy at birth, adult literacy rate, and per capita energy consumption.

Economic profit Total revenue minus explicit and implicit costs.

Economic system The organizations and methods used to determine what goods and services are produced, how they are produced, and for whom they are produced.

Economics The study of how society chooses to allocate its scarce resources to the production of goods and services in order to satisfy unlimited wants.

Economies of scale A situation in which the long-run average cost curve declines as the firm increases output.

Elastic demand A condition in which the percentage change in quantity demanded is greater than the percentage change in price.

Embargo A law that bars trade with another country.

Entrepreneurship The creative ability of individuals to seek profits by taking risks and combining resources to produce innovative products.

Equation of exchange An accounting identity that states the money supply times the velocity of money equals total spending.

Equilibrium A market condition that occurs at any price and quantity at which the quantity demanded and the quantity supplied are equal.

Excess reserves Potential loan balances held in vault cash or on deposit with the Fed in excess of required reserves.

Exchange rate The number of units of one nation's currency that equals one unit of another nation's currency.

Expansion An upturn in the business cycle during which real GDP rises; also called a *recovery*.

Expansionary fiscal policy A deliberate increase in government spending, a deliberate decrease in taxes, or some combination of these two options.

Expenditure approach The national income accounting method that measures GDP by adding all the spending for final goods during a period of time.

Explicit costs Payments to nonowners of a firm for their resources.

External national debt The portion of the national debt owed to foreign citizens.

Externalities A cost or benefit imposed on people other than the consumers and producers of a good or service.

F

Federal Deposit Insurance Corporation (FDIC) A government agency established in 1933 to insure commercial bank deposits up to a specified limit.

Federal funds market A private market in which banks lend reserves to each other for less than 24 hours.

Federal funds rate The interest rate banks charge for overnight loans of reserves to other banks.

Federal Open Market Committee (FOMC) The Federal Reserve's committee that directs the buying and selling of U.S. government securities, which are major instruments for controlling the money supply. The FOMC consists of the seven members of the Federal Reserve's Board of Governors, the president of the New York Federal Reserve Bank, and the presidents of four other Federal Reserve district banks.

Federal Reserve System The 12 Federal Reserve district banks that service banks and other financial institutions within each of the Federal Reserve districts; popularly called the Fed.

Fiat money Money accepted by law and not because of its tangible value.

Final goods Finished goods and services produced for the ultimate user.

Fiscal policy The use of government spending and taxes to influence the nation's output, employment, and price level.

Fixed input Any resource for which the quantity cannot change during the period of time under consideration.

Foreign aid The transfer of money or resources from one government to another with no repayment required.

Fractional reserve banking A system in which banks keep only a percentage of their deposits on reserve as vault cash and deposits at the Fed.

Free trade The flow of goods between countries without restrictions or special taxes.

Frictional unemployment Temporary unemployment caused by the time required of workers to move from one job to another.

Full employment The situation in which an economy operates at an unemployment rate equal to the sum of the frictional and structural unemployment rates. Also called the *natural rate of unemployment*.

G

Game theory A model of the strategic moves and countermoves of rivals.

GDP chain price index A measure that compares changes in the prices of all final goods during a given year to the prices of those goods in a base year.

GDP gap The difference between actual real GDP and potential or full-employment real GDP.

GDP per capita The value of final goods produced (GDP) divided by the total population.

Government expenditures Federal, state, and local government outlays for goods and services, including transfer payments.

Gross domestic product (GDP) The market value of all final goods and services produced in a nation during a period of time, usually a year.

H

Human capital The accumulation of education, training, experience, and health that enables a worker to enter an occupation and be productive.

Hyperinflation An extremely rapid rise in the general price level.

I

Implicit costs The opportunity costs of using resources owned by a firm.

Independent relationship A zero association between two variables. When one variable changes, the other variable remains unchanged.

Industrially advanced countries (IACs) High-income nations that have market economies based on large stocks of technologically advanced capital and well-educated labor. The United States, Canada, Australia, New Zealand, Japan, and most of the countries of Western Europe are IACs.

Inelastic demand A condition in which the percentage change in quantity demanded is less than the percentage change in price.

Inferior goods Any good for which there is an inverse relationship between changes in income and its demand curve.

Inflation An increase in the general (average) price level of goods and services in the economy.

Infrastructure Capital goods usually provided by the government, including highways, bridges, waste and water systems, and airports.

In-kind transfers Government payments in the form of goods and services, rather than cash, including such government programs as food stamps, Medicaid, and housing.

Interest-rate effect The impact on total spending (real GDP) caused by the direct relationship between the price level and the interest rate.

Intermediate goods Goods and services used as inputs for the production of final goods.

Intermediate range The rising segment of the aggregate supply curve, which represents an economy as it approaches full-employment output.

Internal national debt The portion of the national debt owed to a nation's own citizens.

International Monetary Fund (IMF) The lending agency that makes short-term conditional low-interest loans to developing countries.

Inverse relationship A negative association between two variables. When one variable increases, the other variable decreases, and when one variable decreases, the other variable increases.

Investment The accumulation of capital, such as factories, machines, and inventories, used to produce goods and services.

Invisible hand A phrase that expresses the belief that the best interests of a society are served when individual consumers and producers compete to achieve their own private interests.

K

Keynesian economics The theory, first advanced by John Maynard Keynes, that the role of the federal government is to increase or decrease aggregate demand to achieve economic goals

Keynesian range The horizontal segment of the aggregate supply curve, which represents an economy in a severe recession.

L

Labor The mental and physical capacity of workers to produce goods and services.

Laffer curve A graph depicting the relationship between tax rates and total tax revenues.

Lagging indicators Variables that change after real GDP changes.

Land Any natural resource provided by nature used to produce goods and services.

Law of demand The principle that there is an inverse relationship between the price of a good and the quantity buyers are willing to purchase in a defined time period, ceteris paribus.

Law of diminishing returns The principle that beyond some point the marginal product decreases as additional units of a variable factor are added to a fixed factor.

Law of increasing opportunity costs The principle that the opportunity cost increases as production of one output expands.

Law of supply The principle that there is a direct relationship between the price of a good and the quantity sellers are willing to offer for sale in a defined time period, ceteris paribus.

Leading indicators Variables that change before real GDP changes.

Less-developed countries (LDCs) Nations without large stocks of technologically advanced capital and well-educated labor. LDCs are economies based on agriculture, such as most countries of Africa, Asia, and Latin America.

Long run A period of time so long that all inputs are variable.

Long-run aggregate supply curve (LRAS) The curve that shows the level of real GDP produced at different possible price levels during a time period in which nominal incomes change by the same percentage as the price level changes.

Long-run average cost curve (LRAC) The curve that traces the lowest cost per unit at which a firm can produce any level of output when the firm can build any desired plant size.

Long-run perfectly competitive equilibrium It occurs when a firm earns a normal profit by producing where price equals minimum long-run average cost equals minimum short-run average total cost equals short-run marginal cost.

Long-run profit-maximizing monopolist Earns a profit because of barriers to entry. If demand and cost conditions prevent the monopolist from earning a profit, the monopolist will leave the industry.

M

M1 The narrowest definition of the money supply. It includes currency and checkable deposits.

M2 The definition of the money supply that equals M1 plus near monies, such as savings deposits and small time deposits of less than $100,000.

Macroeconomics The branch of economics that studies decision making for the economy as a whole.

Marginal analysis An examination of the effects of additions to or subtractions from a current situation.

Marginal cost (MC) The change in total cost when one additional unit of output is produced.

Marginal product The change in total output produced by adding one unit of a variable input, with all other inputs used being held constant.

Marginal propensity to consume (MPC) The change in consumption spending resulting from a given change in income.

Marginal revenue (MR) The change in total revenue from the sale of one additional unit of output.

Marginal revenue product (MRP) The increase in a firm's total revenue resulting from hiring an additional unit of labor or other variable resource.

Marginal tax rate The fraction of additional income paid in taxes.

Market Any arrangement in which buyers and sellers interact to determine the price and quantity of goods and services exchanged.

Market economy An economic system that answers the *What, How,* and *For Whom* questions using prices determined by the interaction of the forces of supply and demand.

Market failure A situation in which market equilibrium results in too few or too many resources being used in the production of a good or service. This inefficiency may justify government intervention.

Market structure A classification system for the key traits of a market, including the number of firms, the similarity of the products they sell, and the ease of entry into and exit from the market.

Medium of exchange The primary function of money to be widely accepted in exchange for goods and services.

Microeconomics The branch of economics that studies decision making by a single individual, household, firm, industry, or level of government.

Mixed economy An economic system that answers the *What, How,* and *For Whom* questions through a mixture of traditional, command, and market systems.

Model A simplified description of reality used to understand and predict the relationship between variables.

Monetarism The theory that changes in the money supply directly determine changes in prices, real GDP, and employment.

Monetary Control Act A law, formally titled the Depository Institutions Deregulation and Monetary Control Act of 1980, that gave the Federal Reserve System greater control over nonmember banks and made all financial institutions more competitive.

Monetary policy The Federal Reserve's use of open market operations, changes in the discount rate, and changes in the required reserve ratio to change the money supply (M1).

Money Anything that serves as a medium of exchange, unit of account, and store of value.

Money multiplier The maximum change in the money supply (checkable deposits) due to an initial change in the excess reserves banks hold. The money multiplier is equal to 1 divided by the required reserve ratio.

Monopolistic competition A market structure characterized by (1) many small sellers, (2) a differentiated product, and (3) easy market entry and exit.

Monopoly A market structure characterized by (1) a single seller, (2) a unique product, and (3) impossible entry into the market.

Mutual interdependence A condition in which an action by one firm may cause a reaction from other firms.

N

National debt The total amount owed by the federal government to owners of government securities.

National income (NI) The total income earned by resource owners, including wages, rents, interest, and profits. NI is calculated as gross domestic product minus depreciation of the capital worn out in producing output.

Nationalization The act of transforming a private enterprise's assets into government ownership.

Natural monopoly An industry in which the long-run average cost of production declines throughout the entire market. As a result, a single firm can supply the entire market demand at a lower cost than two or more smaller firms.

Net exports effect The impact on total spending (real GDP) caused by the inverse relationship between the price level and the net exports of an economy.

Net public debt National debt minus all government interagency borrowing.

Network good A good that increases in value to each user as the total number of users increases. As a result, a firm can achieve economies of scale.

Nominal GDP The value of all final goods based on the prices existing during the time period of production.

Nominal income The actual number of dollars received over a period of time.

Nominal interest rate The actual rate of interest without adjustment for the inflation rate.

Nonprice competition The situation in which a firm competes using advertising, packaging, product development, better quality, and better service rather than lower prices.

Normal goods Any good for which there is a direct relationship between changes in income and its demand curve.

Normal profit The minimum profit necessary to keep a firm in operation. A firm that earns normal profits earns total revenue equal to its total opportunity cost.

Normative economics An analysis based on value judgment.

O

Offshoring The practice of having work for a company performed by the company's employees located in another country.

Oligopoly A market structure characterized by (1) few large sellers, (2) either a homogeneous or a differentiated product, and (3) difficult market entry.

Open market operations The buying and selling of government securities by the Federal Reserve System.

Opportunity cost The best alternative sacrificed for a chosen alternative.

Outsourcing The practice of a company having its work done by another company in another country.

P

Peak The phase of the business cycle in which real GDP reaches its maximum after rising during a recovery.

Perfect competition A market structure characterized by (1) a large number of small firms, (2) a homogeneous product, and (3) very easy entry into or exit from the market. Perfect competition is also referred to as *pure competition*.

Perfectly competitive firm's short-run supply curve The firm's marginal cost curve above the minimum point on its average variable cost curve.

Perfectly competitive industry's short-run supply curve The supply curve derived from horizontal summation of the marginal cost curves of all firms in the industry above the minimum point of each firm's average variable cost curve.

Perfectly elastic demand A condition in which a small percentage change in price brings about an infinite percentage change in quantity demanded.

Perfectly inelastic demand A condition in which the quantity demanded does not change as the price changes.

Personal income (PI) The total income received by households that is available for consumption, saving, and payment of personal taxes.

Positive economics An analysis limited to statements that are verifiable.

Poverty line The level of income below which a person or a family is considered to be poor.

Precautionary demand for money The stock of money people hold to pay unpredictable expenses.

Price ceiling A legally established maximum price a seller can charge.

Price discrimination The practice of a seller charging different prices for the same product that are not justified by cost differences.

Price elasticity of demand The ratio of the percentage change in the quantity demanded of a product to a percentage change in its price.

Price floor A legally established minimum price a seller can be paid.

Price leadership A pricing strategy in which a dominant firm sets the price for an industry and the other firms follow.

Price maker A firm that faces a downward-sloping demand curve and therefore it can choose among price and output combinations along the demand curve.

Price system A mechanism that uses the forces of supply and demand to create an equilibrium through rising and falling prices.

Price taker A seller that has no control over the price of the product it sells.

Privatization The process of turning a government enterprise into a private enterprise.

Product differentiation The process of creating real or apparent differences between goods and services.

Production function The relationship between the maximum amounts of output that a firm can produce and various quantities of inputs.

Production possibilities curve A curve that shows the maximum combinations of two outputs an economy can produce in a given period of time with its available resources and technology.

Progressive tax A tax that charges a higher percentage of income as income rises.

Proportional tax A tax that charges the same percentage of income, regardless of the size of income. Also called a *flat-tax rate* or simply a *flat tax*.

Protectionism The government's use of embargoes, tariffs, quotas, and other restrictions to protect domestic producers from foreign competition.

Public choice theory The analysis of the government's decision-making process for allocating resources.

Public good A good or service with two properties: (1) users collectively consume benefits, and (2) there is no way to bar people who do not pay (free riders) from consuming the good or service.

Q

Quantity theory of money The theory that changes in the money supply are directly related to changes in the price level.

Quota A limit on the quantity of a good that may be imported in a given time period.

R

Rational ignorance The voter's choice to remain uninformed because the marginal cost of obtaining information is higher than the marginal benefit from knowing it.

Real balances effect The impact on total spending (real GDP) caused by the inverse relationship between the price level and the real value of financial assets with fixed nominal value.

Real GDP The value of all final goods produced during a given time period based on the prices existing in a selected base year.

Real income The actual number of dollars received (nominal income) adjusted for changes in the CPI.

Real interest rate The nominal rate of interest minus the inflation rate.

Recession A downturn in the business cycle during which real GDP declines, and the unemployment rate rises. Also called a *contraction*.

Regressive tax A tax that charges a lower percentage of income as income rises.

Required reserve ratio The percentage of deposits that the Fed requires a bank to hold in vault cash or on deposit with the Fed.

Required reserves The minimum balance that the Fed requires a bank to hold in vault cash or on deposit with the Fed.

Resources The basic categories of inputs used to produce goods and services. Resources are also called *factors of production*. Economists divide resources into three categories: land, labor, and capital.

S

Scarcity The condition in which human wants are forever greater than the available supply of time, goods, and resources.

Shifts in supply and demand for foreign exchange Shifts in supply and demand for foreign exchange result from changes in such factors as tastes, relative price levels, relative real interest rates, and relative income levels.

Short run A period of time so short that there is at least one fixed input.

Short-run aggregate supply curve (SRAS) The curve that shows the level of real GDP produced at different possible price levels during a time period in which nominal incomes do not change in response to changes in the price level.

Short-run equilibrium for a monopolistic competitor It can yield economic losses, zero economic profits, or economic profits. In the long run, monopolistic competitors make zero economic profits.

Short-run profit-maximizing monopolist The perfectly competitive firm, locates the profit-maximizing price by producing the output where the MR and MC curves intersect.

Shortage A market condition existing at any price at where the quantity supplied is less than the quantity demanded.

Slope The ratio of the change in the variable on the vertical axis (the rise or fall) to the change in the variable on the horizontal axis (the run).

Socialism An economic system characterized by government ownership of resources and centralized decision making.

Speculative demand for money The stock of money people hold to take advantage of expected future changes in the price of bonds, stocks, or other nonmoney financial assets.

Spending multiplier (SM) The change in aggregate demand (total spending) resulting from an initial change in any component of aggregate demand, including consumption, investment, government spending, and net exports. As a formula, the spending multiplier equals 1/(1-MPC).

Stagflation The condition that occurs when an economy experiences the twin maladies of high unemployment and rapid inflation simultaneously.

Store of value The ability of money to hold value over time.

Structural unemployment Unemployment caused by a mismatch of the skills of workers out of work and the skills required for existing job opportunities.

Substitute goods A good that competes with another good for consumer purchases. As a result, there is a direct relationship between a price change for one good and the demand for its "competitor" good.

Supply A curve or schedule showing the various quantities of a product sellers are willing to produce and offer for sale at possible prices during a specified period of time, ceteris paribus.

Supply curve of labor A curve showing the different quantities of labor workers are willing to offer employers at different wage rates in a given time period, ceteris paribus.

Supply-side fiscal policy A fiscal policy that emphasizes government policies that increase aggregate supply in order to achieve long-run growth in real output, full employment, and a lower price level.

Surplus A market condition existing at any price where the quantity supplied is greater than the quantity demanded.

T

Tariff A tax on an import.

Tax multiplier (TM) The change in aggregate demand (total spending) resulting from an initial change in taxes. As a formula, the tax multiplier equals 1-spending multiplier.

Technology The body of knowledge applied to how goods are produced.

Total cost (TC) The sum of total fixed cost and total variable cost at each level of output.

Total fixed cost (TFC) Costs that do not vary as output varies and that must be paid even if output is zero. These are payments that the firm must make in the short run, regardless of the level of output.

Total revenue (TR) The total number of dollars a firm earns from the sale of a good or service, which is equal to its price multiplied by the quantity demanded.

Total variable cost (TVC) Costs that are zero when output is zero and vary as output varies.

Traditional economy An economic system that answers the What, How, and For Whom questions the way they always have been answered.

Transactions demand for money The stock of money people hold to pay everyday predictable expenses.

Transfer payment A government payment to individuals not in exchange for goods or services currently produced.

Trough The phase of the business cycle in which real GDP reaches its minimum after falling during a recession.

U

Unemployment rate The percentage of people in the civilian labor force who are without jobs and are actively seeking jobs.

Unit of account The function of money to provide a common measurement of the relative value of goods and services.

Unitary elastic demand A condition in which the percentage change in quantity demanded is equal to the percentage change in price.

V

Variable input Any resource for which the quantity can change during the period of time under consideration.

Velocity of money The average number of times per year a dollar of the money supply is spent on final goods and services.

Vicious circle of poverty The trap in which countries are poor because they cannot afford to save and invest, but they cannot save and invest because they are poor.

W

Wage–price spiral A situation that occurs when increases in nominal wage rates are passed on in higher prices, which, in turn, result in even higher nominal wage rates and prices.

Wealth The value of the stock of assets owned at some point in time.

World Bank The lending agency that makes long-term, low-interest loans and provides technical assistance to less-developed countries.

World Trade Organization (WTO) An international organization of member countries that oversees international trade agreements and rules on trade disputes.

INDEX